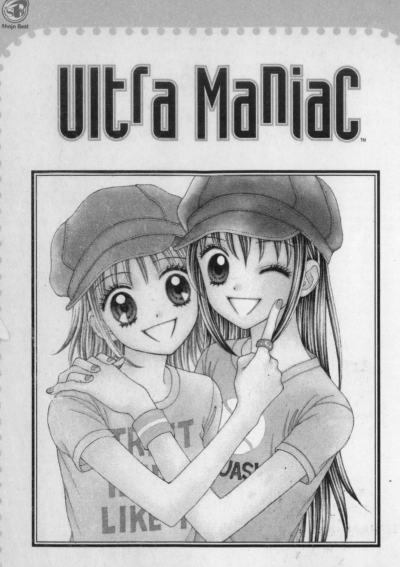

Shojo Beat

Ultra Maniac™

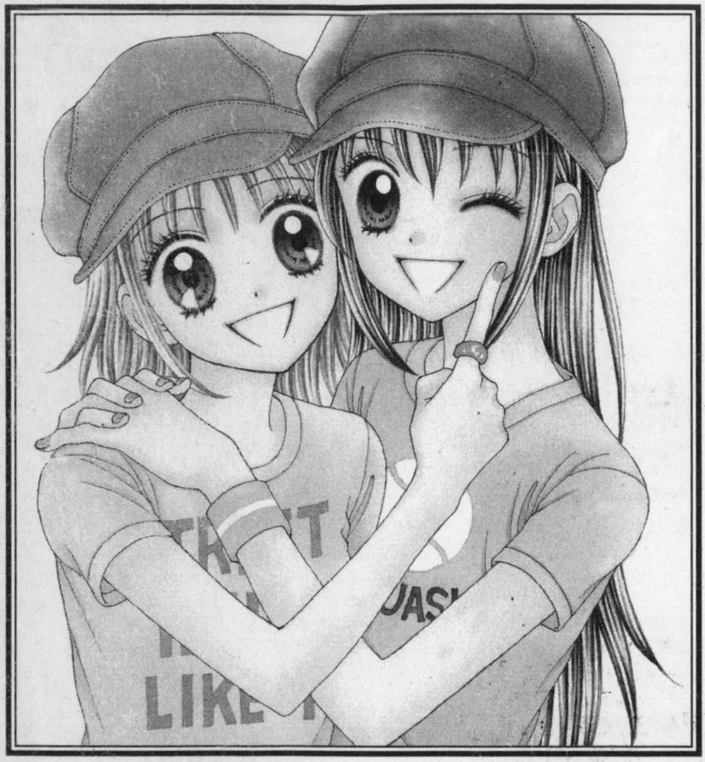
LIKE

Vol. 2

Story and Art by

Wataru Yoshizumi

Characters

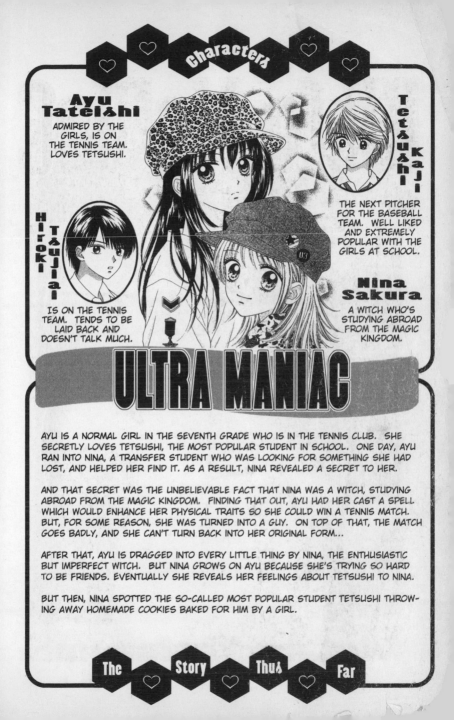

Ayu Tateishi

ADMIRED BY THE GIRLS, IS ON THE TENNIS TEAM. LOVES TETSUSHI.

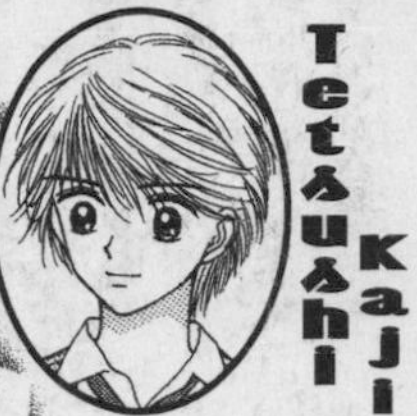

Tetsushi Kaji

THE NEXT PITCHER FOR THE BASEBALL TEAM. WELL LIKED AND EXTREMELY POPULAR WITH THE GIRLS AT SCHOOL.

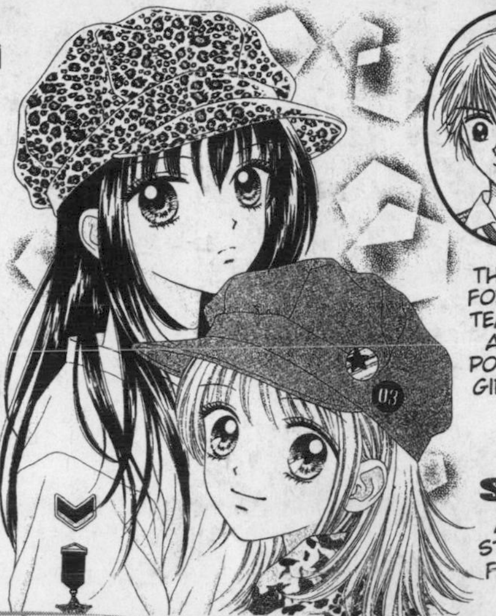

03

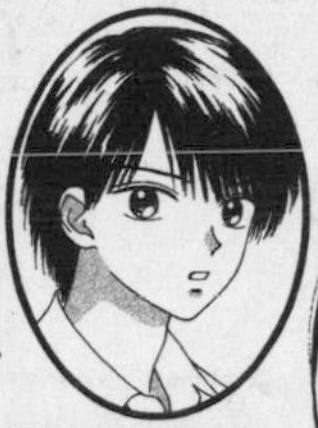

Hiroki Tsujiai

IS ON THE TENNIS TEAM. TENDS TO BE LAID BACK AND DOESN'T TALK MUCH.

Nina Sakura

A WITCH WHO'S STUDYING ABROAD FROM THE MAGIC KINGDOM.

ULTRA MANIAC

AYU IS A NORMAL GIRL IN THE SEVENTH GRADE WHO IS IN THE TENNIS CLUB. SHE SECRETLY LOVES TETSUSHI, THE MOST POPULAR STUDENT IN SCHOOL. ONE DAY, AYU RAN INTO NINA, A TRANSFER STUDENT WHO WAS LOOKING FOR SOMETHING SHE HAD LOST, AND HELPED HER FIND IT. AS A RESULT, NINA REVEALED A SECRET TO HER.

AND THAT SECRET WAS THE UNBELIEVABLE FACT THAT NINA WAS A WITCH, STUDYING ABROAD FROM THE MAGIC KINGDOM. FINDING THAT OUT, AYU HAD HER CAST A SPELL WHICH WOULD ENHANCE HER PHYSICAL TRAITS SO SHE COULD WIN A TENNIS MATCH. BUT, FOR SOME REASON, SHE WAS TURNED INTO A GUY. ON TOP OF THAT, THE MATCH GOES BADLY, AND SHE CAN'T TURN BACK INTO HER ORIGINAL FORM...

AFTER THAT, AYU IS DRAGGED INTO EVERY LITTLE THING BY NINA, THE ENTHUSIASTIC BUT IMPERFECT WITCH. BUT NINA GROWS ON AYU BECAUSE SHE'S TRYING SO HARD TO BE FRIENDS. EVENTUALLY SHE REVEALS HER FEELINGS ABOUT TETSUSHI TO NINA.

BUT THEN, NINA SPOTTED THE SO-CALLED MOST POPULAR STUDENT TETSUSHI THROWING AWAY HOMEMADE COOKIES BAKED FOR HIM BY A GIRL.

The Story Thus Far

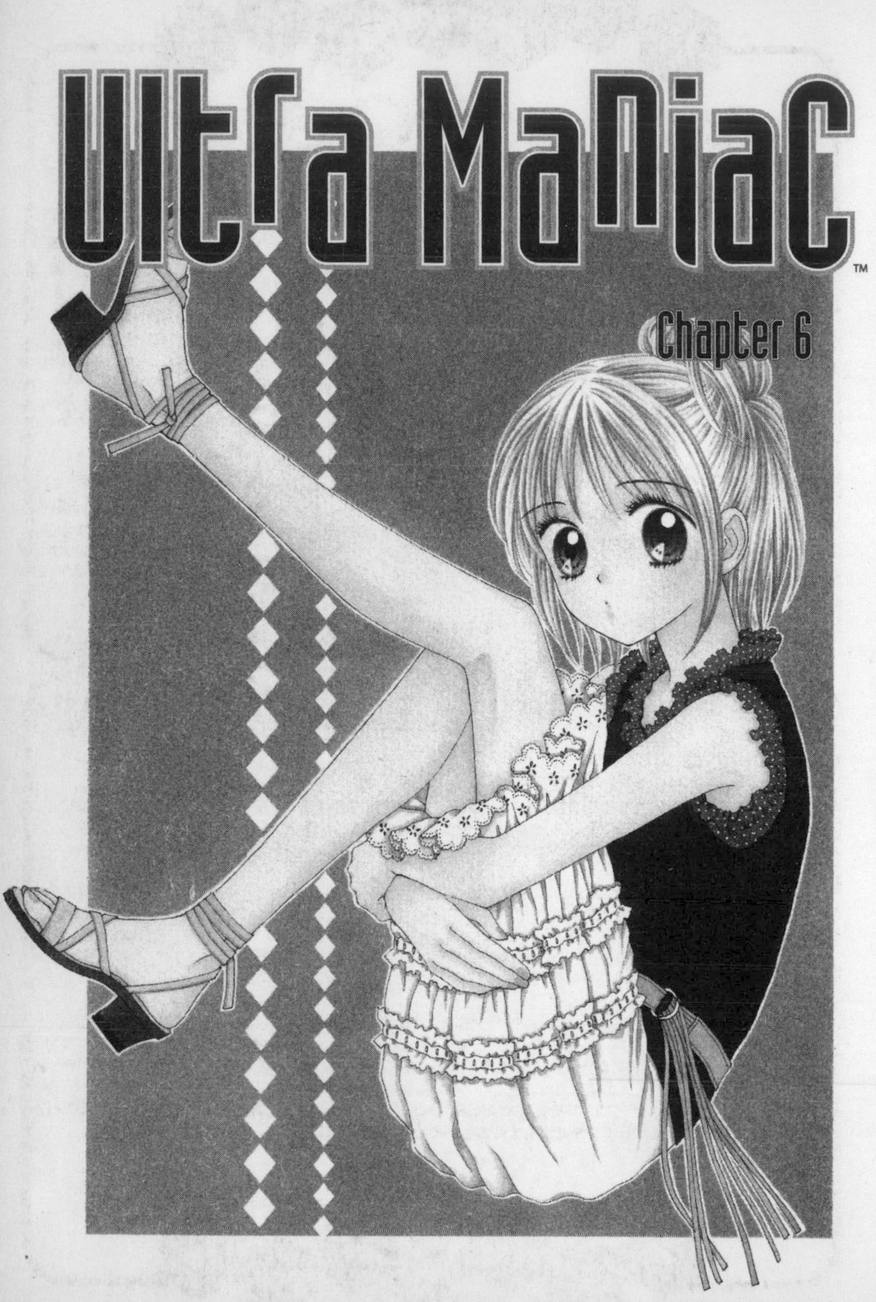
Ultra Maniac™
Chapter 6

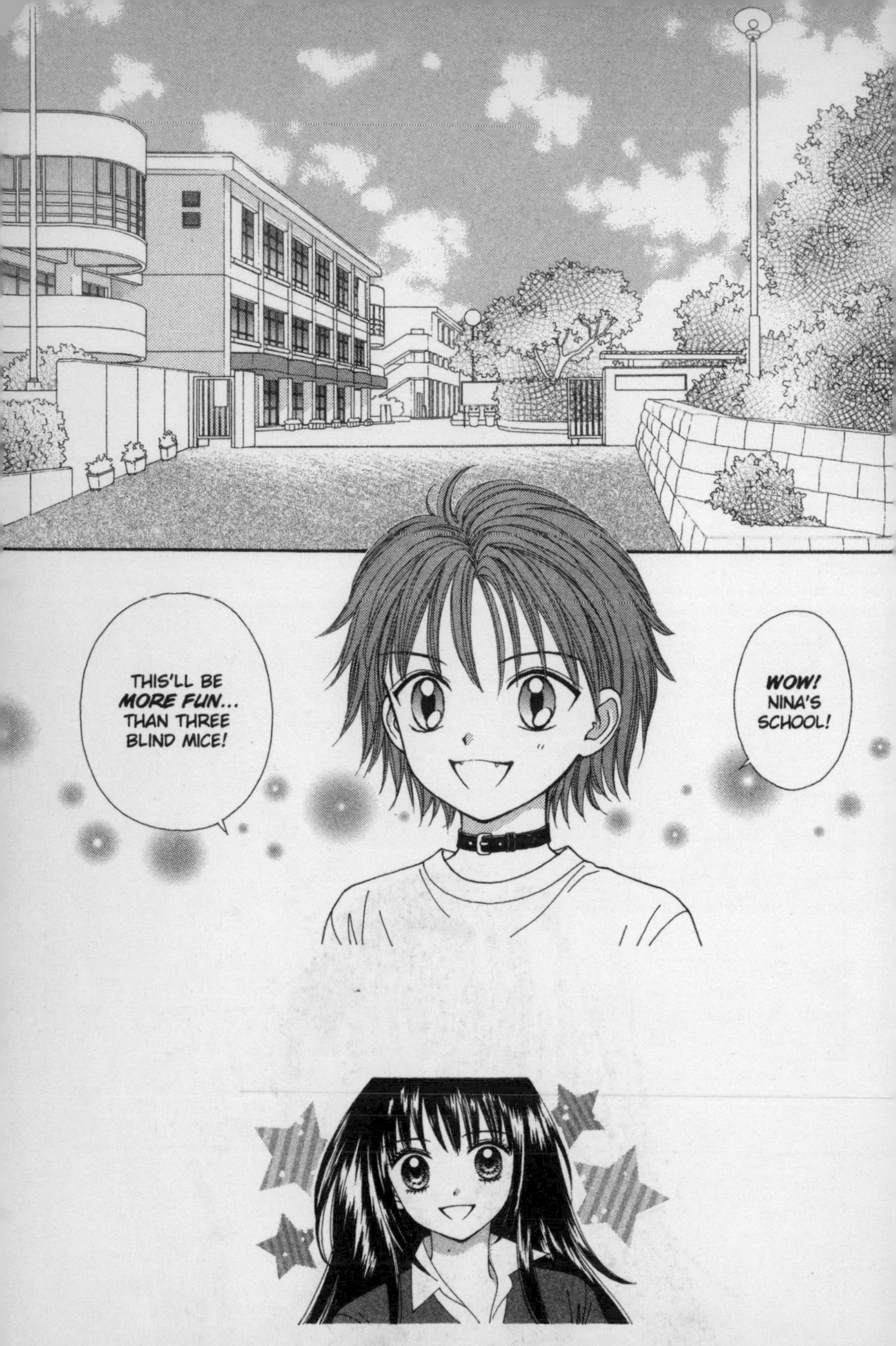
WOW! NINA'S SCHOOL!
THIS'LL BE MORE FUN... THAN THREE BLIND MICE!

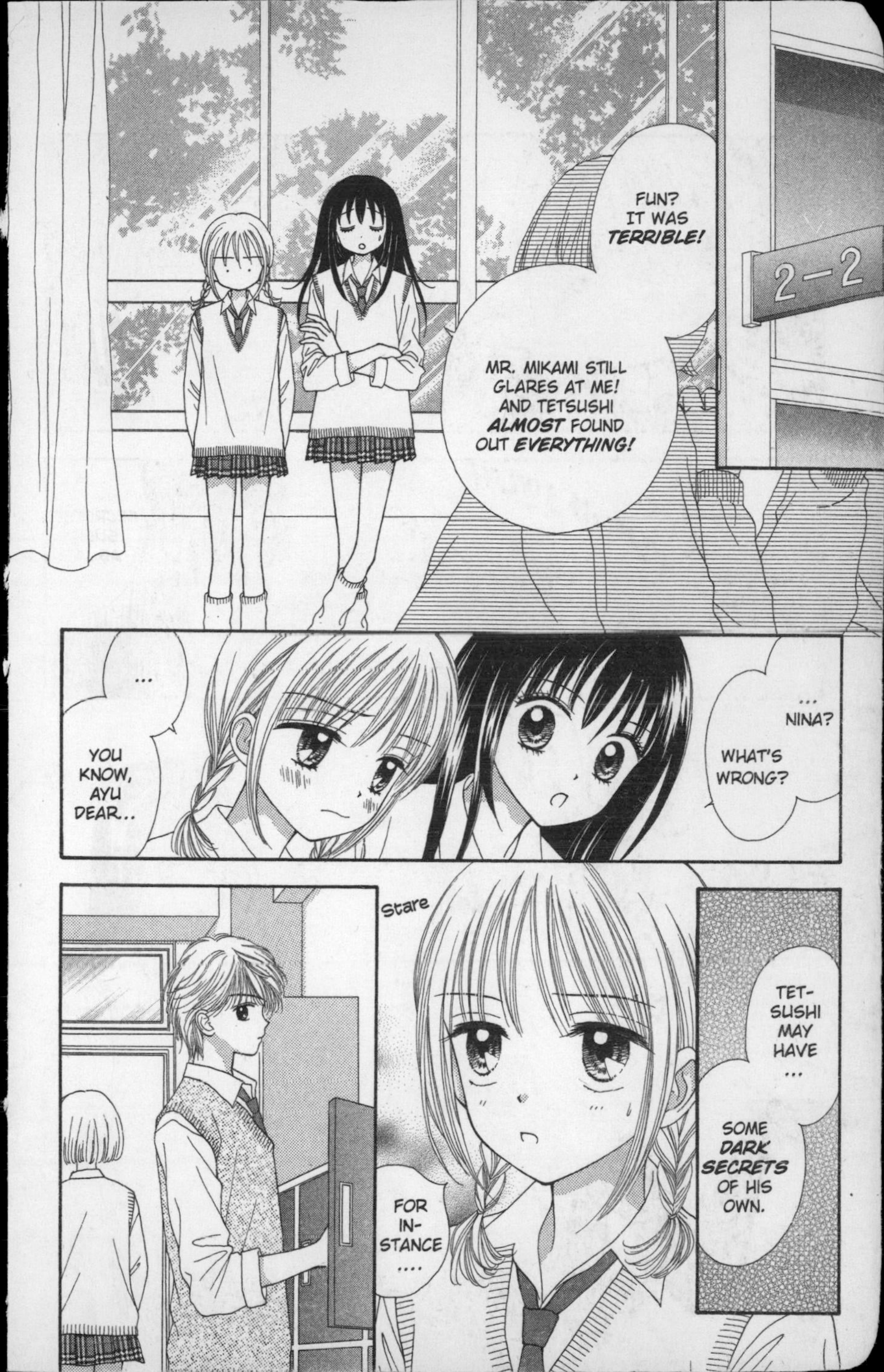
FUN? IT WAS TERRIBLE!
MR. MIKAMI STILL GLARES AT ME! AND TETSUSHI ALMOST FOUND OUT EVERYTHING!
... NINA?
WHAT'S WRONG?
...
YOU KNOW, AYU DEAR...
TET-SUSHI MAY HAVE ...
SOME DARK SECRETS OF HIS OWN.
...
Stare
FOR IN-STANCE ....

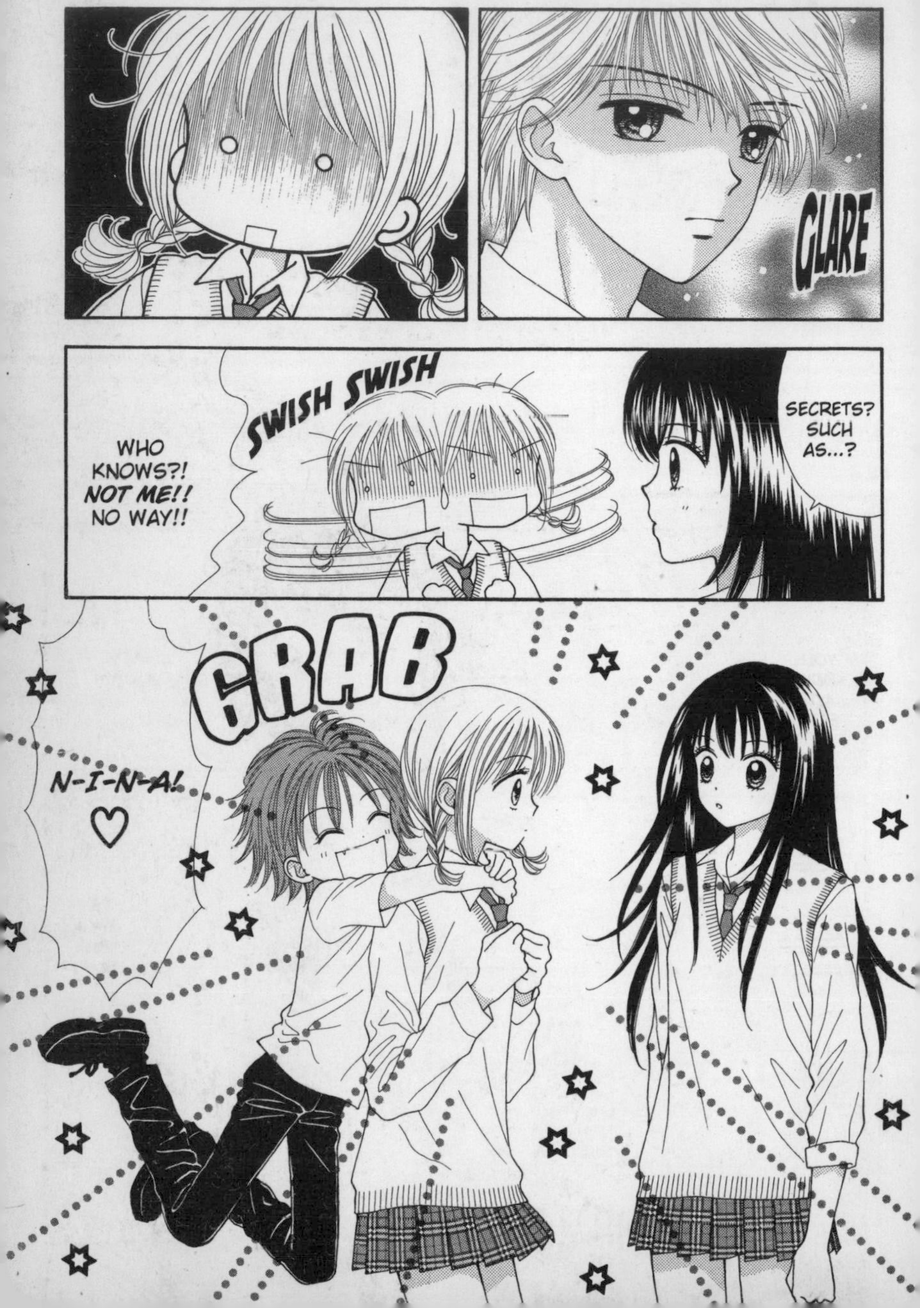
GLARE
SECRETS? SUCH AS...?
SWISH SWISH
WHO KNOWS?! NOT ME!! NO WAY!!
GRAB
N-I-N-A! ♡

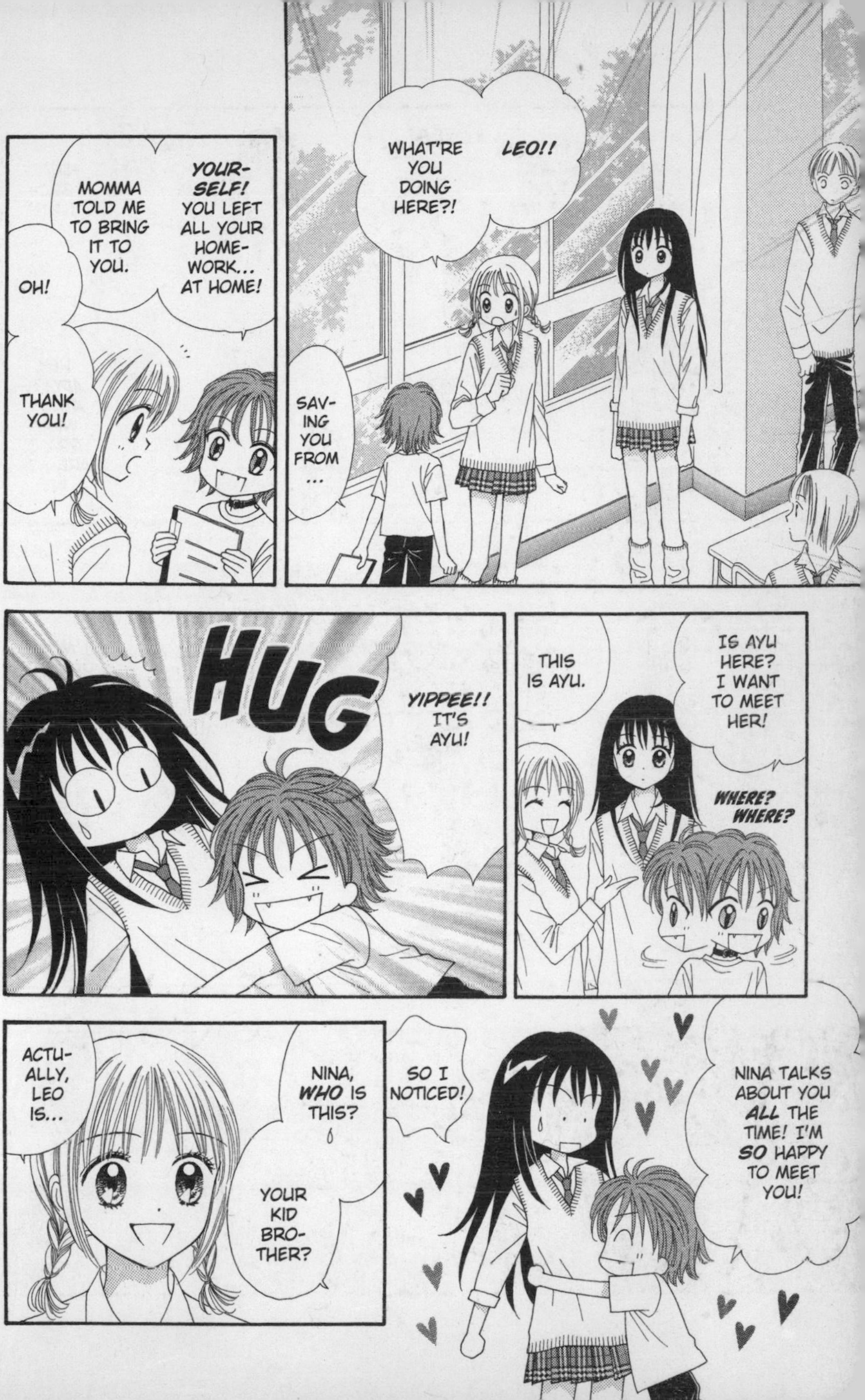
LEO!!
WHAT'RE YOU DOING HERE?!
SAV-ING YOU FROM ...
YOUR-SELF! YOU LEFT ALL YOUR HOME-WORK... AT HOME!
MOMMA TOLD ME TO BRING IT TO YOU.
OH!
THANK YOU!
IS AYU HERE? I WANT TO MEET HER!
THIS IS AYU.
WHERE? WHERE?
YIPPEE!! IT'S AYU!
HUG
NINA TALKS ABOUT YOU ALL THE TIME! I'M SO HAPPY TO MEET YOU!
SO I NOTICED!
NINA, WHO IS THIS?
YOUR KID BROTHER?
ACTU-ALLY, LEO IS...

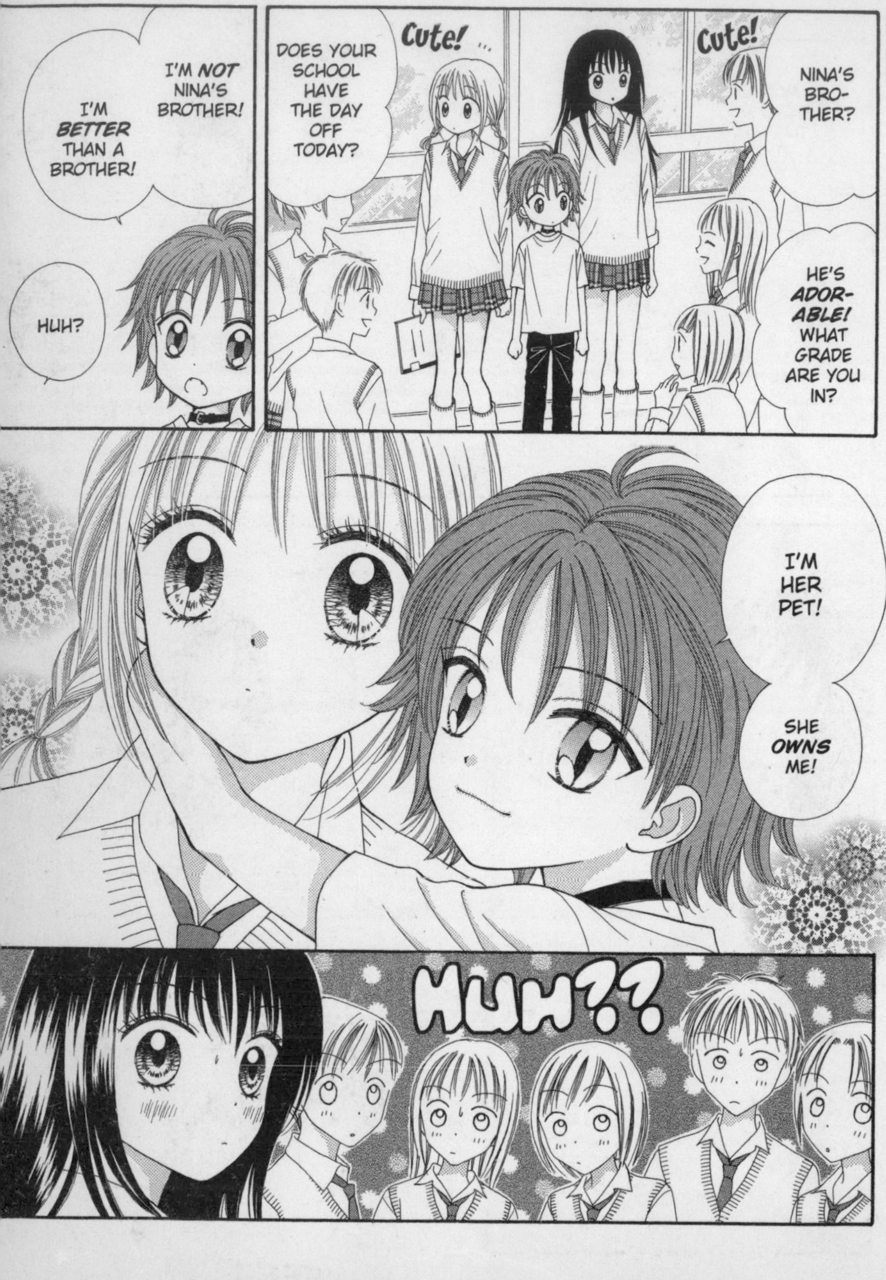
NINA'S BROTHER?
Cute!
HE'S ADORABLE! WHAT GRADE ARE YOU IN?
Cute!
DOES YOUR SCHOOL HAVE THE DAY OFF TODAY?
I'M NOT NINA'S BROTHER!
I'M BETTER THAN A BROTHER!
HUH?
I'M HER PET!
SHE OWNS ME!
HUH??

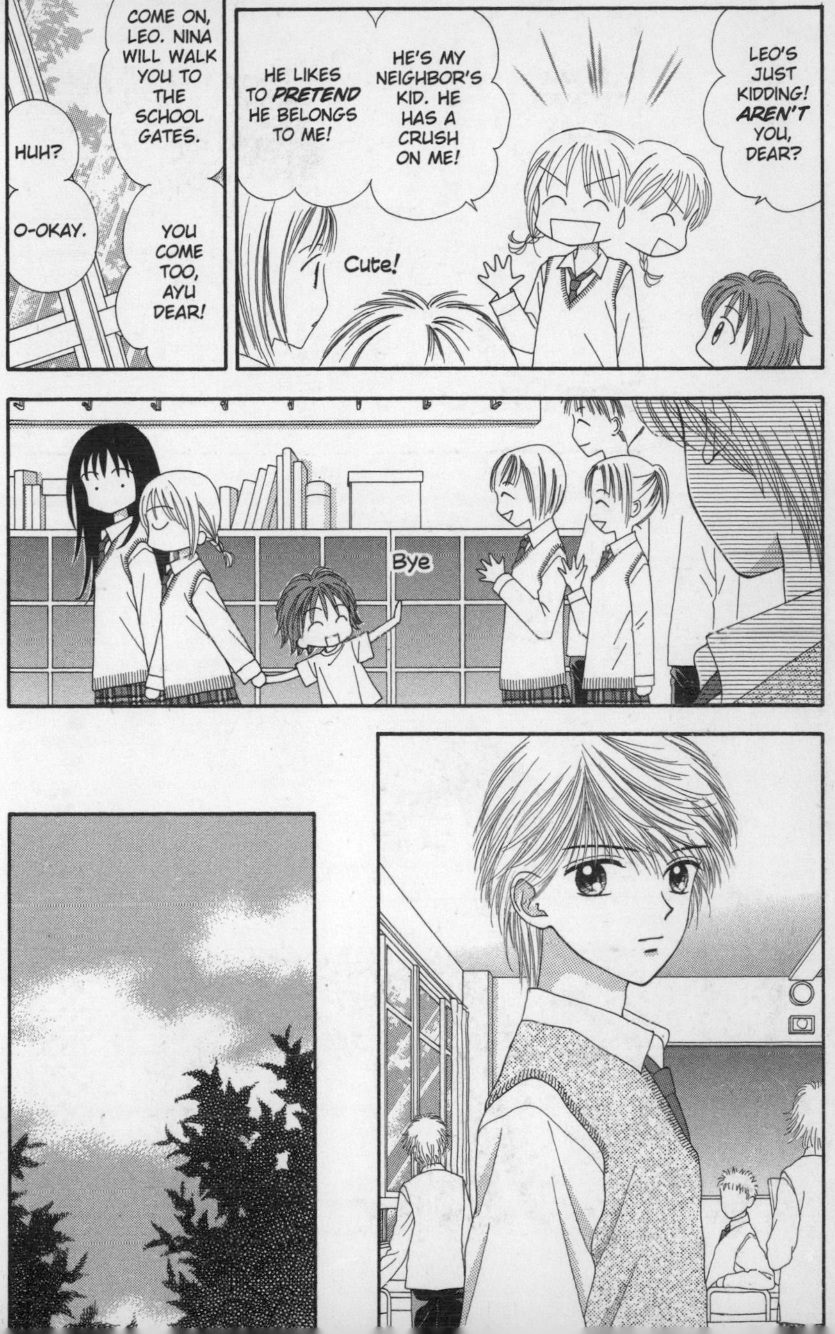
LEO'S JUST KIDDING! AREN'T YOU, DEAR?
HE'S MY NEIGHBOR'S KID. HE HAS A CRUSH ON ME!
HE LIKES TO PRETEND HE BELONGS TO ME!
Cute!
COME ON, LEO. NINA WILL WALK YOU TO THE SCHOOL GATES.
HUH?
YOU COME TOO, AYU DEAR!
O-OKAY.
Bye

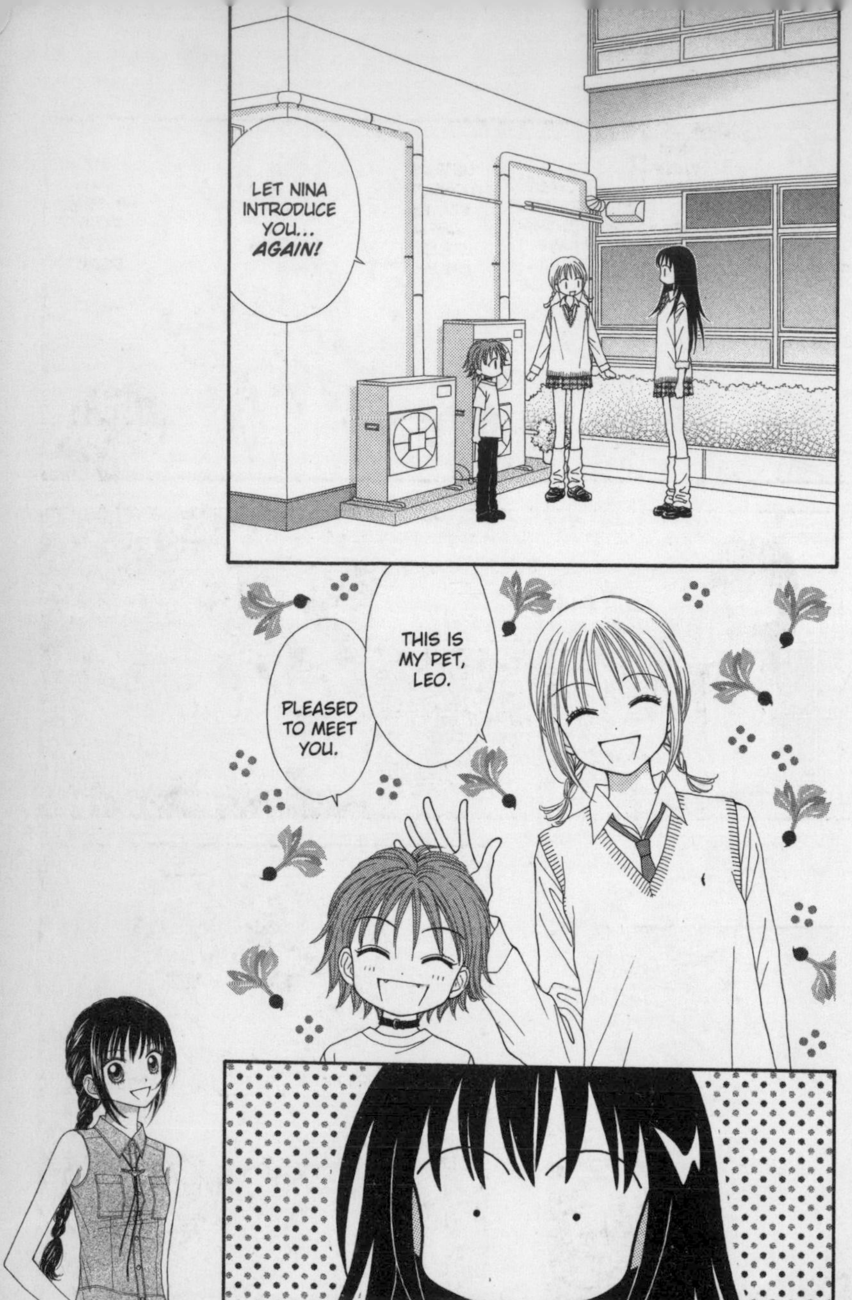
LET NINA INTRODUCE YOU... *AGAIN!*
THIS IS MY PET, LEO.
PLEASED TO MEET YOU.

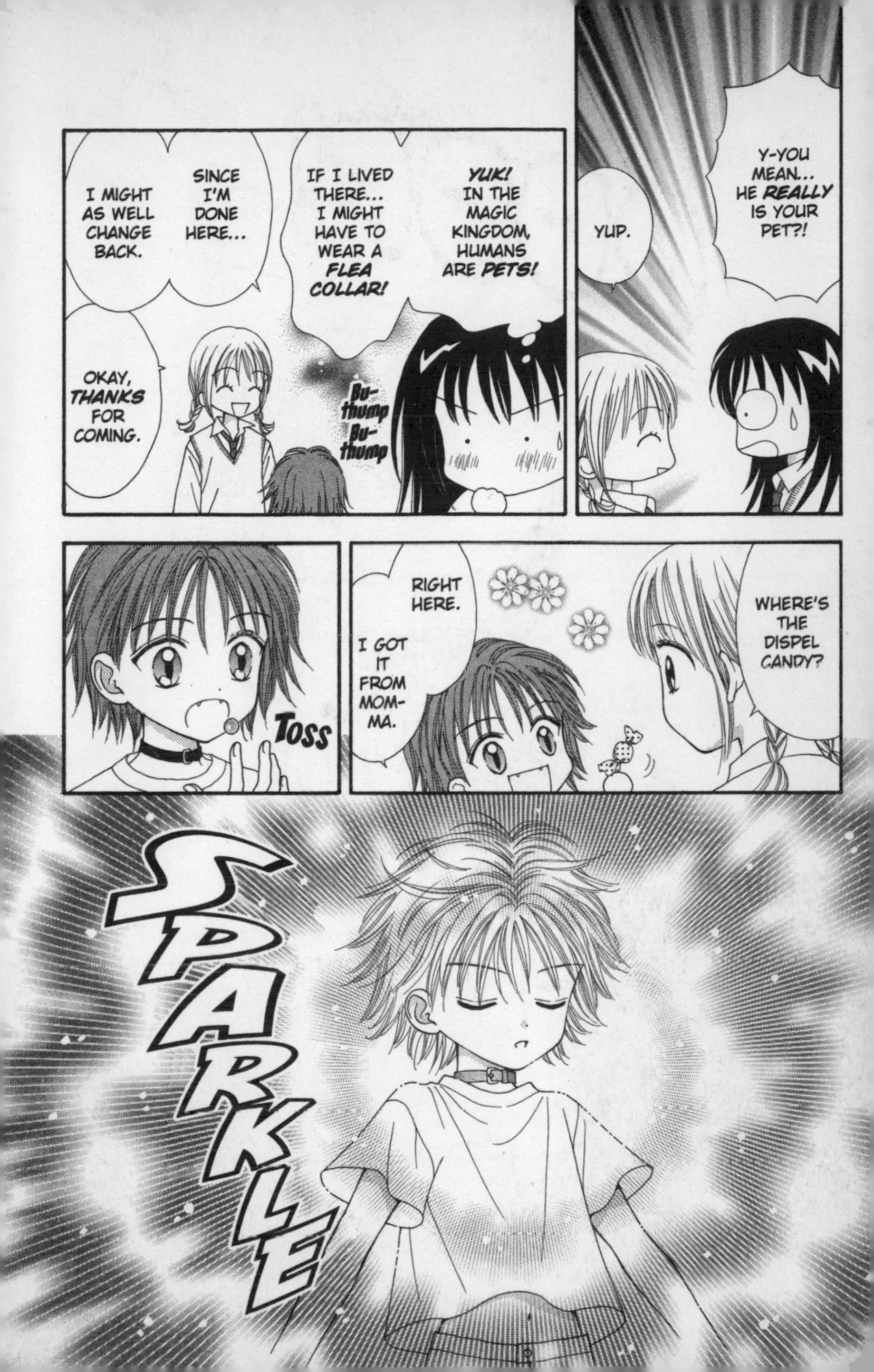
Y-YOU MEAN... HE REALLY IS YOUR PET?!
YUP.
YUK! IN THE MAGIC KINGDOM, HUMANS ARE PETS!
IF I LIVED THERE... I MIGHT HAVE TO WEAR A FLEA COLLAR!
Bu-thump Bu-thump
SINCE I'M DONE HERE...
I MIGHT AS WELL CHANGE BACK.
OKAY, THANKS FOR COMING.
WHERE'S THE DISPEL CANDY?
RIGHT HERE.
I GOT IT FROM MOM-MA.
TOSS
SPARKLE

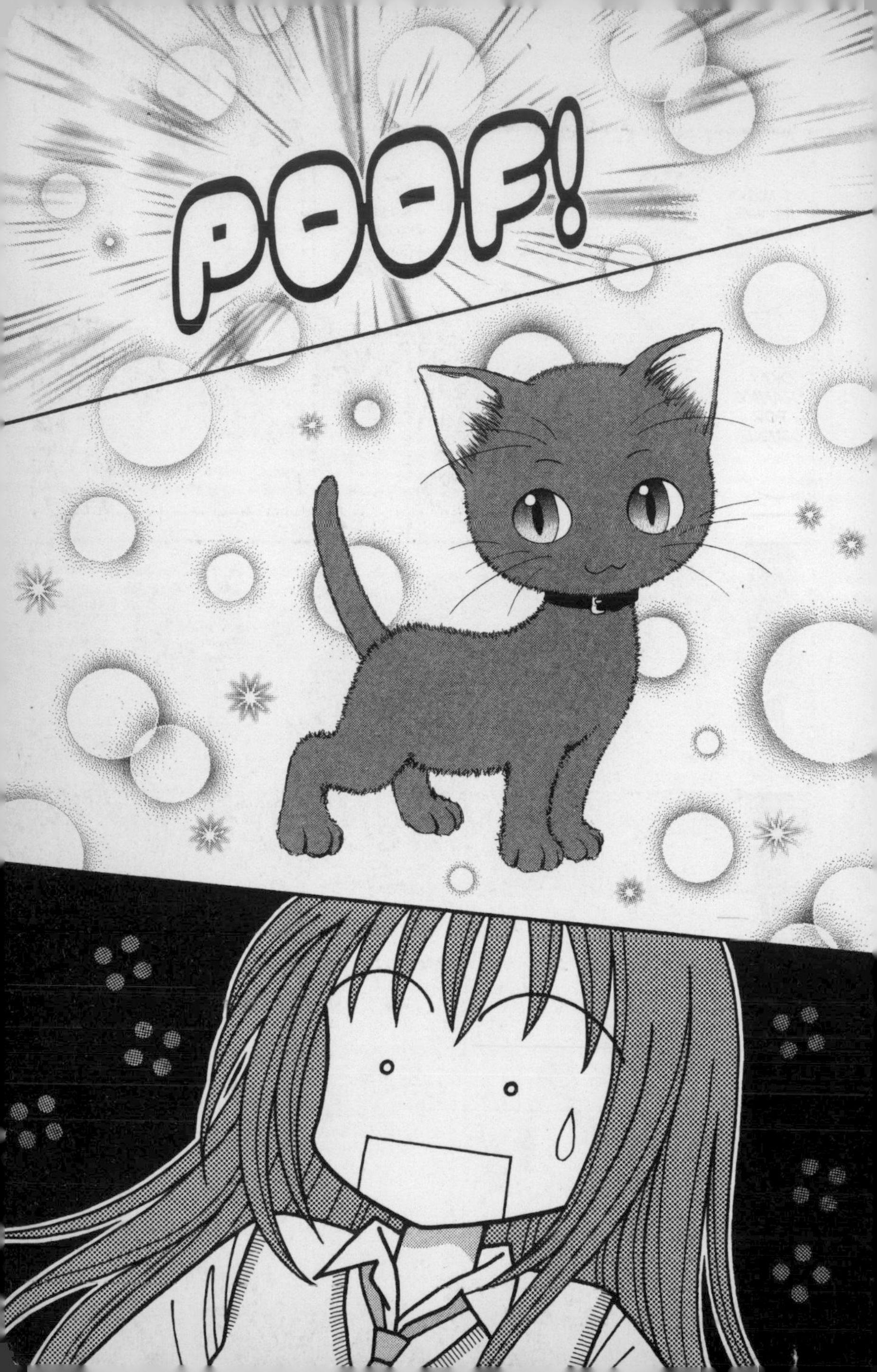
POOF!

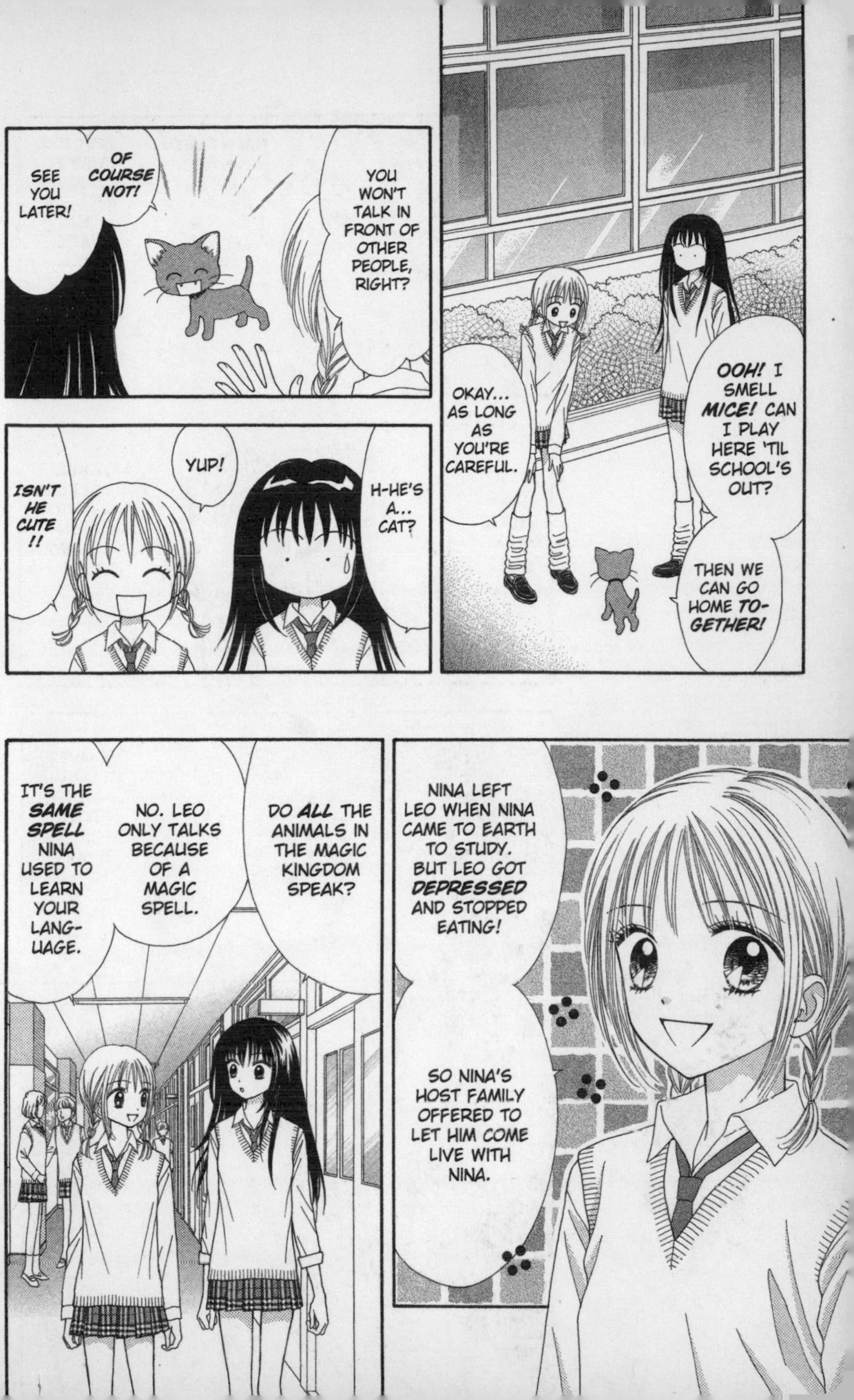
OOH! I SMELL MICE! CAN I PLAY HERE 'TIL SCHOOL'S OUT?
OKAY... AS LONG AS YOU'RE CAREFUL.
THEN WE CAN GO HOME TO-GETHER!
YOU WON'T TALK IN FRONT OF OTHER PEOPLE, RIGHT?
OF COURSE NOT!
SEE YOU LATER!
H-HE'S A... CAT?
YUP!
ISN'T HE CUTE!!
NINA LEFT LEO WHEN NINA CAME TO EARTH TO STUDY. BUT LEO GOT DEPRESSED AND STOPPED EATING!
SO NINA'S HOST FAMILY OFFERED TO LET HIM COME LIVE WITH NINA.
DO ALL THE ANIMALS IN THE MAGIC KINGDOM SPEAK?
NO. LEO ONLY TALKS BECAUSE OF A MAGIC SPELL.
IT'S THE SAME SPELL NINA USED TO LEARN YOUR LANG-UAGE.

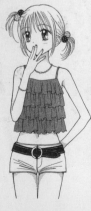

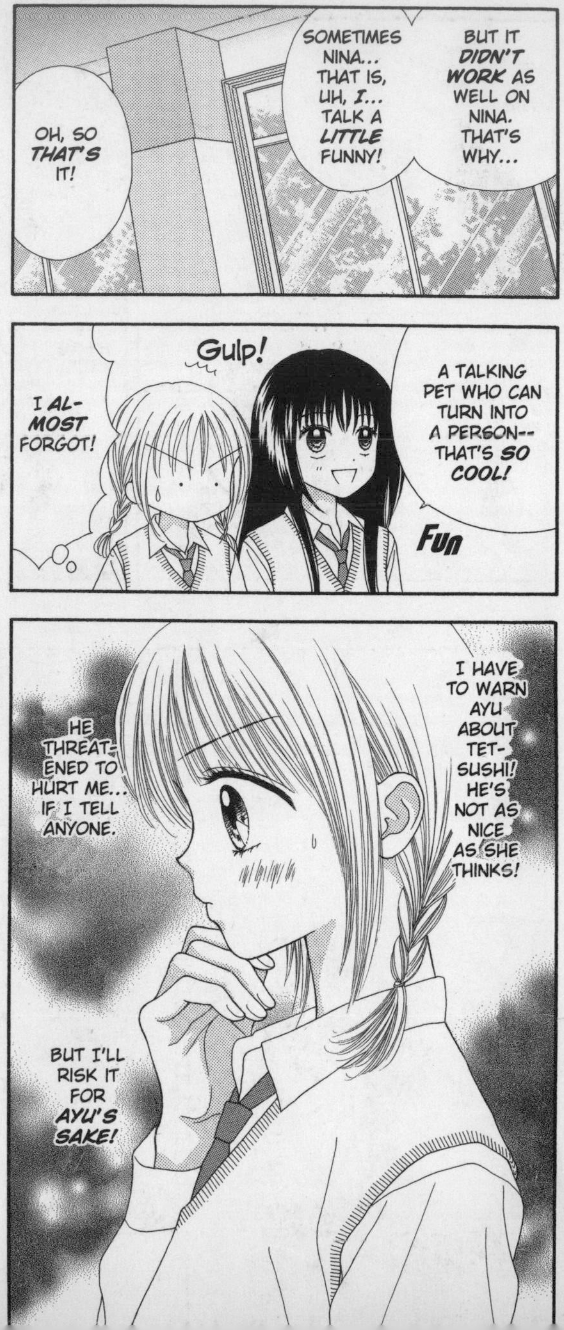
SOMETIMES NINA... THAT IS, UH, *I*... TALK A *LITTLE* FUNNY!
BUT IT *DIDN'T WORK* AS WELL ON NINA. THAT'S WHY...
OH, SO *THAT'S* IT!
A TALKING PET WHO CAN TURN INTO A PERSON-- THAT'S *SO COOL!*
Fun
Gulp!
I *AL-MOST* FORGOT!
I HAVE TO WARN AYU ABOUT TET-SUSHI! HE'S NOT AS NICE AS SHE THINKS!
HE THREAT-ENED TO HURT ME... IF I TELL ANYONE.
BUT I'LL RISK IT FOR *AYU'S SAKE!*
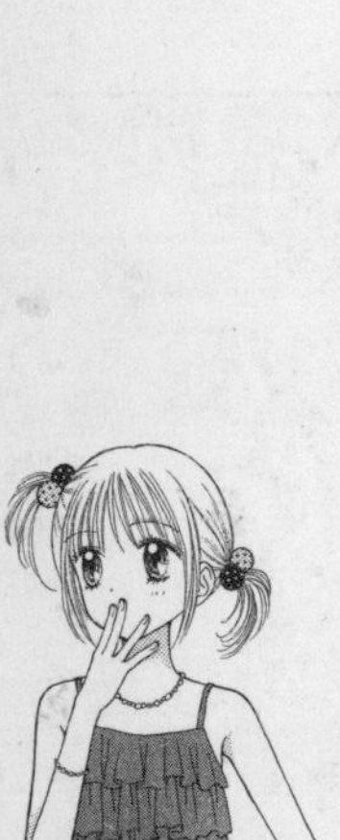

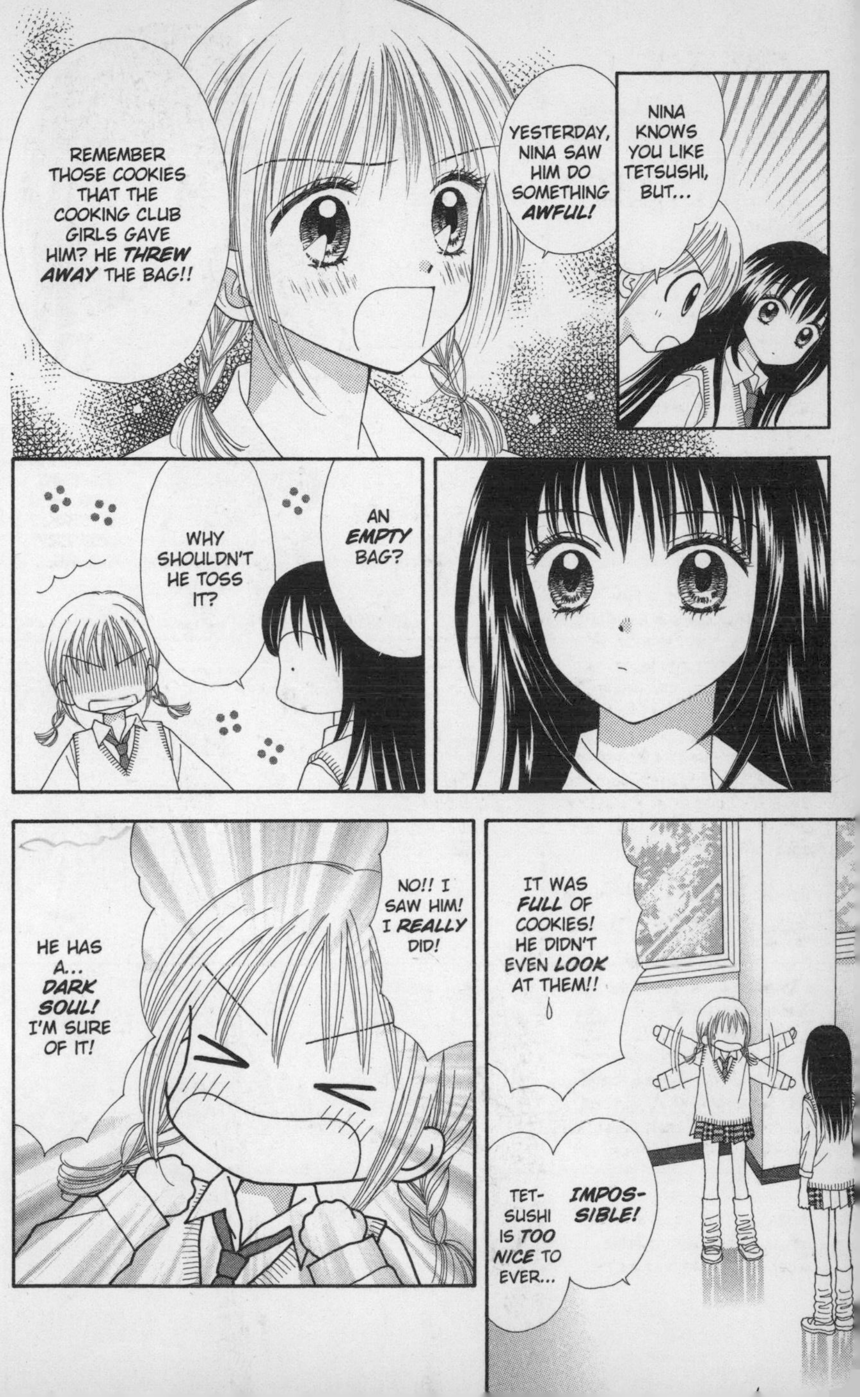
NINA KNOWS YOU LIKE TETSUSHI, BUT...
YESTERDAY, NINA SAW HIM DO SOMETHING AWFUL!
REMEMBER THOSE COOKIES THAT THE COOKING CLUB GIRLS GAVE HIM? HE THREW AWAY THE BAG!!
AN EMPTY BAG?
WHY SHOULDN'T HE TOSS IT?
IT WAS FULL OF COOKIES! HE DIDN'T EVEN LOOK AT THEM!!
IMPOSSIBLE!
TETSUSHI IS TOO NICE TO EVER...
NO!! I SAW HIM! I REALLY DID!
HE HAS A... DARK SOUL! I'M SURE OF IT!

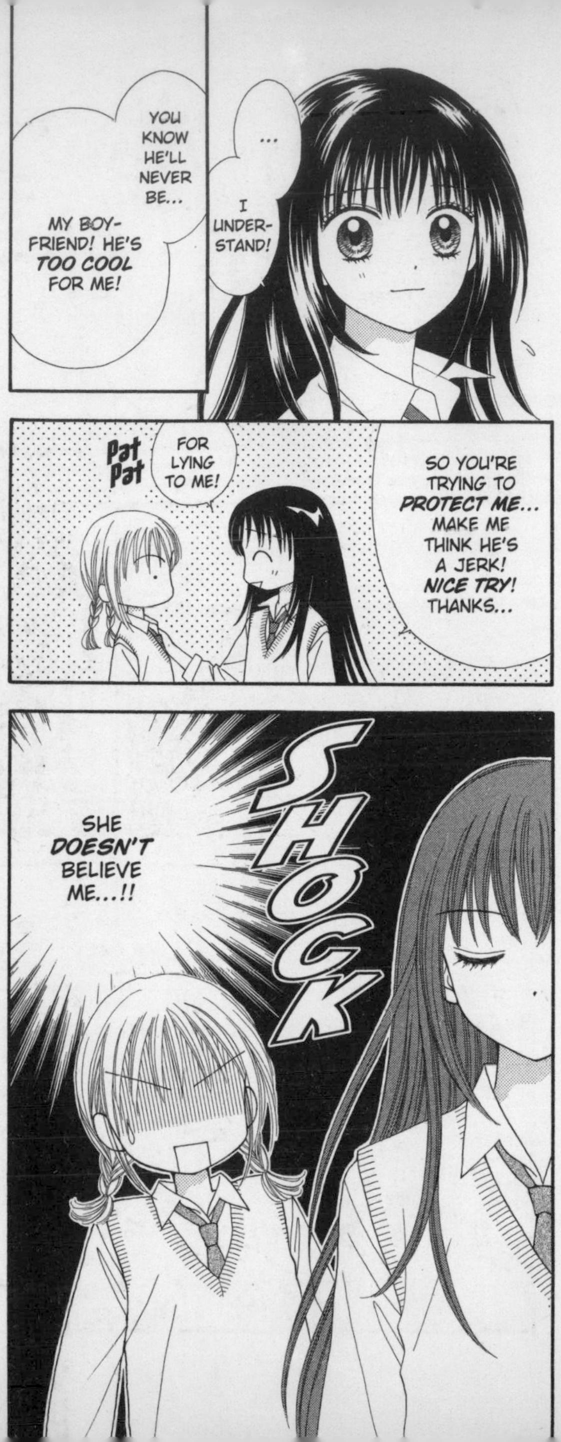
...
I UNDERSTAND!
YOU KNOW HE'LL NEVER BE...
MY BOY-FRIEND! HE'S TOO COOL FOR ME!
SO YOU'RE TRYING TO PROTECT ME... MAKE ME THINK HE'S A JERK! NICE TRY! THANKS...
FOR LYING TO ME!
Pat Pat
SHOCK
SHE DOESN'T BELIEVE ME...!!

FREE TALK 1

Hello. It's me--Wataru. I hope you're enjoying Volume 2 of *Ultra Maniac.*

Nina's cat, Leo, who first appears in Chapter 6--is my **very first** animal character.

I've drawn a lot of animals in bonus material for magazines, but having one as a character in a story is a first for me.

Most cartoon animals don't look exactly like their counterparts in the real world. They're changed to look cuter or so that their facial expressions and movements are more like humans. I wasn't sure how much I should distort Leo, so I just went ahead and drew him.

Because I didn't make a model sheet of how he should look, Leo changed more and more as I drew him. As a result, I got **quite a shock** recently. It happened when I was drawing his transformation scene in Chapter 11. I couldn't remember what kind of screen tone I'd used for his first transformation. So I looked back at the scene in Chapter 6 and freaked myself out when I realized, **"Ack! He's totally different!"**♭

I decided it might be fun for people to see him gradually changing, so I left him as is.

The reason I gave Leo a grey screen tone is because white would make him look **too plain**. A pattern would be a **pain** to draw. And, I figured, a black cat would be **even more** difficult. But when I introduced a black cat character in Chapter 12, I found that it was **actually** a lot easier to draw. . . .♭

When I draw Leo in color, I color him in a grayish color with the image of a Russian Blue in mind.

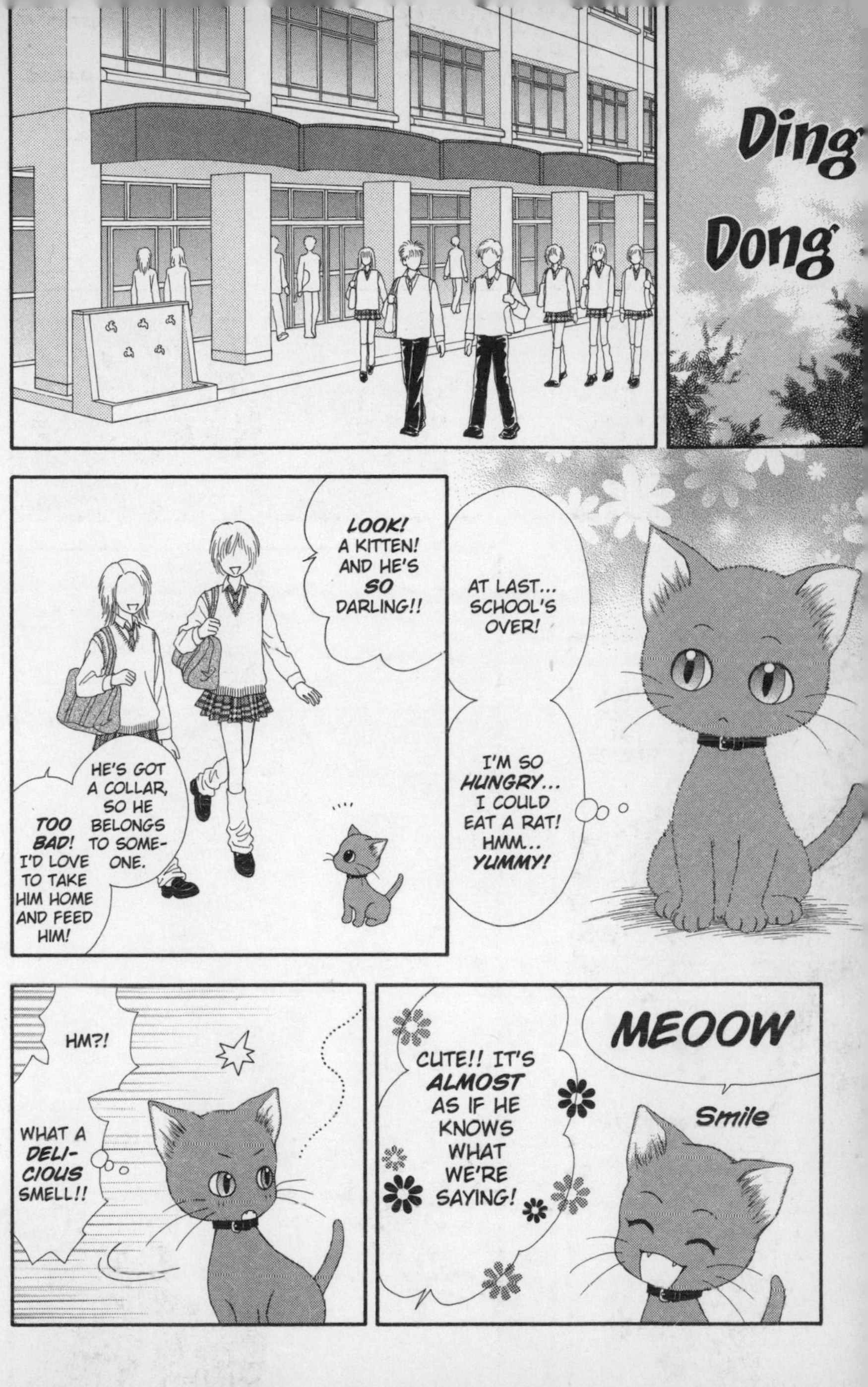
Ding Dong
AT LAST... SCHOOL'S OVER!
I'M SO HUNGRY... I COULD EAT A RAT! HMM.. YUMMY!
LOOK! A KITTEN! AND HE'S SO DARLING!!
HE'S GOT A COLLAR, SO HE BELONGS TO SOME-ONE.
TOO BAD! I'D LOVE TO TAKE HIM HOME AND FEED HIM!
MEOOW
Smile
CUTE!! IT'S ALMOST AS IF HE KNOWS WHAT WE'RE SAYING!
HM?!
WHAT A DELI-CIOUS SMELL!!

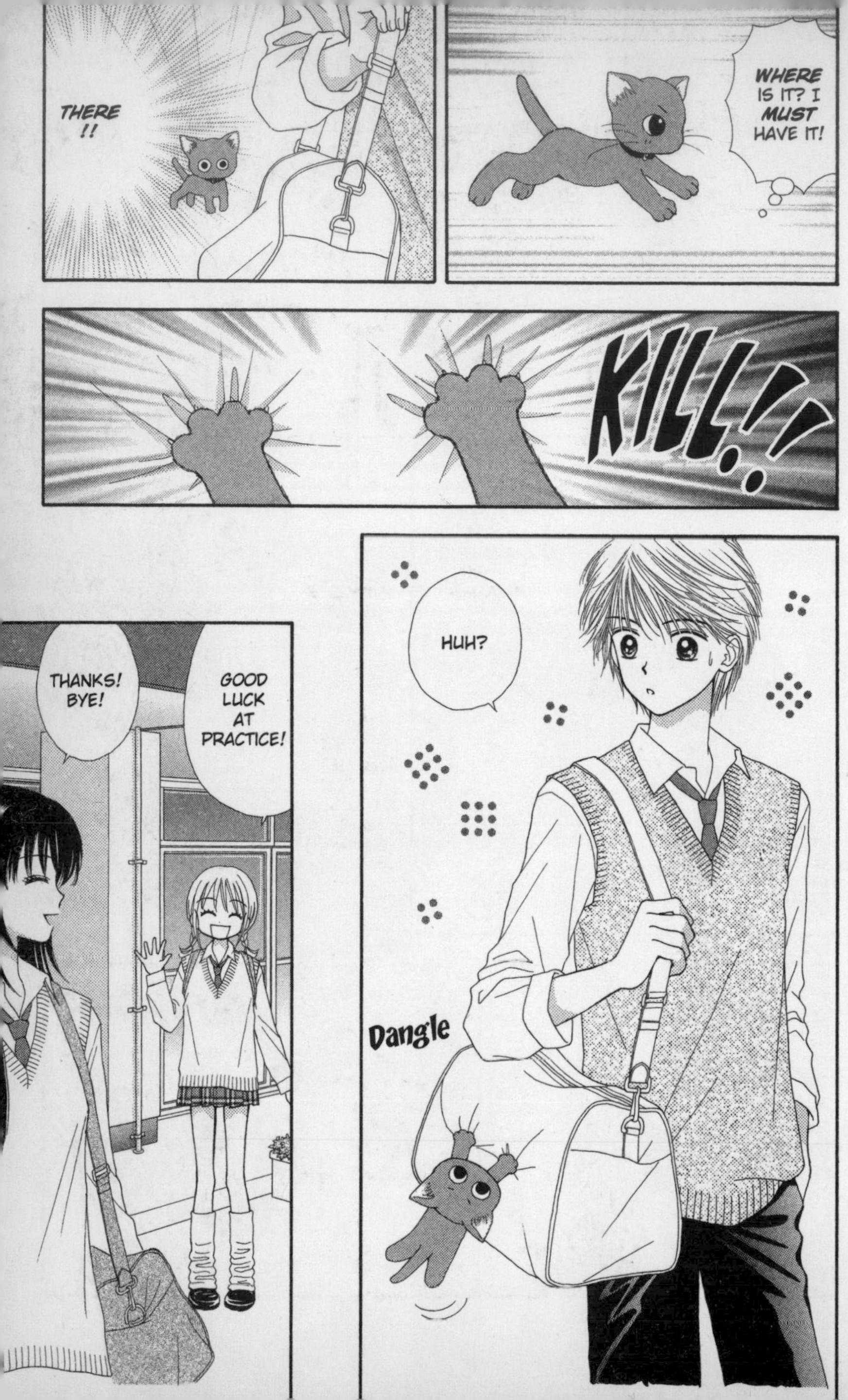
WHERE IS IT? I MUST HAVE IT!
THERE!!
KILL!!!
HUH?
Dangle
GOOD LUCK AT PRACTICE!
THANKS! BYE!

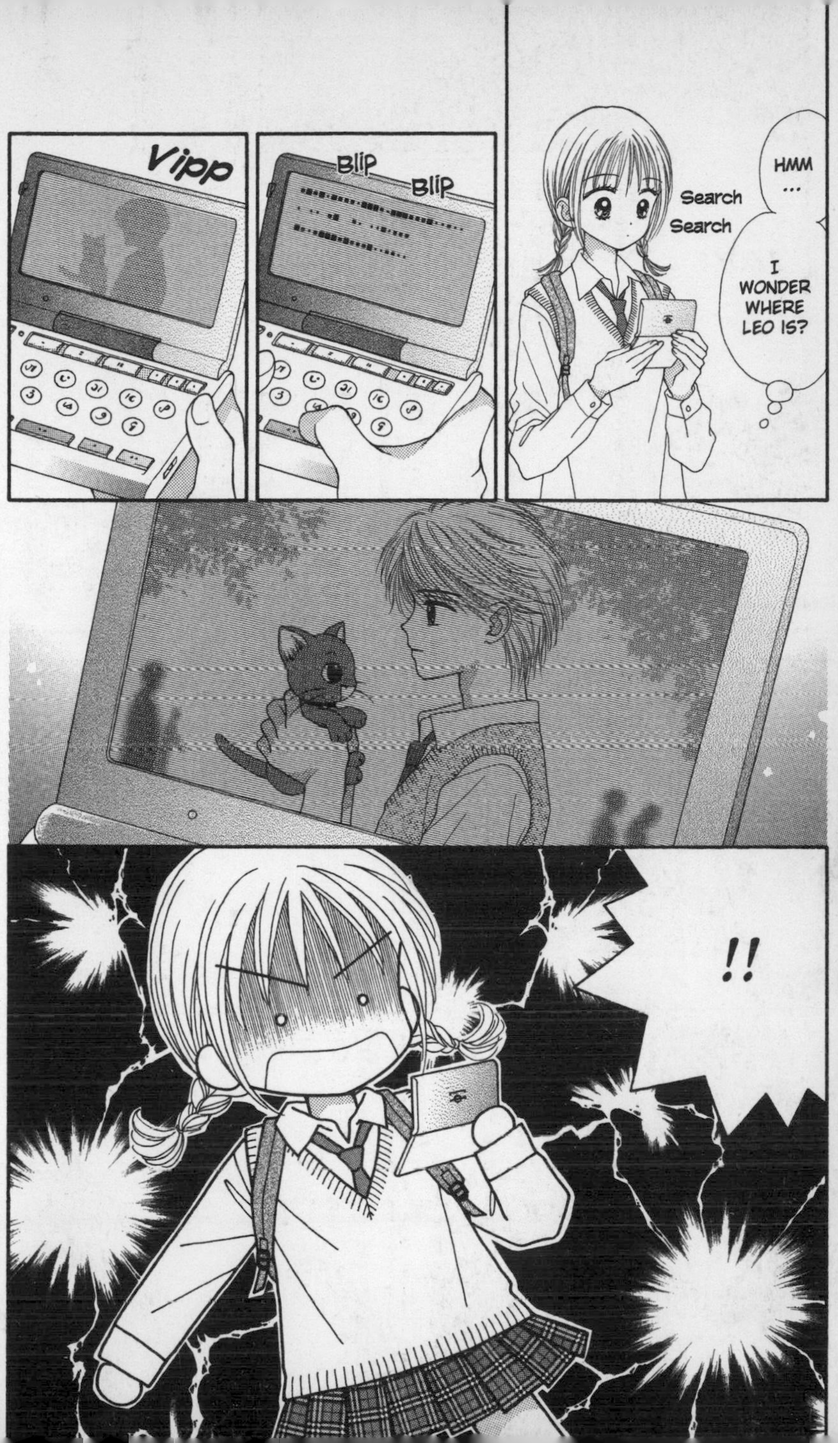
HMM ...
I WONDER WHERE LEO IS?
Search
Search
Blip
Blip
Vipp
!!

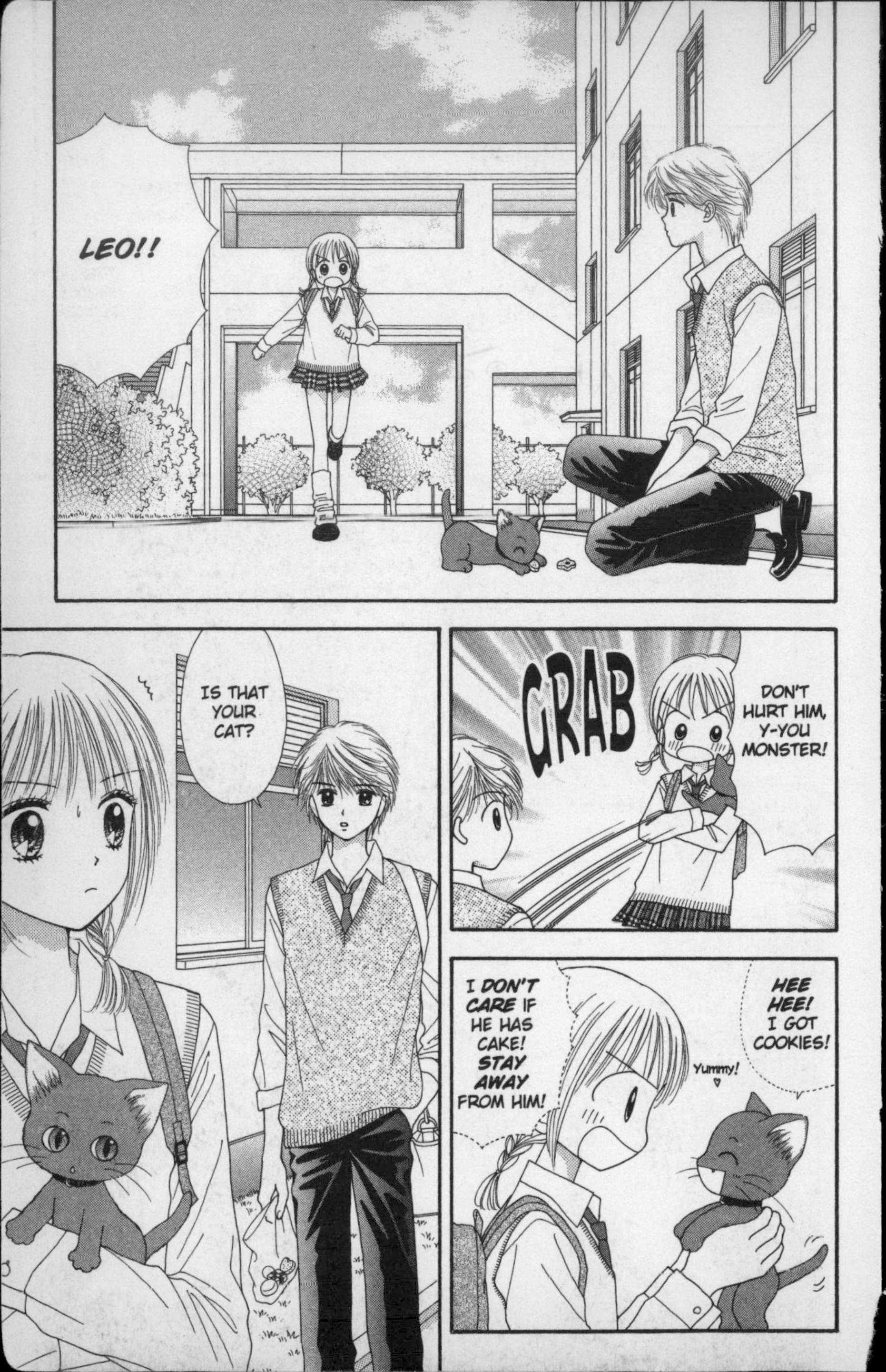
LEO!!
GRAB
DON'T HURT HIM, Y-YOU MONSTER!
HEE HEE! I GOT COOKIES!
Yummy!
I DON'T CARE IF HE HAS CAKE! STAY AWAY FROM HIM!
IS THAT YOUR CAT?

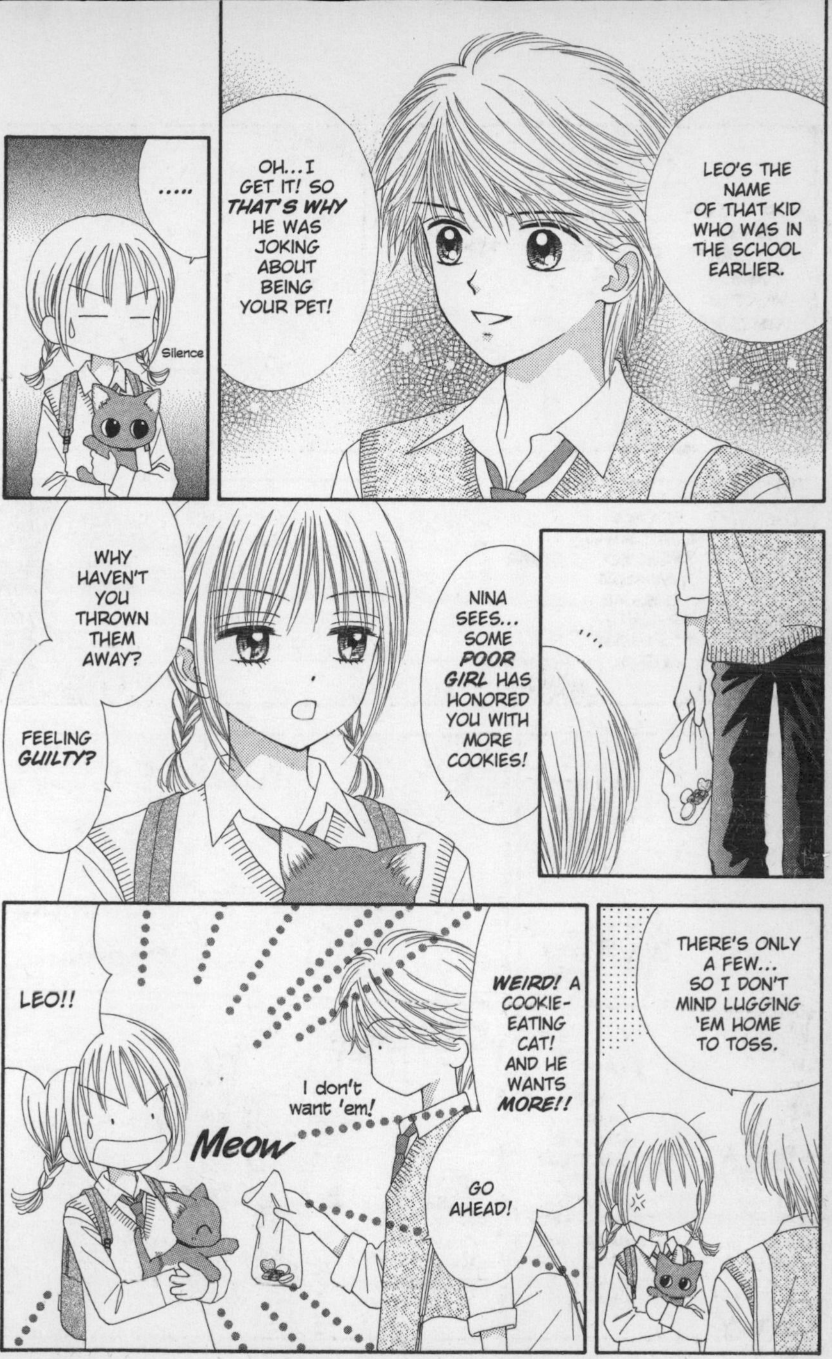
LEO'S THE NAME OF THAT KID WHO WAS IN THE SCHOOL EARLIER.
OH...I GET IT! SO THAT'S WHY HE WAS JOKING ABOUT BEING YOUR PET!
.....
Silence
...
NINA SEES... SOME POOR GIRL HAS HONORED YOU WITH MORE COOKIES!
WHY HAVEN'T YOU THROWN THEM AWAY?
FEELING GUILTY?
THERE'S ONLY A FEW... SO I DON'T MIND LUGGING 'EM HOME TO TOSS.
WEIRD! A COOKIE-EATING CAT! AND HE WANTS MORE!!
GO AHEAD!
I don't want 'em!
Meow
LEO!!

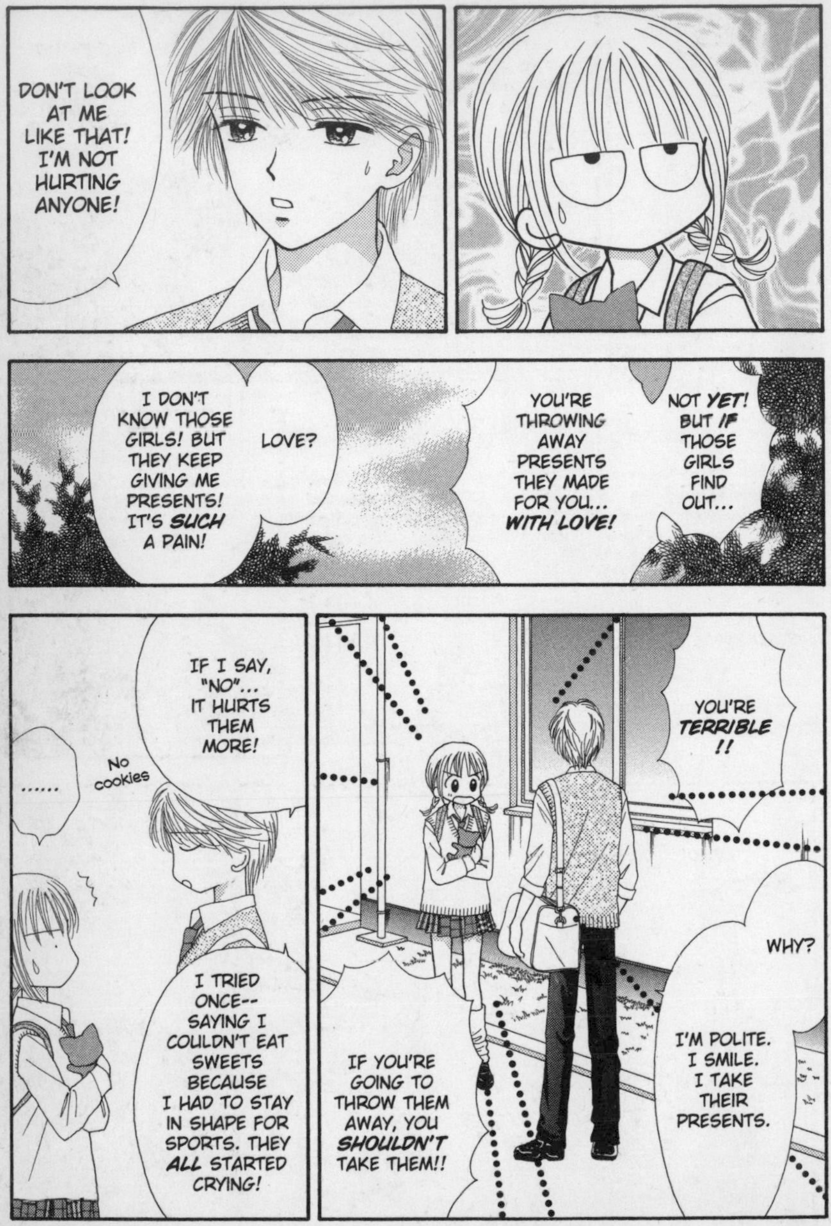
DON'T LOOK AT ME LIKE THAT! I'M NOT HURTING ANYONE!
NOT *YET*! BUT *IF* THOSE GIRLS FIND OUT...
YOU'RE THROWING AWAY PRESENTS THEY MADE FOR YOU... ***WITH LOVE!***
LOVE?
I DON'T KNOW THOSE GIRLS! BUT THEY KEEP GIVING ME PRESENTS! IT'S ***SUCH*** A PAIN!
YOU'RE ***TERRIBLE*** !!
WHY?
I'M POLITE. I SMILE. I TAKE THEIR PRESENTS.
IF YOU'RE GOING TO THROW THEM AWAY, YOU ***SHOULDN'T*** TAKE THEM!!
IF I SAY, "NO"... IT HURTS THEM MORE!
No cookies
......
I TRIED ONCE-- SAYING I COULDN'T EAT SWEETS BECAUSE I HAD TO STAY IN SHAPE FOR SPORTS. THEY ***ALL*** STARTED CRYING!

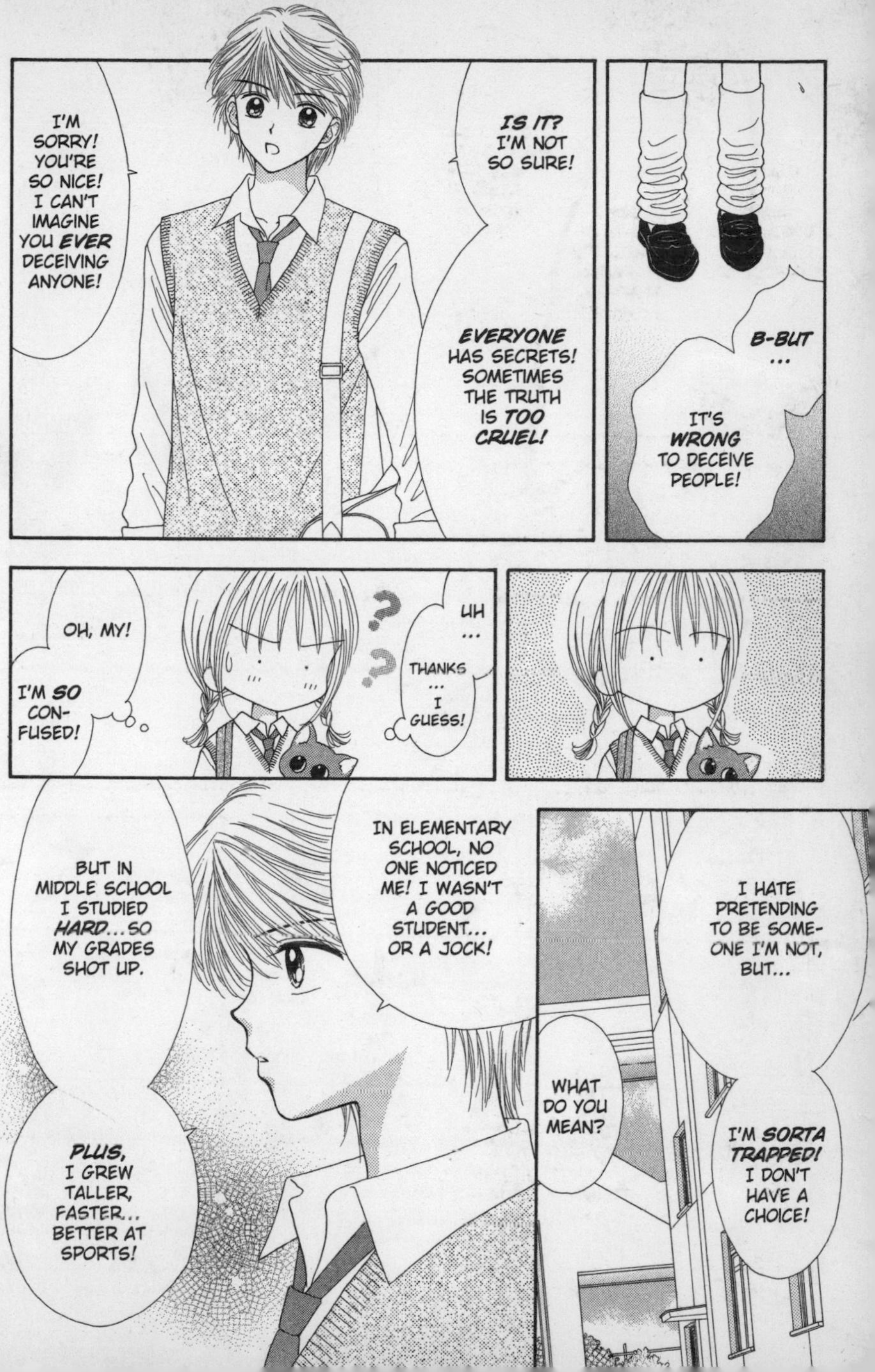
B-BUT...
IT'S WRONG TO DECEIVE PEOPLE!
IS IT? I'M NOT SO SURE!
EVERYONE HAS SECRETS! SOMETIMES THE TRUTH IS TOO CRUEL!
I'M SORRY! YOU'RE SO NICE! I CAN'T IMAGINE YOU EVER DECEIVING ANYONE!
UH... THANKS... I GUESS!
OH, MY!
I'M SO CON-FUSED!
I HATE PRETENDING TO BE SOME-ONE I'M NOT, BUT...
I'M SORTA TRAPPED! I DON'T HAVE A CHOICE!
WHAT DO YOU MEAN?
IN ELEMENTARY SCHOOL, NO ONE NOTICED ME! I WASN'T A GOOD STUDENT... OR A JOCK!
BUT IN MIDDLE SCHOOL I STUDIED HARD...SO MY GRADES SHOT UP.
PLUS, I GREW TALLER, FASTER... BETTER AT SPORTS!

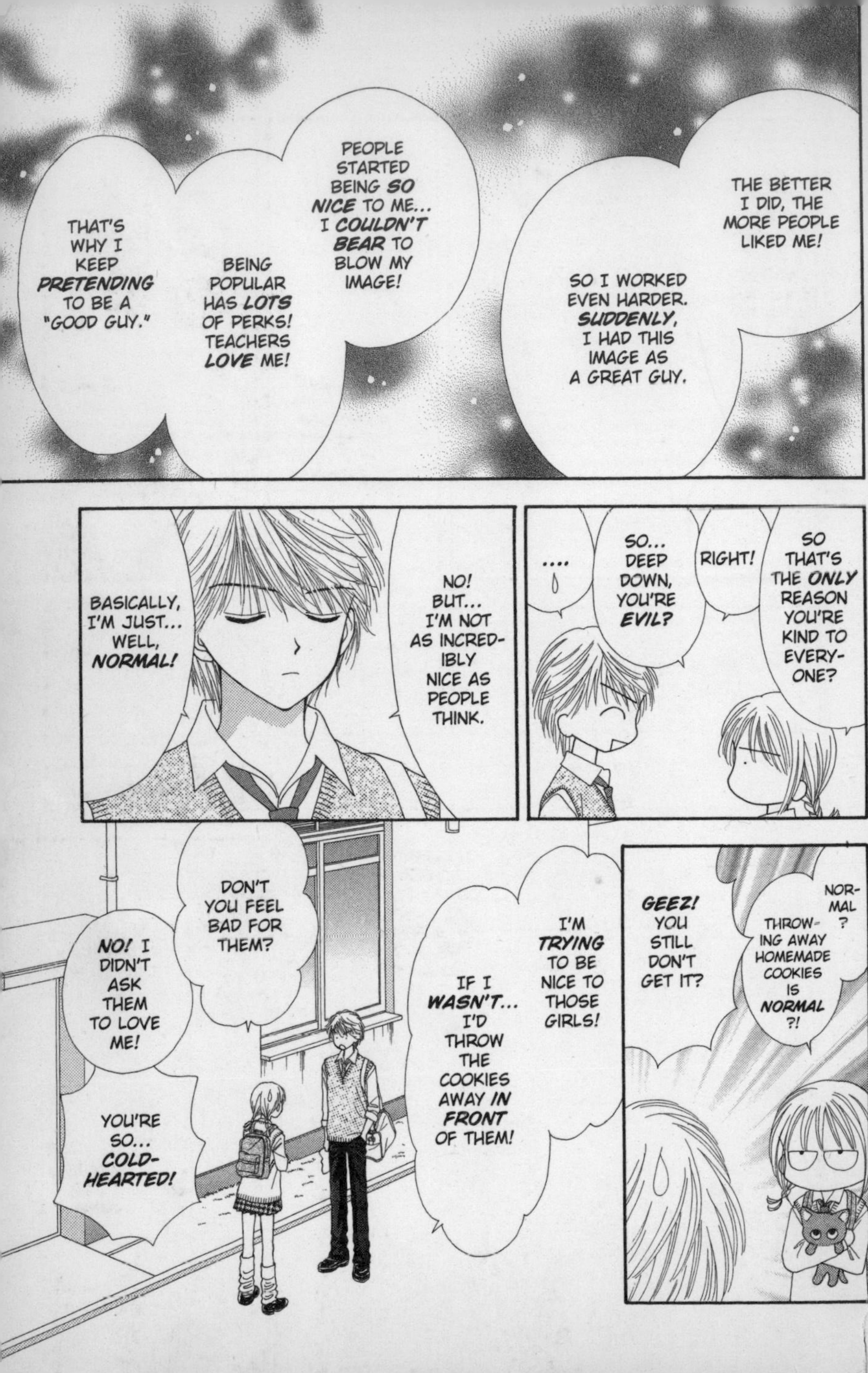
THE BETTER I DID, THE MORE PEOPLE LIKED ME!
SO I WORKED EVEN HARDER. SUDDENLY, I HAD THIS IMAGE AS A GREAT GUY.
PEOPLE STARTED BEING SO NICE TO ME... I COULDN'T BEAR TO BLOW MY IMAGE!
BEING POPULAR HAS LOTS OF PERKS! TEACHERS LOVE ME!
THAT'S WHY I KEEP PRETENDING TO BE A "GOOD GUY."
SO THAT'S THE ONLY REASON YOU'RE KIND TO EVERYONE?
RIGHT!
SO... DEEP DOWN, YOU'RE EVIL?
....
NO! BUT... I'M NOT AS INCREDIBLY NICE AS PEOPLE THINK.
BASICALLY, I'M JUST... WELL, NORMAL!
NORMAL?
THROWING AWAY HOMEMADE COOKIES IS NORMAL?!
GEEZ! YOU STILL DON'T GET IT?
I'M TRYING TO BE NICE TO THOSE GIRLS!
IF I WASN'T... I'D THROW THE COOKIES AWAY IN FRONT OF THEM!
DON'T YOU FEEL BAD FOR THEM?
NO! I DIDN'T ASK THEM TO LOVE ME!
YOU'RE SO... COLD-HEARTED!

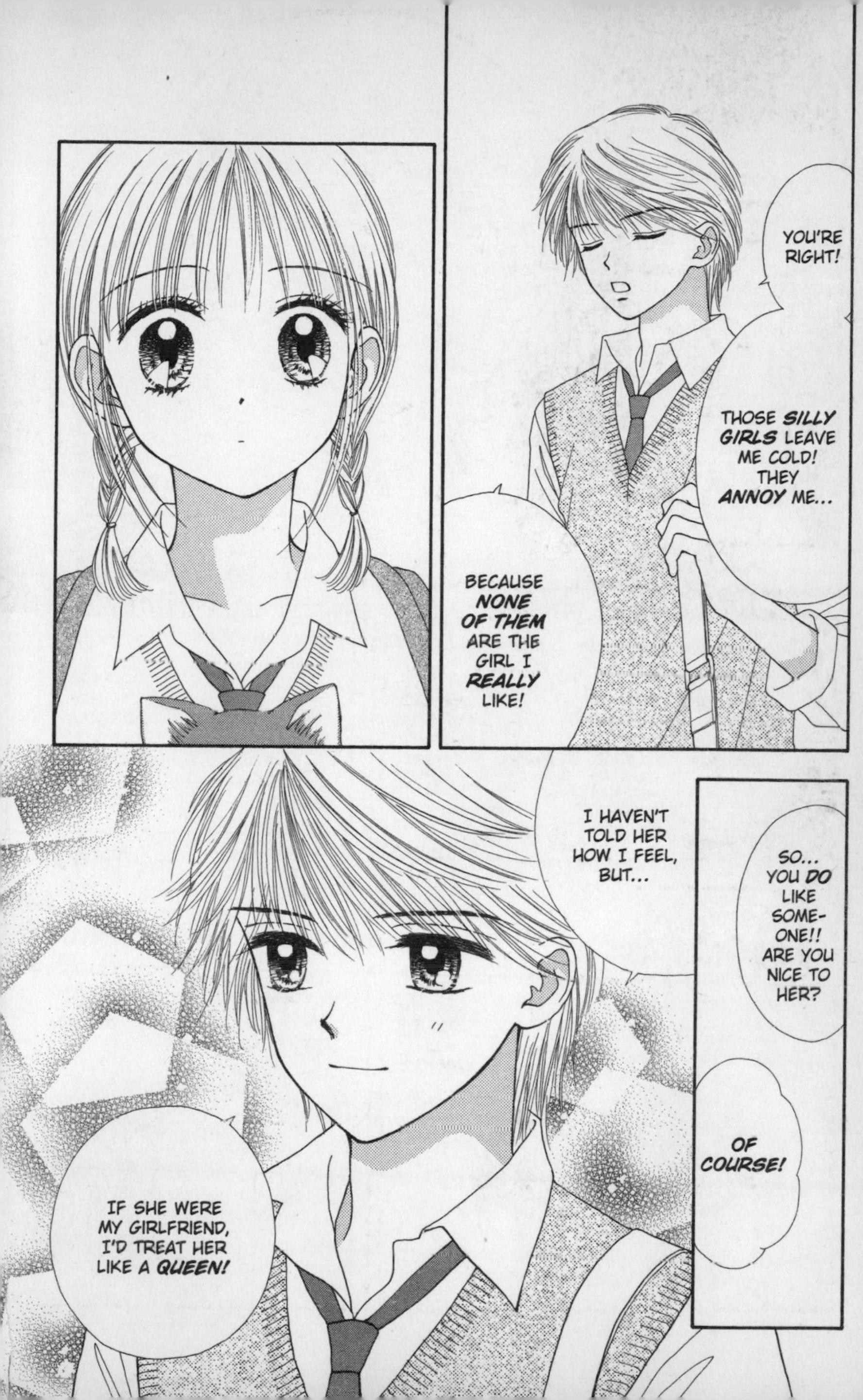
YOU'RE RIGHT!
THOSE SILLY GIRLS LEAVE ME COLD! THEY ANNOY ME...
BECAUSE NONE OF THEM ARE THE GIRL I REALLY LIKE!
SO... YOU DO LIKE SOME-ONE!! ARE YOU NICE TO HER?
OF COURSE!
I HAVEN'T TOLD HER HOW I FEEL, BUT...
IF SHE WERE MY GIRLFRIEND, I'D TREAT HER LIKE A QUEEN!

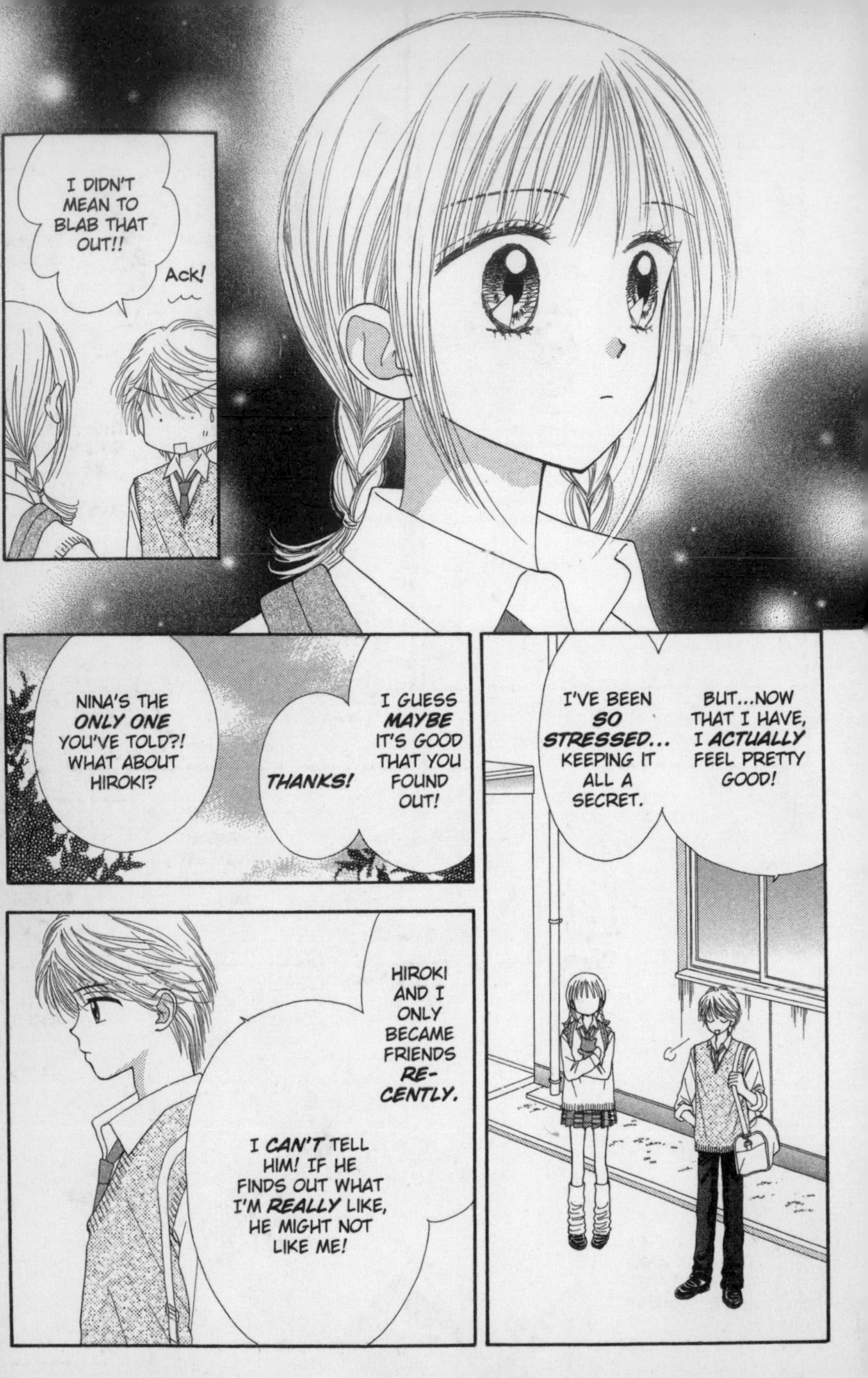
I DIDN'T MEAN TO BLAB THAT OUT!!
Ack!
I'VE BEEN SO STRESSED... KEEPING IT ALL A SECRET.
BUT...NOW THAT I HAVE, I ACTUALLY FEEL PRETTY GOOD!
I GUESS MAYBE IT'S GOOD THAT YOU FOUND OUT!
THANKS!
NINA'S THE ONLY ONE YOU'VE TOLD?! WHAT ABOUT HIROKI?
HIROKI AND I ONLY BECAME FRIENDS RE-CENTLY.
I CAN'T TELL HIM! IF HE FINDS OUT WHAT I'M REALLY LIKE, HE MIGHT NOT LIKE ME!

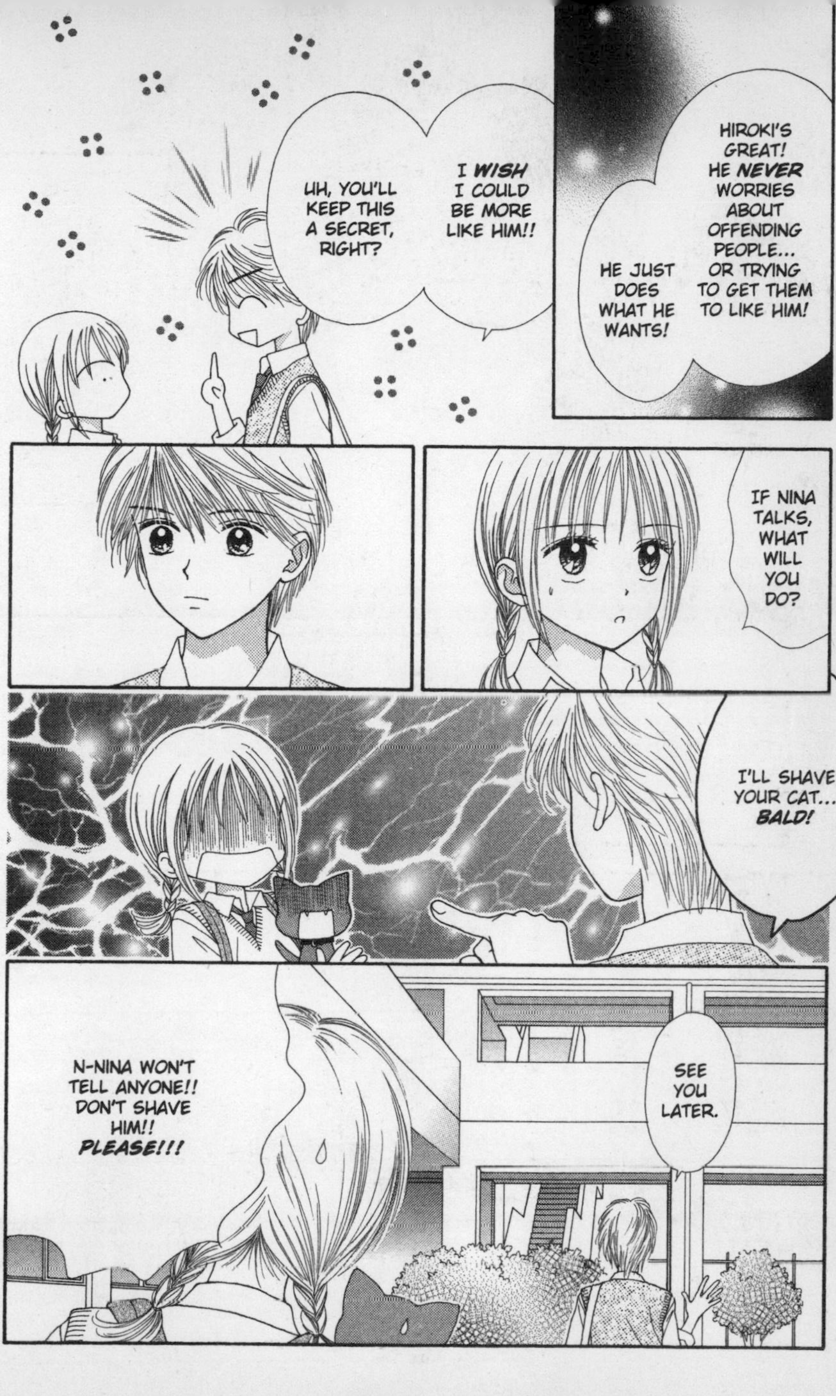
HIROKI'S GREAT! HE **NEVER** WORRIES ABOUT OFFENDING PEOPLE... OR TRYING TO GET THEM TO LIKE HIM!
HE JUST DOES WHAT HE WANTS!
I **WISH** I COULD BE MORE LIKE HIM!!
UH, YOU'LL KEEP THIS A SECRET, RIGHT?
IF NINA TALKS, WHAT WILL YOU DO?
I'LL SHAVE YOUR CAT... **BALD!**
SEE YOU LATER.
N-NINA WON'T TELL ANYONE!! DON'T SHAVE HIM!! **PLEASE!!!**

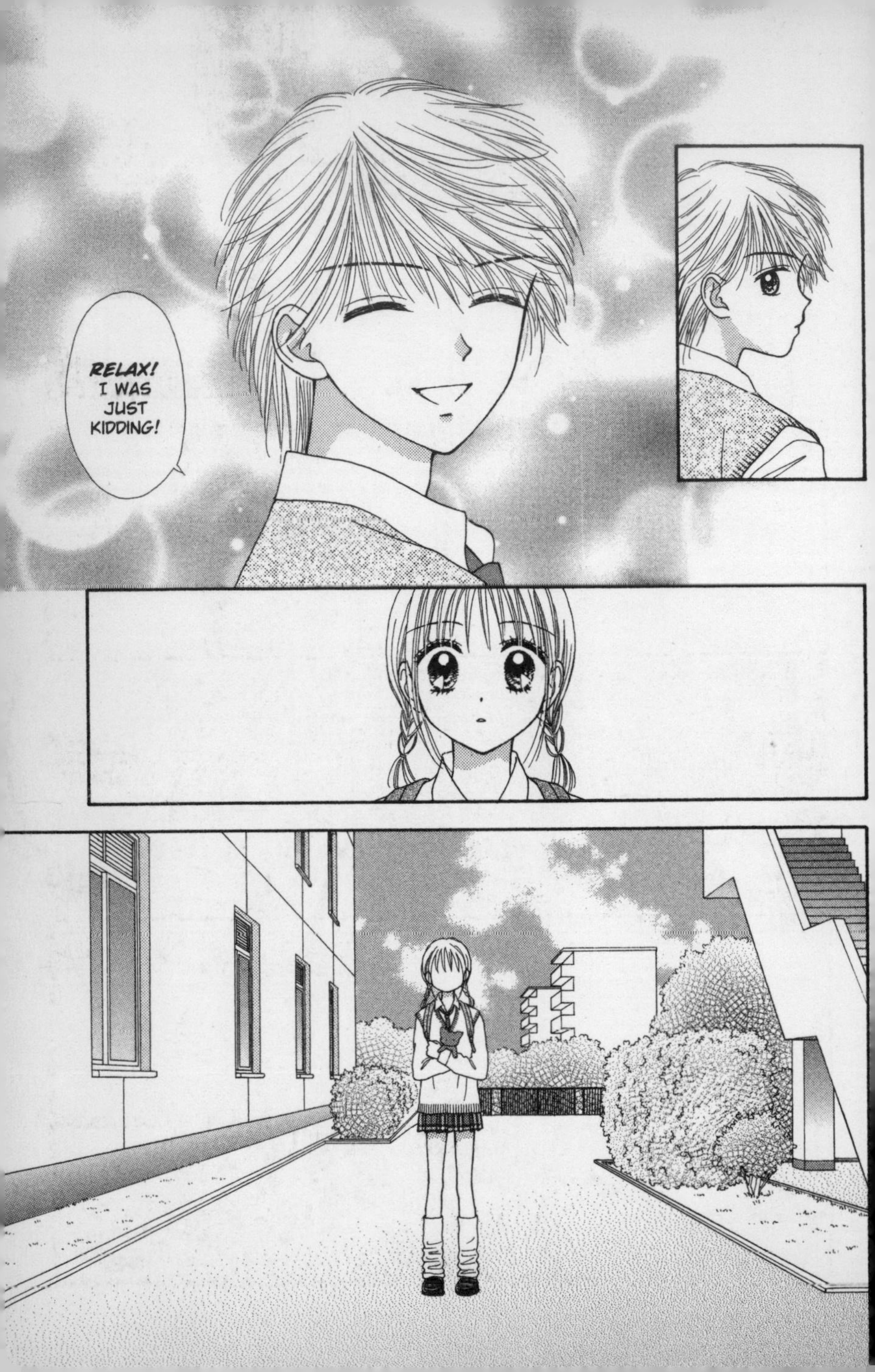
RELAX! I WAS JUST KIDDING!

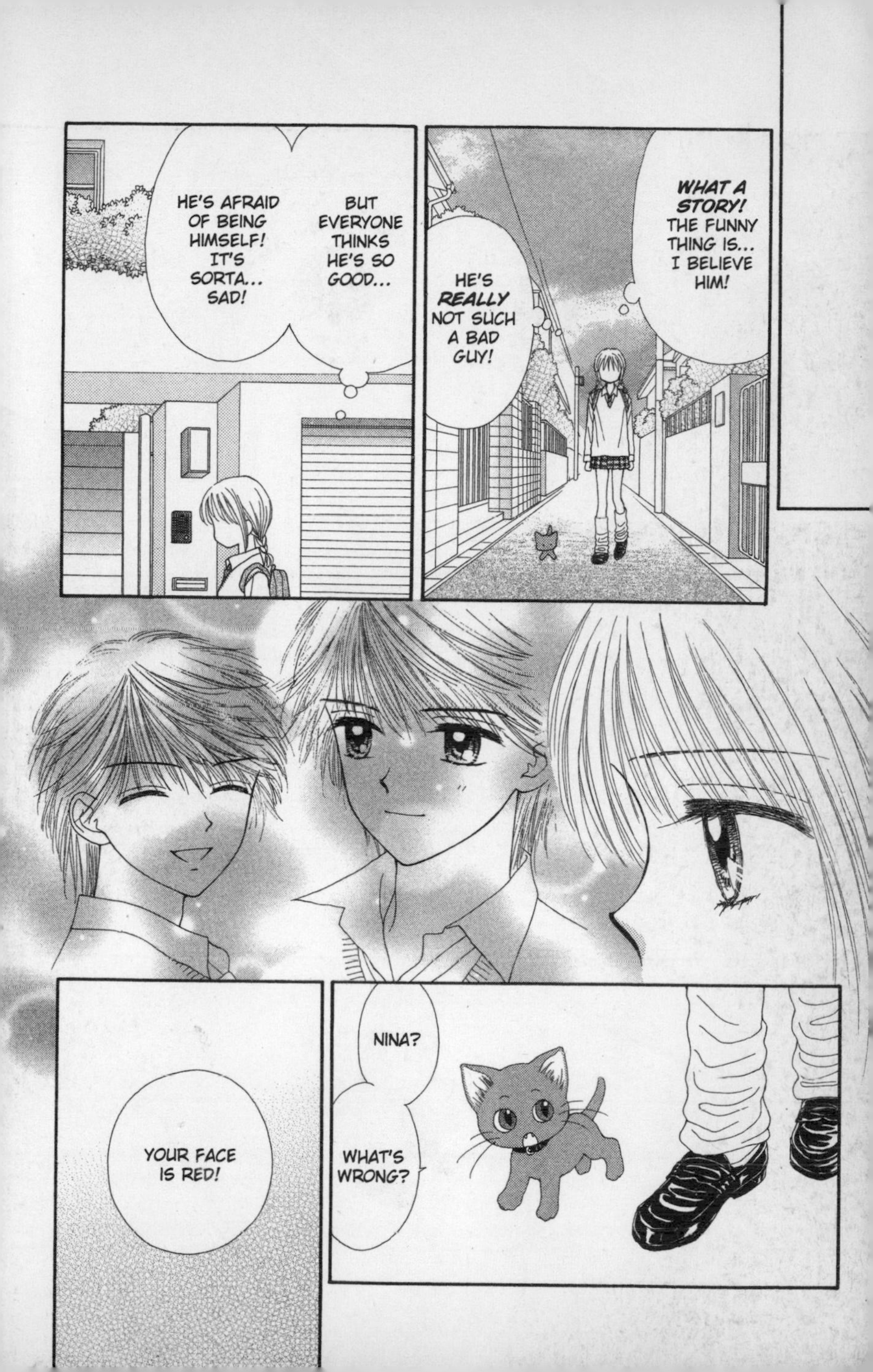

WHAT A STORY! THE FUNNY THING IS... I BELIEVE HIM!
HE'S REALLY NOT SUCH A BAD GUY!
BUT EVERYONE THINKS HE'S SO GOOD...
HE'S AFRAID OF BEING HIMSELF! IT'S SORTA... SAD!
NINA?
WHAT'S WRONG?
YOUR FACE IS RED!

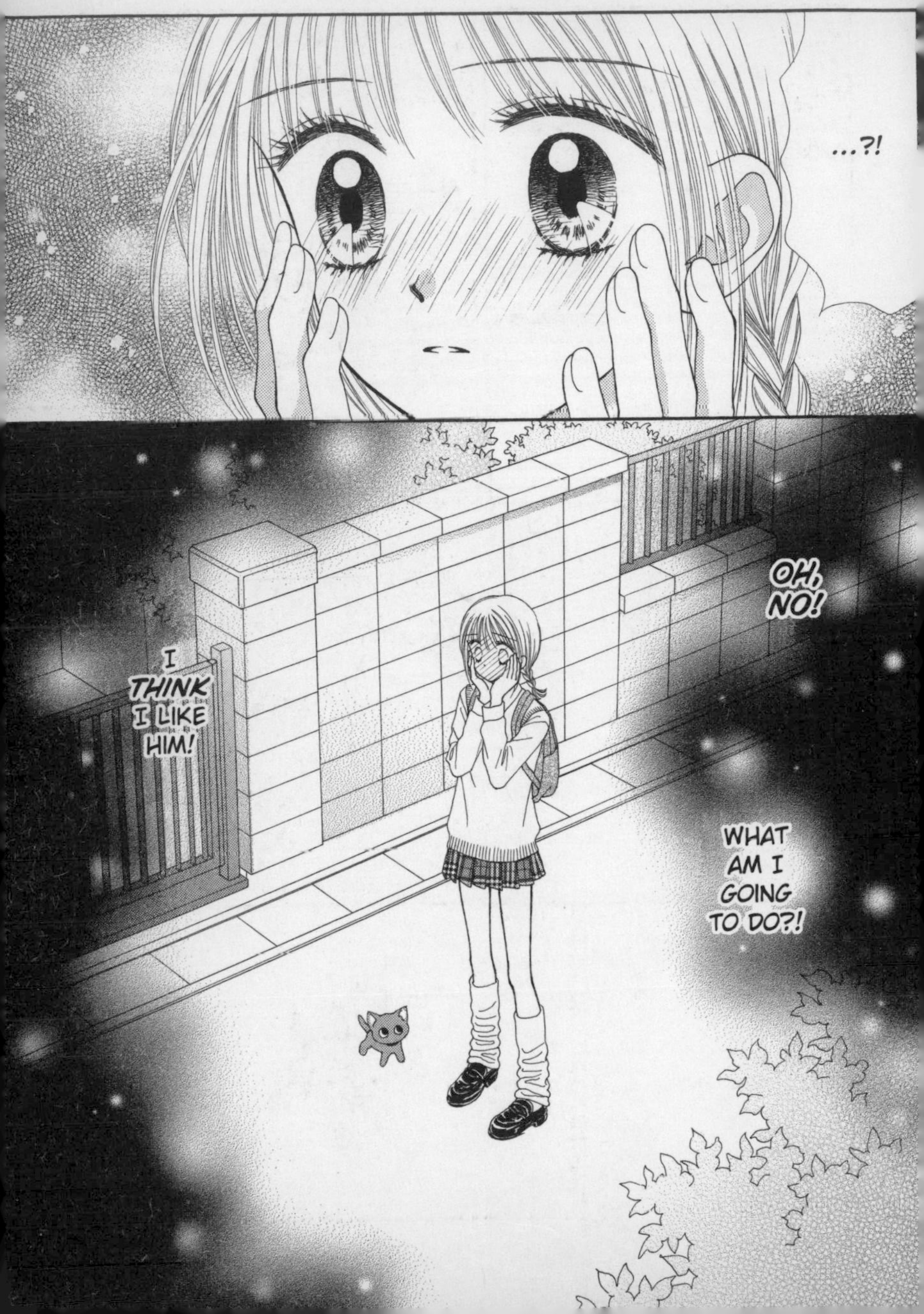
...?!
OH, NO!
WHAT AM I GOING TO DO?!
I THINK I LIKE HIM!

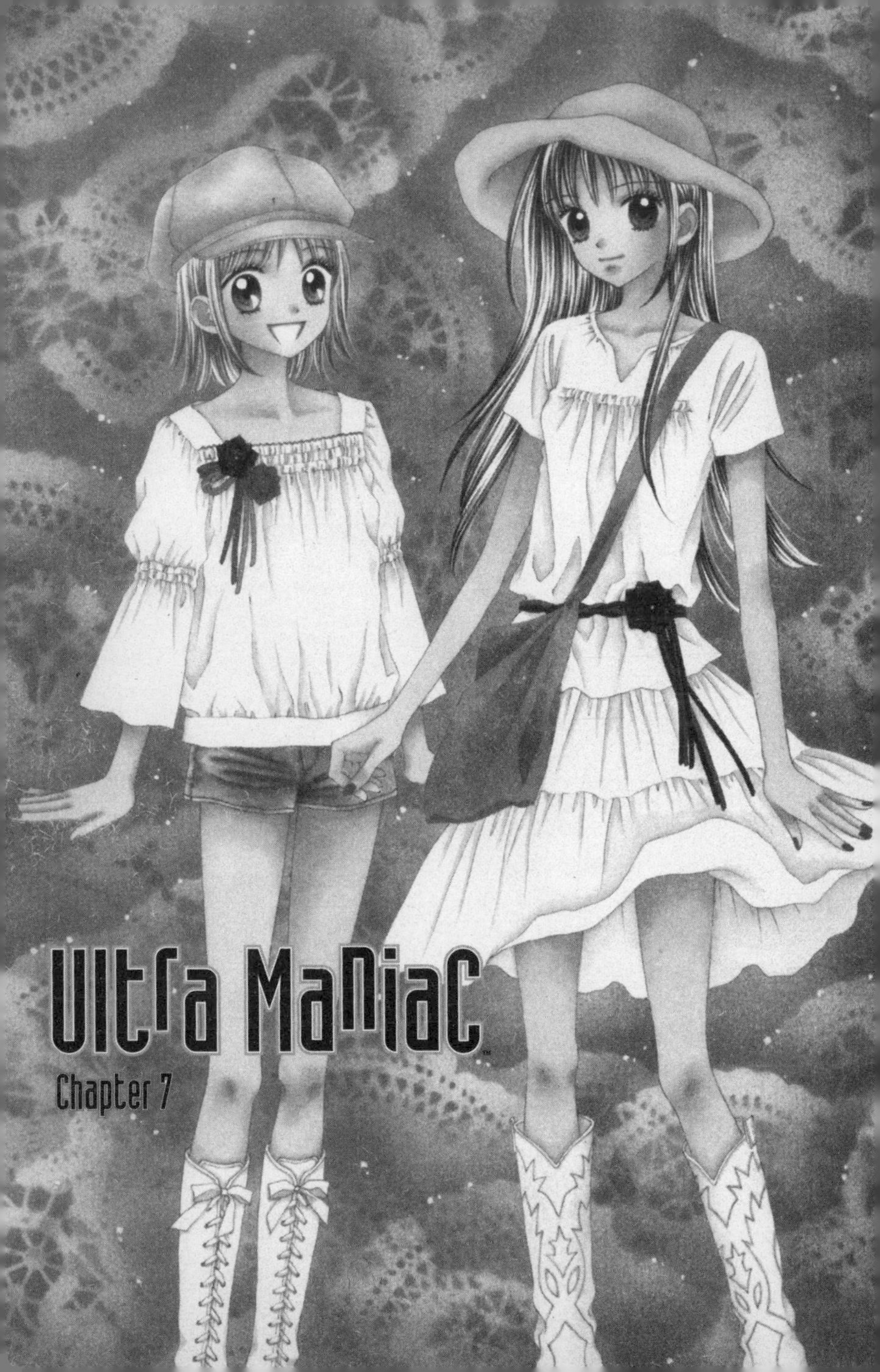
Ultra Maniac™
Chapter 7

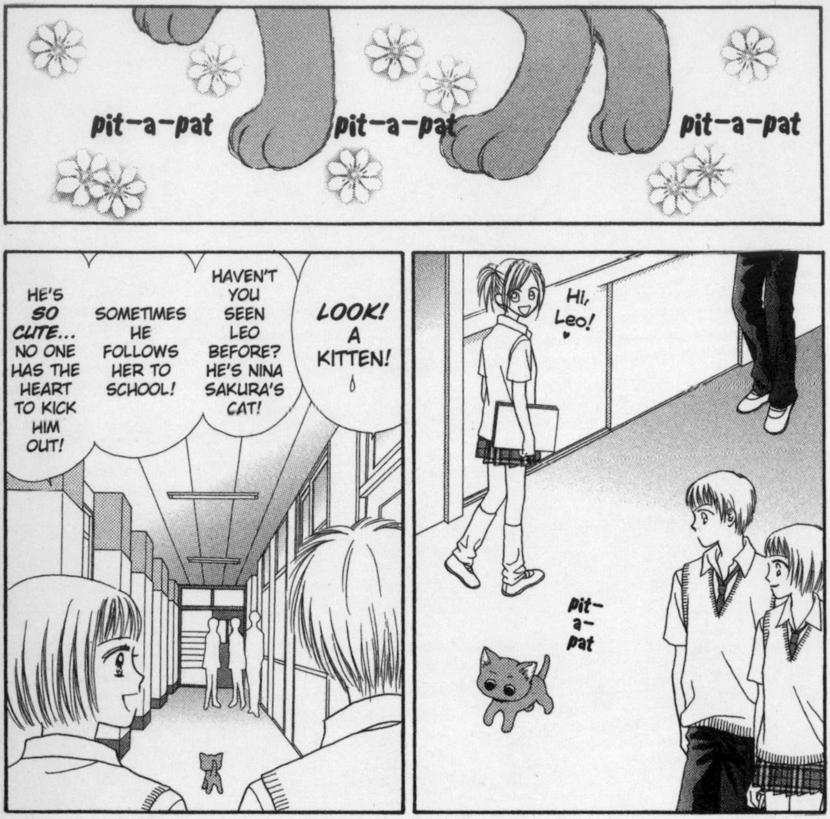
pit-a-pat
pit-a-pat
pit-a-pat
Hi, Leo!
pit-a-pat
LOOK! A KITTEN!
HAVEN'T YOU SEEN LEO BEFORE? HE'S NINA SAKURA'S CAT!
SOMETIMES HE FOLLOWS HER TO SCHOOL!
HE'S SO CUTE... NO ONE HAS THE HEART TO KICK HIM OUT!

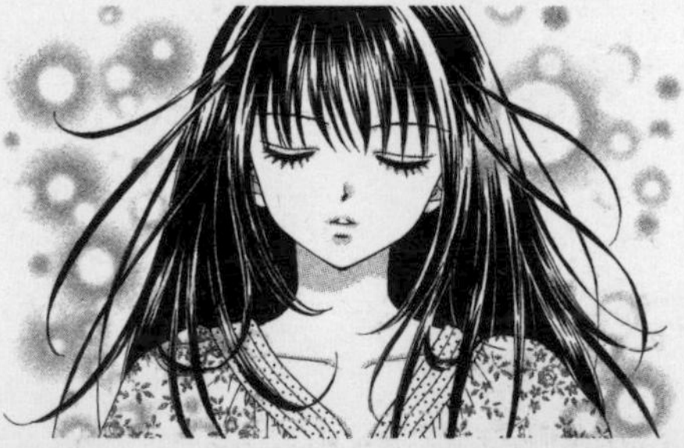

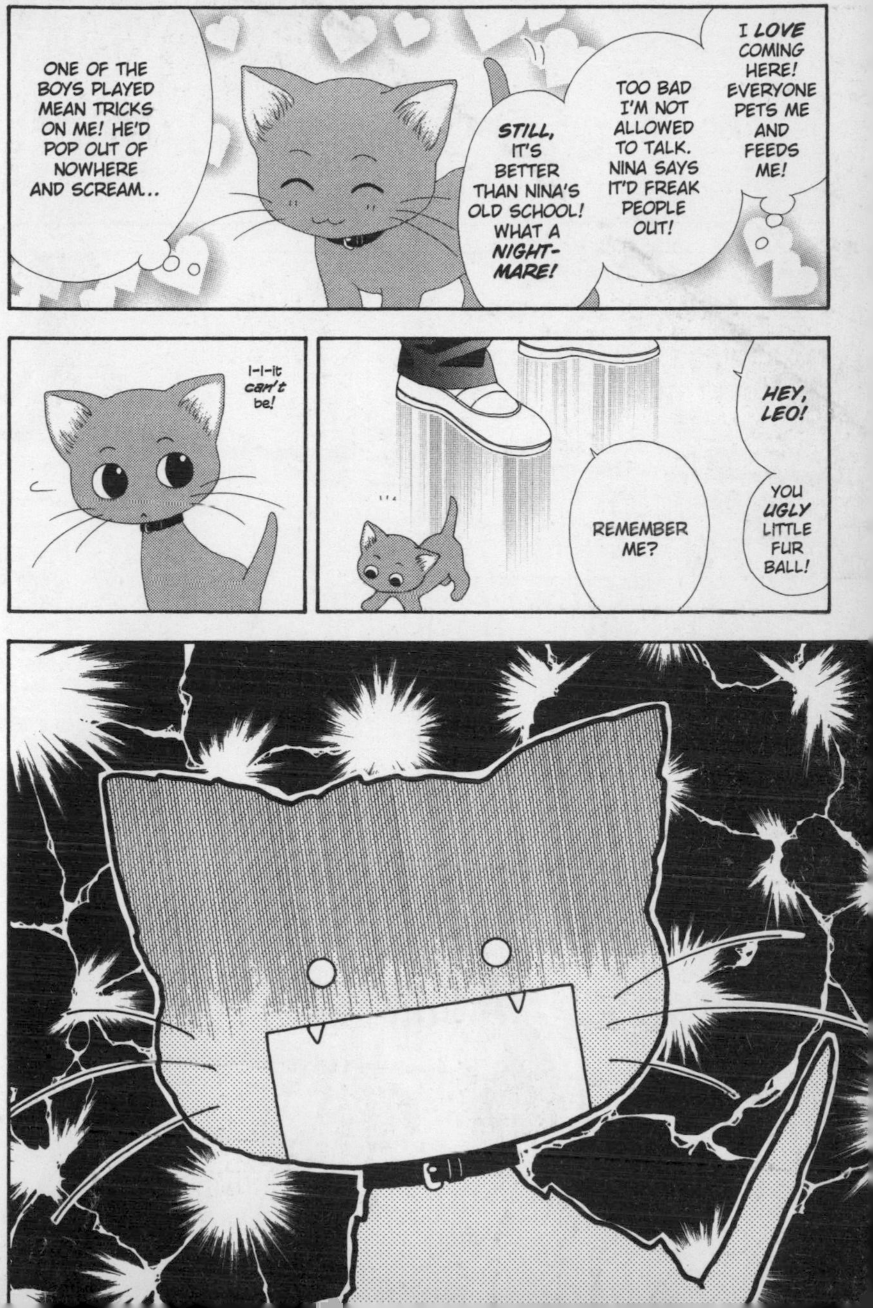
I LOVE COMING HERE! EVERYONE PETS ME AND FEEDS ME!
TOO BAD I'M NOT ALLOWED TO TALK. NINA SAYS IT'D FREAK PEOPLE OUT!
STILL, IT'S BETTER THAN NINA'S OLD SCHOOL! WHAT A NIGHT-MARE!
ONE OF THE BOYS PLAYED MEAN TRICKS ON ME! HE'D POP OUT OF NOWHERE AND SCREAM..
HEY, LEO!
YOU UGLY LITTLE FUR BALL!
REMEMBER ME?
I-I-it can't be!

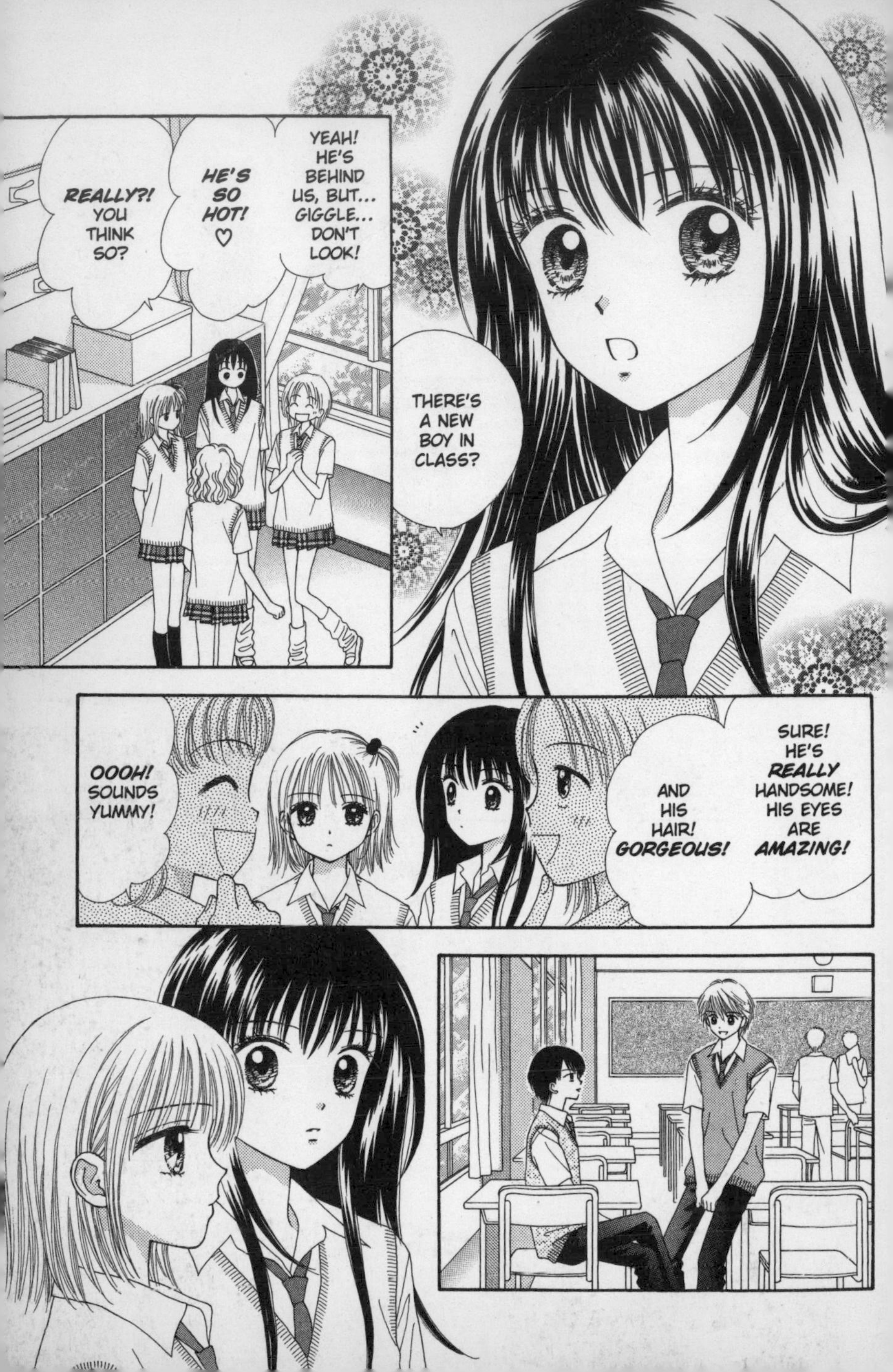
THERE'S A NEW BOY IN CLASS?
YEAH! HE'S BEHIND US, BUT... GIGGLE... DON'T LOOK!
HE'S SO HOT! ♡
REALLY?! YOU THINK SO?
SURE! HE'S *REALLY* HANDSOME! HIS EYES ARE *AMAZING!*
AND HIS HAIR! *GORGEOUS!*
OOOH! SOUNDS YUMMY!

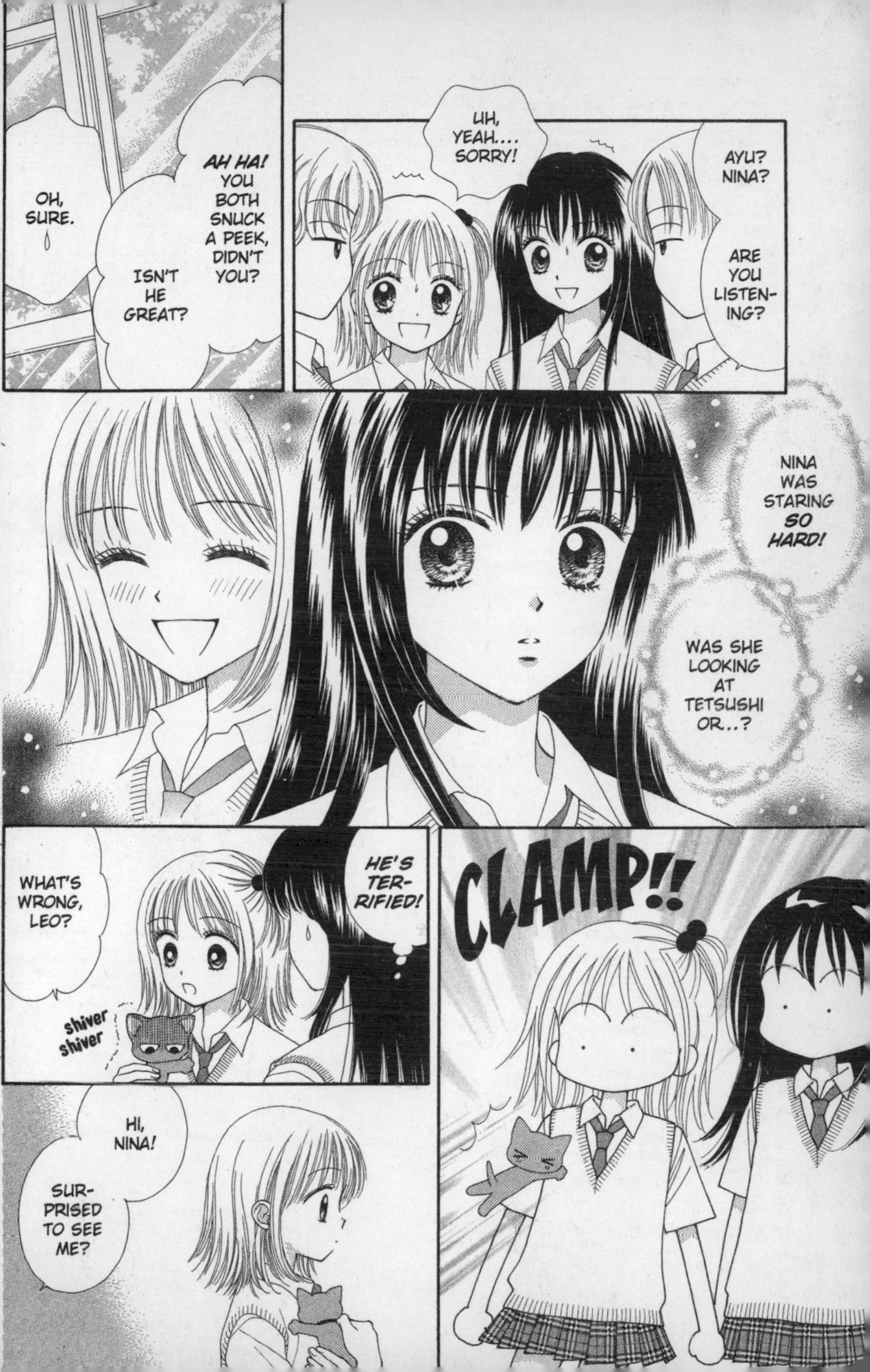
AYU? NINA?
ARE YOU LISTENING?
UH, YEAH.... SORRY!
AH HA! YOU BOTH SNUCK A PEEK, DIDN'T YOU?
ISN'T HE GREAT?
OH, SURE.
NINA WAS STARING SO HARD!
WAS SHE LOOKING AT TETSUSHI OR..?
CLAMP!!
HE'S TERRIFIED!
WHAT'S WRONG, LEO?
shiver shiver
HI, NINA!
SURPRISED TO SEE ME?

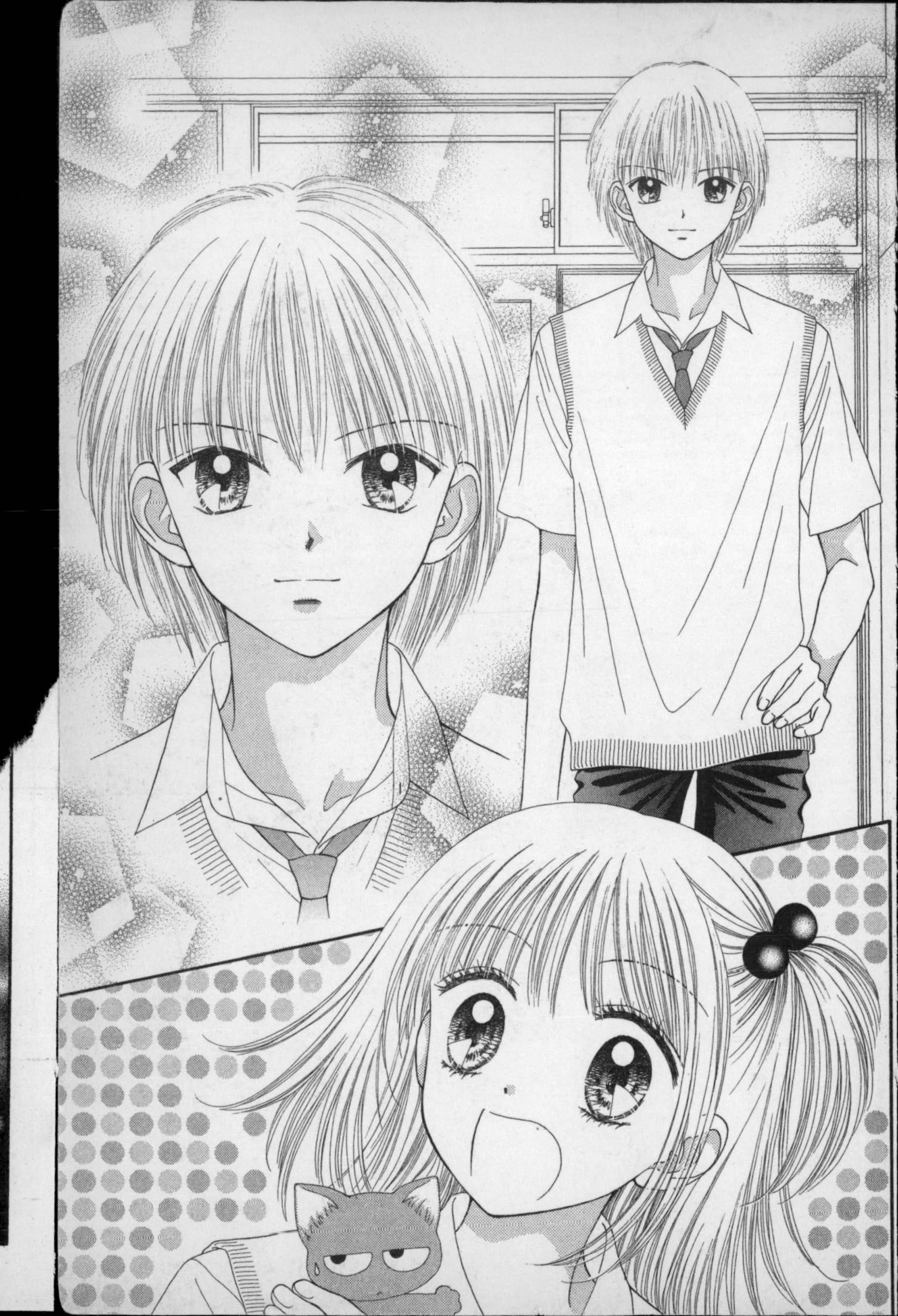

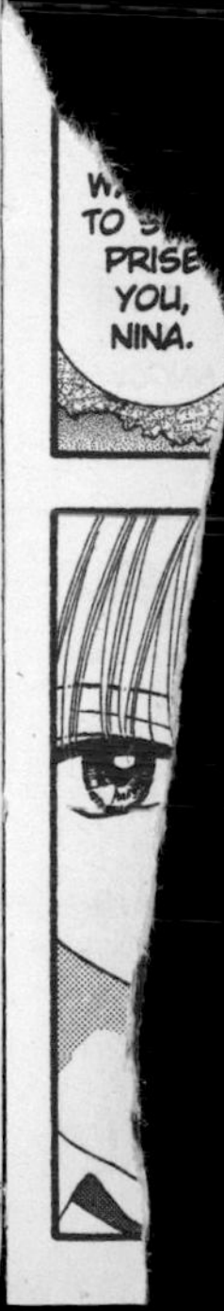
PRISE
YOU,
NINA.
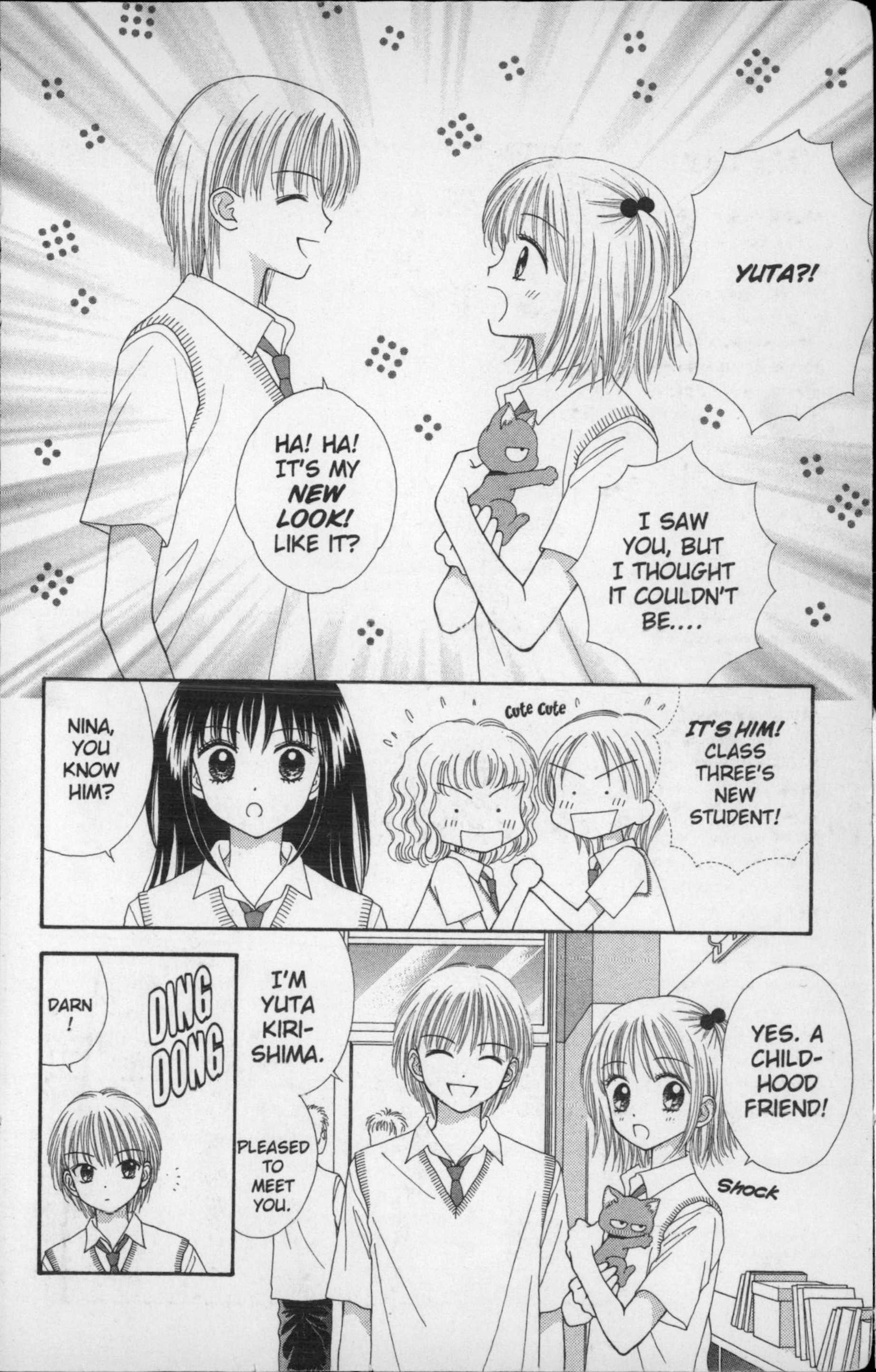
YUTA?!
I SAW YOU, BUT I THOUGHT IT COULDN'T BE....
HA! HA! IT'S MY *NEW LOOK!* LIKE IT?
IT'S HIM! CLASS THREE'S NEW STUDENT!
Cute Cute
NINA, YOU KNOW HIM?
YES. A CHILDHOOD FRIEND!
Shock
I'M YUTA KIRI-SHIMA.
PLEASED TO MEET YOU.
DING DONG
DARN!

FREE TALK 2

I think this is the first time I've written about a character who owns a pet. I suppose it's because I've only ever owned birds or guppies. So I don't have any warm, cuddly pet memories to draw on. (My parents wouldn't allow me to have any cats or dogs.)

I'd like to own a cat now, but I'm afraid I might get busy and neglect it. Plus, it would tie me down. I couldn't be away from the house for long. And I'd be sad if anything happened to the cat. Someday, though, I definitely want to own one! ♡

By the way, it's not an accident that Nina refers to herself as "Nina" instead of "I". I know it's a little on the cutesy girl side, but Nina's from a different world, so she's different from normal. Also, I wanted to bring out her silliness. Sometimes, though, I completely forget about the plan and have her say "I".

Occasionally, I think the dialogue would sound better to not use "Nina". But it does make Nina stand out. So I've decided to keep having her talk that way.

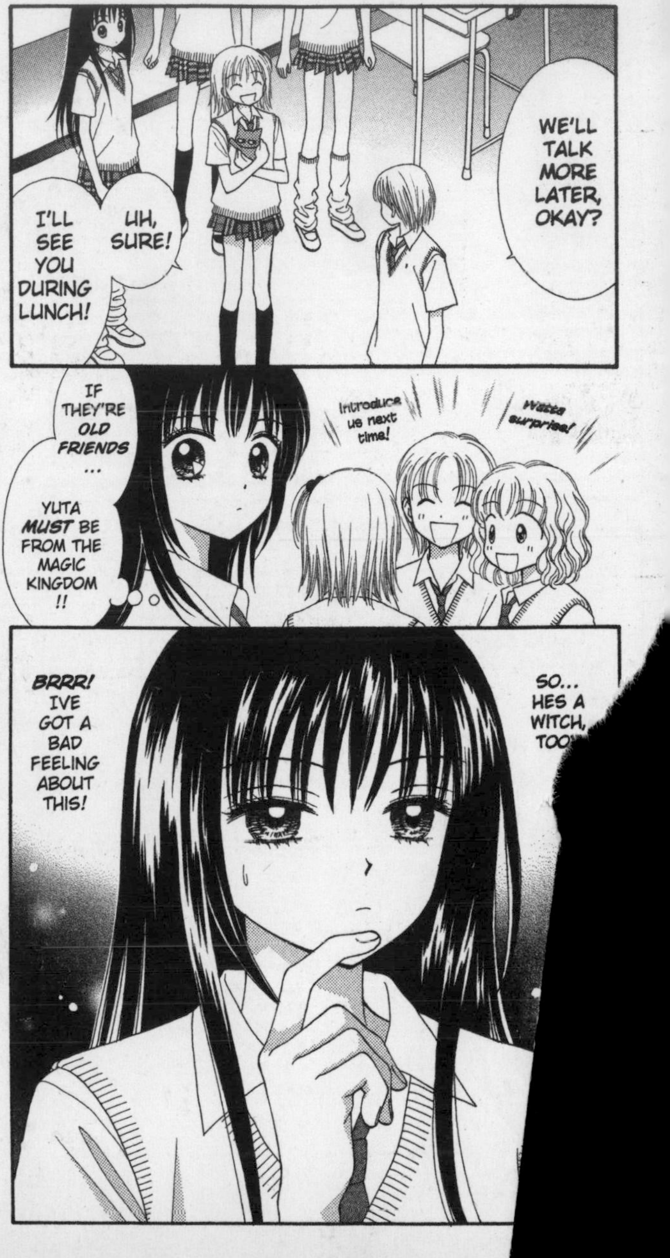
WE'LL TALK MORE LATER, OKAY?
UH, SURE!
I'LL SEE YOU DURING LUNCH!
Watta surprise!
Introduce us next time!
IF THEY'RE OLD FRIENDS ...
YUTA MUST BE FROM THE MAGIC KINGDOM !!
SO... HES A WITCH, TOO
BRRR! IVE GOT A BAD FEELING ABOUT THIS!

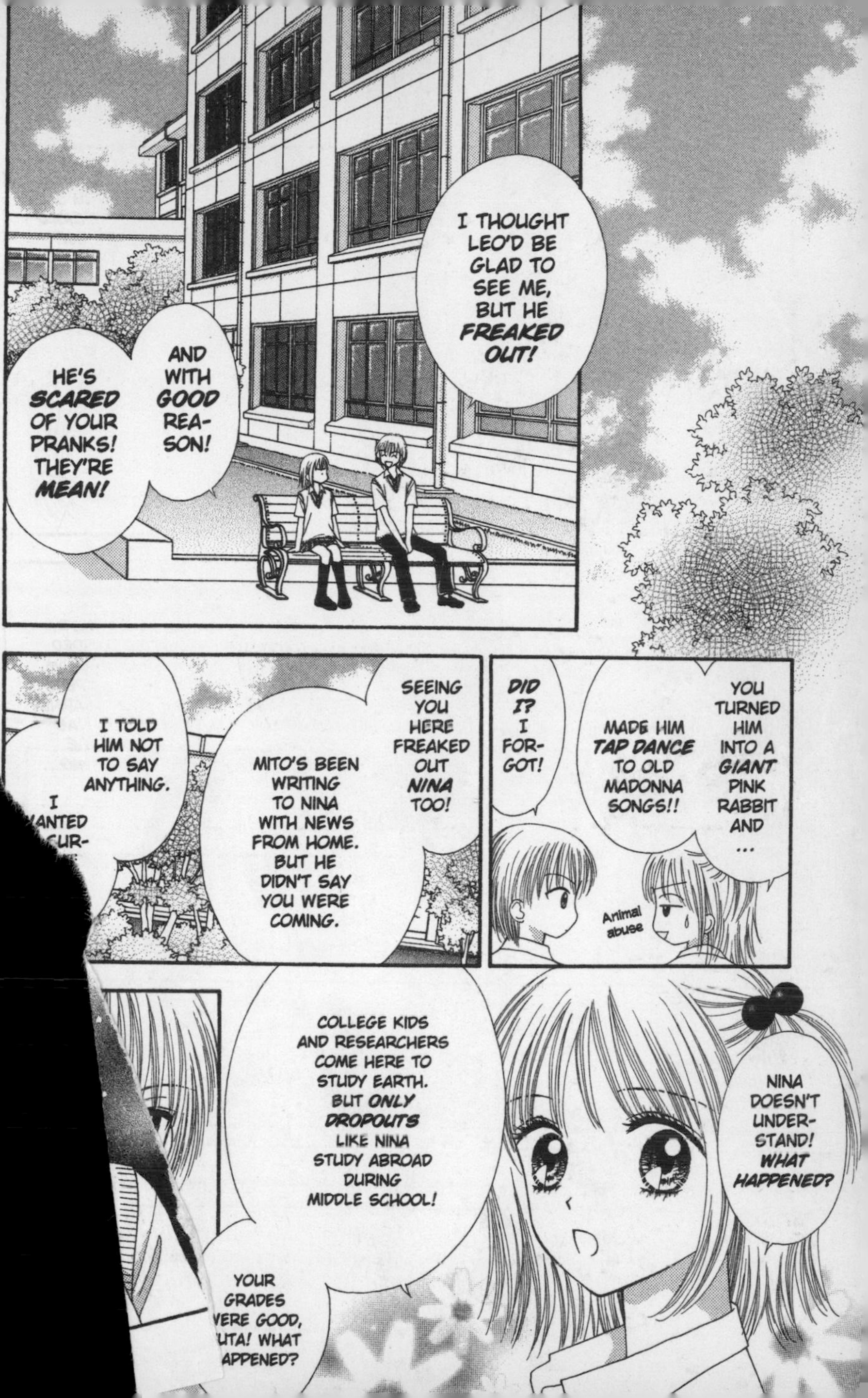
I THOUGHT LEO'D BE GLAD TO SEE ME, BUT HE FREAKED OUT!
AND WITH GOOD REASON!
HE'S SCARED OF YOUR PRANKS! THEY'RE MEAN!
YOU TURNED HIM INTO A GIANT PINK RABBIT AND ...
MADE HIM TAP DANCE TO OLD MADONNA SONGS!!
DID I? I FORGOT!
Animal abuse
SEEING YOU HERE FREAKED OUT NINA TOO!
MITO'S BEEN WRITING TO NINA WITH NEWS FROM HOME. BUT HE DIDN'T SAY YOU WERE COMING.
I TOLD HIM NOT TO SAY ANYTHING.
NINA DOESN'T UNDERSTAND! WHAT HAPPENED?
COLLEGE KIDS AND RESEARCHERS COME HERE TO STUDY EARTH. BUT ONLY DROPOUTS LIKE NINA STUDY ABROAD DURING MIDDLE SCHOOL!
YOUR GRADES VERE GOOD, UTA! WHAT APPENED?

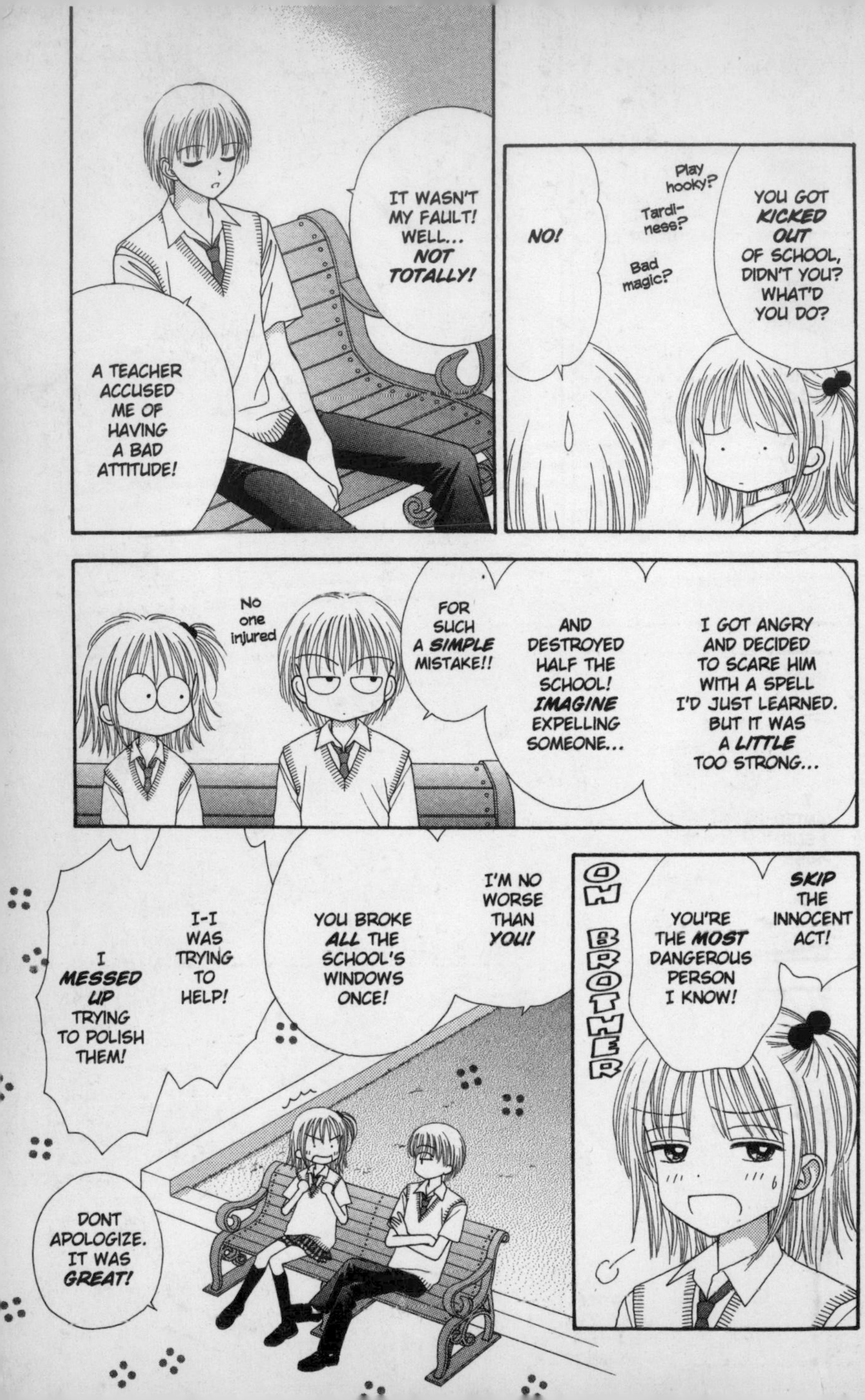
YOU GOT KICKED OUT OF SCHOOL, DIDN'T YOU? WHAT'D YOU DO?
Play hooky?
Tardiness?
Bad magic?
NO!
IT WASN'T MY FAULT! WELL... NOT TOTALLY!
A TEACHER ACCUSED ME OF HAVING A BAD ATTITUDE!
I GOT ANGRY AND DECIDED TO SCARE HIM WITH A SPELL I'D JUST LEARNED. BUT IT WAS A LITTLE TOO STRONG...
AND DESTROYED HALF THE SCHOOL! IMAGINE EXPELLING SOMEONE...
FOR SUCH A SIMPLE MISTAKE!!
No one injured
SKIP THE INNOCENT ACT!
YOU'RE THE MOST DANGEROUS PERSON I KNOW!
OH BROTHER
I'M NO WORSE THAN YOU!
YOU BROKE ALL THE SCHOOL'S WINDOWS ONCE!
I-I WAS TRYING TO HELP!
I MESSED UP TRYING TO POLISH THEM!
DONT APOLOGIZE. IT WAS GREAT!

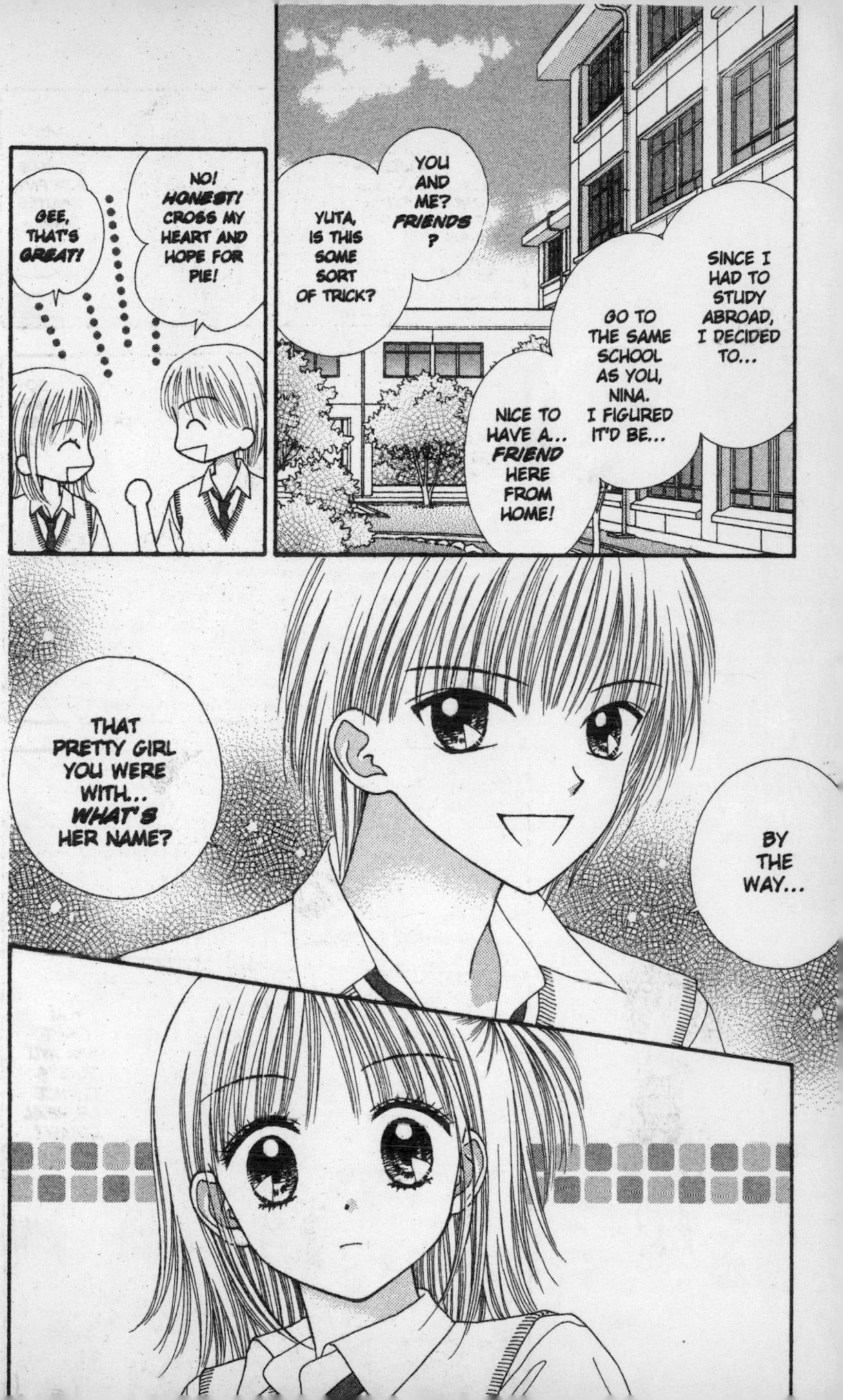
SINCE I HAD TO STUDY ABROAD, I DECIDED TO...
GO TO THE SAME SCHOOL AS YOU, NINA. I FIGURED IT'D BE...
NICE TO HAVE A... FRIEND HERE FROM HOME!
YOU AND ME? FRIENDS?
YUTA, IS THIS SOME SORT OF TRICK?
NO! HONEST! CROSS MY HEART AND HOPE FOR PIE!
GEE, THAT'S GREAT!
BY THE WAY...
THAT PRETTY GIRL YOU WERE WITH... WHAT'S HER NAME?

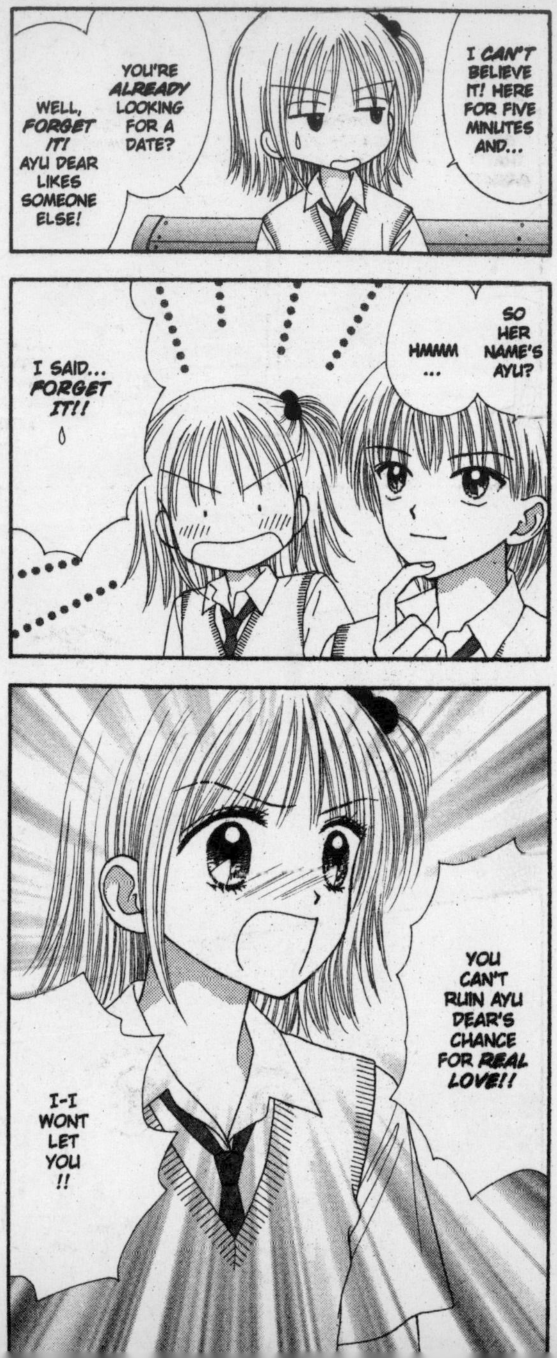
I CAN'T BELIEVE IT! HERE FOR FIVE MINUTES AND...
YOU'RE ALREADY LOOKING FOR A DATE?
WELL, FORGET IT! AYU DEAR LIKES SOMEONE ELSE!
SO HER NAME'S AYU?
HMMM ...
I SAID... FORGET IT!!
YOU CAN'T RUIN AYU DEAR'S CHANCE FOR REAL LOVE!!
I-I WONT LET YOU !!

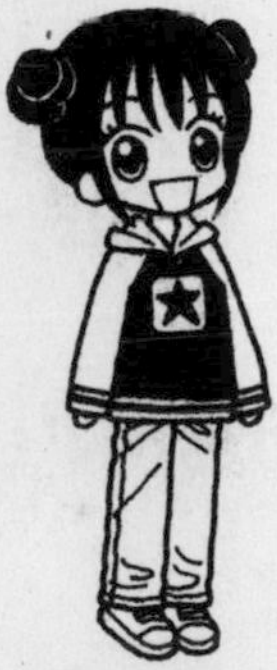

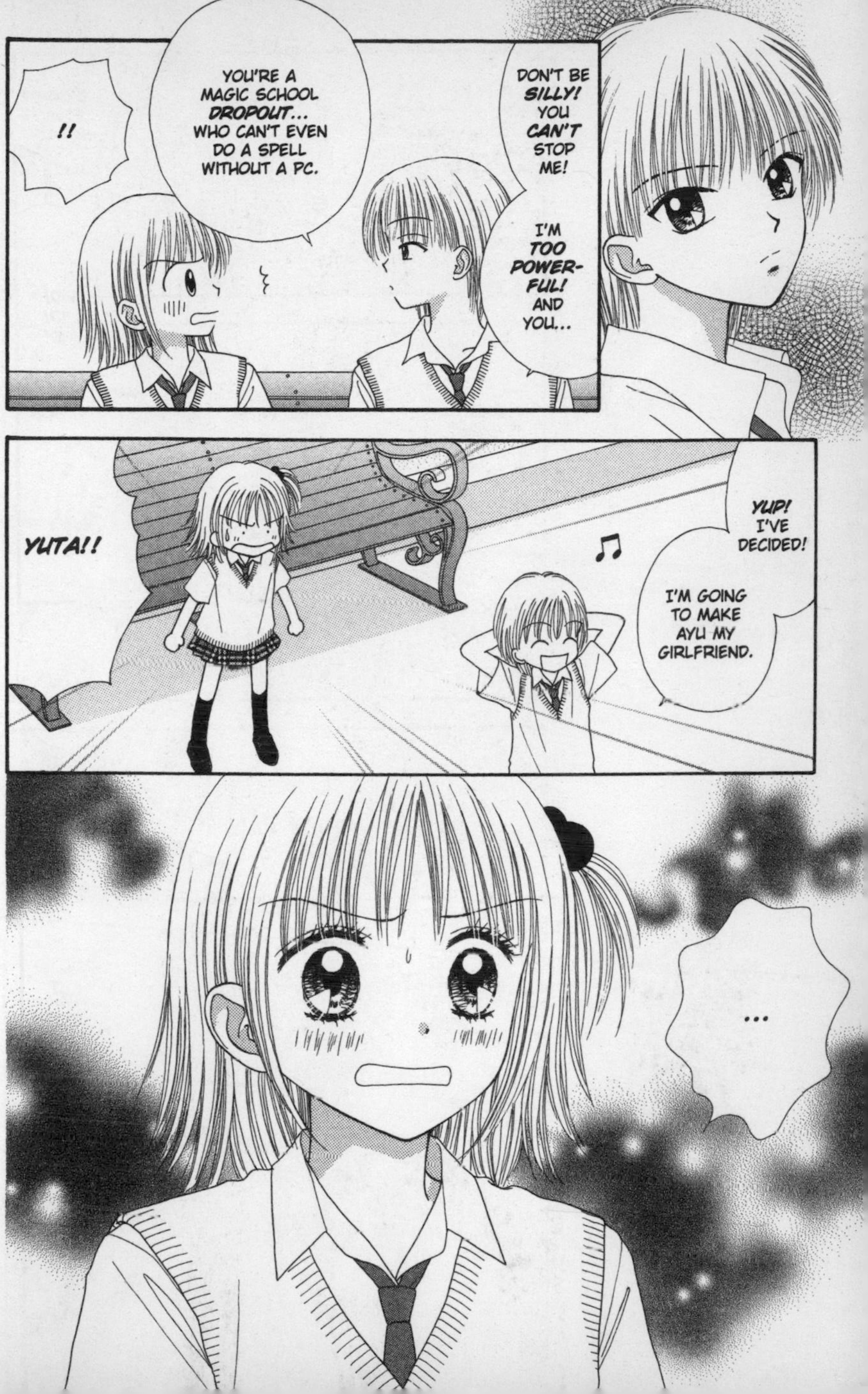
DON'T BE SILLY! YOU CAN'T STOP ME!
I'M TOO POWERFUL! AND YOU...
YOU'RE A MAGIC SCHOOL DROPOUT... WHO CAN'T EVEN DO A SPELL WITHOUT A PC.
!!
YUP! I'VE DECIDED!
I'M GOING TO MAKE AYU MY GIRLFRIEND.
♫
YUTA!!
...

I'M STUPID! STUPID! STUPID!
I *ACTUALLY* THOUGHT YUTA COULD BE NICE!
HI, NINA!
DOES LEO EAT CUP-CAKES?
UH, PROB-ABLY ....
GOOD! I'VE GOT SOME FOR HIM!
I'LL GIVE THEM TO YOU LATER.

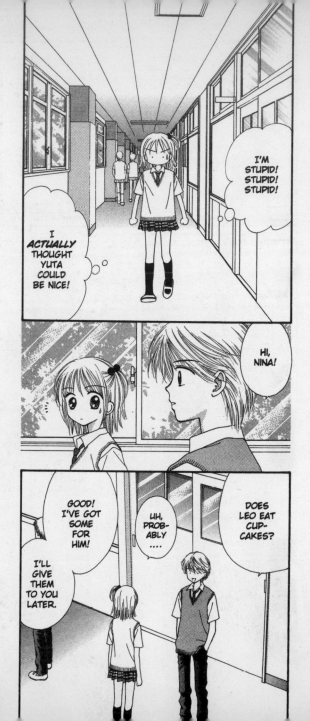

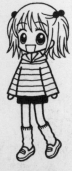

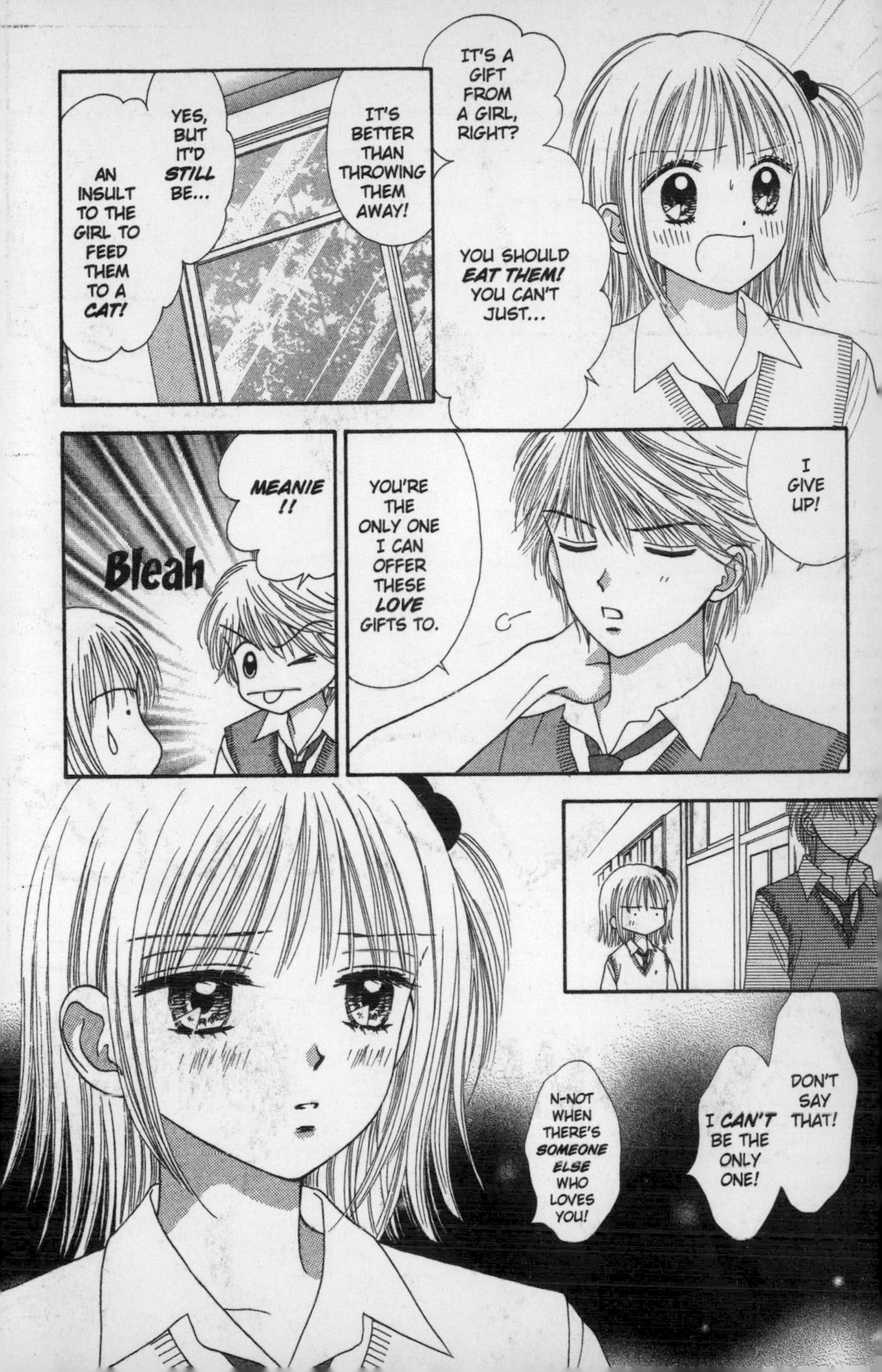
IT'S A GIFT FROM A GIRL, RIGHT?
YOU SHOULD EAT THEM! YOU CAN'T JUST...
IT'S BETTER THAN THROWING THEM AWAY!
YES, BUT IT'D STILL BE...
AN INSULT TO THE GIRL TO FEED THEM TO A CAT!
I GIVE UP!
YOU'RE THE ONLY ONE I CAN OFFER THESE LOVE GIFTS TO.
MEANIE!!
Bleah
DON'T SAY THAT!
I CAN'T BE THE ONLY ONE!
N-NOT WHEN THERE'S SOMEONE ELSE WHO LOVES YOU!

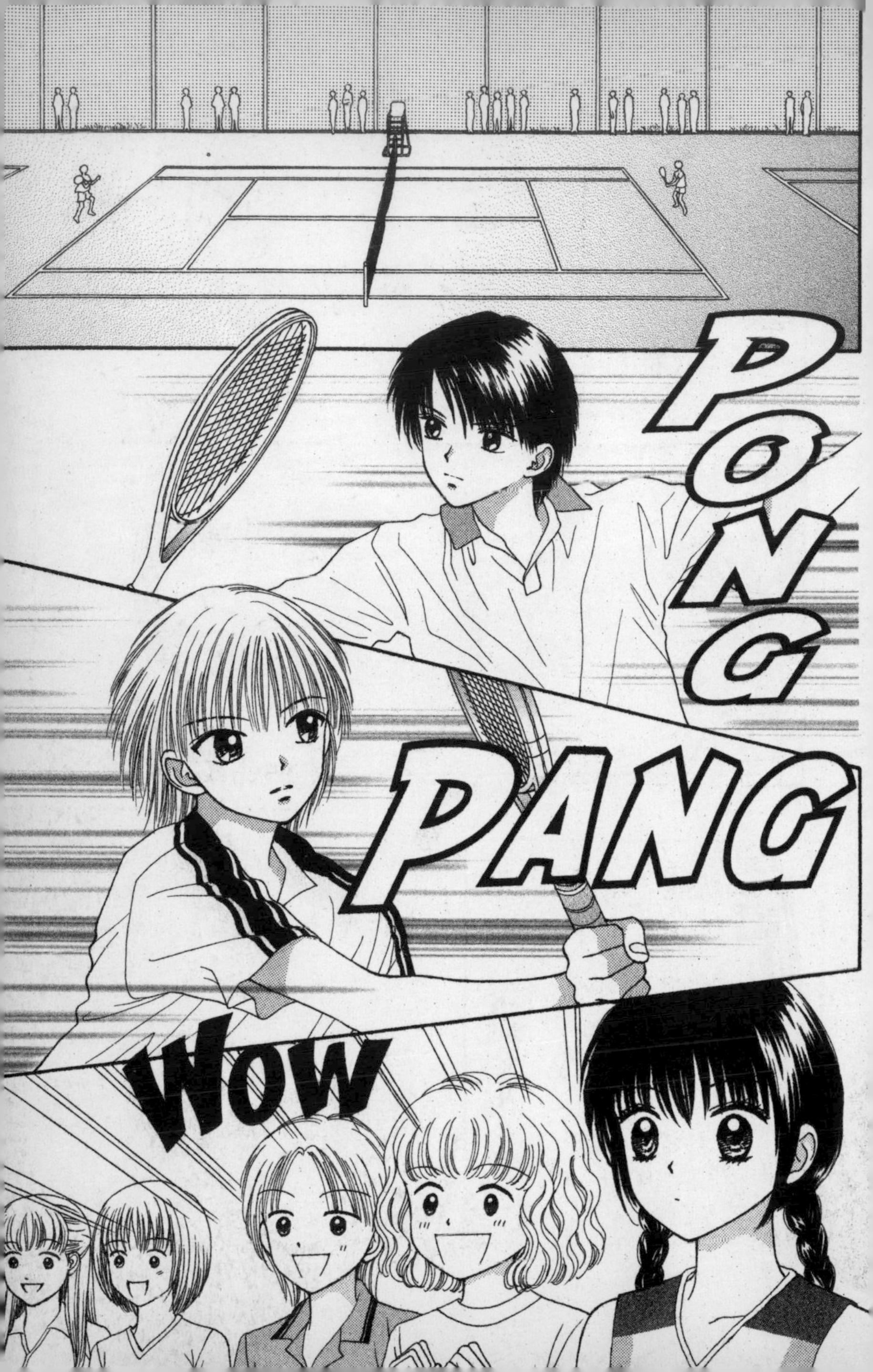
PONG
PANG
WOW

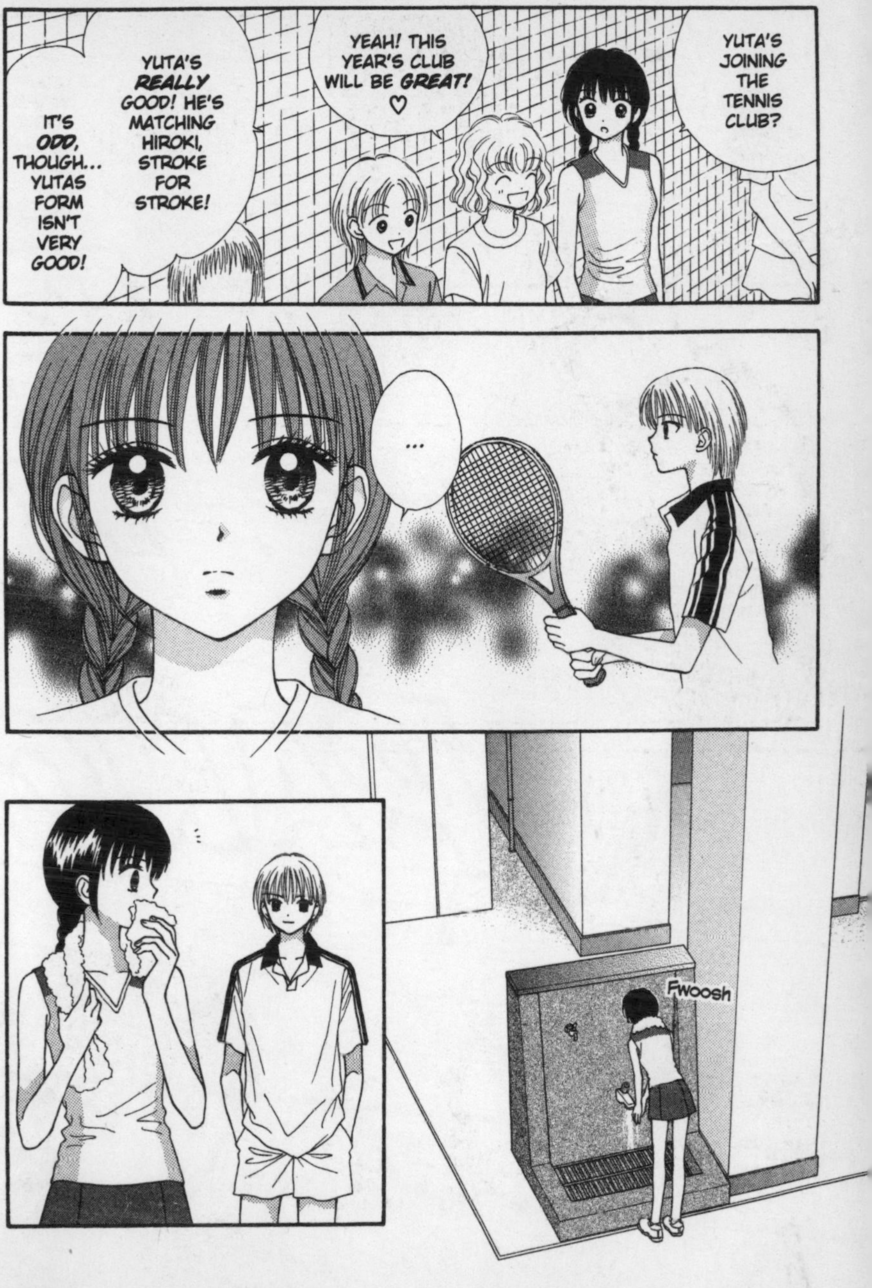
YUTA'S JOINING THE TENNIS CLUB?
YEAH! THIS YEAR'S CLUB WILL BE *GREAT!* ♡
YUTA'S ***REALLY*** GOOD! HE'S MATCHING HIROKI, STROKE FOR STROKE!
IT'S ***ODD***, THOUGH... YUTAS FORM ISN'T VERY GOOD!
...
Fwoosh

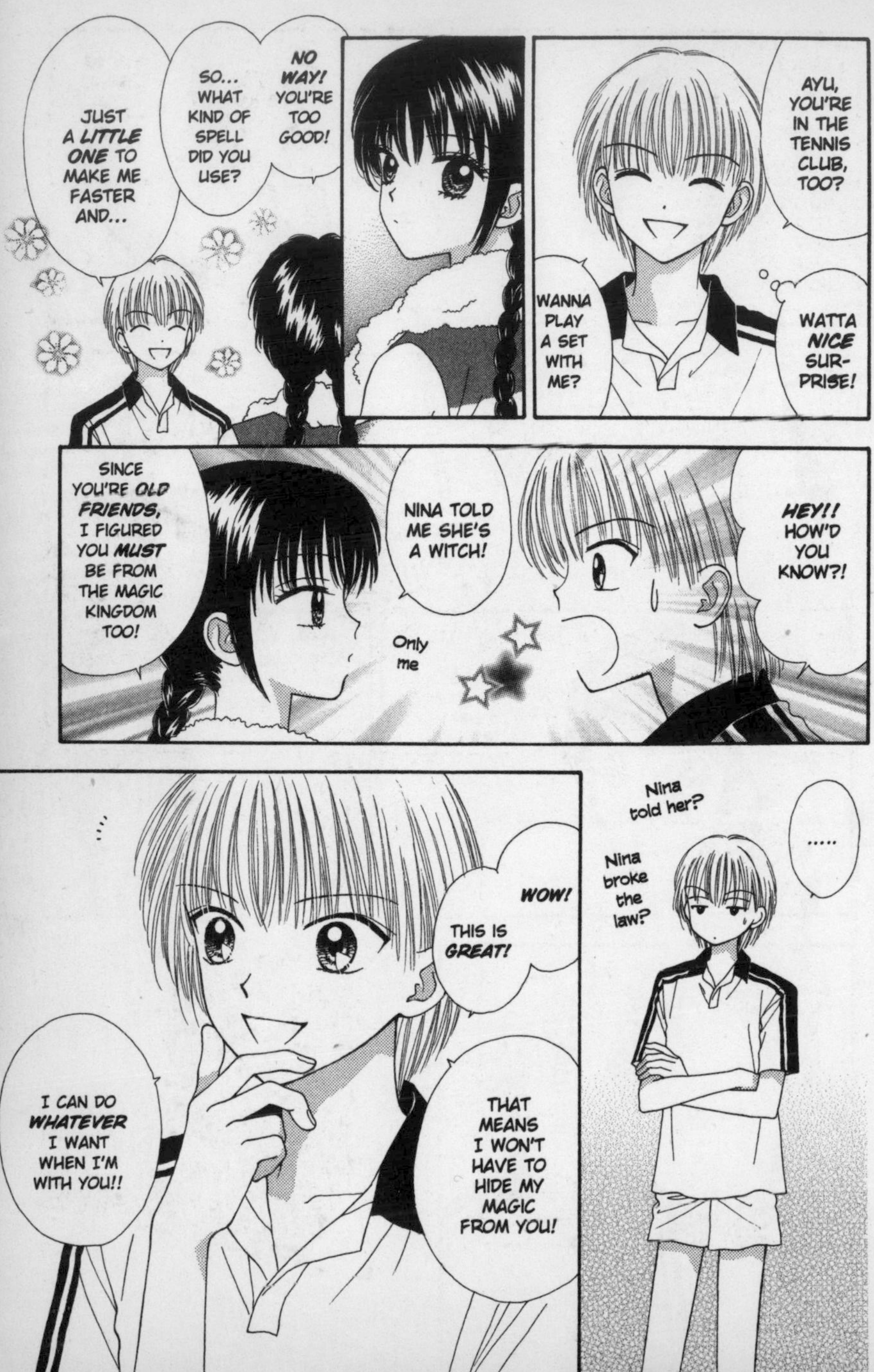
AYU, YOU'RE IN THE TENNIS CLUB, TOO?
WATTA NICE SURPRISE!
WANNA PLAY A SET WITH ME?
NO WAY! YOU'RE TOO GOOD!
SO... WHAT KIND OF SPELL DID YOU USE?
JUST A LITTLE ONE TO MAKE ME FASTER AND...
HEY!! HOW'D YOU KNOW?!
NINA TOLD ME SHE'S A WITCH!
Only me
SINCE YOU'RE OLD FRIENDS, I FIGURED YOU MUST BE FROM THE MAGIC KINGDOM TOO!
.....
Nina told her?
Nina broke the law?
...
WOW! THIS IS GREAT!
THAT MEANS I WON'T HAVE TO HIDE MY MAGIC FROM YOU!
I CAN DO WHATEVER I WANT WHEN I'M WITH YOU!!

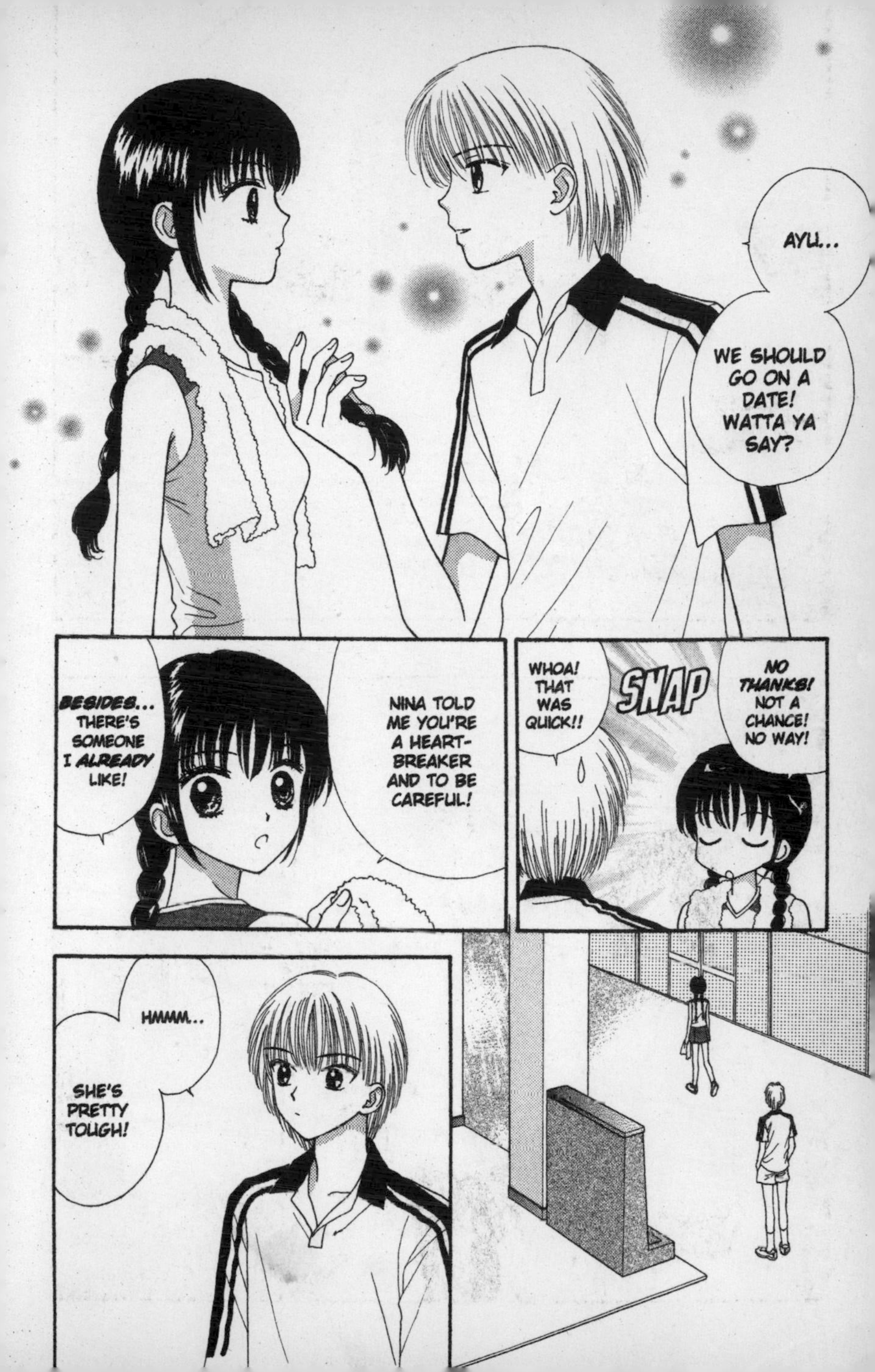
AYU...
WE SHOULD GO ON A DATE! WATTA YA SAY?
NO THANKS! NOT A CHANCE! NO WAY!
SNAP
WHOA! THAT WAS QUICK!!
NINA TOLD ME YOU'RE A HEART-BREAKER AND TO BE CAREFUL!
BESIDES... THERE'S SOMEONE I ALREADY LIKE!
HMMM...
SHE'S PRETTY TOUGH!

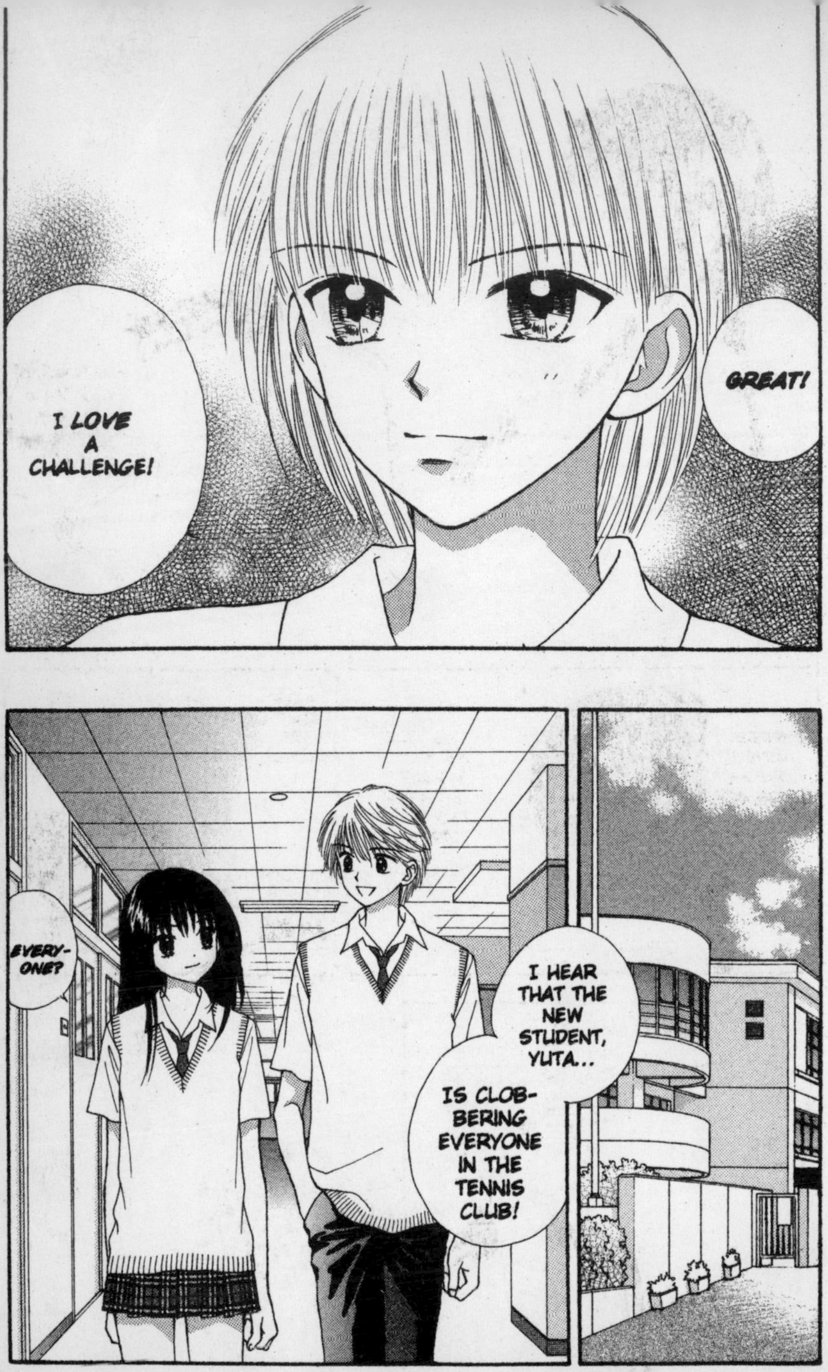
GREAT!
I LOVE A CHALLENGE!
I HEAR THAT THE NEW STUDENT, YUTA...
IS CLOBBERING EVERYONE IN THE TENNIS CLUB!
EVERY-ONE?

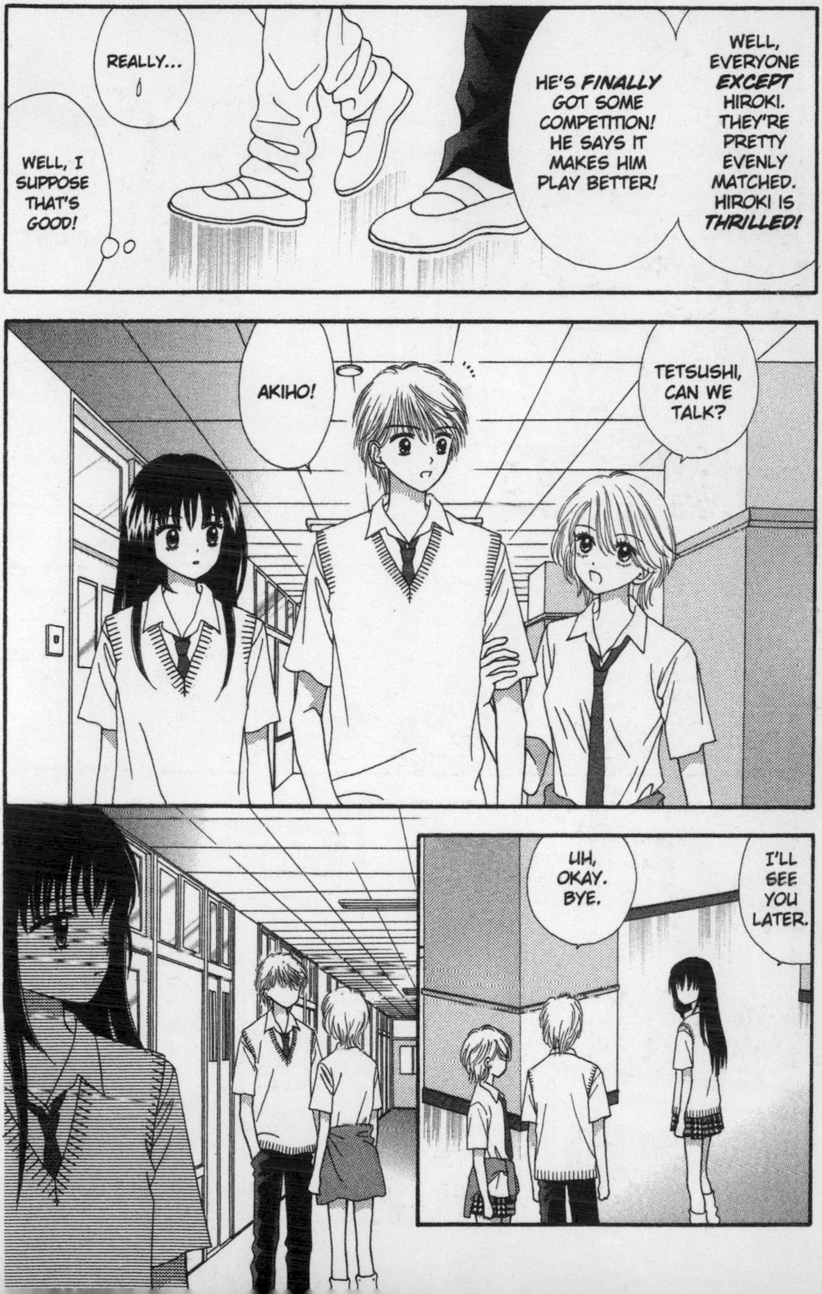
WELL, EVERYONE *EXCEPT* HIROKI. THEY'RE PRETTY EVENLY MATCHED. HIROKI IS *THRILLED!*
HE'S *FINALLY* GOT SOME COMPETITION! HE SAYS IT MAKES HIM PLAY BETTER!
REALLY...
WELL, I SUPPOSE THAT'S GOOD!
TETSUSHI, CAN WE TALK?
AKIHO!
I'LL SEE YOU LATER.
UH, OKAY. BYE.

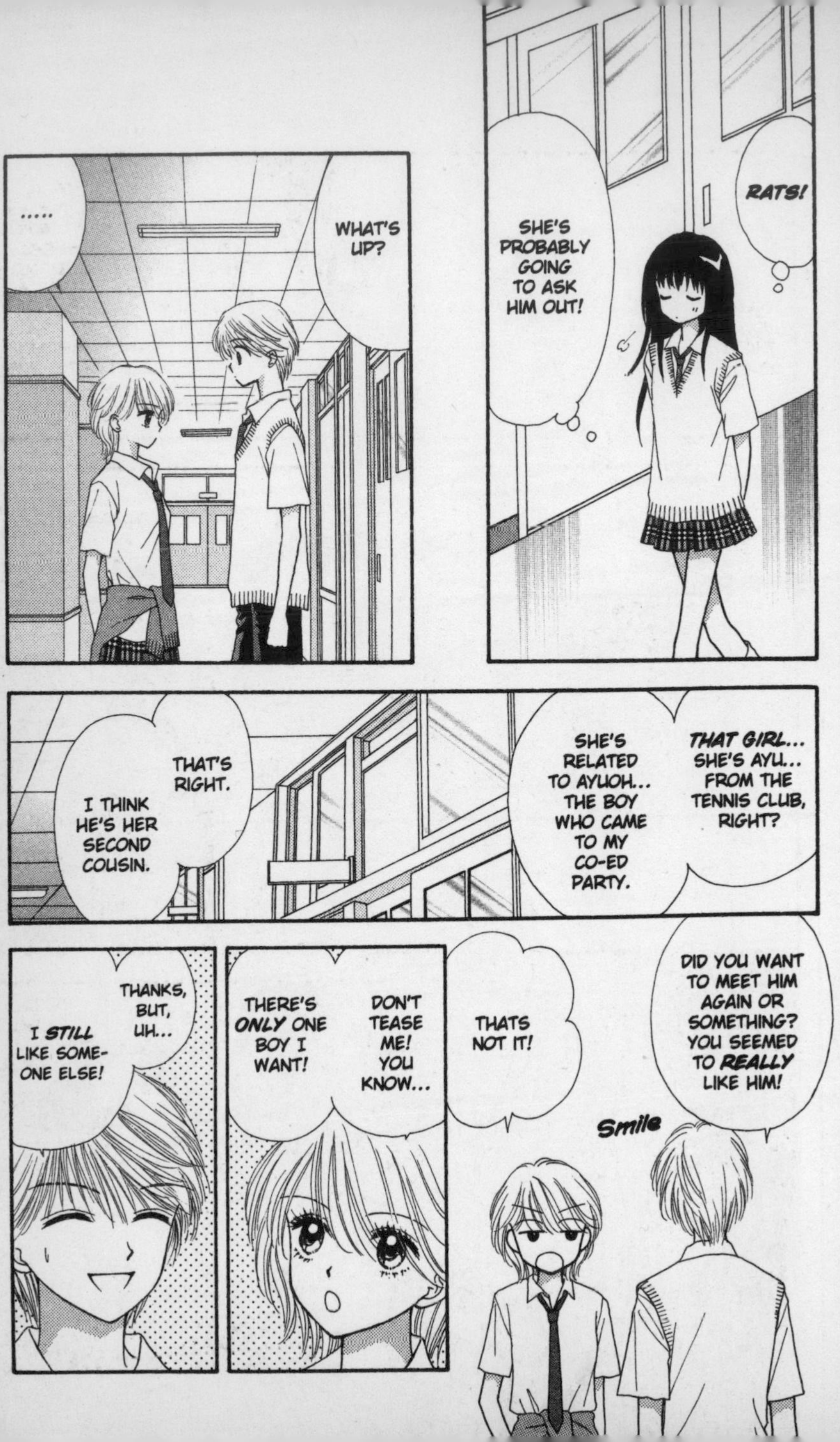
RATS!
SHE'S PROBABLY GOING TO ASK HIM OUT!
WHAT'S UP?
.....
THAT GIRL... SHE'S AYU... FROM THE TENNIS CLUB, RIGHT?
SHE'S RELATED TO AYUOH... THE BOY WHO CAME TO MY CO-ED PARTY.
THAT'S RIGHT.
I THINK HE'S HER SECOND COUSIN.
DID YOU WANT TO MEET HIM AGAIN OR SOMETHING? YOU SEEMED TO REALLY LIKE HIM!
Smile
THATS NOT IT!
DON'T TEASE ME! YOU KNOW...
THERE'S ONLY ONE BOY I WANT!
THANKS, BUT, UH...
I STILL LIKE SOME-ONE ELSE!

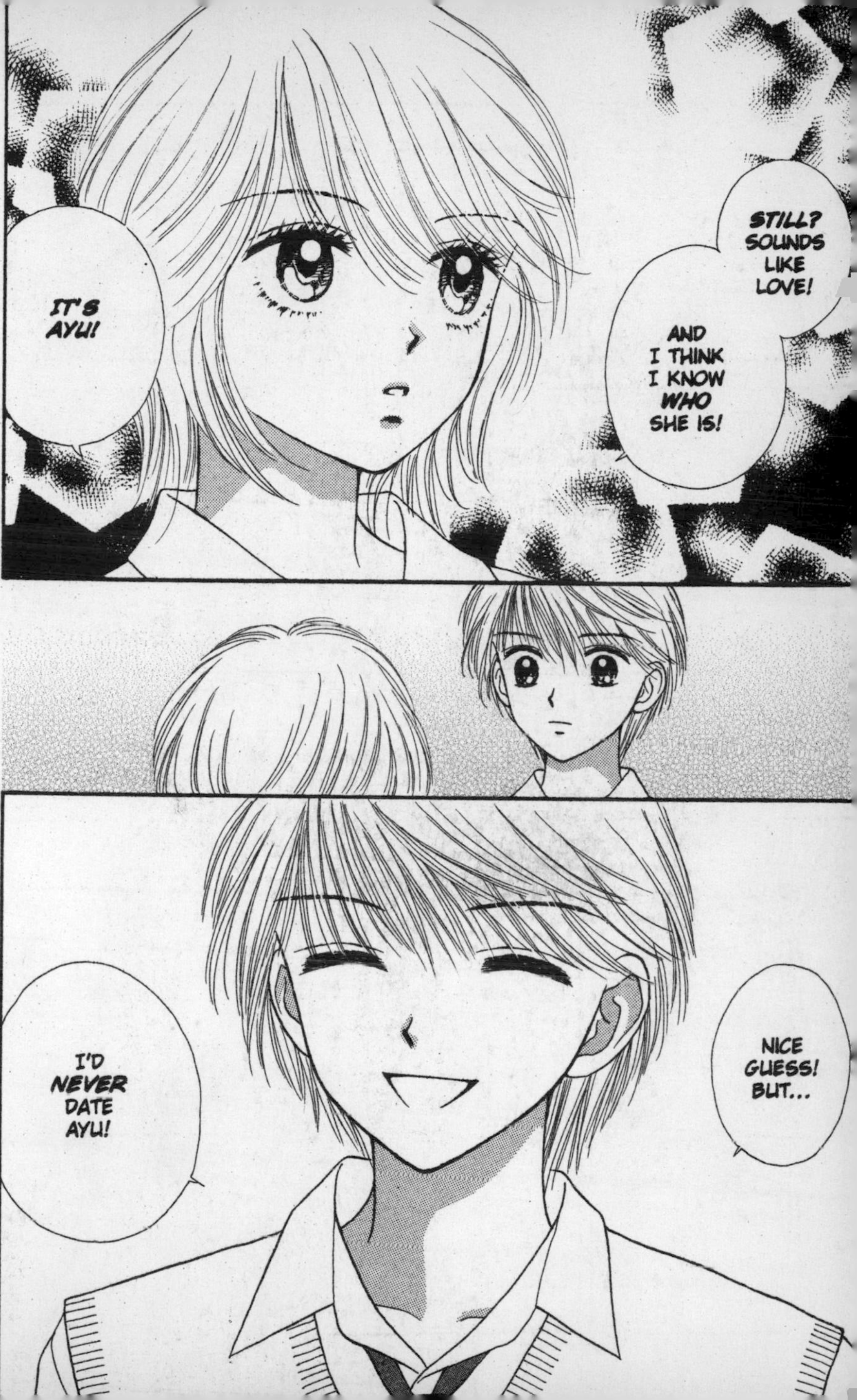
STILL? SOUNDS LIKE LOVE!
AND I THINK I KNOW *WHO* SHE IS!
IT'S AYU!
NICE GUESS! BUT...
I'D *NEVER* DATE AYU!

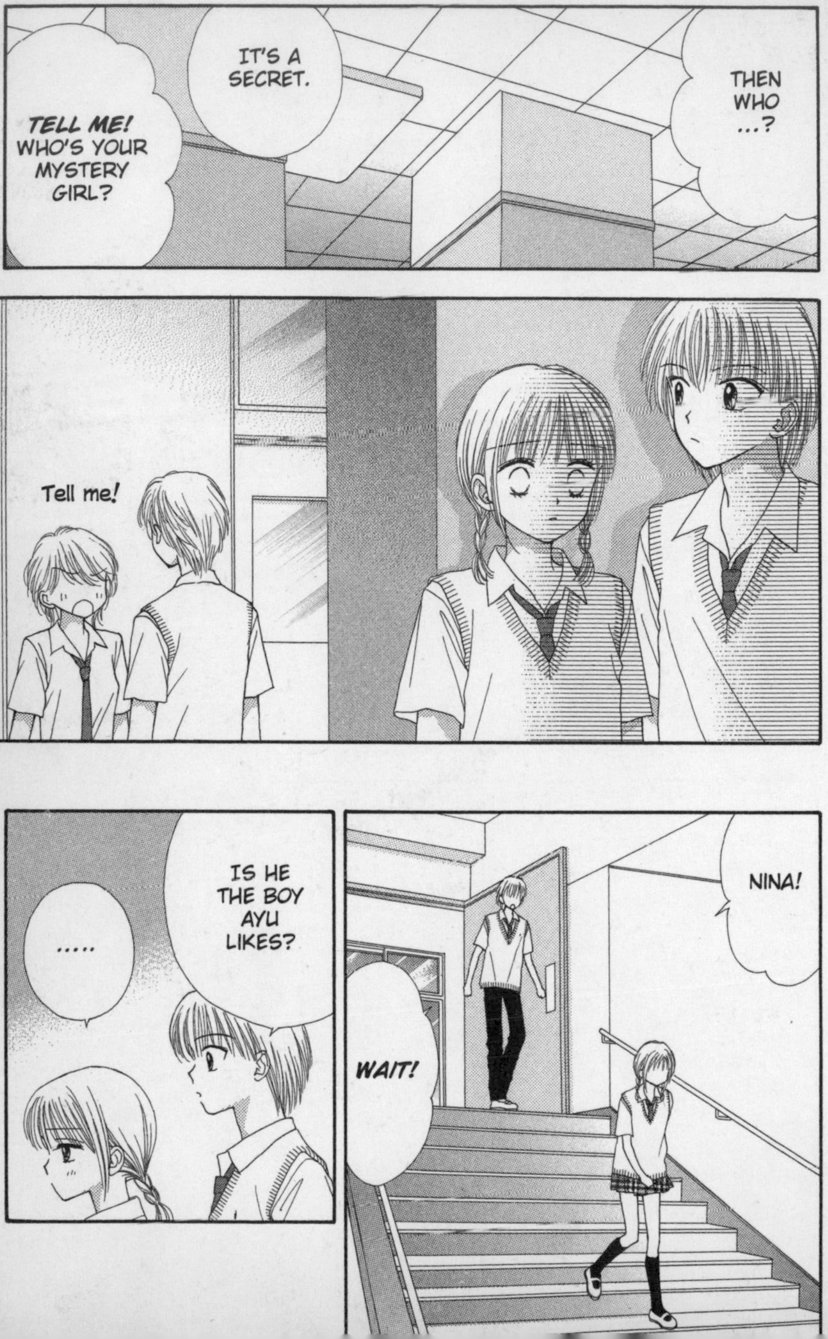
THEN WHO ...?
IT'S A SECRET.
TELL ME! WHO'S YOUR MYSTERY GIRL?
Tell me!
NINA!
WAIT!
IS HE THE BOY AYU LIKES?
.....

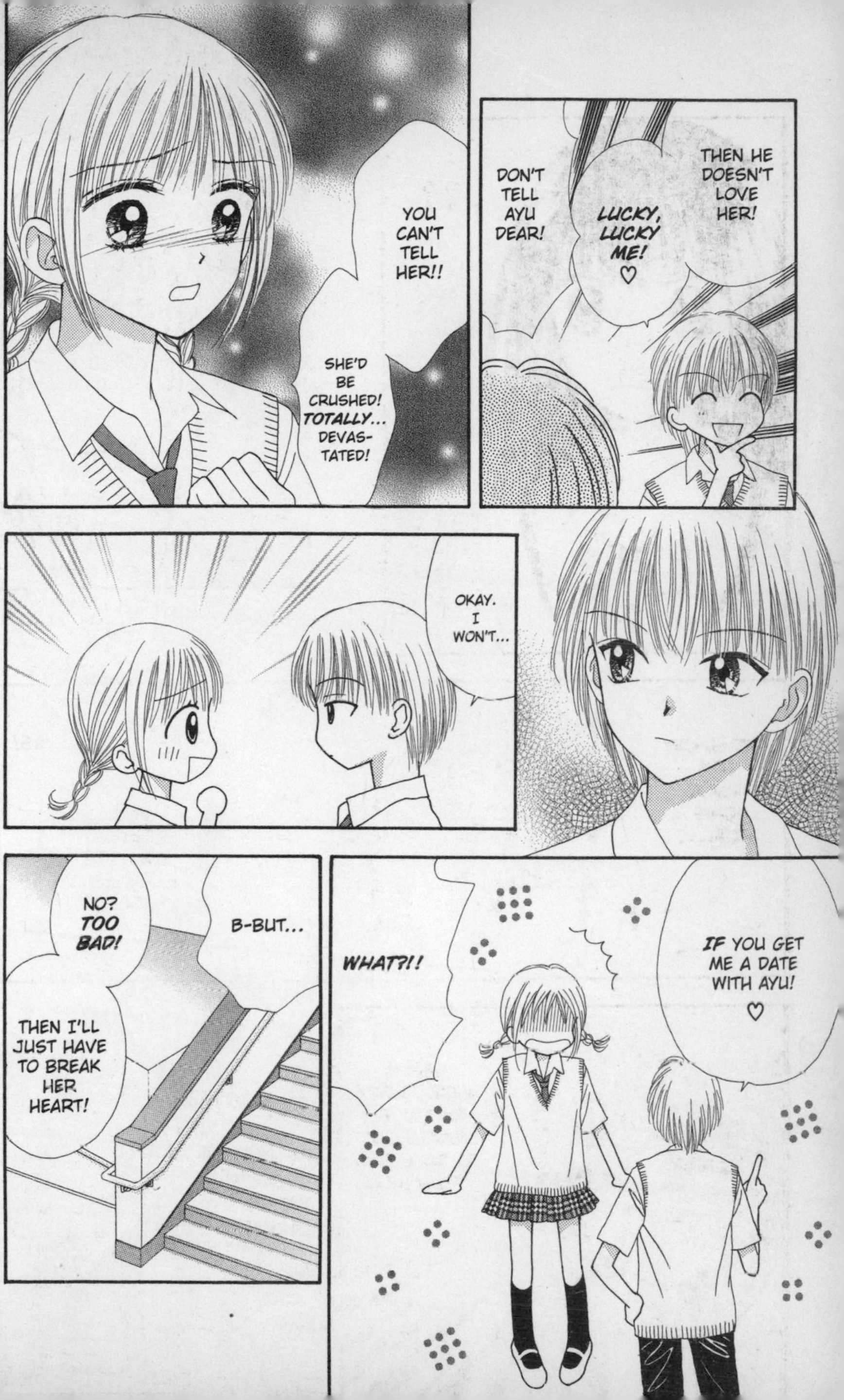
THEN HE DOESN'T LOVE HER!
LUCKY, LUCKY ME! ♡
DON'T TELL AYU DEAR!
YOU CAN'T TELL HER!!
SHE'D BE CRUSHED! TOTALLY... DEVASTATED!
OKAY. I WON'T...
IF YOU GET ME A DATE WITH AYU! ♡
WHAT?!!
B-BUT...
NO? TOO BAD!
THEN I'LL JUST HAVE TO BREAK HER HEART!

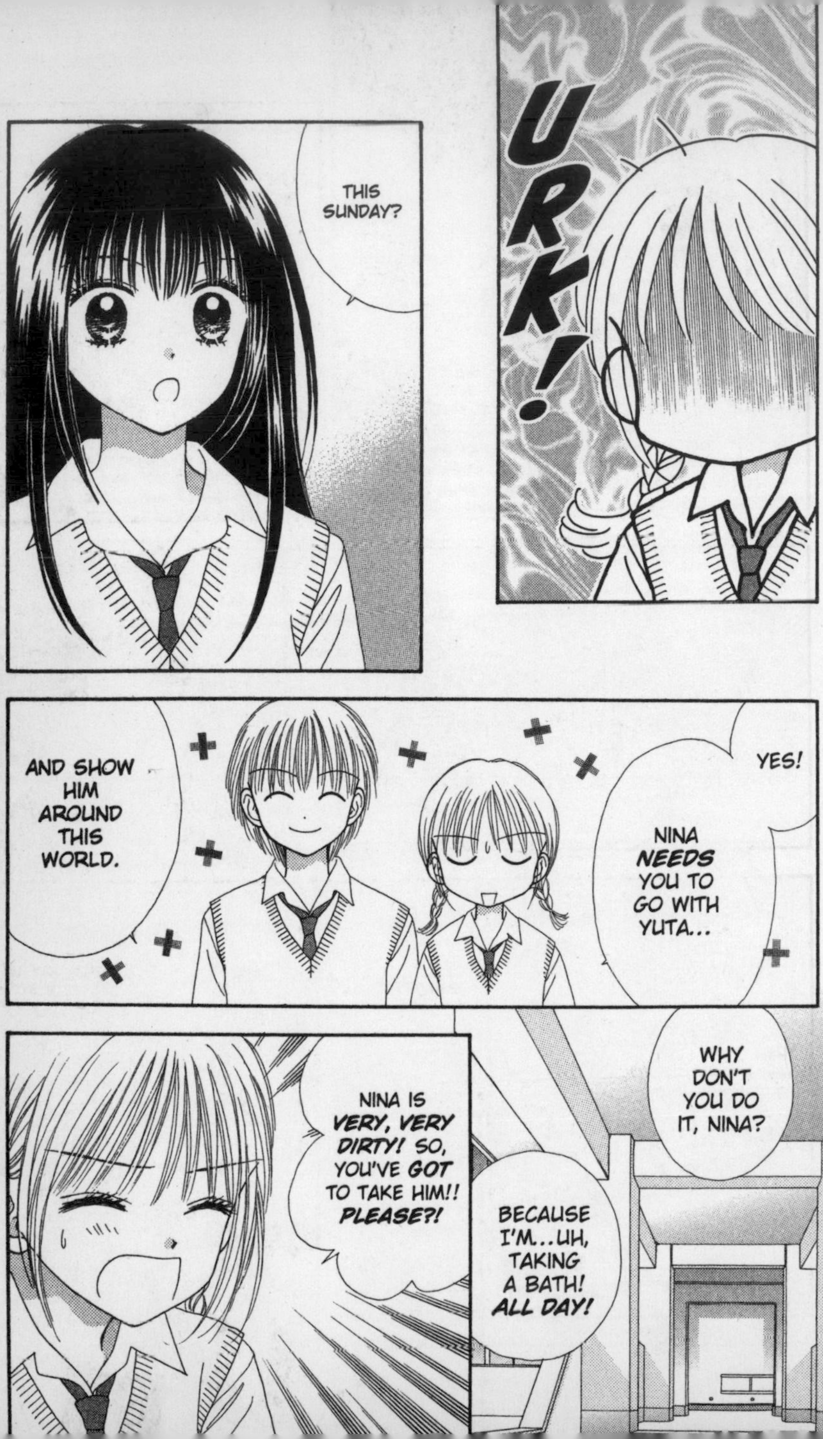
URK!
THIS SUNDAY?
YES!
NINA **NEEDS** YOU TO GO WITH YUTA...
AND SHOW HIM AROUND THIS WORLD.
WHY DON'T YOU DO IT, NINA?
BECAUSE I'M...UH, TAKING A BATH! **ALL DAY!**
NINA IS **VERY, VERY DIRTY!** SO, YOU'VE **GOT** TO TAKE HIM!! **PLEASE?!**

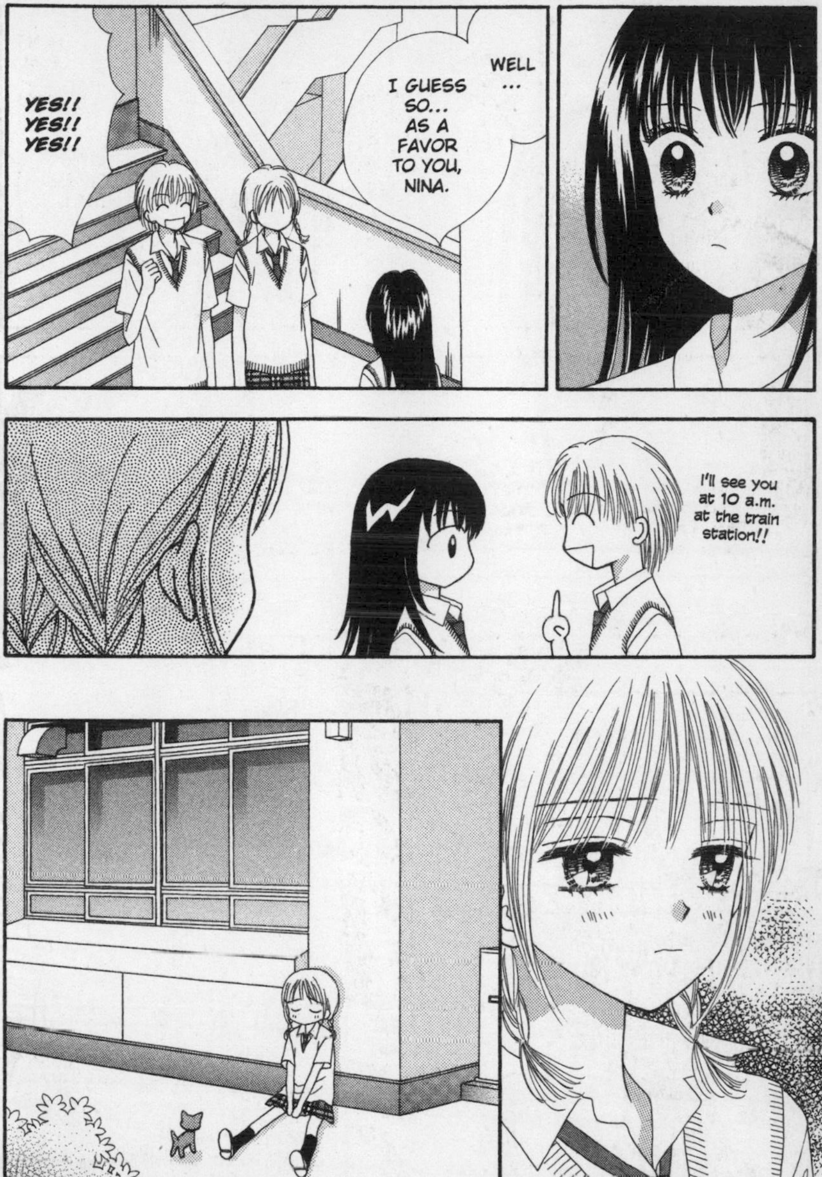
WELL ...
I GUESS SO... AS A FAVOR TO YOU, NINA.
YES!! YES!! YES!!
I'll see you at 10 a.m. at the train station!!

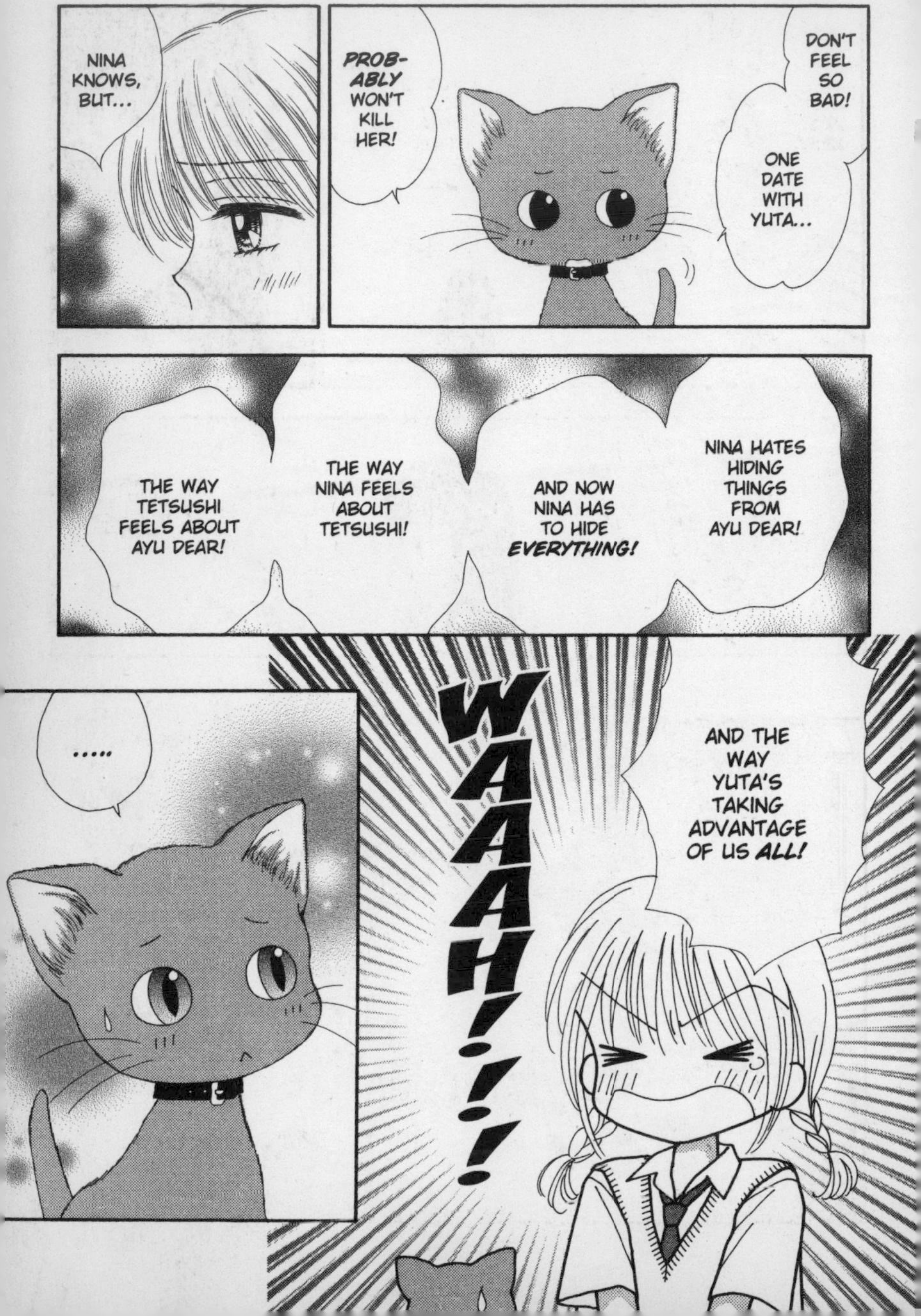
DON'T FEEL SO BAD!
ONE DATE WITH YUTA...
PROBABLY WON'T KILL HER!
NINA KNOWS, BUT...
NINA HATES HIDING THINGS FROM AYU DEAR!
AND NOW NINA HAS TO HIDE *EVERYTHING!*
THE WAY NINA FEELS ABOUT TETSUSHI!
THE WAY TETSUSHI FEELS ABOUT AYU DEAR!
AND THE WAY YUTA'S TAKING ADVANTAGE OF US *ALL!*
WAAAH!!!!!
.....

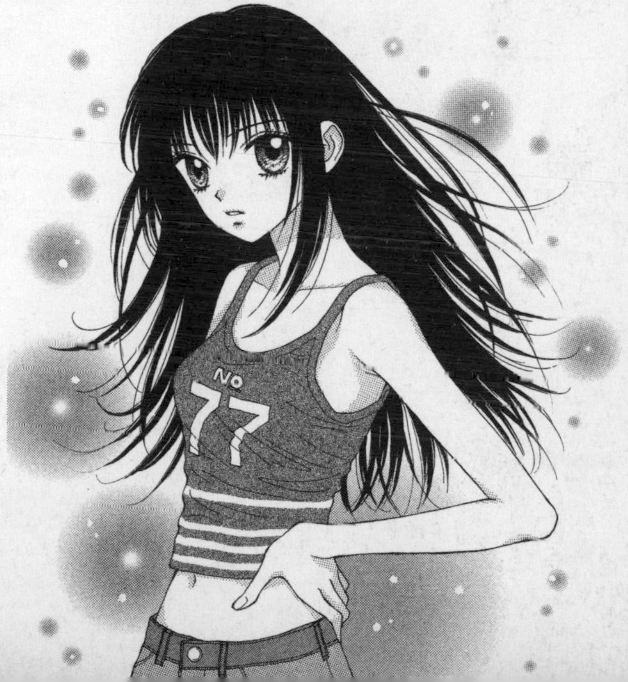
No 77

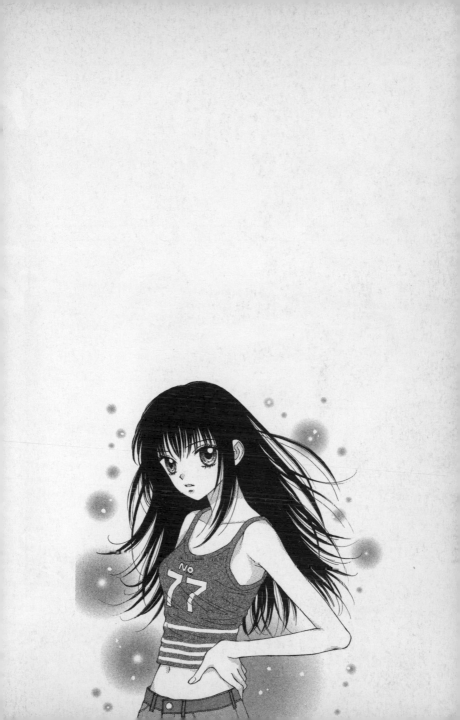

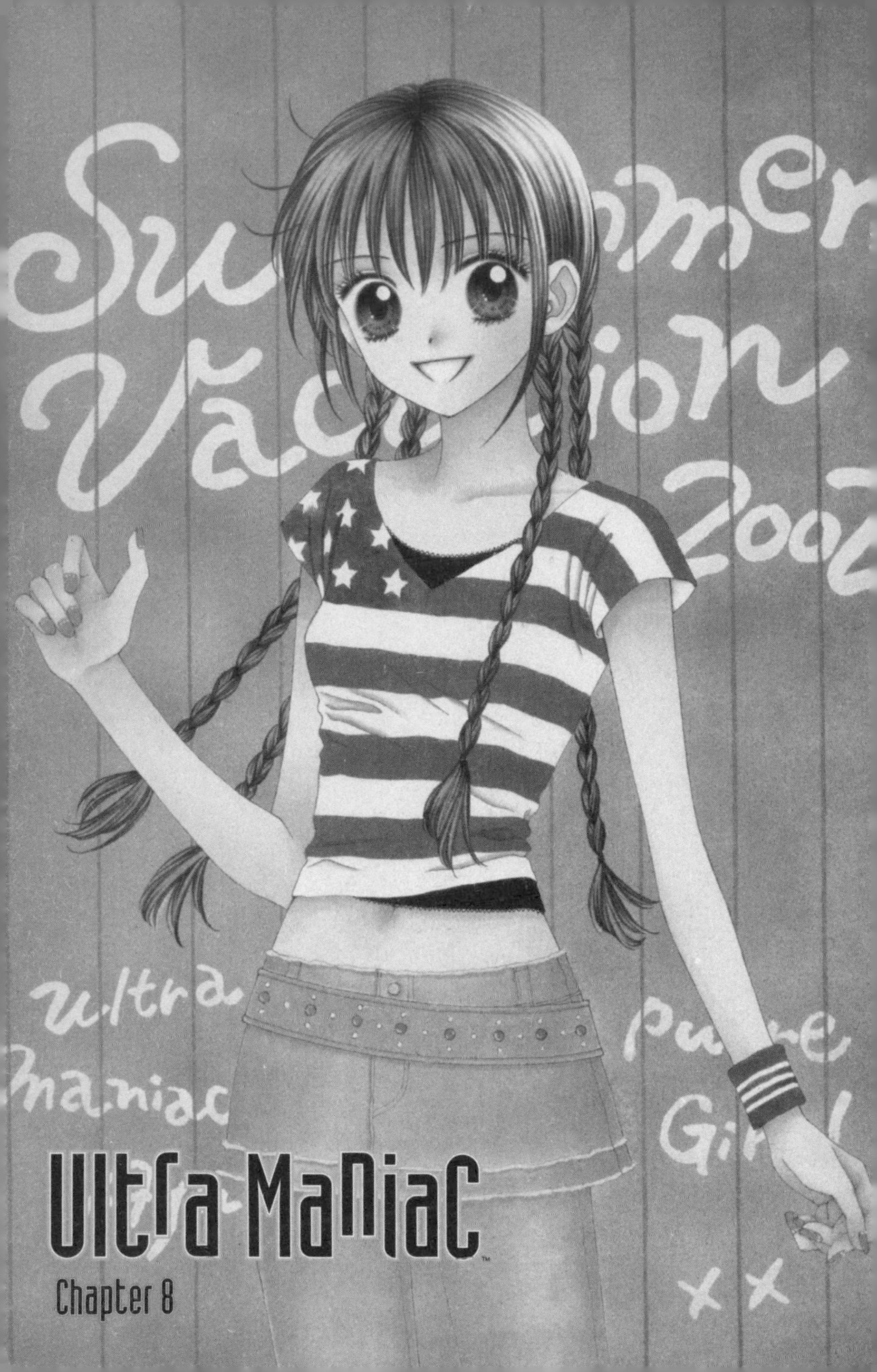
ultra maniac
Ultra Maniac
Chapter 8

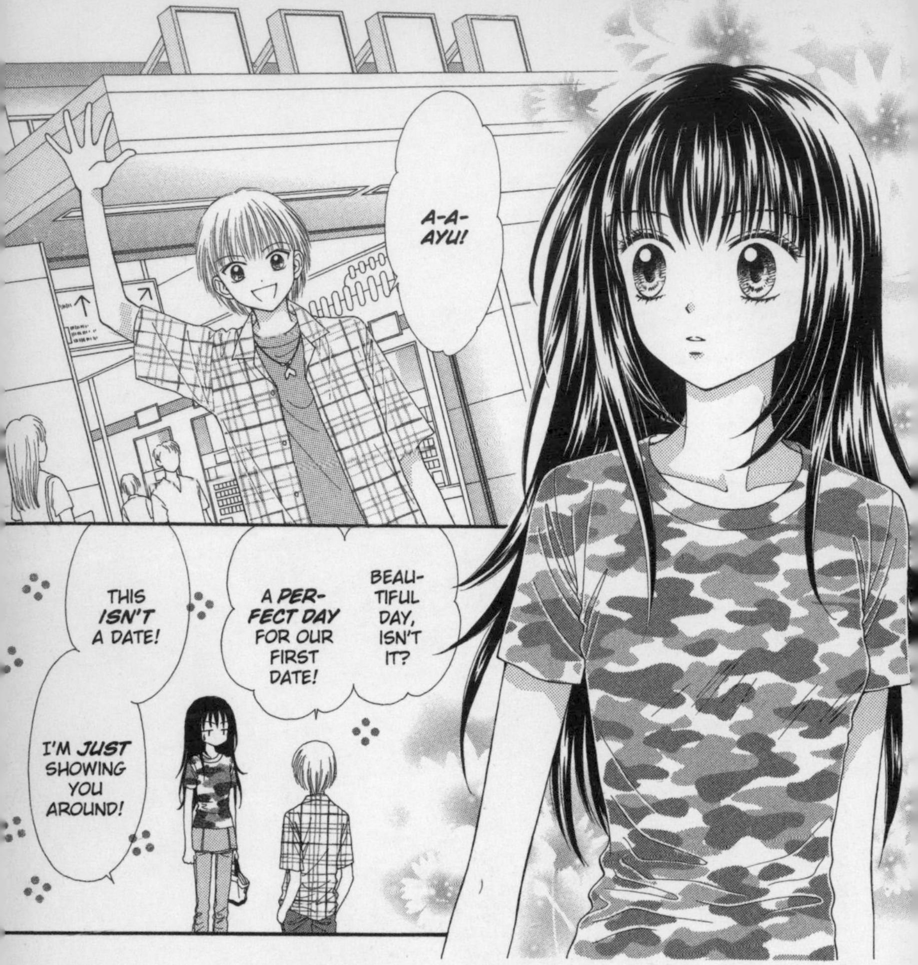
A-A-AYU!
BEAU-TIFUL DAY, ISN'T IT?
A PERFECT DAY FOR OUR FIRST DATE!
THIS ISN'T A DATE!
I'M JUST SHOWING YOU AROUND!

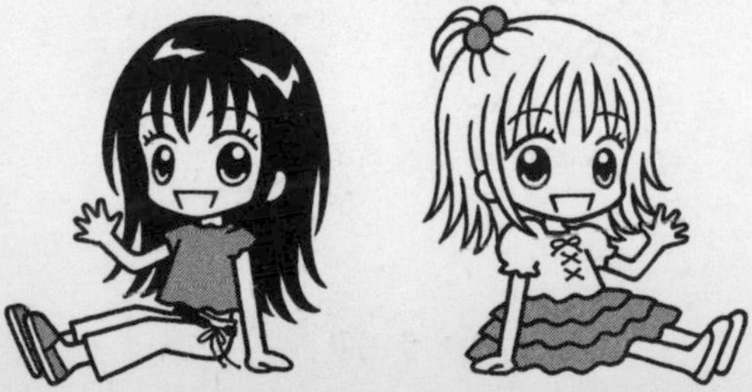

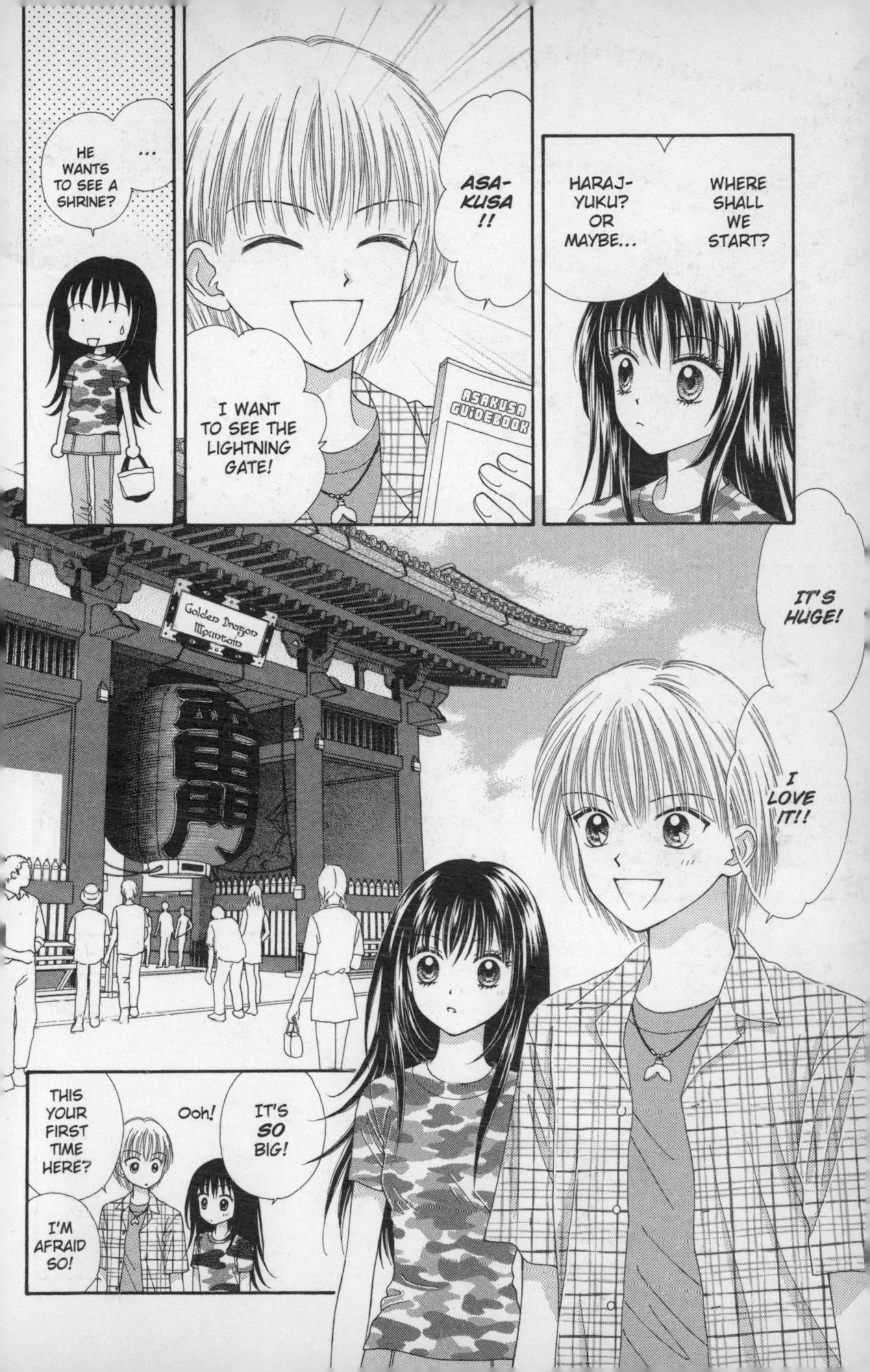
WHERE SHALL WE START?
HARAJ-YUKU? OR MAYBE...
ASA-KUSA!!
ASAKUSA GUIDEBOOK
I WANT TO SEE THE LIGHTNING GATE!
...
HE WANTS TO SEE A SHRINE?
Golden Dragon Mountain
IT'S HUGE!
I LOVE IT!!
IT'S SO BIG!
Ooh!
THIS YOUR FIRST TIME HERE?
I'M AFRAID SO!

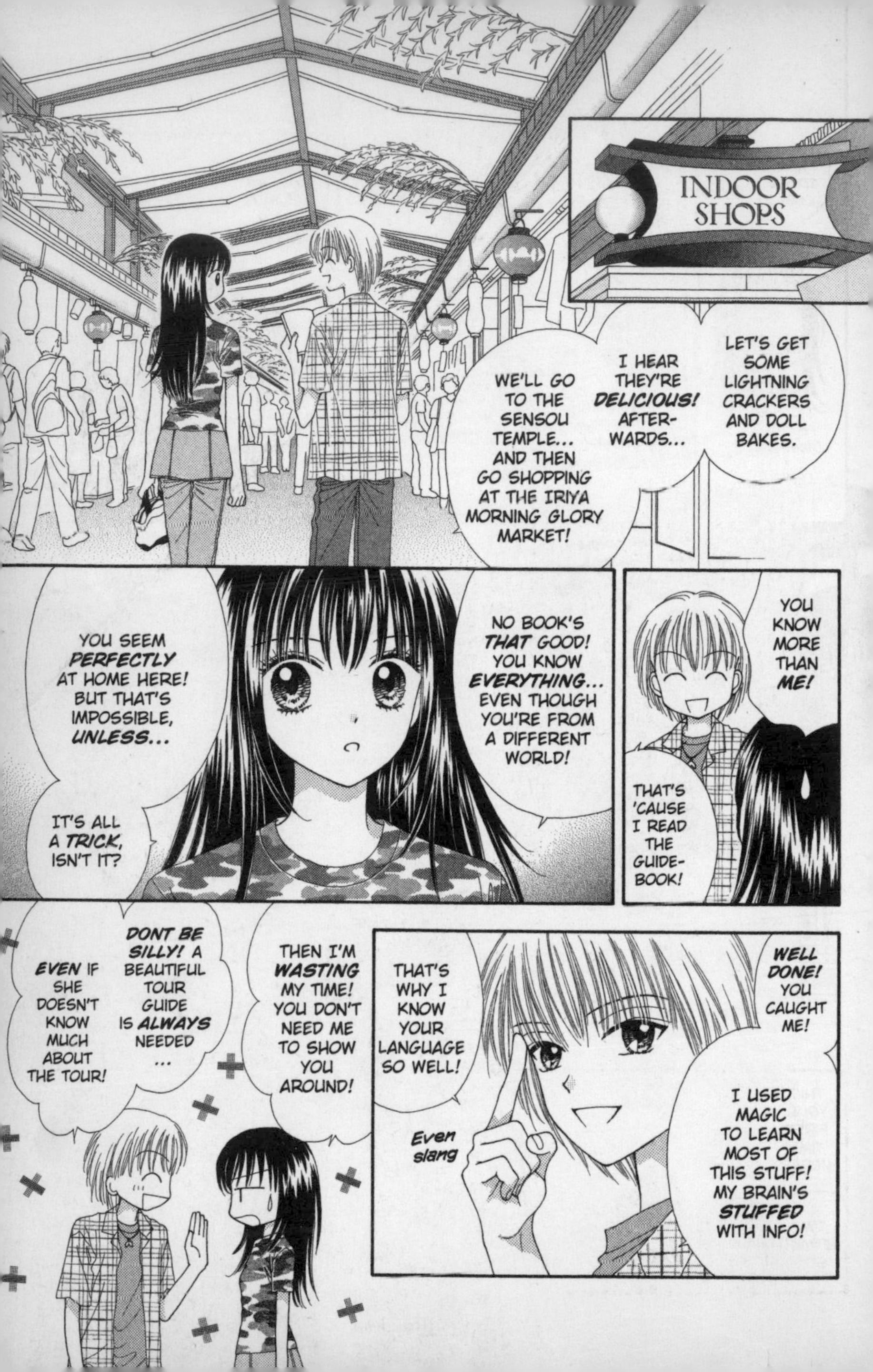
INDOOR SHOPS
LET'S GET SOME LIGHTNING CRACKERS AND DOLL BAKES.
I HEAR THEY'RE *DELICIOUS!* AFTER-WARDS...
WE'LL GO TO THE SENSOU TEMPLE... AND THEN GO SHOPPING AT THE IRIYA MORNING GLORY MARKET!
YOU KNOW MORE THAN *ME!*
THAT'S 'CAUSE I READ THE GUIDE-BOOK!
NO BOOK'S *THAT* GOOD! YOU KNOW *EVERYTHING...* EVEN THOUGH YOU'RE FROM A DIFFERENT WORLD!
YOU SEEM *PERFECTLY* AT HOME HERE! BUT THAT'S IMPOSSIBLE, *UNLESS...*
IT'S ALL A *TRICK,* ISN'T IT?
WELL DONE! YOU CAUGHT ME!
I USED MAGIC TO LEARN MOST OF THIS STUFF! MY BRAIN'S *STUFFED* WITH INFO!
THAT'S WHY I KNOW YOUR LANGUAGE SO WELL!
Even slang
THEN I'M *WASTING* MY TIME! YOU DON'T NEED ME TO SHOW YOU AROUND!
DONT BE SILLY! A BEAUTIFUL TOUR GUIDE IS *ALWAYS* NEEDED ...
EVEN IF SHE DOESN'T KNOW MUCH ABOUT THE TOUR!

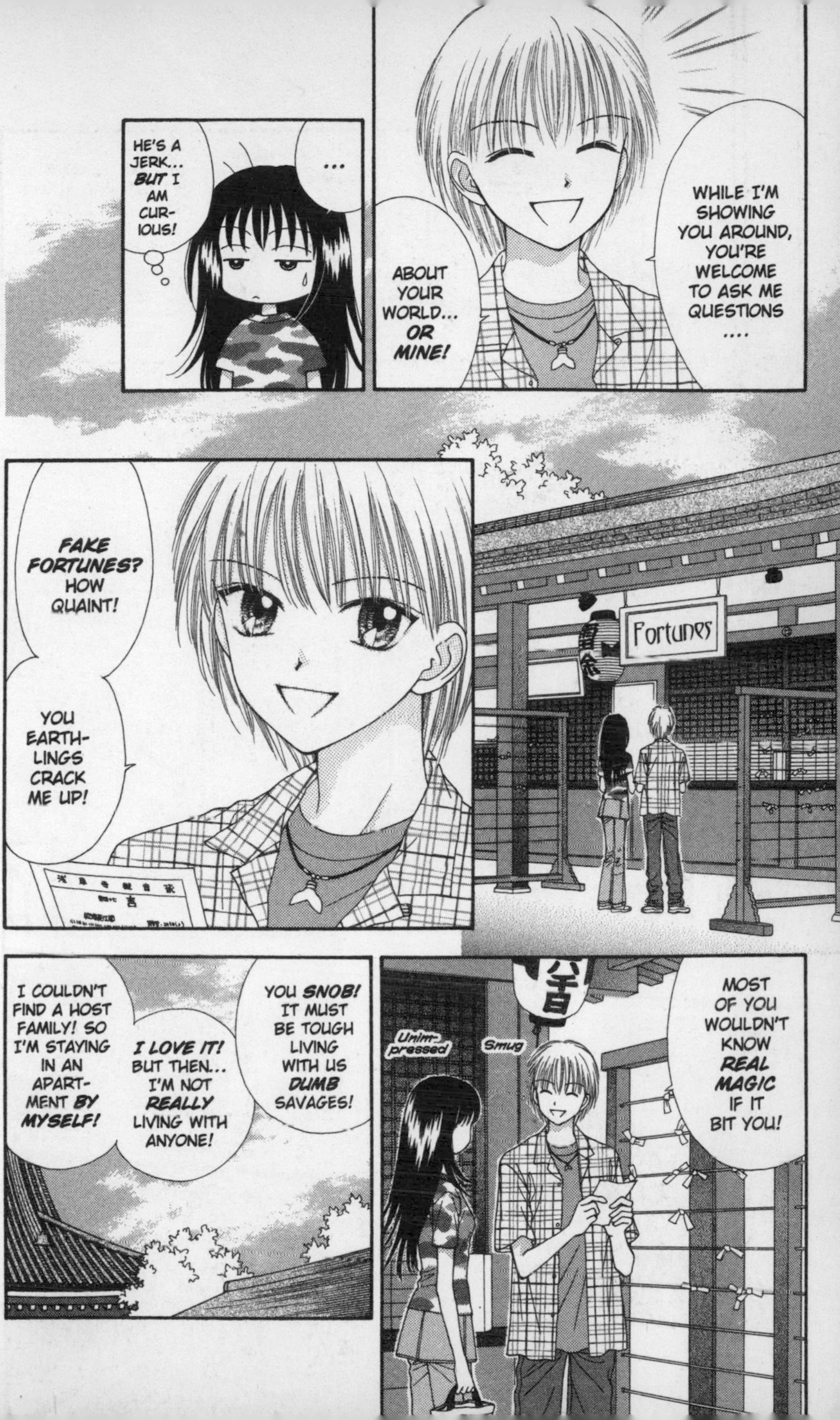
WHILE I'M SHOWING YOU AROUND, YOU'RE WELCOME TO ASK ME QUESTIONS....
ABOUT YOUR WORLD... OR MINE!
...
HE'S A JERK... BUT I AM CURIOUS!
Fortunes
FAKE FORTUNES? HOW QUAINT!
YOU EARTHLINGS CRACK ME UP!
MOST OF YOU WOULDN'T KNOW REAL MAGIC IF IT BIT YOU!
Smug
Unimpressed
YOU SNOB! IT MUST BE TOUGH LIVING WITH US DUMB SAVAGES!
I LOVE IT! BUT THEN... I'M NOT REALLY LIVING WITH ANYONE!
I COULDN'T FIND A HOST FAMILY! SO I'M STAYING IN AN APARTMENT BY MYSELF!

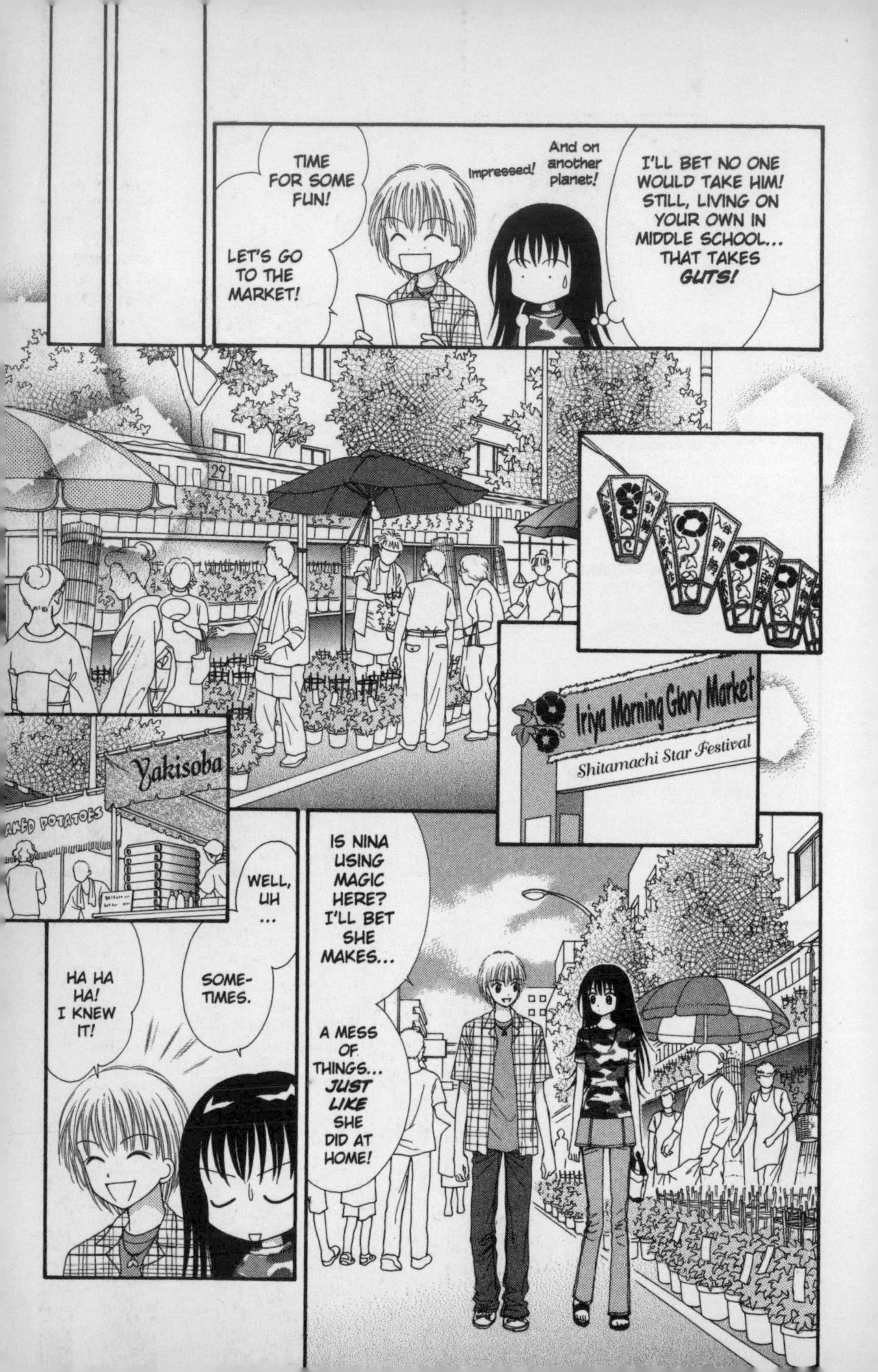
I'LL BET NO ONE WOULD TAKE HIM! STILL, LIVING ON YOUR OWN IN MIDDLE SCHOOL... THAT TAKES **GUTS!**
And on another planet!
Impressed!
TIME FOR SOME FUN!
LET'S GO TO THE MARKET!
Iriya Morning Glory Market
Shitamachi Star Festival
Yakisoba
AKED POTATOES
IS NINA USING MAGIC HERE? I'LL BET SHE MAKES...
A MESS OF THINGS... **JUST LIKE** SHE DID AT HOME!
WELL, UH ...
SOME-TIMES.
HA HA HA! I KNEW IT!

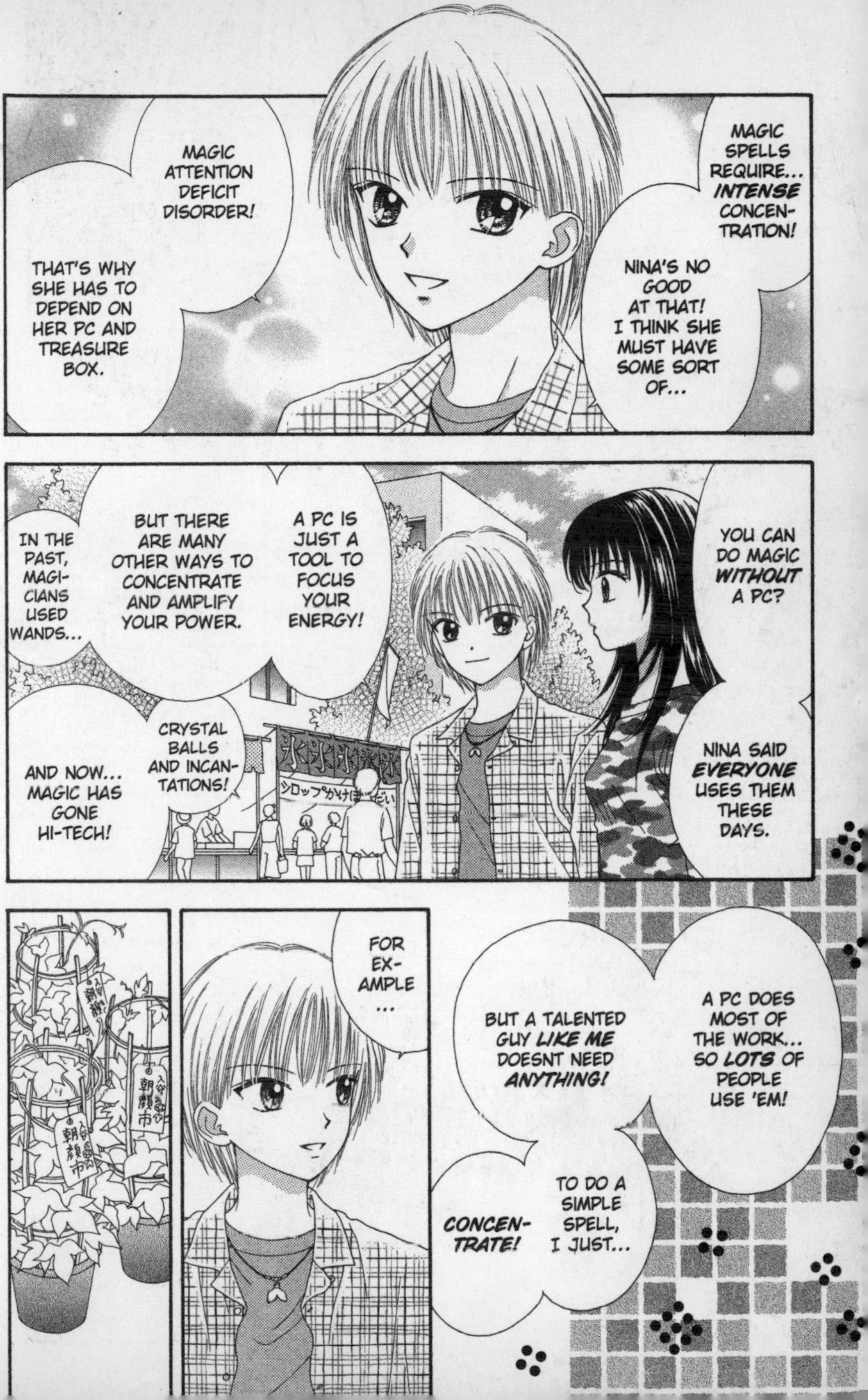
MAGIC SPELLS REQUIRE... *INTENSE* CONCENTRATION!
NINA'S NO GOOD AT THAT! I THINK SHE MUST HAVE SOME SORT OF...
MAGIC ATTENTION DEFICIT DISORDER!
THAT'S WHY SHE HAS TO DEPEND ON HER PC AND TREASURE BOX.
YOU CAN DO MAGIC *WITHOUT* A PC?
NINA SAID *EVERYONE* USES THEM THESE DAYS.
A PC IS JUST A TOOL TO FOCUS YOUR ENERGY!
BUT THERE ARE MANY OTHER WAYS TO CONCENTRATE AND AMPLIFY YOUR POWER.
IN THE PAST, MAGICIANS USED WANDS...
CRYSTAL BALLS AND INCANTATIONS!
AND NOW... MAGIC HAS GONE HI-TECH!
A PC DOES MOST OF THE WORK... SO *LOTS* OF PEOPLE USE 'EM!
BUT A TALENTED GUY *LIKE ME* DOESNT NEED *ANYTHING!*
TO DO A SIMPLE SPELL, I JUST...
CONCENTRATE!
FOR EXAMPLE...

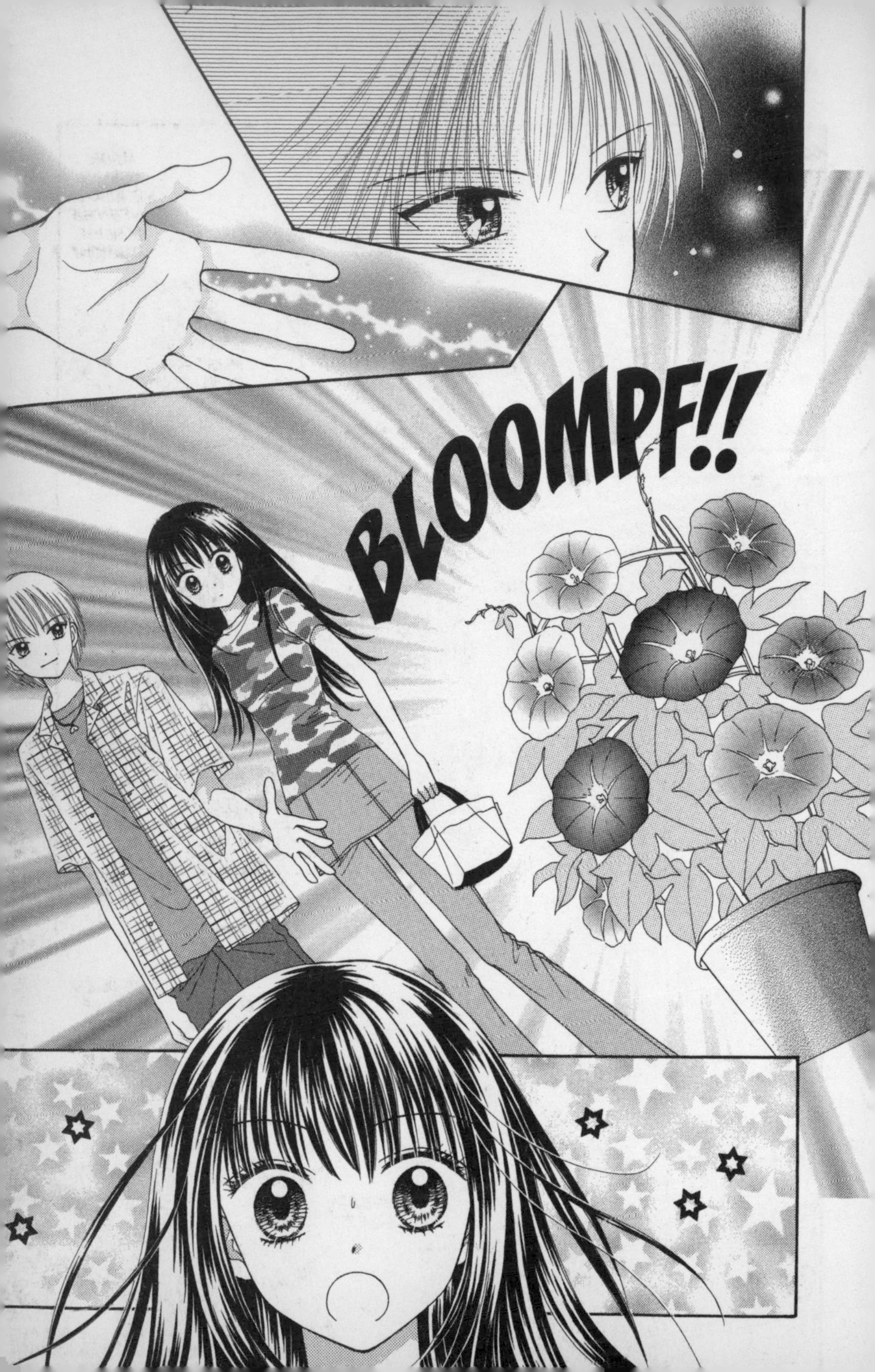
BLOOMPF!!

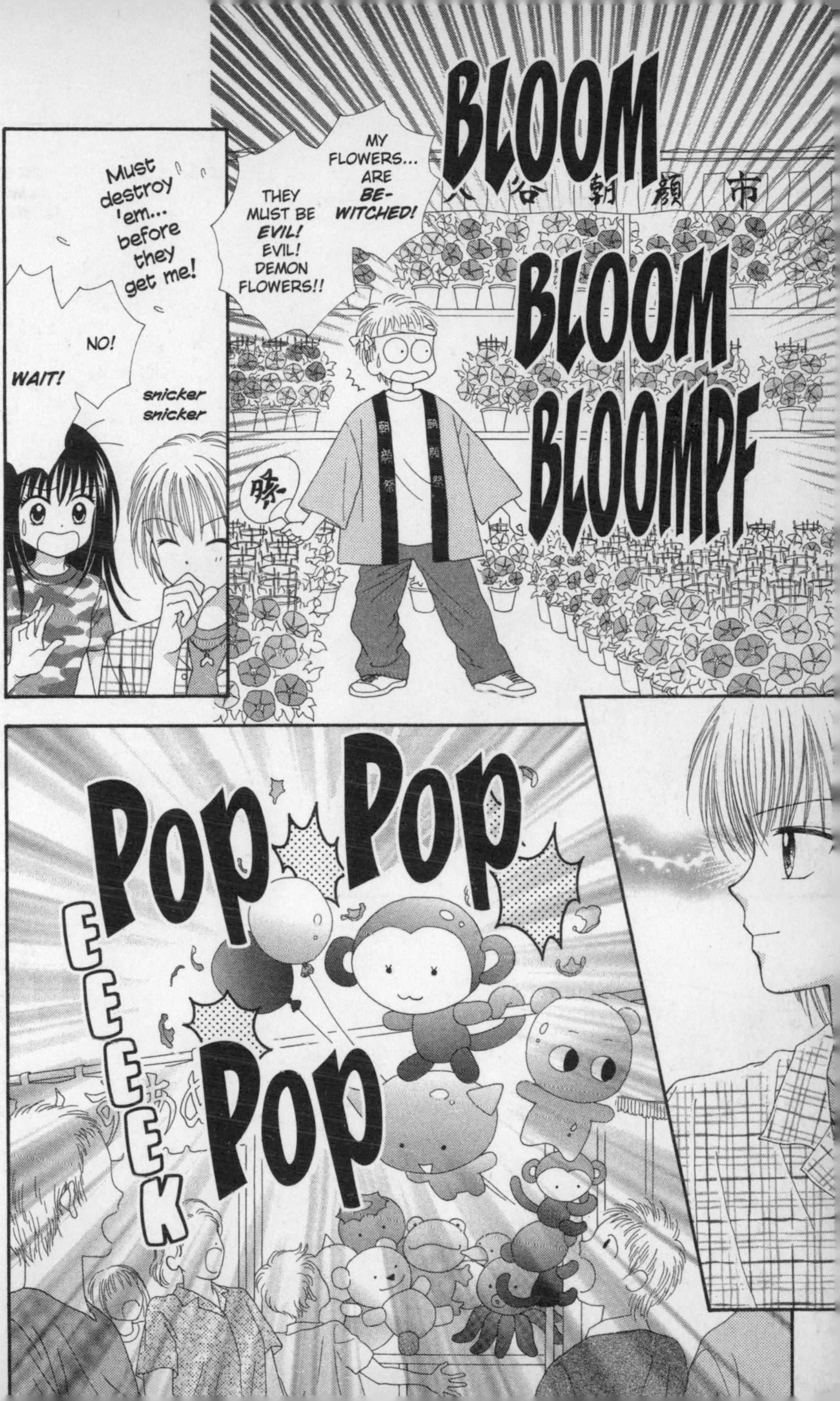
MY FLOWERS... ARE BE-WITCHED!
THEY MUST BE EVIL! EVIL! DEMON FLOWERS!!
BLOOM
入谷朝顔市
BLOOM
BLOOMPF
Must destroy 'em... before they get me!
NO!
WAIT!
snicker snicker
Pop Pop
EEEEEK
Pop

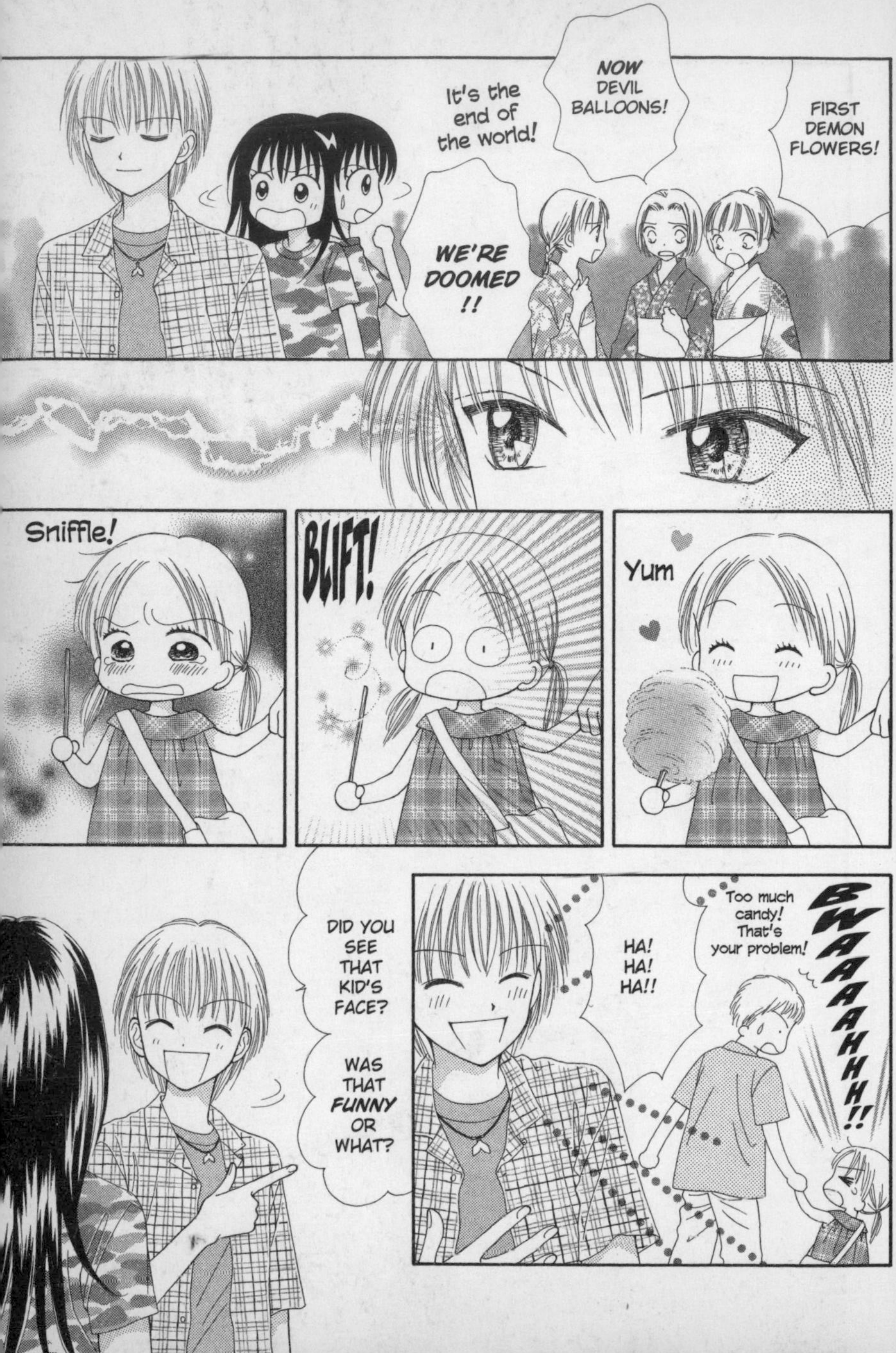
FIRST DEMON FLOWERS!
NOW DEVIL BALLOONS!
It's the end of the world!
WE'RE DOOMED!!
Yum
BLIFT!
Sniffle!
BWAAAAHHH!!
Too much candy! That's your problem!
HA! HA! HA!!
DID YOU SEE THAT KID'S FACE?
WAS THAT *FUNNY* OR WHAT?

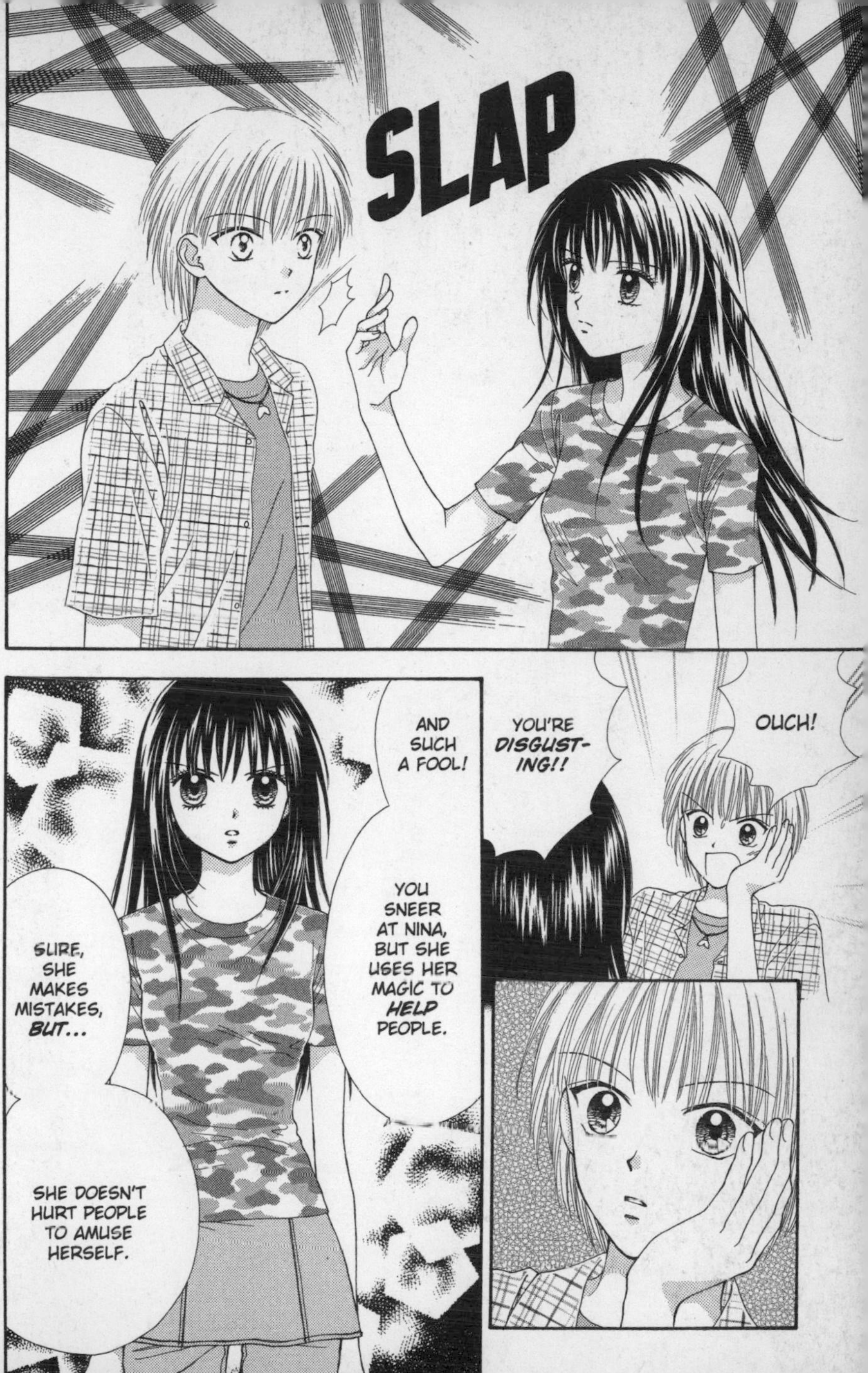
SLAP
OUCH!
YOU'RE *DISGUSTING!!*
AND SUCH A FOOL!
YOU SNEER AT NINA, BUT SHE USES HER MAGIC TO ***HELP*** PEOPLE.
SURE, SHE MAKES MISTAKES, ***BUT...***
SHE DOESN'T HURT PEOPLE TO AMUSE HERSELF.

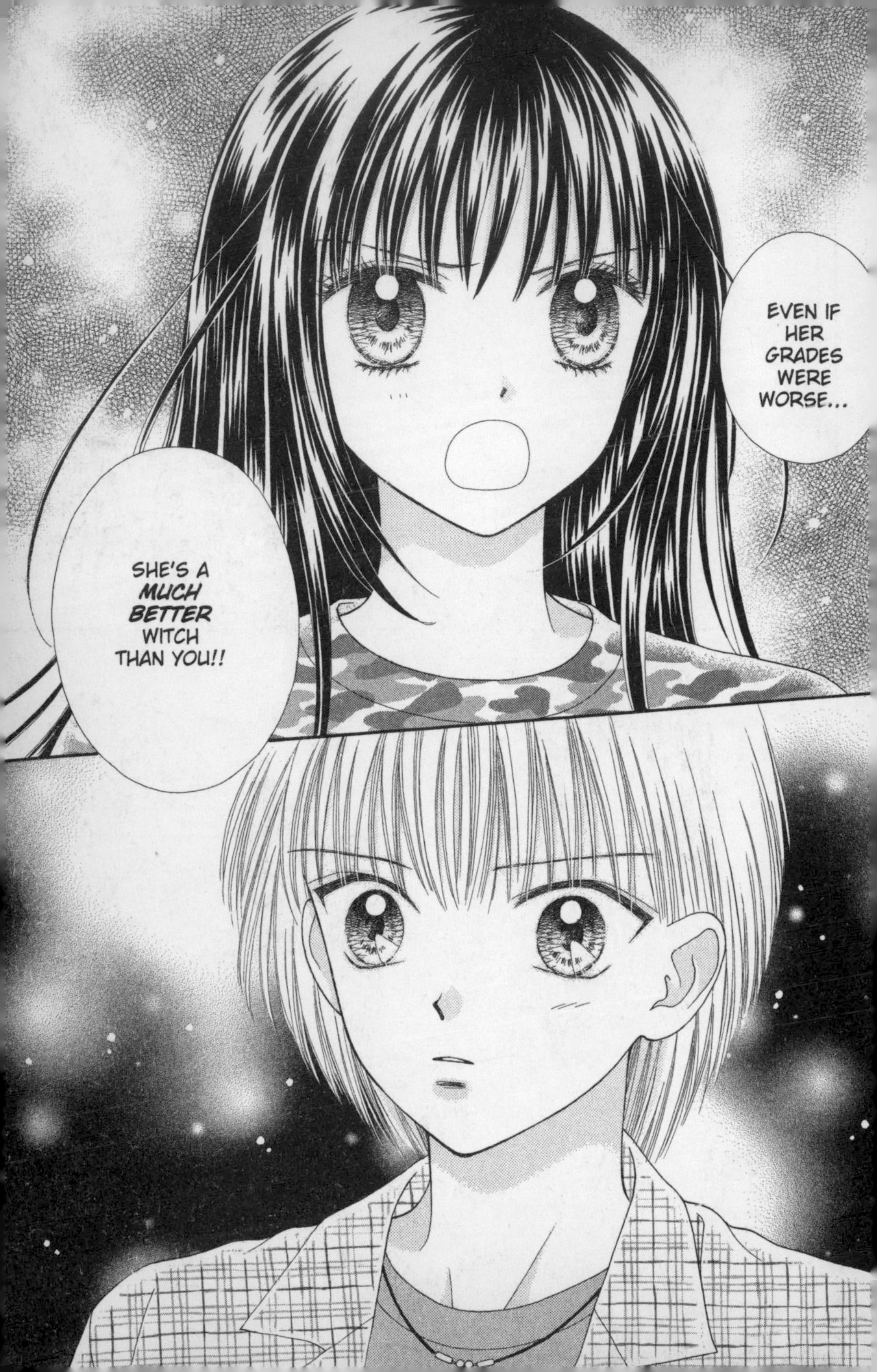
EVEN IF HER GRADES WERE WORSE...
SHE'S A *MUCH BETTER* WITCH THAN YOU!!

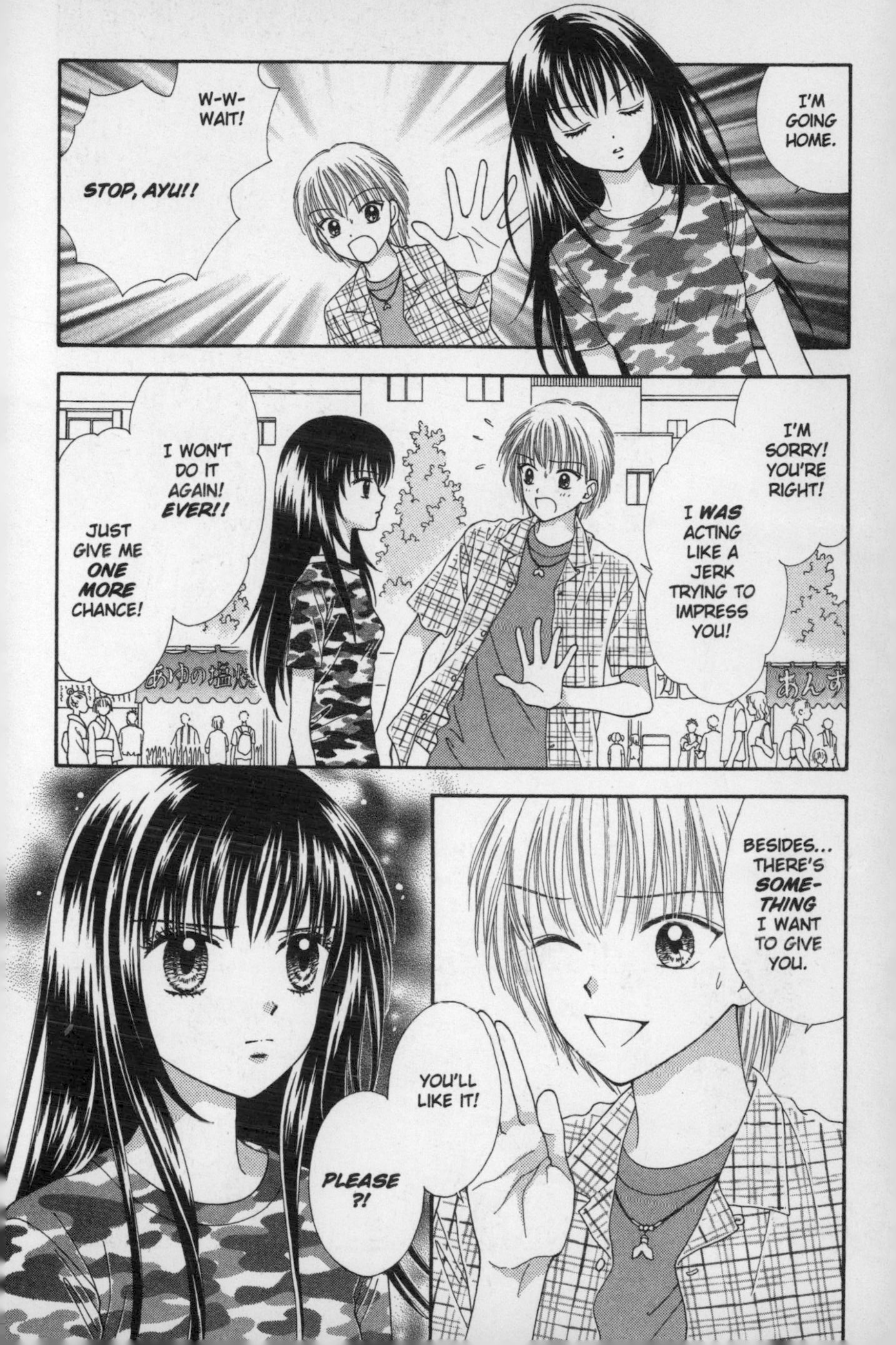
I'M GOING HOME.
W-W-WAIT!
STOP, AYU!!
I'M SORRY! YOU'RE RIGHT!
I *WAS* ACTING LIKE A JERK TRYING TO IMPRESS YOU!
I WON'T DO IT AGAIN! *EVER!!*
JUST GIVE ME *ONE MORE* CHANCE!
あんず
あゆの塩焼
BESIDES... THERE'S *SOMETHING* I WANT TO GIVE YOU.
YOU'LL LIKE IT!
PLEASE ?!

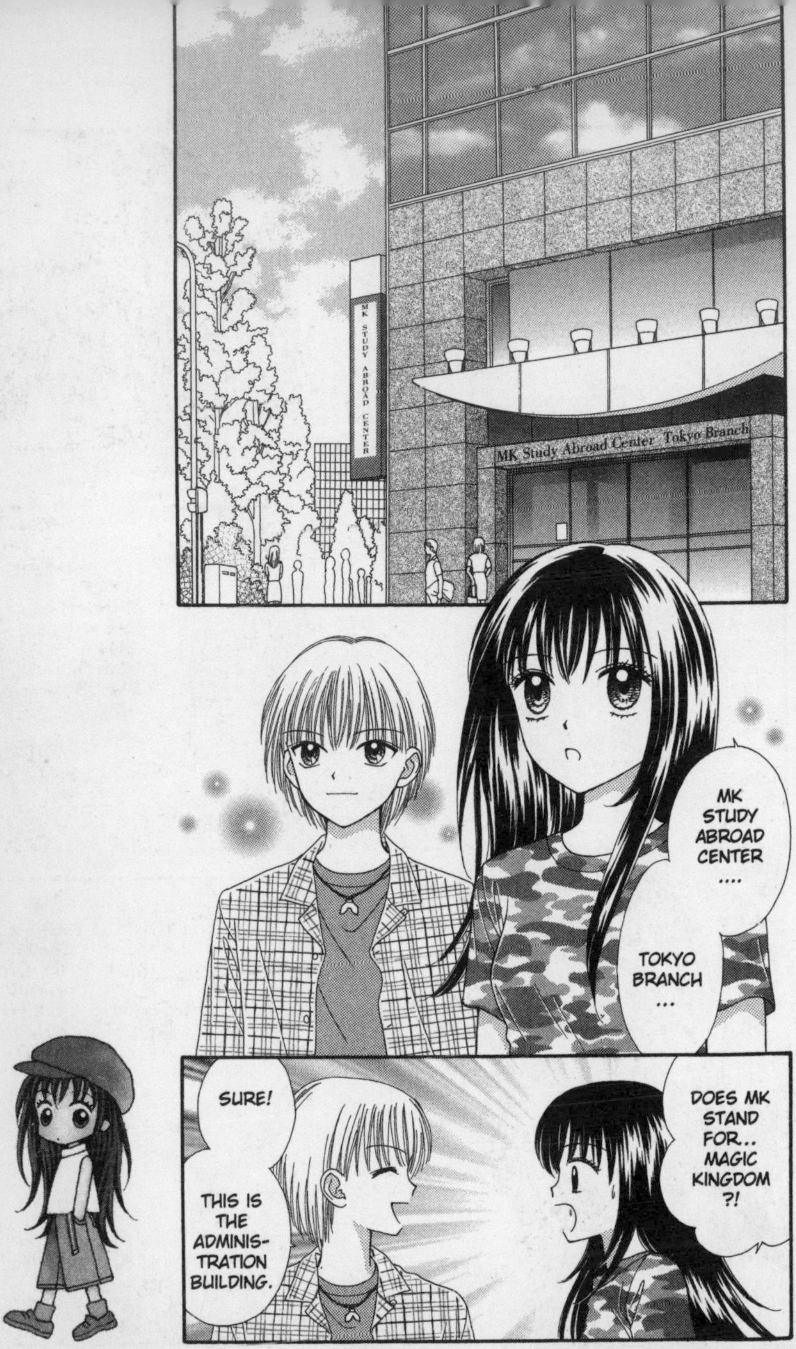
MK STUDY ABROAD CENTER
MK Study Abroad Center Tokyo Branch
MK STUDY ABROAD CENTER ....
TOKYO BRANCH ...
DOES MK STAND FOR... MAGIC KINGDOM ?!
SURE!
THIS IS THE ADMINIS-TRATION BUILDING.

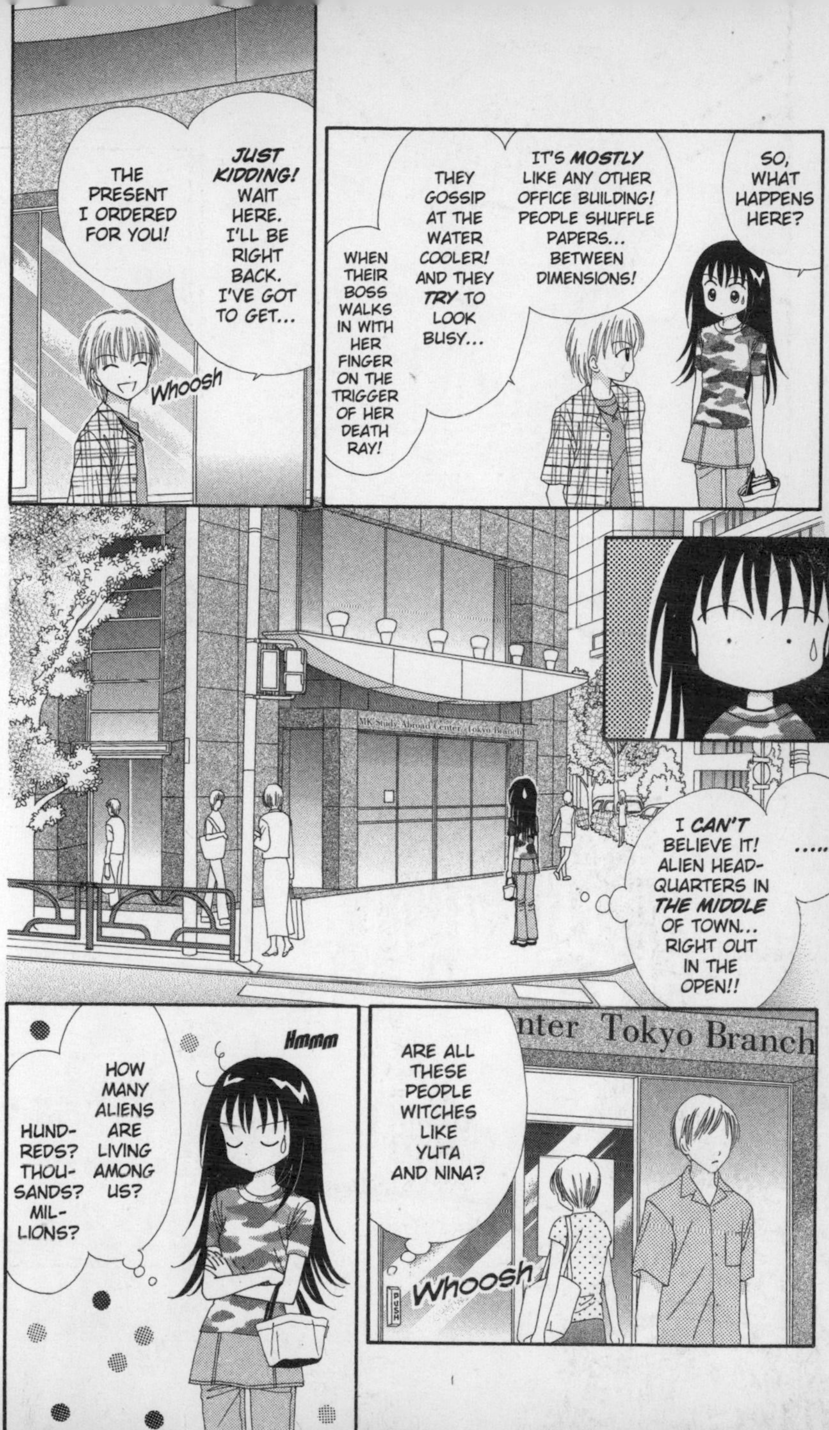
SO, WHAT HAPPENS HERE?
IT'S MOSTLY LIKE ANY OTHER OFFICE BUILDING! PEOPLE SHUFFLE PAPERS... BETWEEN DIMENSIONS!
THEY GOSSIP AT THE WATER COOLER! AND THEY TRY TO LOOK BUSY...
WHEN THEIR BOSS WALKS IN WITH HER FINGER ON THE TRIGGER OF HER DEATH RAY!
JUST KIDDING! WAIT HERE. I'LL BE RIGHT BACK. I'VE GOT TO GET...
THE PRESENT I ORDERED FOR YOU!
Whoosh
MK Study Abroad Center · Tokyo Branch
.....
I CAN'T BELIEVE IT! ALIEN HEAD-QUARTERS IN THE MIDDLE OF TOWN... RIGHT OUT IN THE OPEN!!
nter Tokyo Branch
ARE ALL THESE PEOPLE WITCHES LIKE YUTA AND NINA?
PUSH
Whoosh
Hmmm
HOW MANY ALIENS ARE LIVING AMONG US?
HUND-REDS? THOU-SANDS? MIL-LIONS?

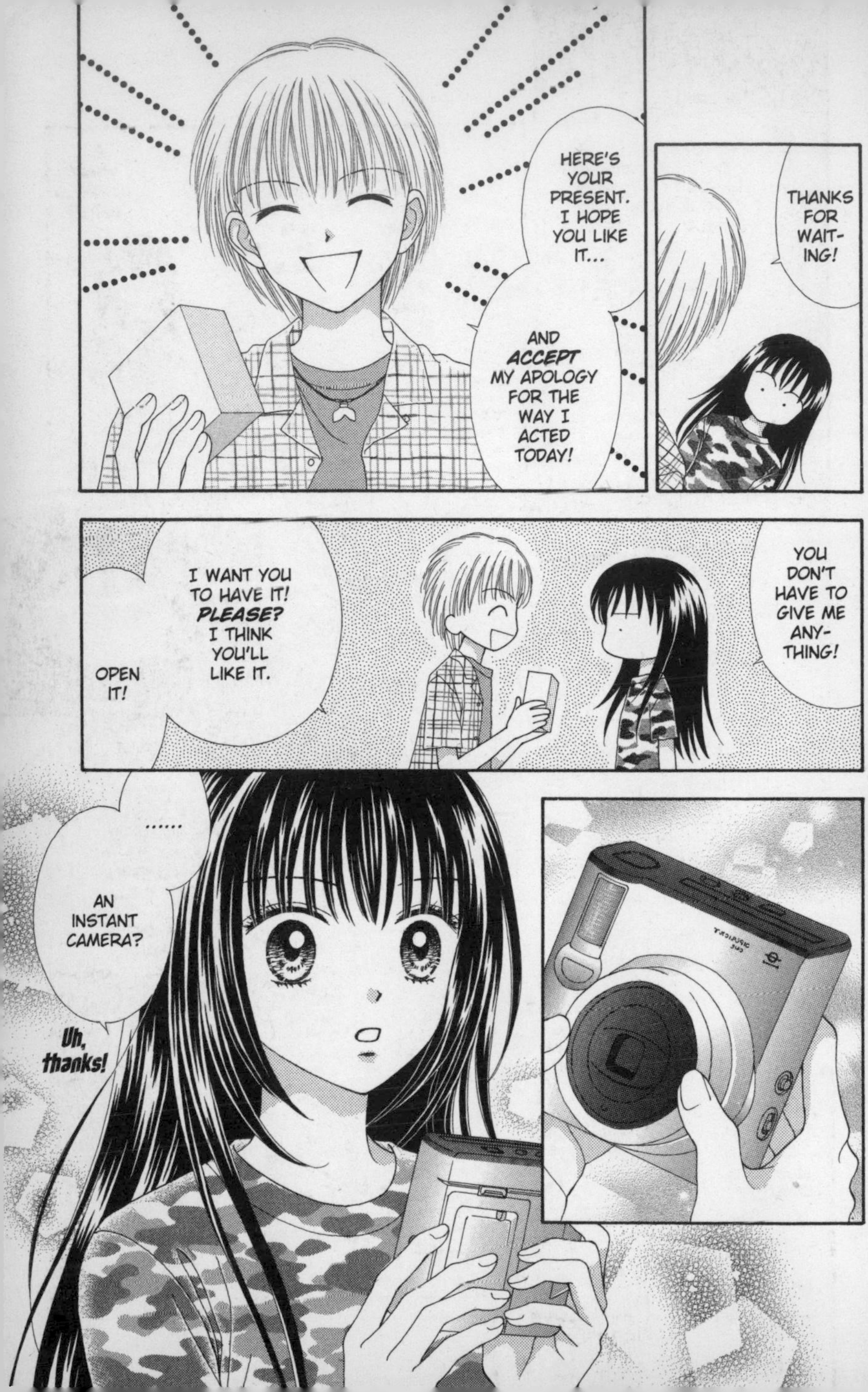
THANKS FOR WAIT-ING!
HERE'S YOUR PRESENT. I HOPE YOU LIKE IT...
AND ACCEPT MY APOLOGY FOR THE WAY I ACTED TODAY!
YOU DON'T HAVE TO GIVE ME ANY-THING!
I WANT YOU TO HAVE IT! PLEASE? I THINK YOU'LL LIKE IT.
OPEN IT!
......
AN INSTANT CAMERA?
Uh, thanks!

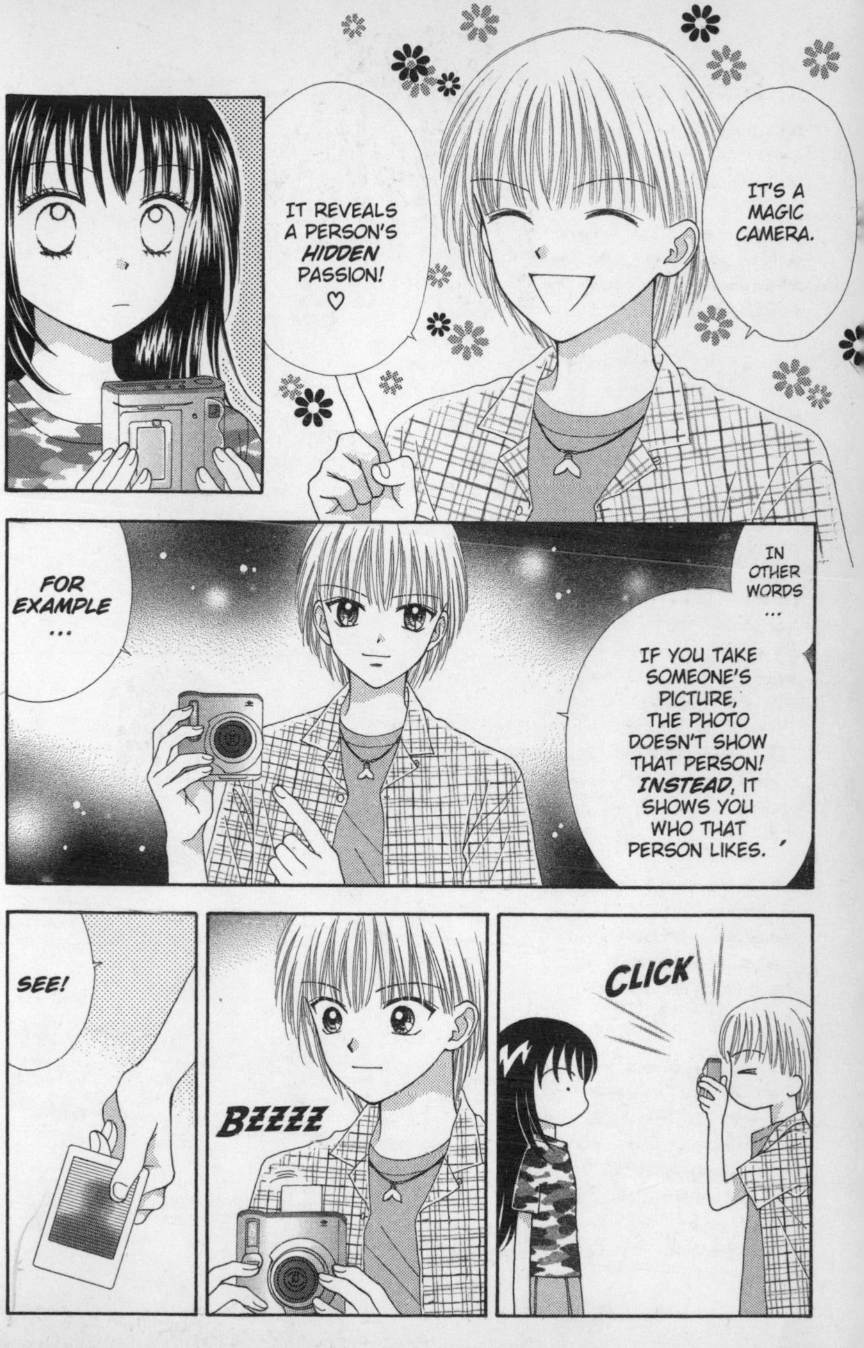
IT'S A MAGIC CAMERA.
IT REVEALS A PERSON'S *HIDDEN* PASSION! ♡
IN OTHER WORDS ...
IF YOU TAKE SOMEONE'S PICTURE, THE PHOTO DOESN'T SHOW THAT PERSON! *INSTEAD*, IT SHOWS YOU WHO THAT PERSON LIKES.
FOR EXAMPLE ...
CLICK
BZZZZ
SEE!

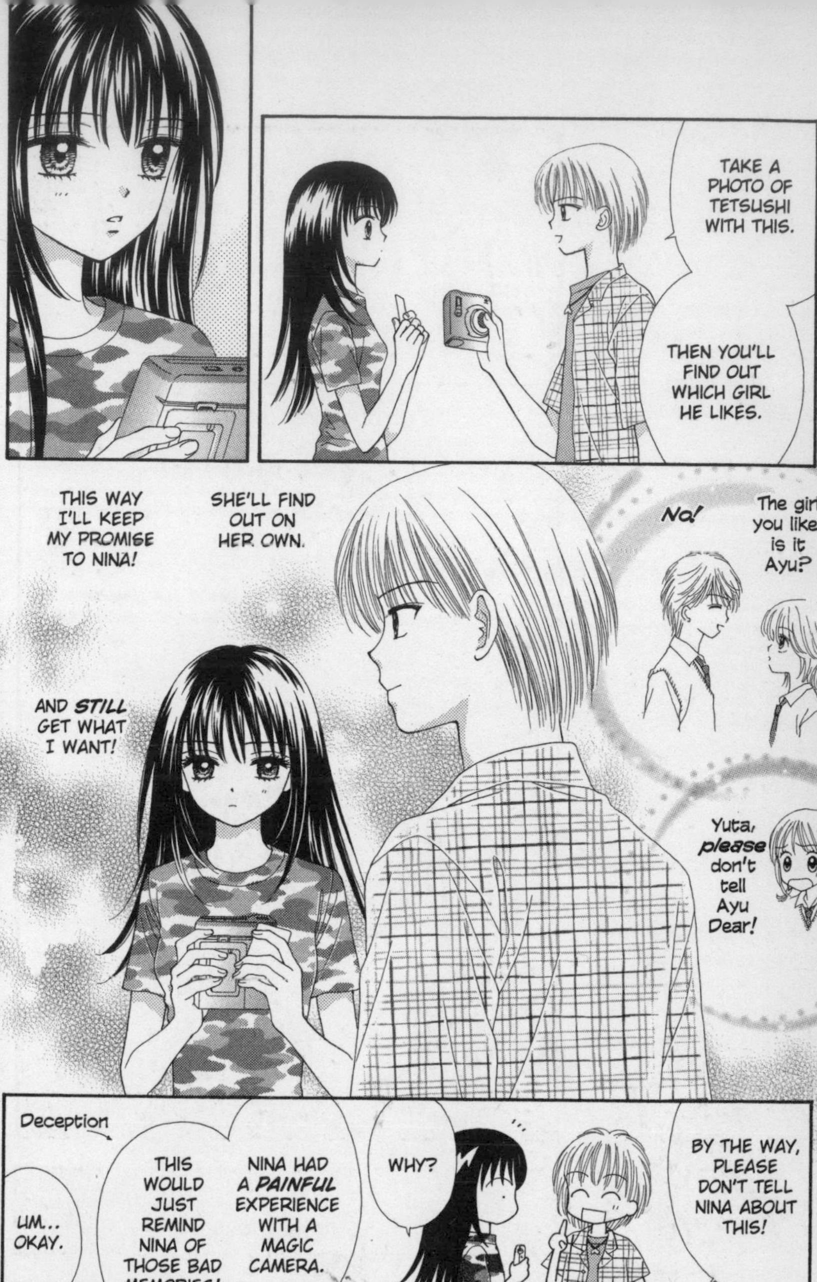
TAKE A PHOTO OF TETSUSHI WITH THIS.
THEN YOU'LL FIND OUT WHICH GIRL HE LIKES.
The girl you like, is it Ayu?
No!
Yuta, please don't tell Ayu Dear!
SHE'LL FIND OUT ON HER OWN.
THIS WAY I'LL KEEP MY PROMISE TO NINA!
AND STILL GET WHAT I WANT!
BY THE WAY, PLEASE DON'T TELL NINA ABOUT THIS!
...
WHY?
NINA HAD A PAINFUL EXPERIENCE WITH A MAGIC CAMERA.
THIS WOULD JUST REMIND NINA OF THOSE BAD MEMORIES!
UM.. OKAY.
Deception

FREE TALK 3

Before I wrote Chapter 8, I went to Asakusa for research. I discovered that the Iriya Morning Glory Market Festival was going on, so I went there, too. (The festival takes place July 6-8.) During the festival, one side of a wide street is lined with morning glory stores, while the other side is lined with food stalls.

It was a lot of fun and reminded me of festivals I attended when I was in elementary school. Our local shrine's summer festival wasn't very big probably because it was a small shrine. But it was **so much fun!** Nostalgic memories of those celebrations came back to me as I visited the Iriya festival.

Still, there were some big differences between the Iriya festival and the festivals from my childhood. There were more stalls and they carried things (like colorful drinks) that we'd never had when I was a girl. And some types of food stalls were missing . . . like caramel makers. I used to love watching caramel being made. At the Iriya festival I didn't see **any** caramel maker at all.

Oddly enough, around the time of the Iriya festival my friend, Yôko Ôkawa, was working on a very entertaining book about temple festivals. (The Illustrated Book of Walking Through a Temple Festival.)

I ended up going with her to the Black-Eyed Fudo Temple Festival. In the book, you can see a photo of a tako-yaki stand we visited. There was a **huge** line of people waiting to buy tako-yaki (small chunks of boiled octopus baked inside a flour and seasoning coating.) The crust is crunchy, while the inside is creamy. It's **very tasty!**

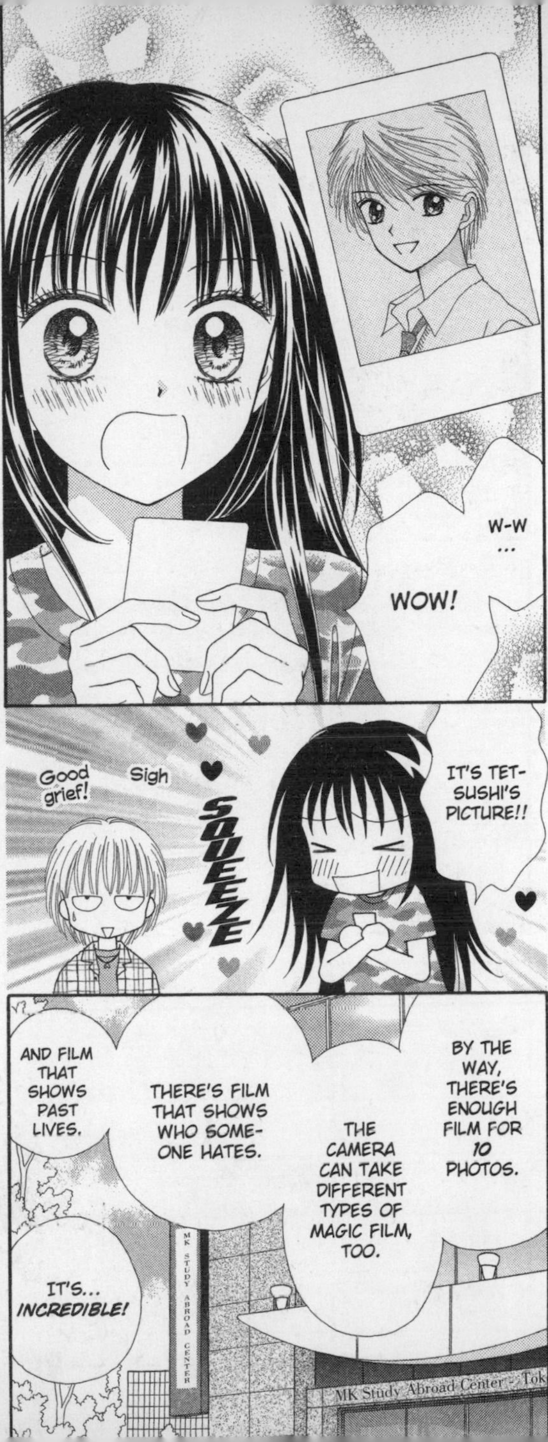
W-W ...
WOW!
IT'S TET-SUSHI'S PICTURE!!
SQUEEZE
Sigh
Good grief!
BY THE WAY, THERE'S ENOUGH FILM FOR 10 PHOTOS.
THE CAMERA CAN TAKE DIFFERENT TYPES OF MAGIC FILM, TOO.
THERE'S FILM THAT SHOWS WHO SOME-ONE HATES.
AND FILM THAT SHOWS PAST LIVES.
IT'S... INCREDIBLE!
MK STUDY ABROAD CENTER
MK Study Abroad Center - Tok

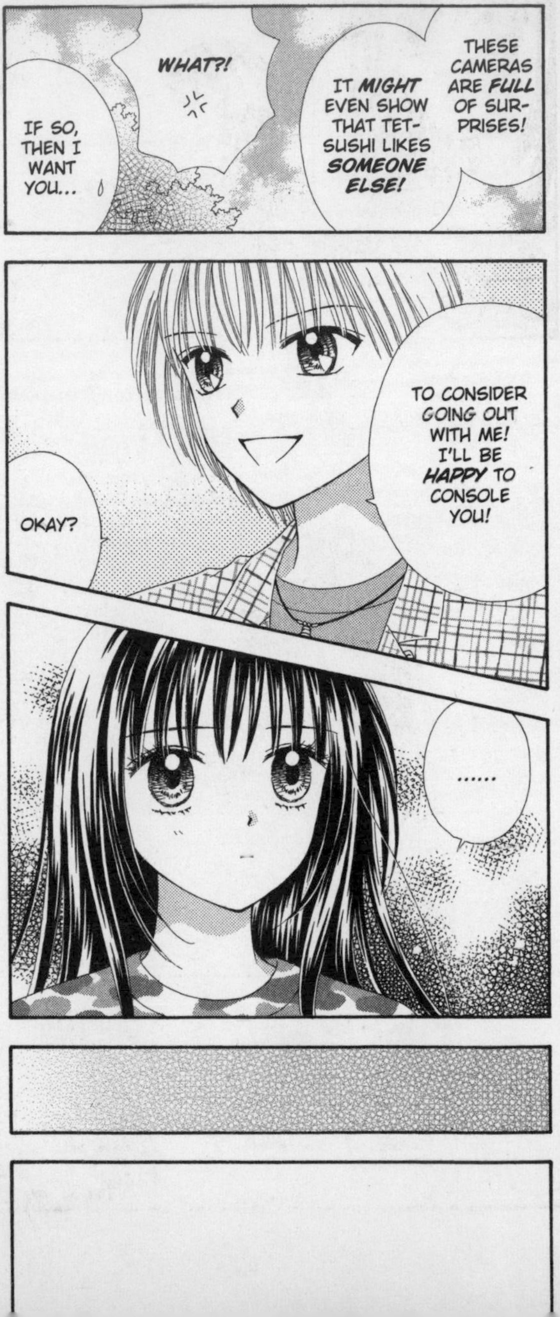
THESE CAMERAS ARE **FULL** OF SUR-PRISES!
IT **MIGHT** EVEN SHOW THAT TET-SUSHI LIKES **SOMEONE ELSE!**
WHAT?!
IF SO, THEN I WANT YOU...
TO CONSIDER GOING OUT WITH ME! I'LL BE **HAPPY** TO CONSOLE YOU!
OKAY?
......

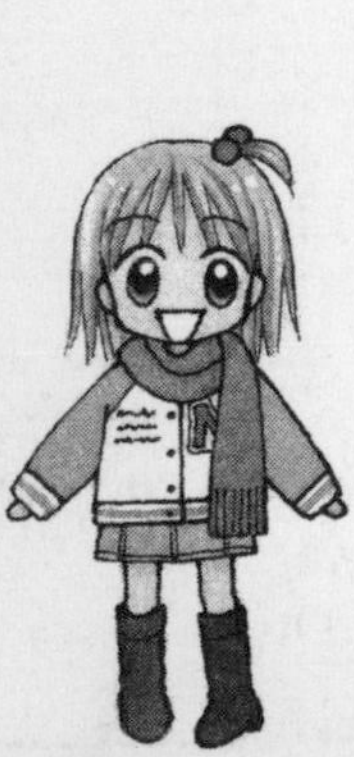

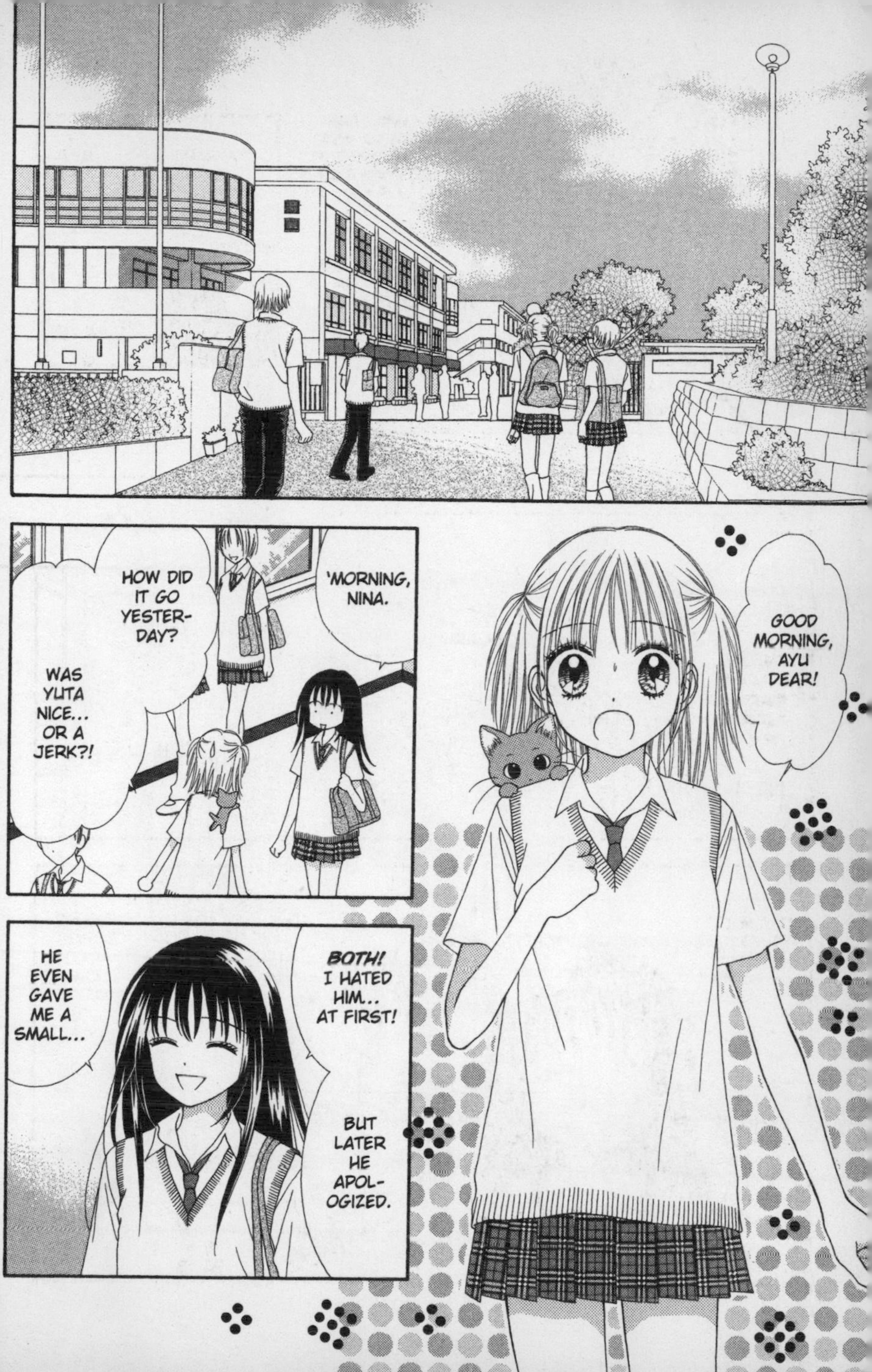
GOOD MORNING, AYU DEAR!
'MORNING, NINA.
HOW DID IT GO YESTER-DAY?
WAS YUTA NICE... OR A JERK?!
BOTH! I HATED HIM... AT FIRST!
BUT LATER HE APOLOG-IZED.
HE EVEN GAVE ME A SMALL...

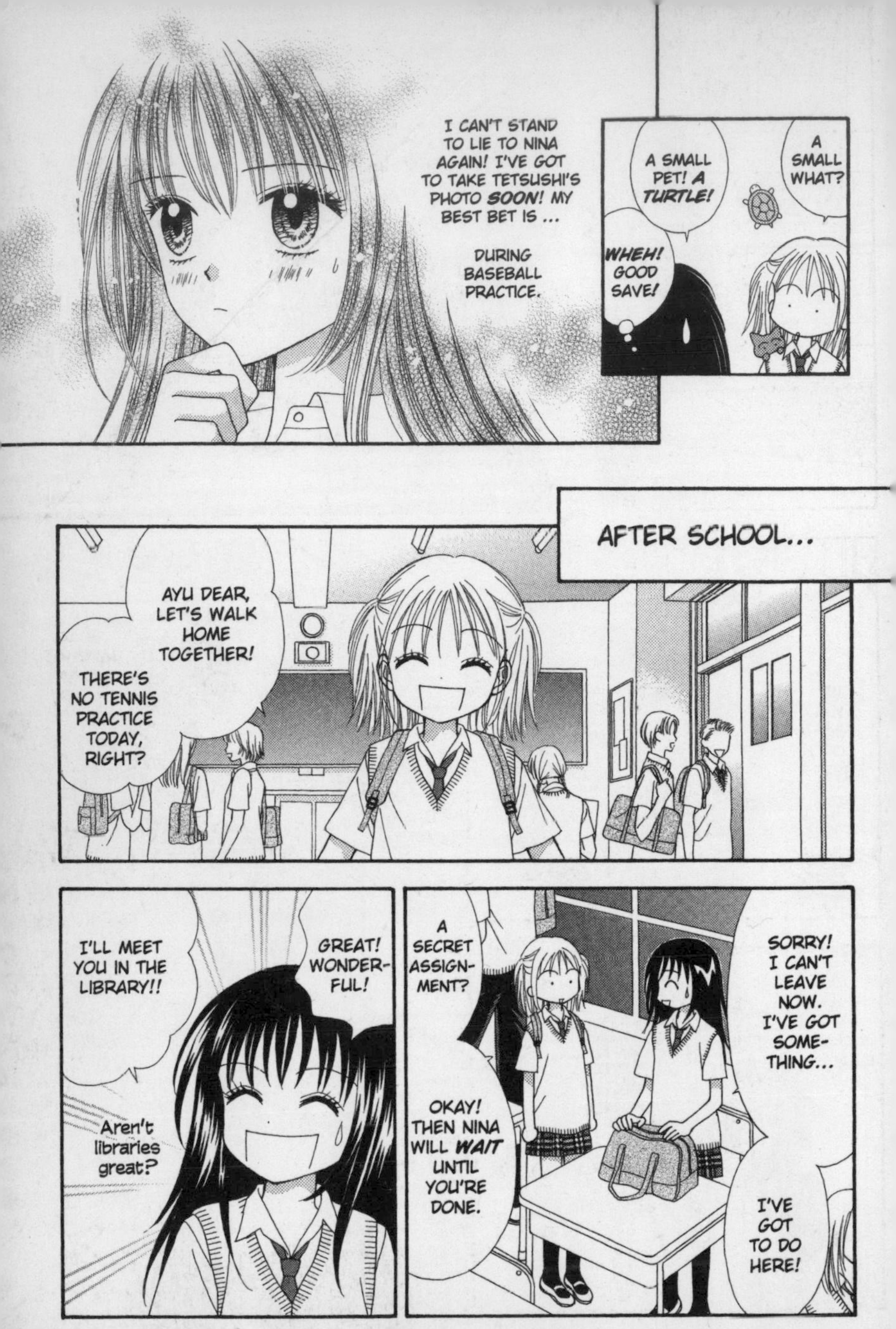
A SMALL WHAT?
A SMALL PET! A TURTLE!
WHEH! GOOD SAVE!
I CAN'T STAND TO LIE TO NINA AGAIN! I'VE GOT TO TAKE TETSUSHI'S PHOTO SOON! MY BEST BET IS ...
DURING BASEBALL PRACTICE.
AFTER SCHOOL...
AYU DEAR, LET'S WALK HOME TOGETHER!
THERE'S NO TENNIS PRACTICE TODAY, RIGHT?
SORRY! I CAN'T LEAVE NOW. I'VE GOT SOME-THING...
I'VE GOT TO DO HERE!
A SECRET ASSIGN-MENT?
OKAY! THEN NINA WILL WAIT UNTIL YOU'RE DONE.
GREAT! WONDER-FUL!
I'LL MEET YOU IN THE LIBRARY!!
Aren't libraries great?

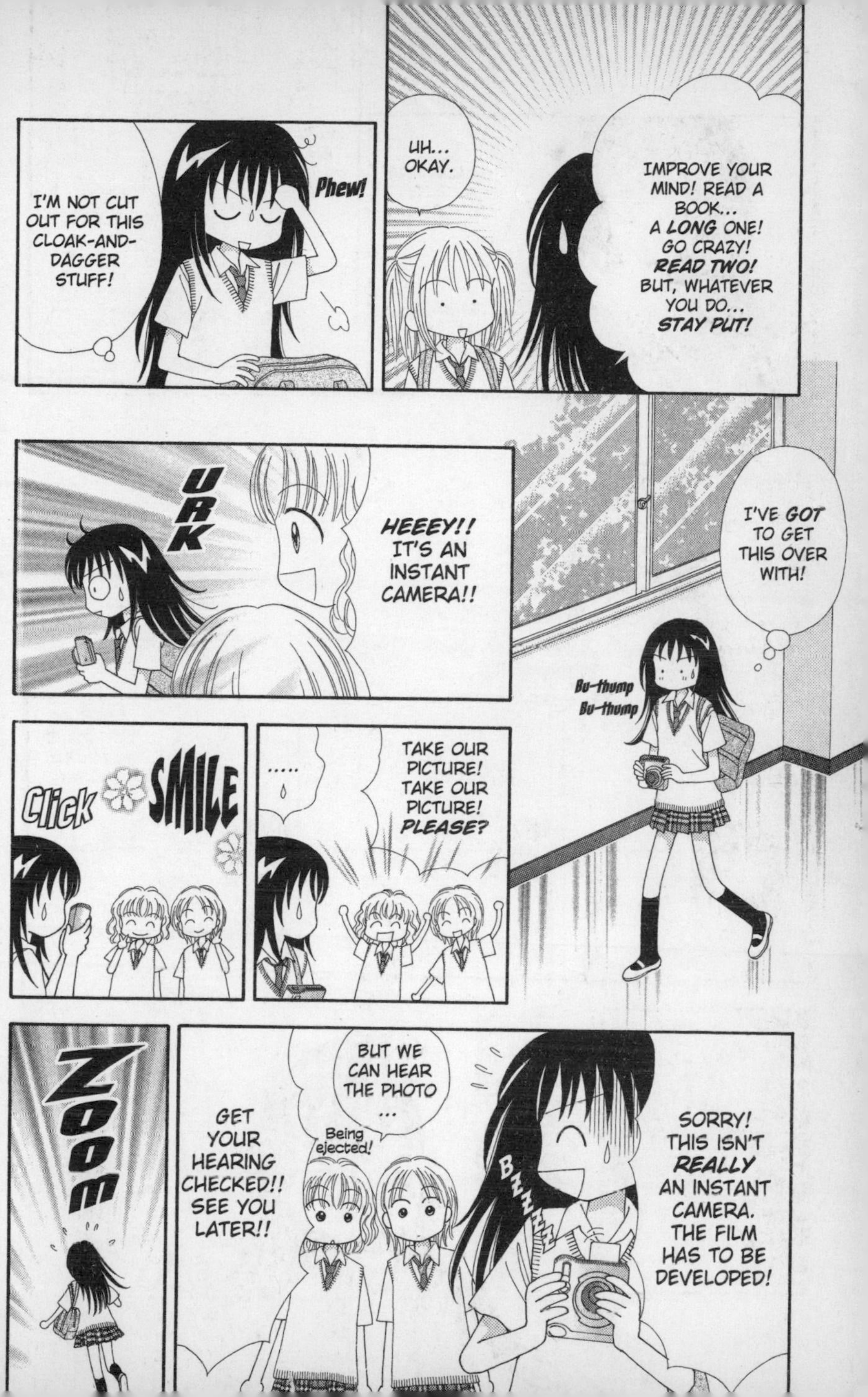

IMPROVE YOUR MIND! READ A BOOK... A LONG ONE! GO CRAZY! READ TWO! BUT, WHATEVER YOU DO... STAY PUT!
UH... OKAY.
Phew!
I'M NOT CUT OUT FOR THIS CLOAK-AND-DAGGER STUFF!
I'VE GOT TO GET THIS OVER WITH!
Bu-thump Bu-thump
HEEEY!! IT'S AN INSTANT CAMERA!!
URK
TAKE OUR PICTURE! TAKE OUR PICTURE! PLEASE?
.....
SMILE
Click
SORRY! THIS ISN'T REALLY AN INSTANT CAMERA. THE FILM HAS TO BE DEVELOPED!
BZZZZ
BUT WE CAN HEAR THE PHOTO ...
Being ejected!
GET YOUR HEARING CHECKED!! SEE YOU LATER!!
ZOOM

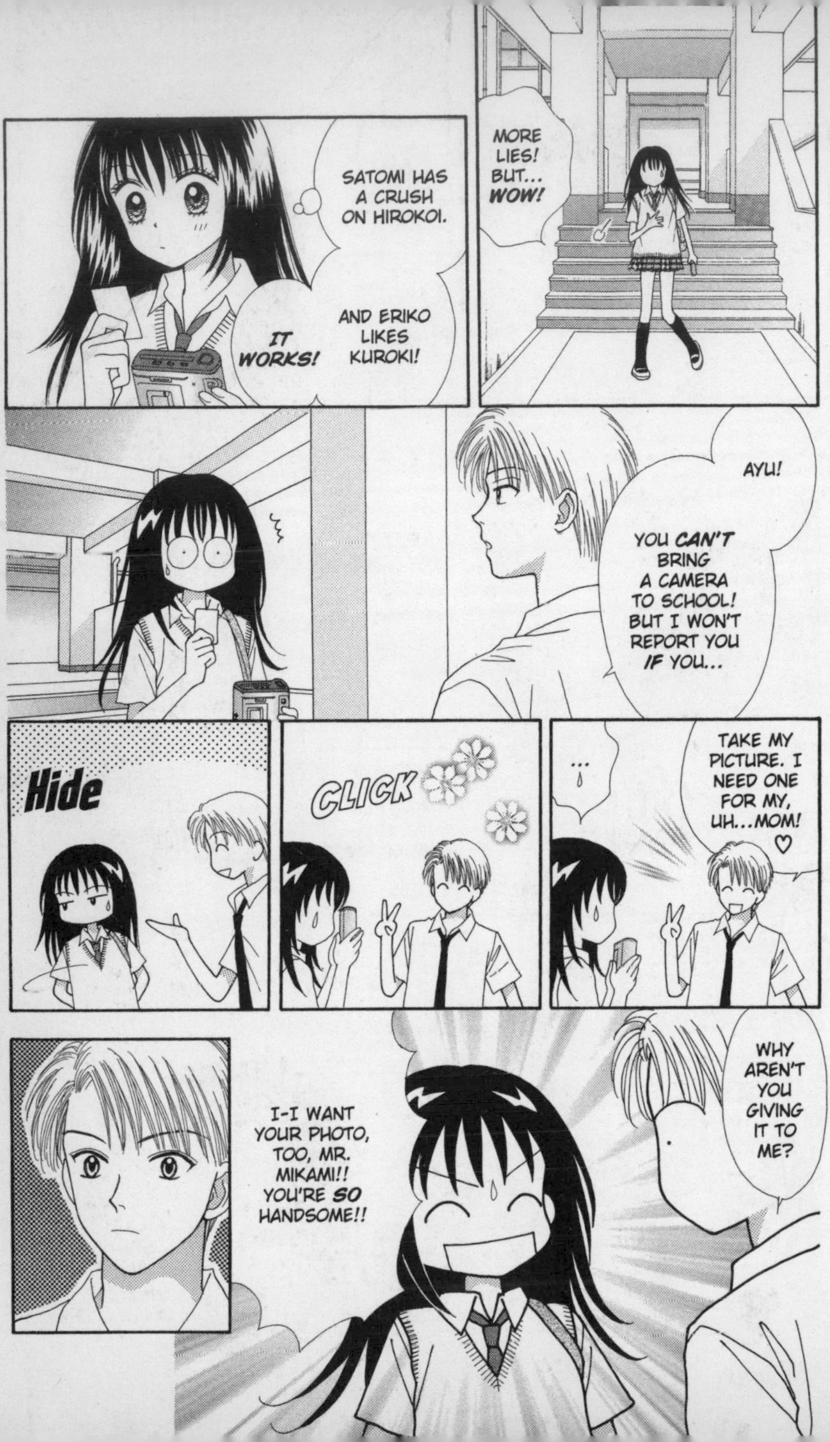
MORE LIES! BUT... WOW!
SATOMI HAS A CRUSH ON HIROKOI.
AND ERIKO LIKES KUROKI!
IT WORKS!
AYU!
YOU CAN'T BRING A CAMERA TO SCHOOL! BUT I WON'T REPORT YOU IF YOU...
TAKE MY PICTURE. I NEED ONE FOR MY, UH...MOM! ♡
...
CLICK
Hide
WHY AREN'T YOU GIVING IT TO ME?
I-I WANT YOUR PHOTO, TOO, MR. MIKAMI!! YOU'RE SO HANDSOME!!

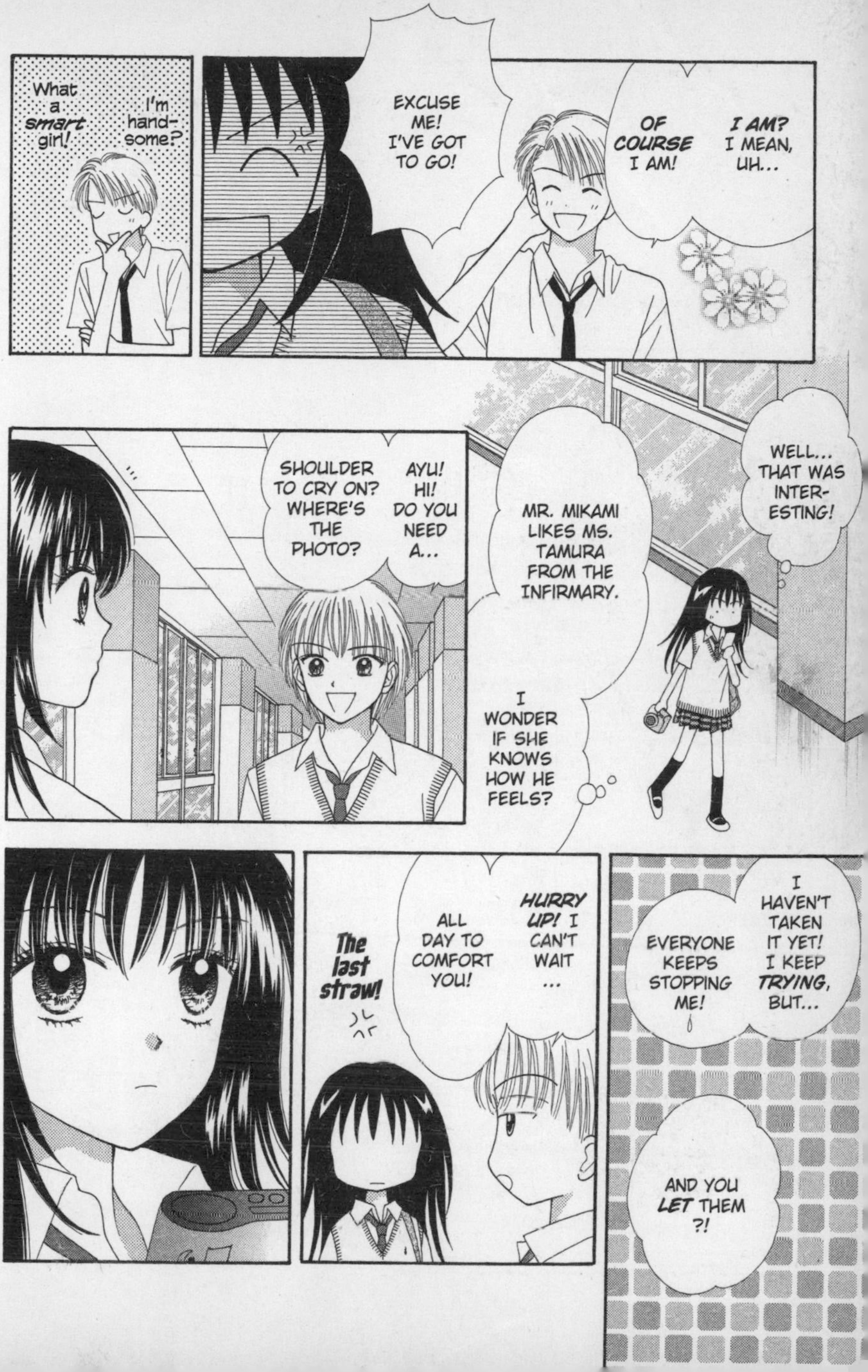
I AM? I MEAN, UH... OF COURSE I AM!
EXCUSE ME! I'VE GOT TO GO!
I'm handsome?
What a smart girl!
WELL... THAT WAS INTERESTING!
MR. MIKAMI LIKES MS. TAMURA FROM THE INFIRMARY.
I WONDER IF SHE KNOWS HOW HE FEELS?
AYU! HI! DO YOU NEED A... SHOULDER TO CRY ON? WHERE'S THE PHOTO?
I HAVEN'T TAKEN IT YET! I KEEP TRYING, BUT... EVERYONE KEEPS STOPPING ME!
AND YOU LET THEM?!
HURRY UP! I CAN'T WAIT ... ALL DAY TO COMFORT YOU!
The last straw!

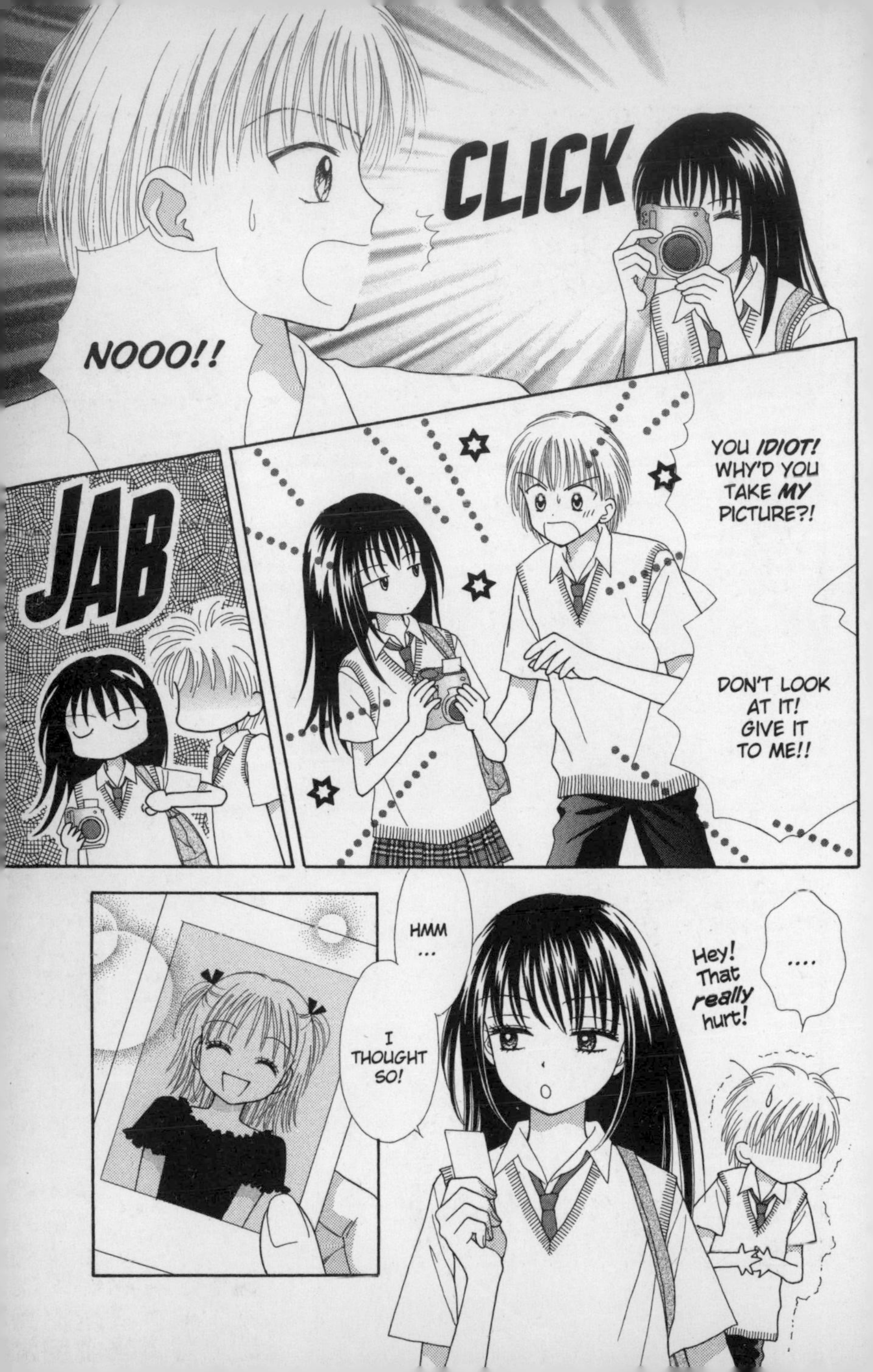
CLICK
NOOO!!
YOU *IDIOT!* WHY'D YOU TAKE *MY* PICTURE?!
DON'T LOOK AT IT! GIVE IT TO ME!!
JAB
....
Hey! That *really* hurt!
HMM ...
I THOUGHT SO!

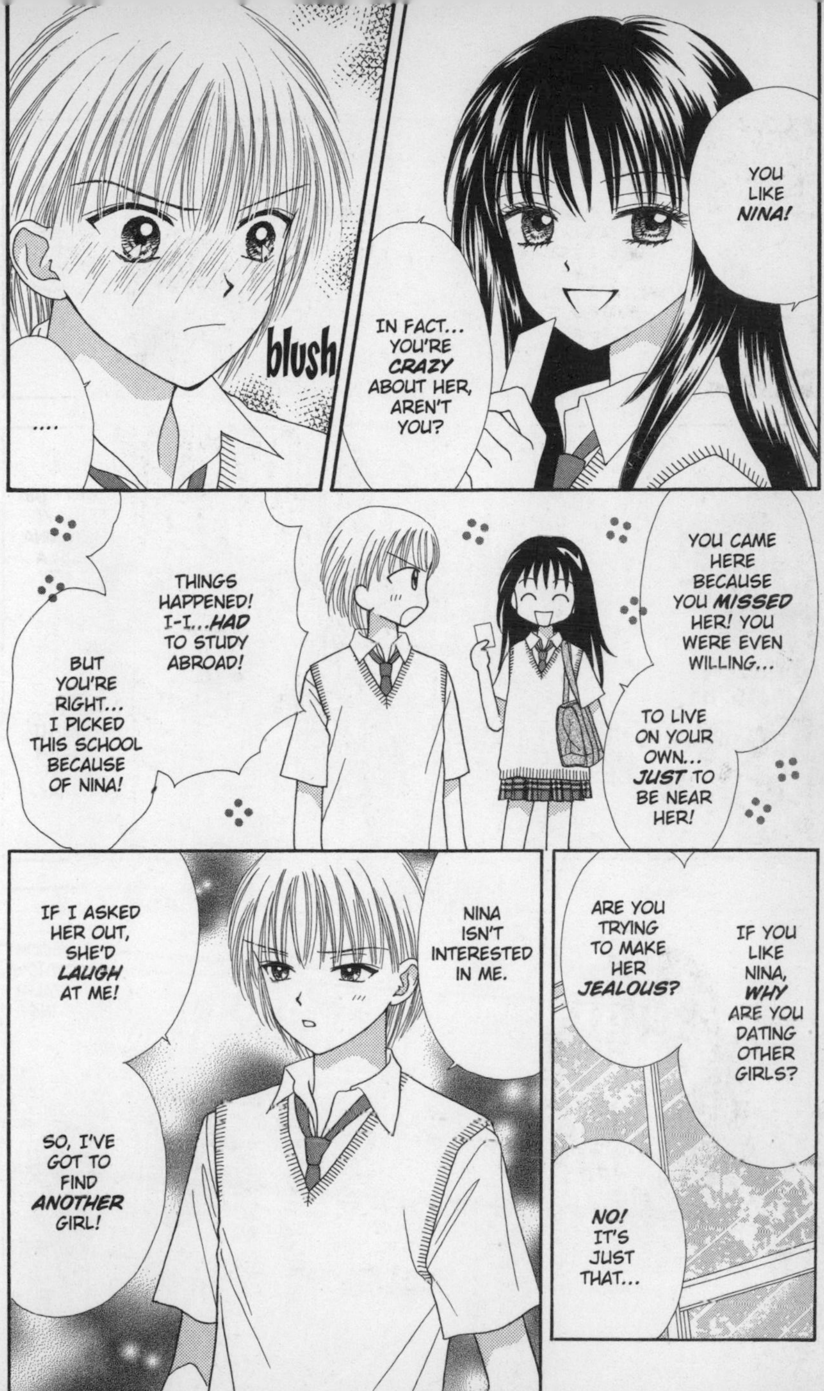
YOU LIKE NINA!
IN FACT... YOU'RE CRAZY ABOUT HER, AREN'T YOU?
blush
....
YOU CAME HERE BECAUSE YOU MISSED HER! YOU WERE EVEN WILLING...
TO LIVE ON YOUR OWN... JUST TO BE NEAR HER!
THINGS HAPPENED! I-I...HAD TO STUDY ABROAD!
BUT YOU'RE RIGHT... I PICKED THIS SCHOOL BECAUSE OF NINA!
IF YOU LIKE NINA, WHY ARE YOU DATING OTHER GIRLS?
ARE YOU TRYING TO MAKE HER JEALOUS?
NO! IT'S JUST THAT...
NINA ISN'T INTERESTED IN ME.
IF I ASKED HER OUT, SHE'D LAUGH AT ME!
SO, I'VE GOT TO FIND ANOTHER GIRL!

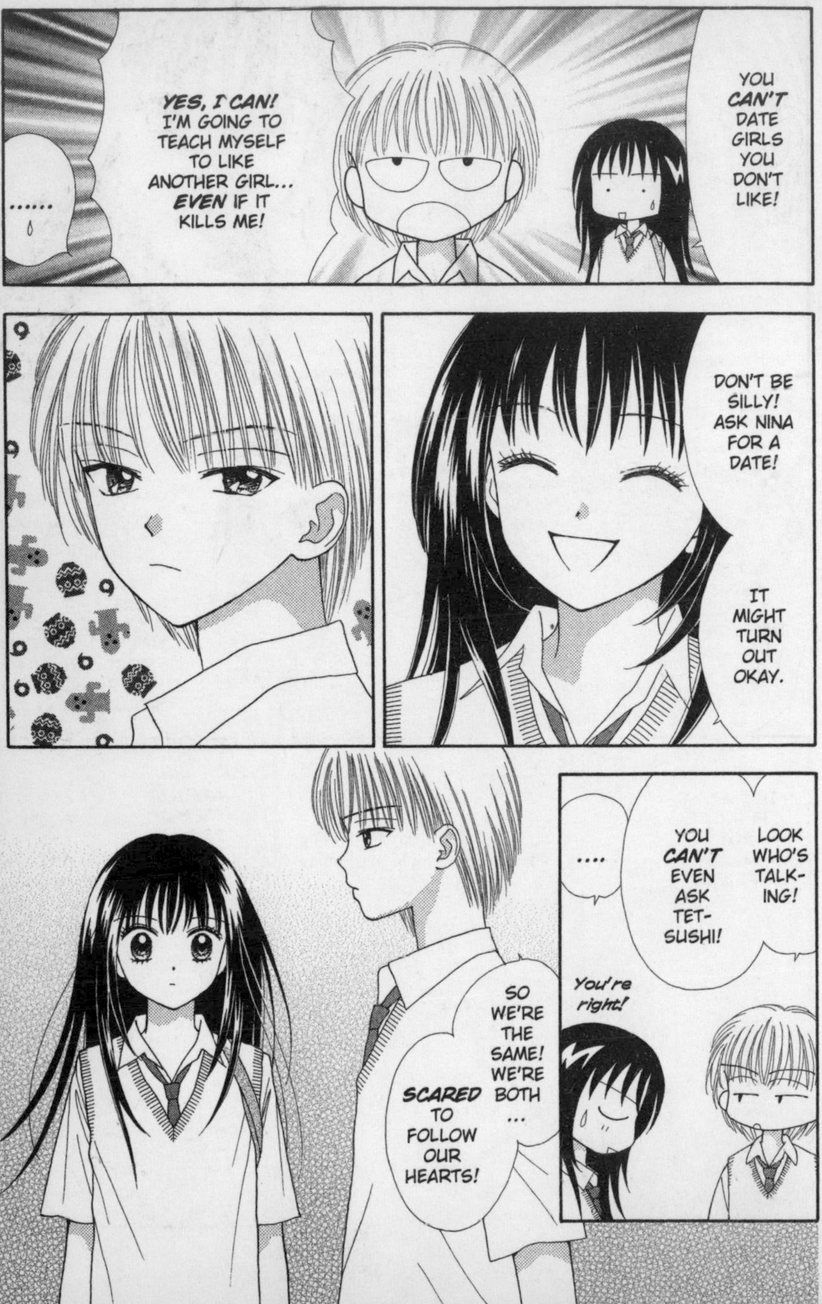
YOU CAN'T DATE GIRLS YOU DON'T LIKE!
YES, I CAN! I'M GOING TO TEACH MYSELF TO LIKE ANOTHER GIRL... EVEN IF IT KILLS ME!
......
DON'T BE SILLY! ASK NINA FOR A DATE!
IT MIGHT TURN OUT OKAY.
LOOK WHO'S TALKING!
YOU CAN'T EVEN ASK TETSUSHI!
....
You're right!
SO WE'RE THE SAME! WE'RE BOTH... SCARED TO FOLLOW OUR HEARTS!

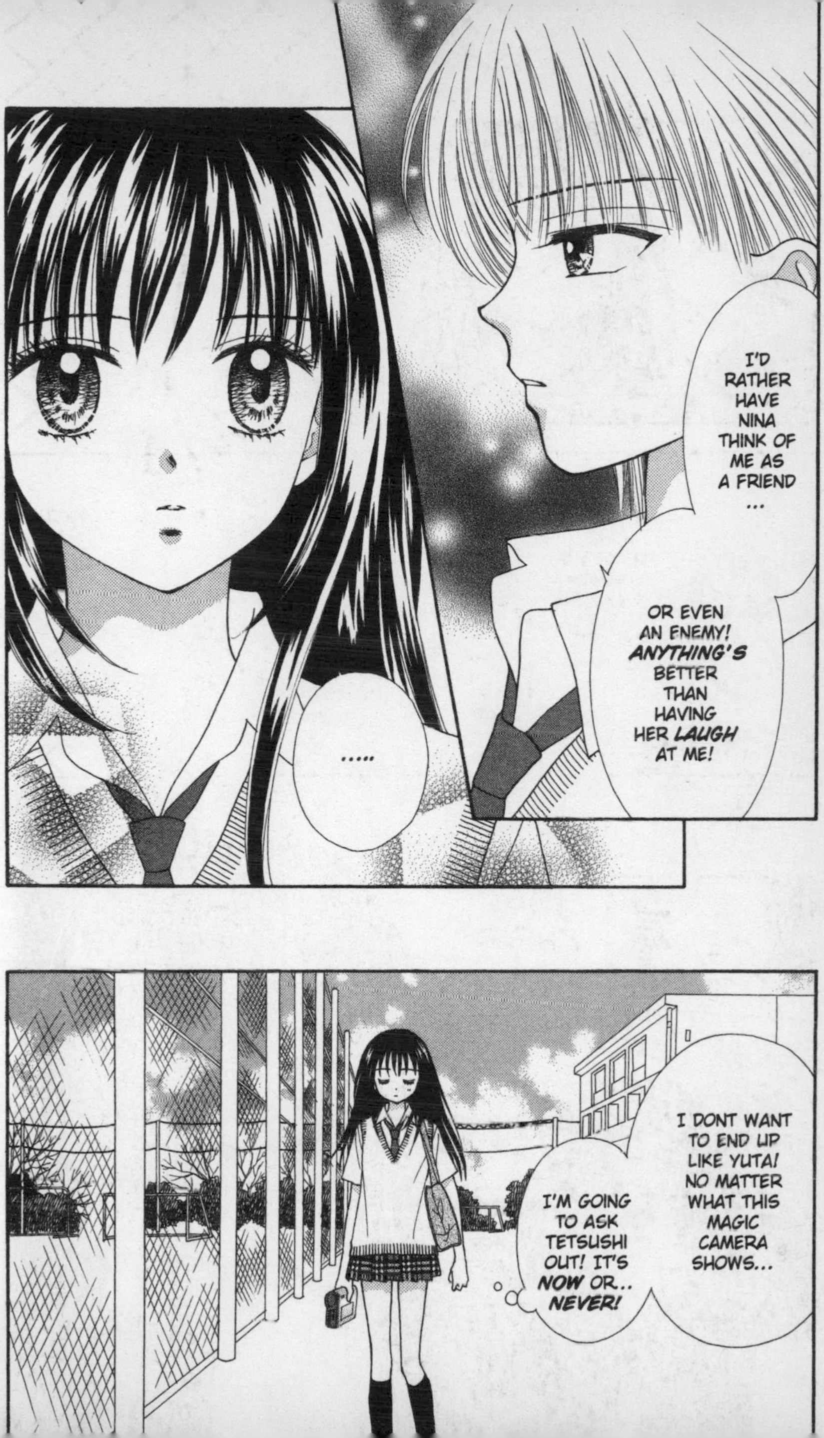
I'D RATHER HAVE NINA THINK OF ME AS A FRIEND ...
OR EVEN AN ENEMY! ANYTHING'S BETTER THAN HAVING HER LAUGH AT ME!
.....
I DONT WANT TO END UP LIKE YUTA! NO MATTER WHAT THIS MAGIC CAMERA SHOWS...
I'M GOING TO ASK TETSUSHI OUT! IT'S NOW OR.. NEVER!

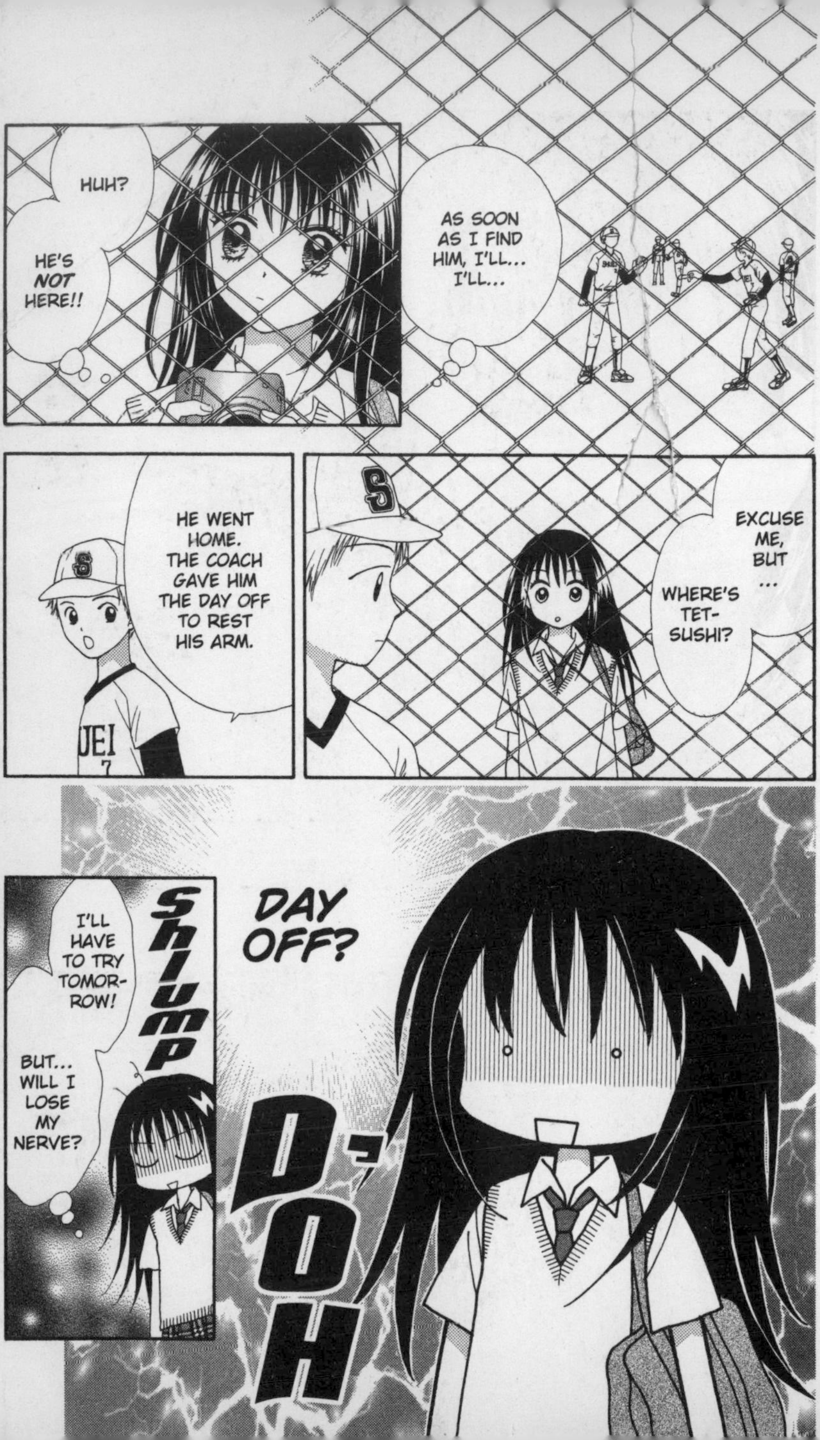
AS SOON AS I FIND HIM, I'LL... I'LL...
HUH?
HE'S *NOT* HERE!!
EXCUSE ME, BUT ...
WHERE'S TET-SUSHI?
HE WENT HOME. THE COACH GAVE HIM THE DAY OFF TO REST HIS ARM.
DAY OFF?
D'OH
SHLUMP
I'LL HAVE TO TRY TOMORROW!
BUT... WILL I LOSE MY NERVE?

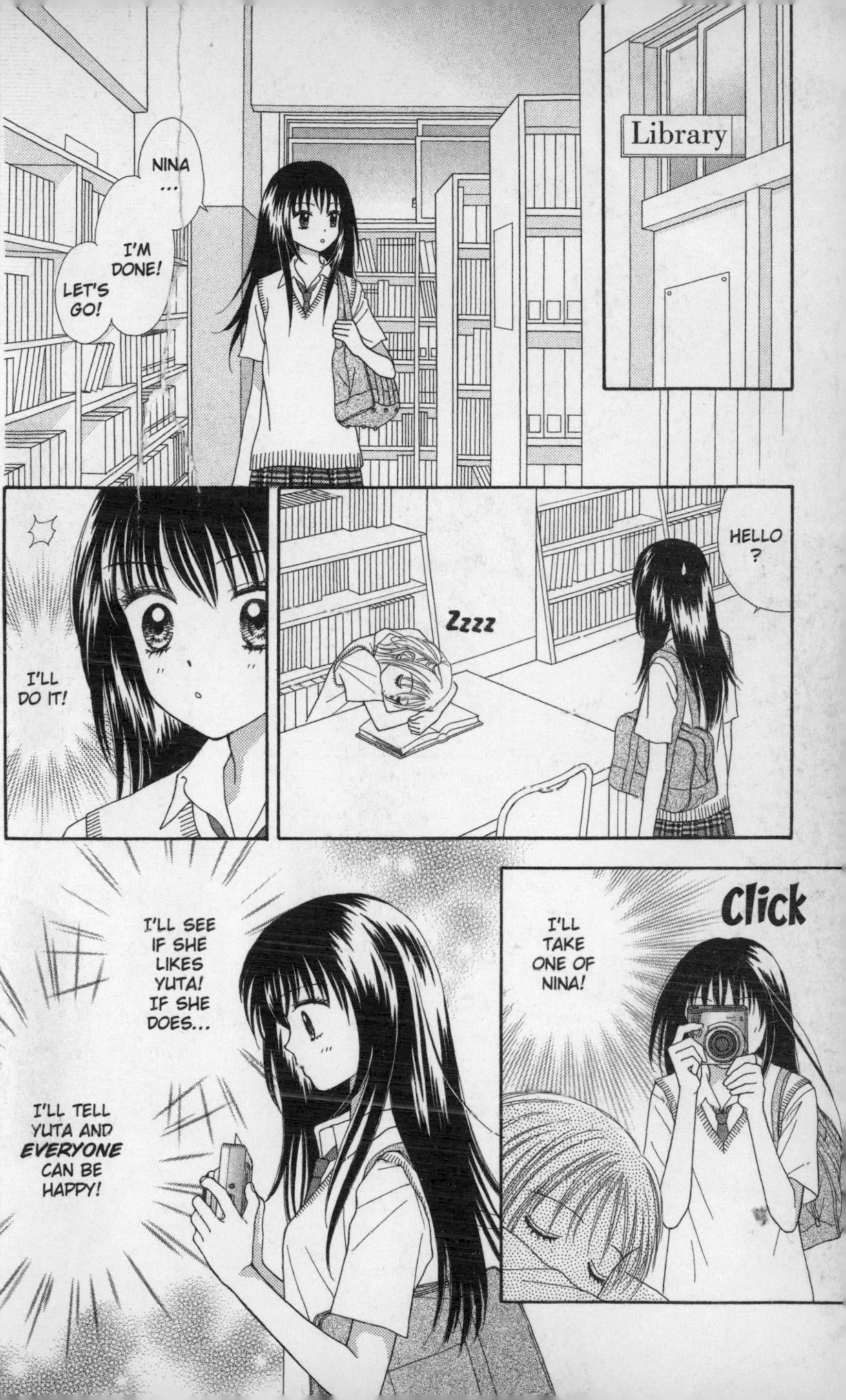
Library
NINA ...
I'M DONE! LET'S GO!
HELLO ?
Zzzz
I'LL DO IT!
Click
I'LL TAKE ONE OF NINA!
I'LL SEE IF SHE LIKES YUTA! IF SHE DOES...
I'LL TELL YUTA AND **EVERYONE** CAN BE HAPPY!

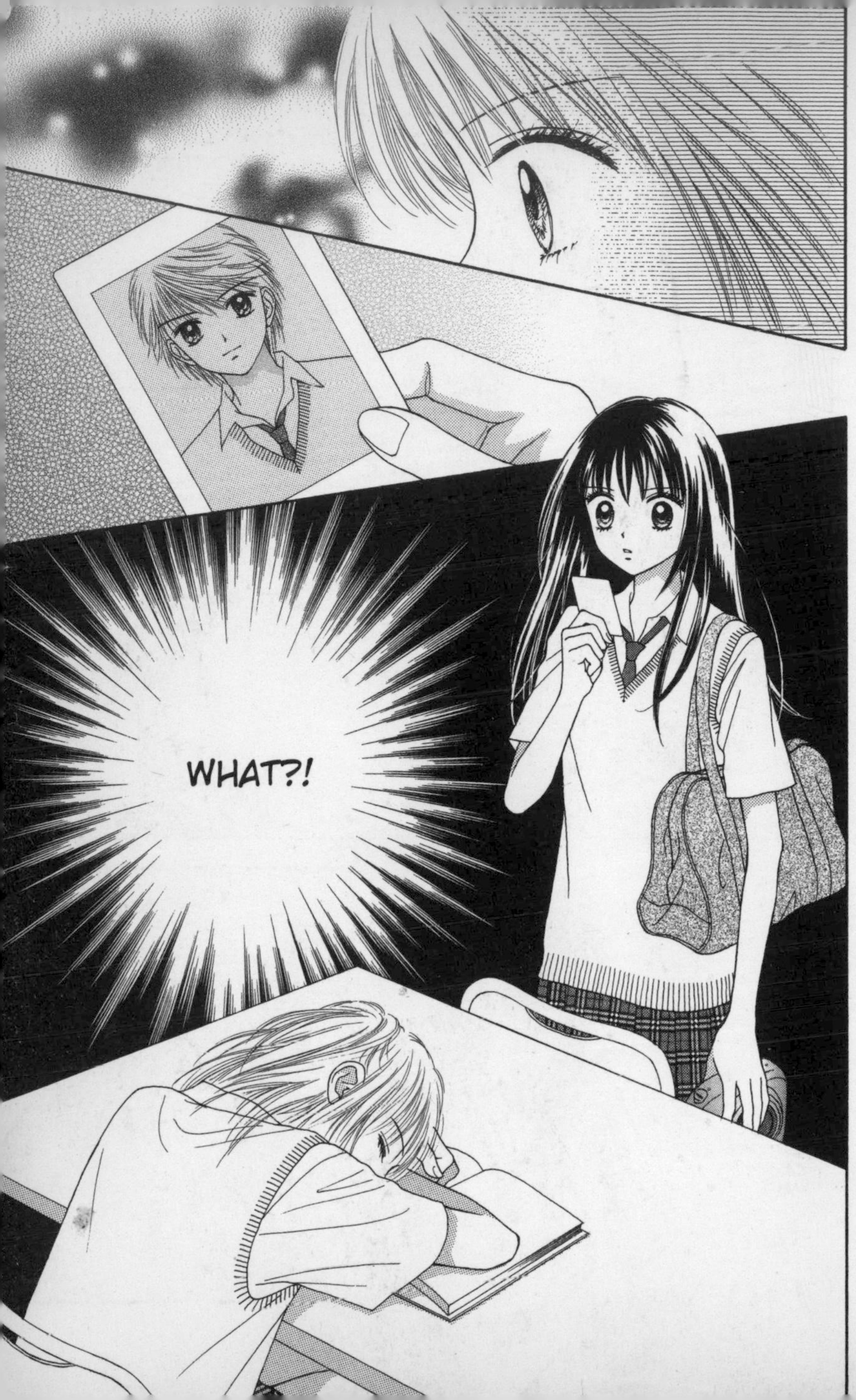
WHAT?!

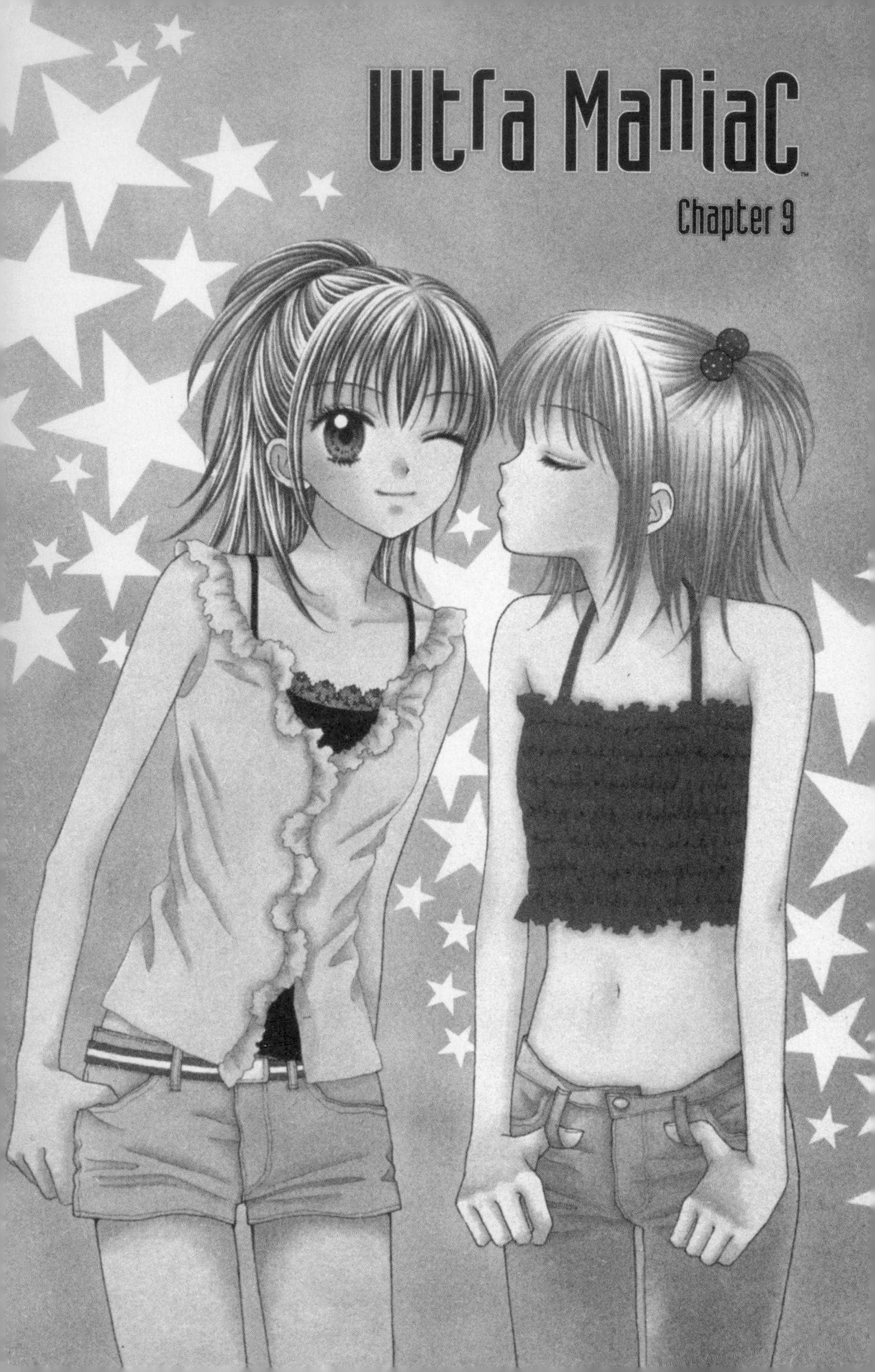
Ultra Maniac™
Chapter 9

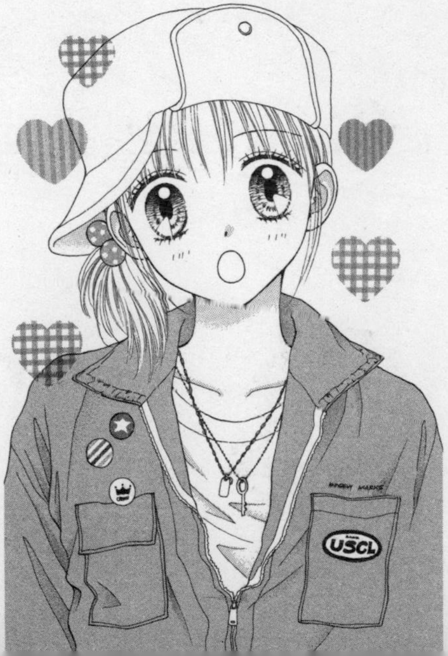
USCL

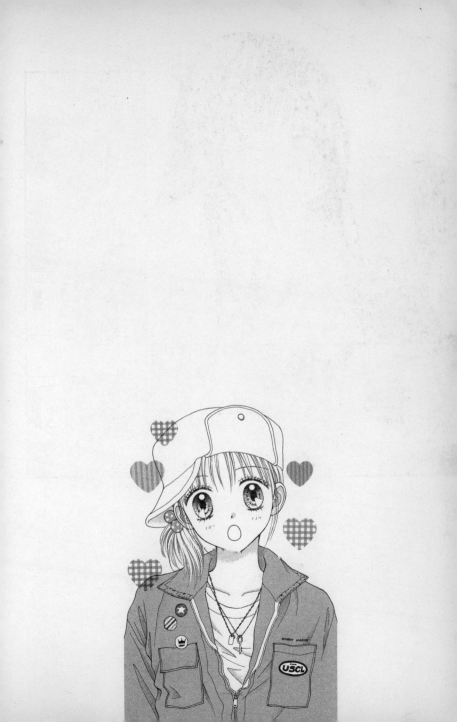

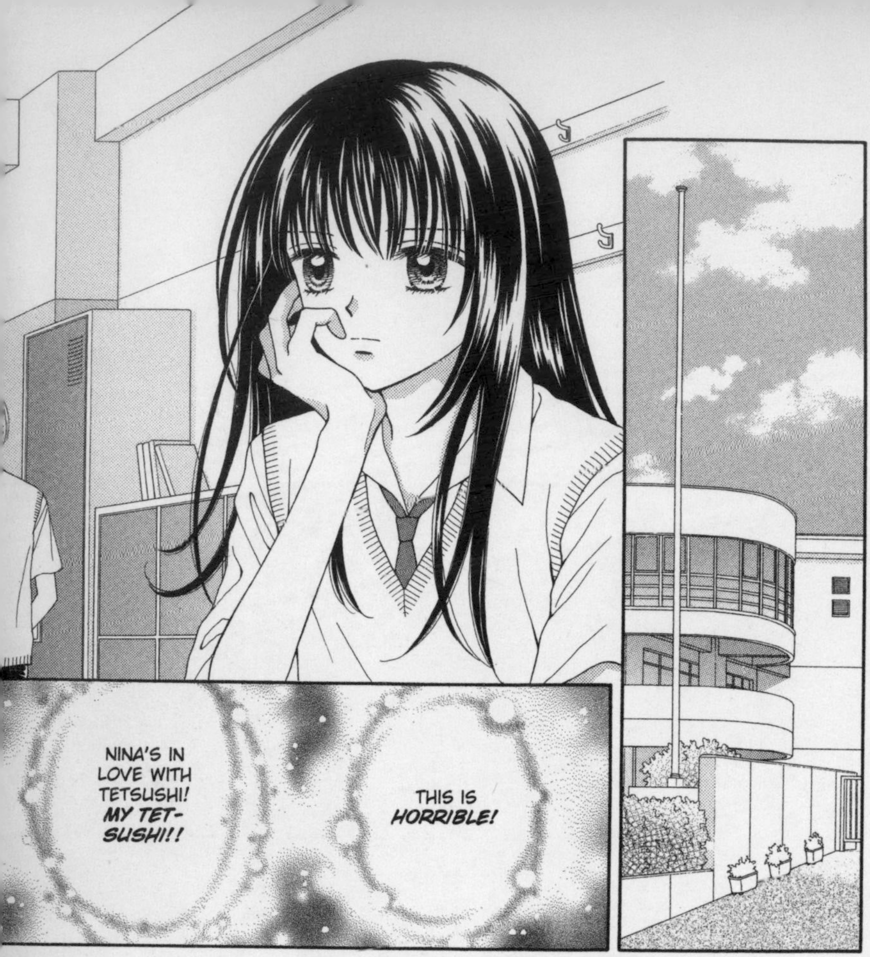
THIS IS HORRIBLE!
NINA'S IN LOVE WITH TETSUSHI! MY TET-SUSHI!!

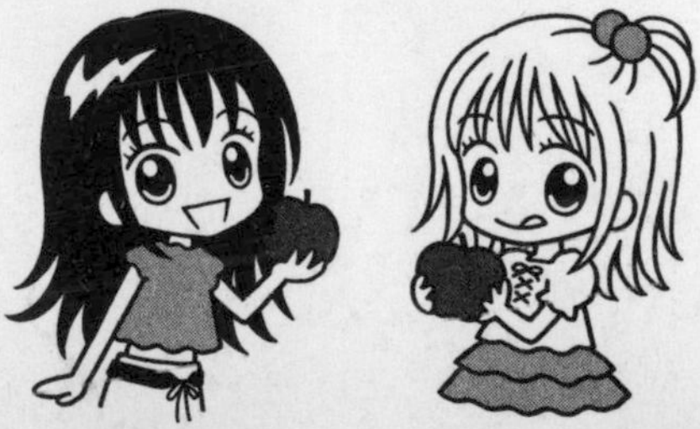

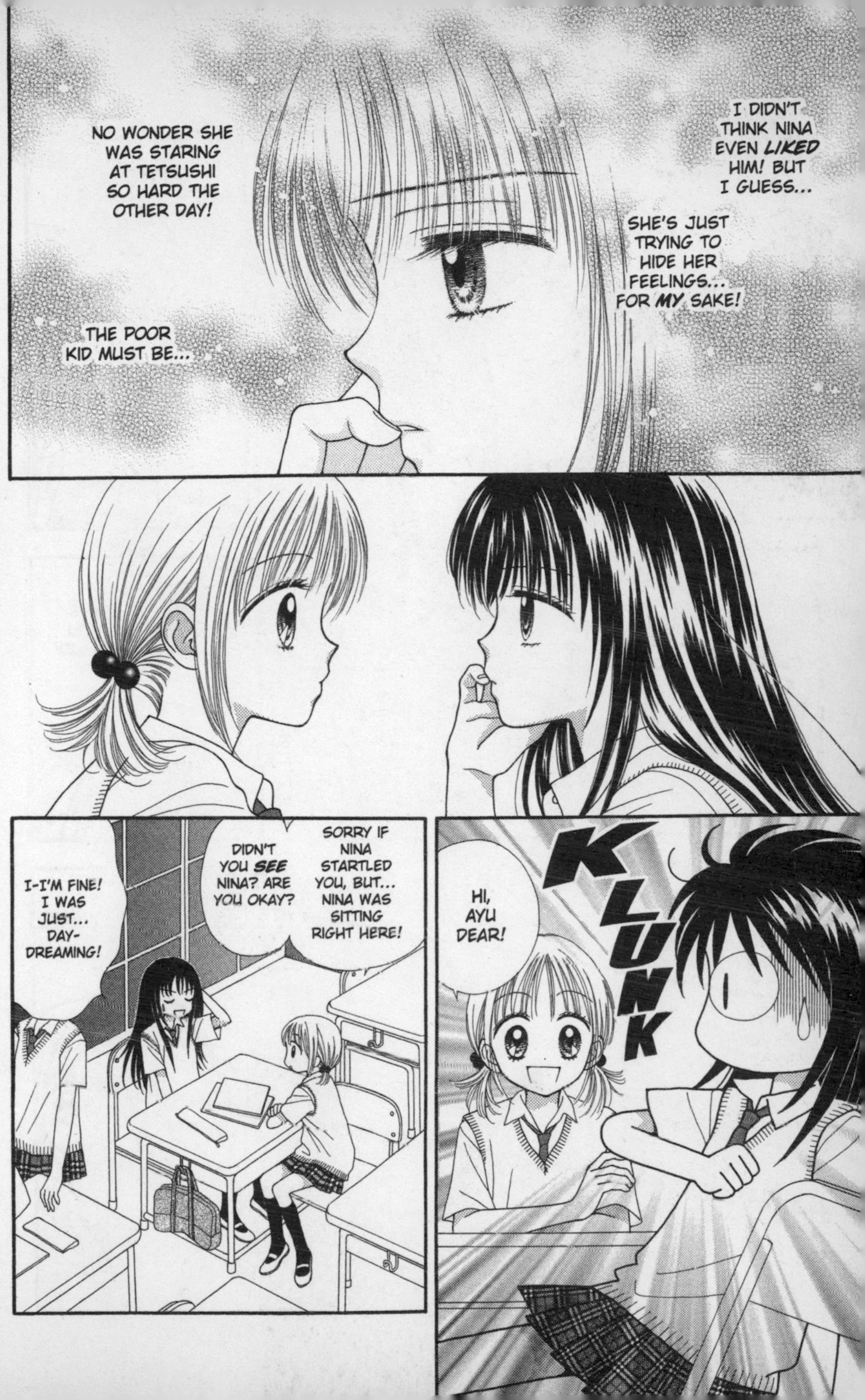
I DIDN'T THINK NINA EVEN *LIKED* HIM! BUT I GUESS...
SHE'S JUST TRYING TO HIDE HER FEELINGS... FOR *MY* SAKE!
NO WONDER SHE WAS STARING AT TETSUSHI SO HARD THE OTHER DAY!
THE POOR KID MUST BE...
KLUNK
HI, AYU DEAR!
SORRY IF NINA STARTLED YOU, BUT... NINA WAS SITTING RIGHT HERE!
DIDN'T YOU *SEE* NINA? ARE YOU OKAY?
I-I'M FINE! I WAS JUST... DAY-DREAMING!

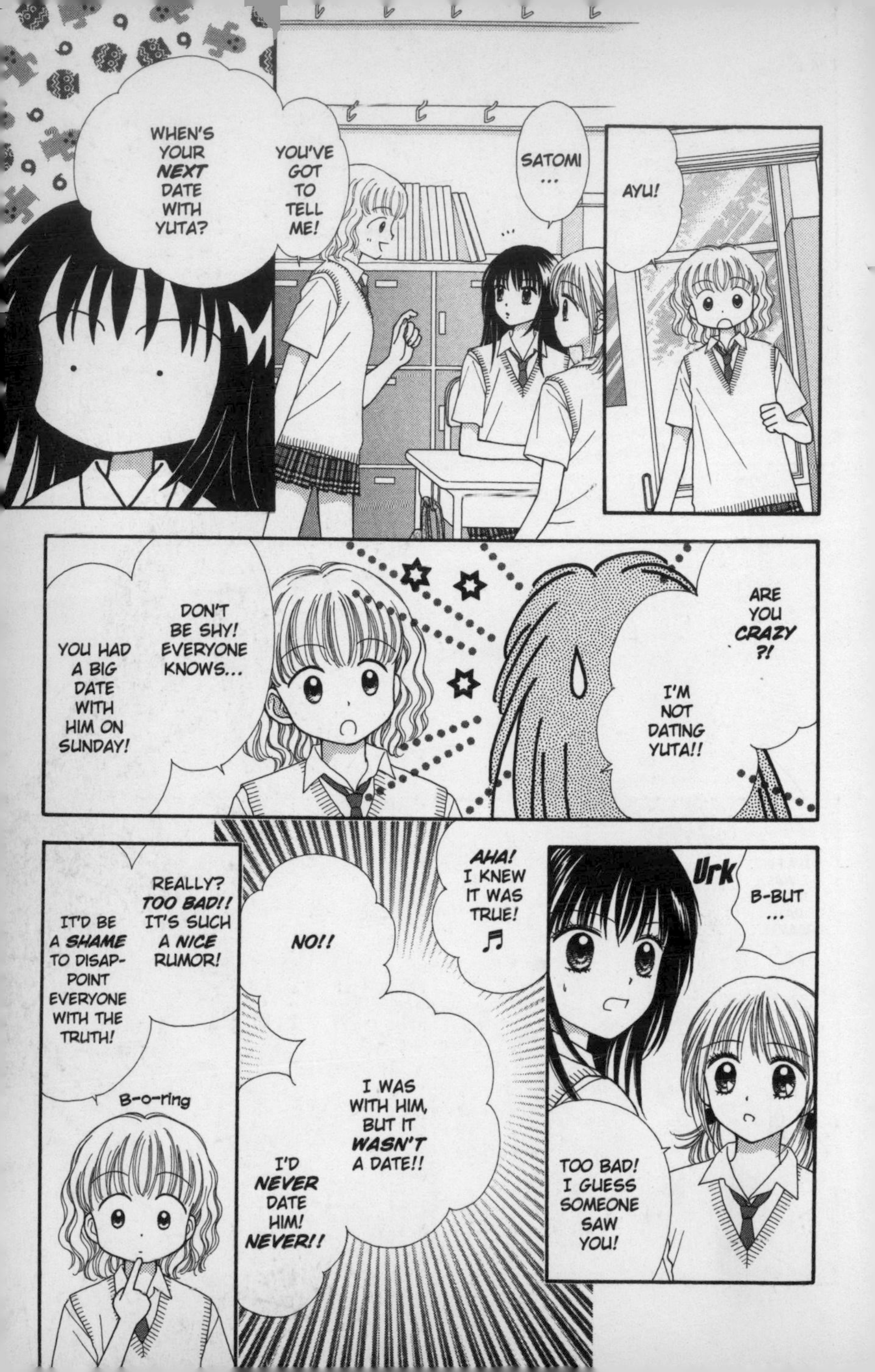
AYU!
SATOMI ...
...
YOU'VE GOT TO TELL ME!
WHEN'S YOUR NEXT DATE WITH YUTA?
ARE YOU CRAZY?!
I'M NOT DATING YUTA!!
DON'T BE SHY! EVERYONE KNOWS...
YOU HAD A BIG DATE WITH HIM ON SUNDAY!
Urk
B-BUT ...
TOO BAD! I GUESS SOMEONE SAW YOU!
AHA! I KNEW IT WAS TRUE! ♪
NO!!
I WAS WITH HIM, BUT IT WASN'T A DATE!!
I'D NEVER DATE HIM! NEVER!!
REALLY? TOO BAD!! IT'S SUCH A NICE RUMOR!
IT'D BE A SHAME TO DISAPPOINT EVERYONE WITH THE TRUTH!
B-o-ring

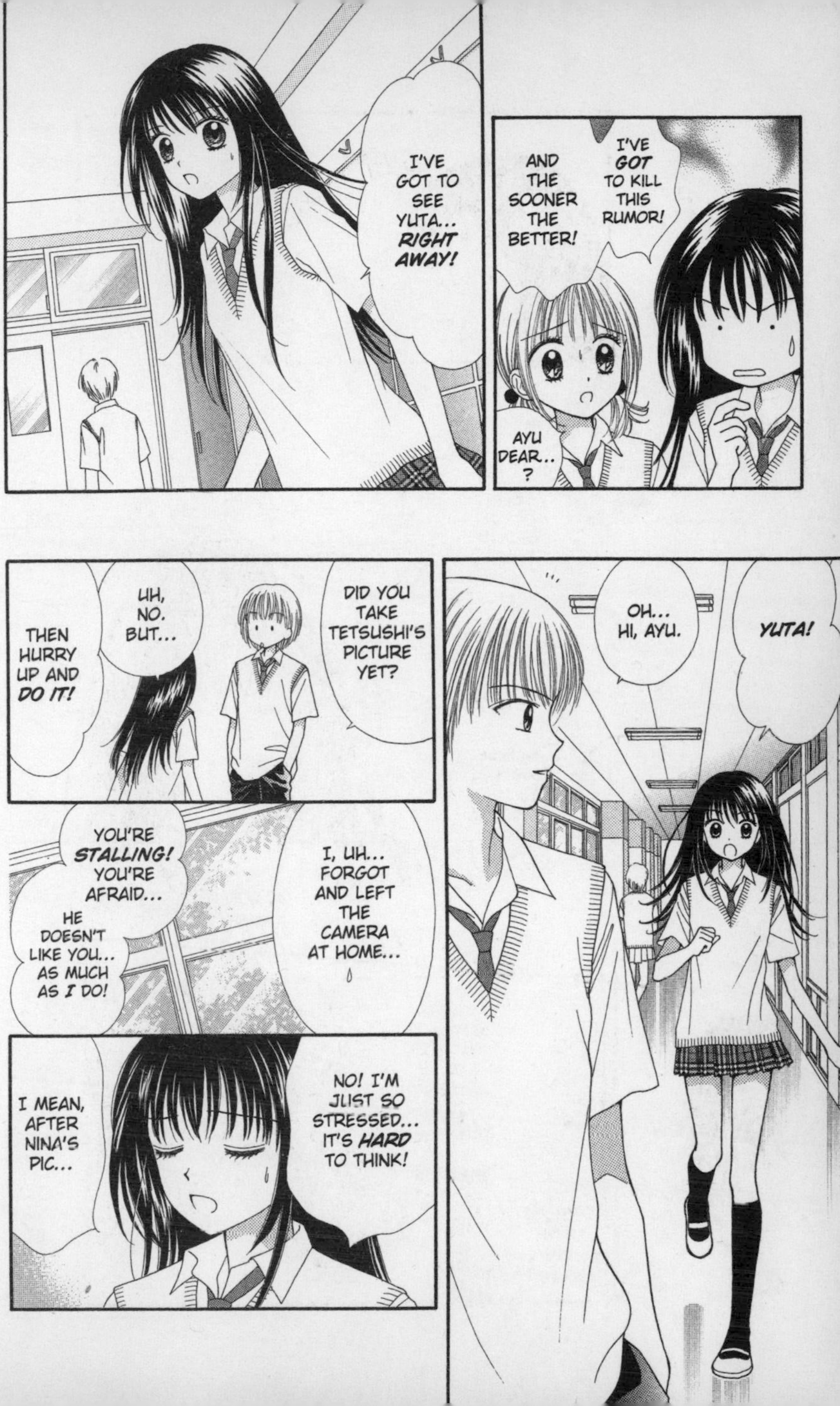
I'VE GOT TO KILL THIS RUMOR!
AND THE SOONER THE BETTER!
AYU DEAR...?
I'VE GOT TO SEE YUTA... RIGHT AWAY!
YUTA!
OH... HI, AYU.
...
DID YOU TAKE TETSUSHI'S PICTURE YET?
UH, NO. BUT...
THEN HURRY UP AND DO IT!
I, UH... FORGOT AND LEFT THE CAMERA AT HOME...
YOU'RE STALLING! YOU'RE AFRAID...
HE DOESN'T LIKE YOU... AS MUCH AS I DO!
NO! I'M JUST SO STRESSED... IT'S HARD TO THINK!
I MEAN, AFTER NINA'S PIC...

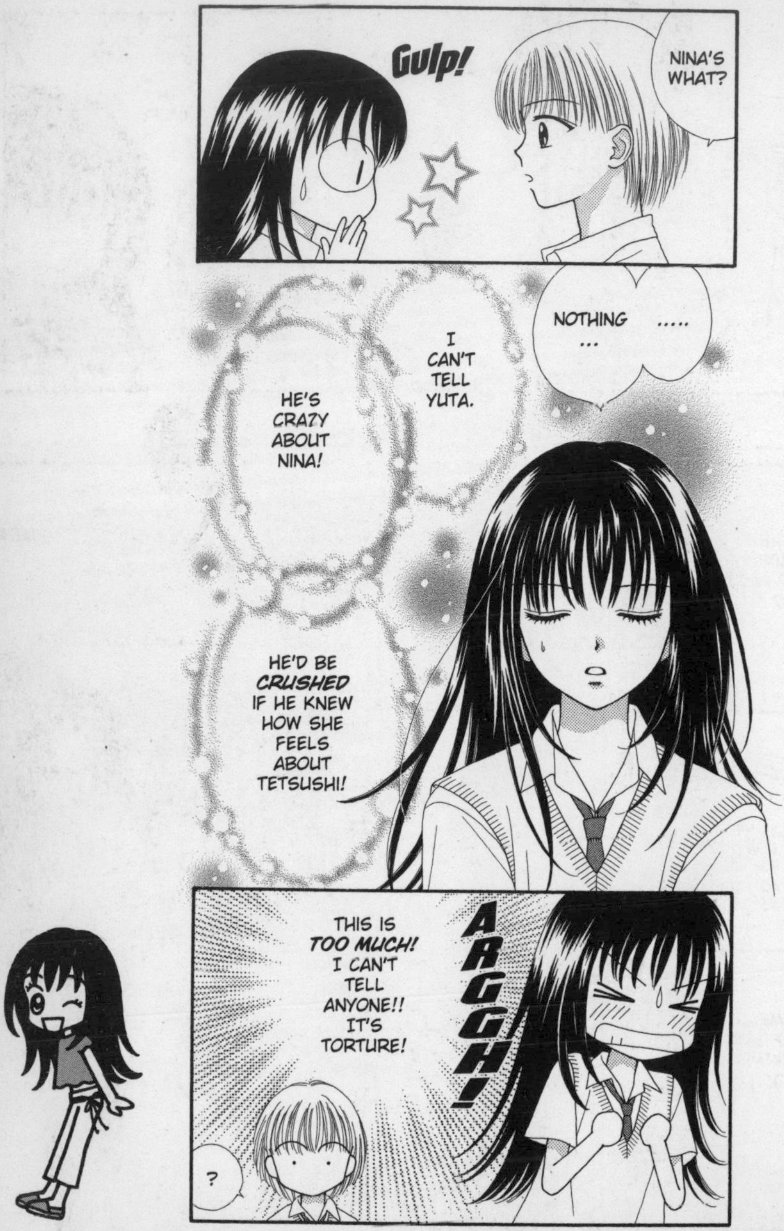
NINA'S WHAT?
GULP!
NOTHING ....
I CAN'T TELL YUTA.
HE'S CRAZY ABOUT NINA!
HE'D BE CRUSHED IF HE KNEW HOW SHE FEELS ABOUT TETSUSHI!
ARGGH!
THIS IS TOO MUCH! I CAN'T TELL ANYONE!! IT'S TORTURE!
?

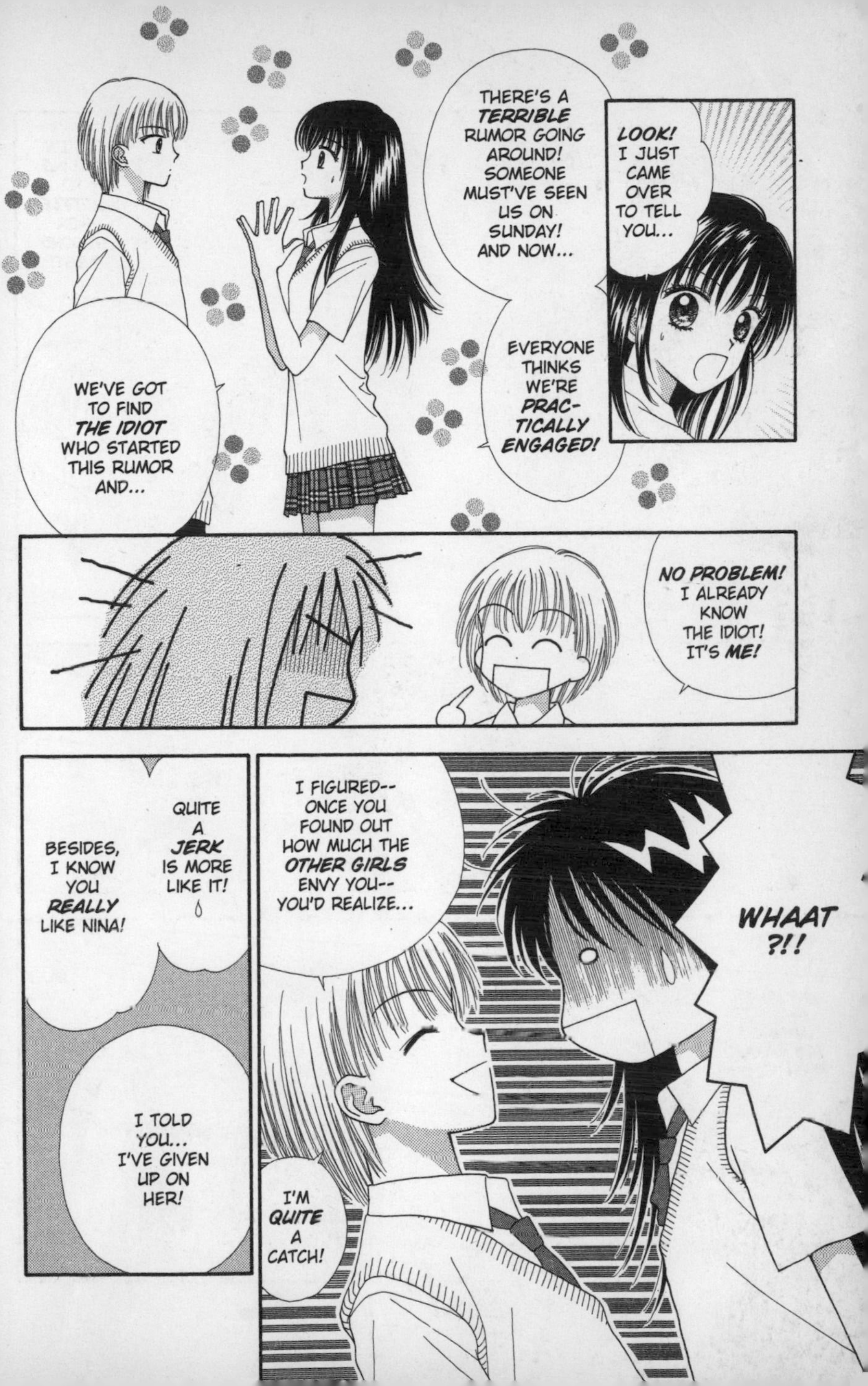
LOOK! I JUST CAME OVER TO TELL YOU...
THERE'S A TERRIBLE RUMOR GOING AROUND! SOMEONE MUST'VE SEEN US ON SUNDAY! AND NOW...
EVERYONE THINKS WE'RE PRAC-TICALLY ENGAGED!
WE'VE GOT TO FIND THE IDIOT WHO STARTED THIS RUMOR AND...
NO PROBLEM! I ALREADY KNOW THE IDIOT! IT'S ME!
WHAAT ?!!
I FIGURED-- ONCE YOU FOUND OUT HOW MUCH THE OTHER GIRLS ENVY YOU-- YOU'D REALIZE...
I'M QUITE A CATCH!
QUITE A JERK IS MORE LIKE IT!
BESIDES, I KNOW YOU REALLY LIKE NINA!
I TOLD YOU... I'VE GIVEN UP ON HER!

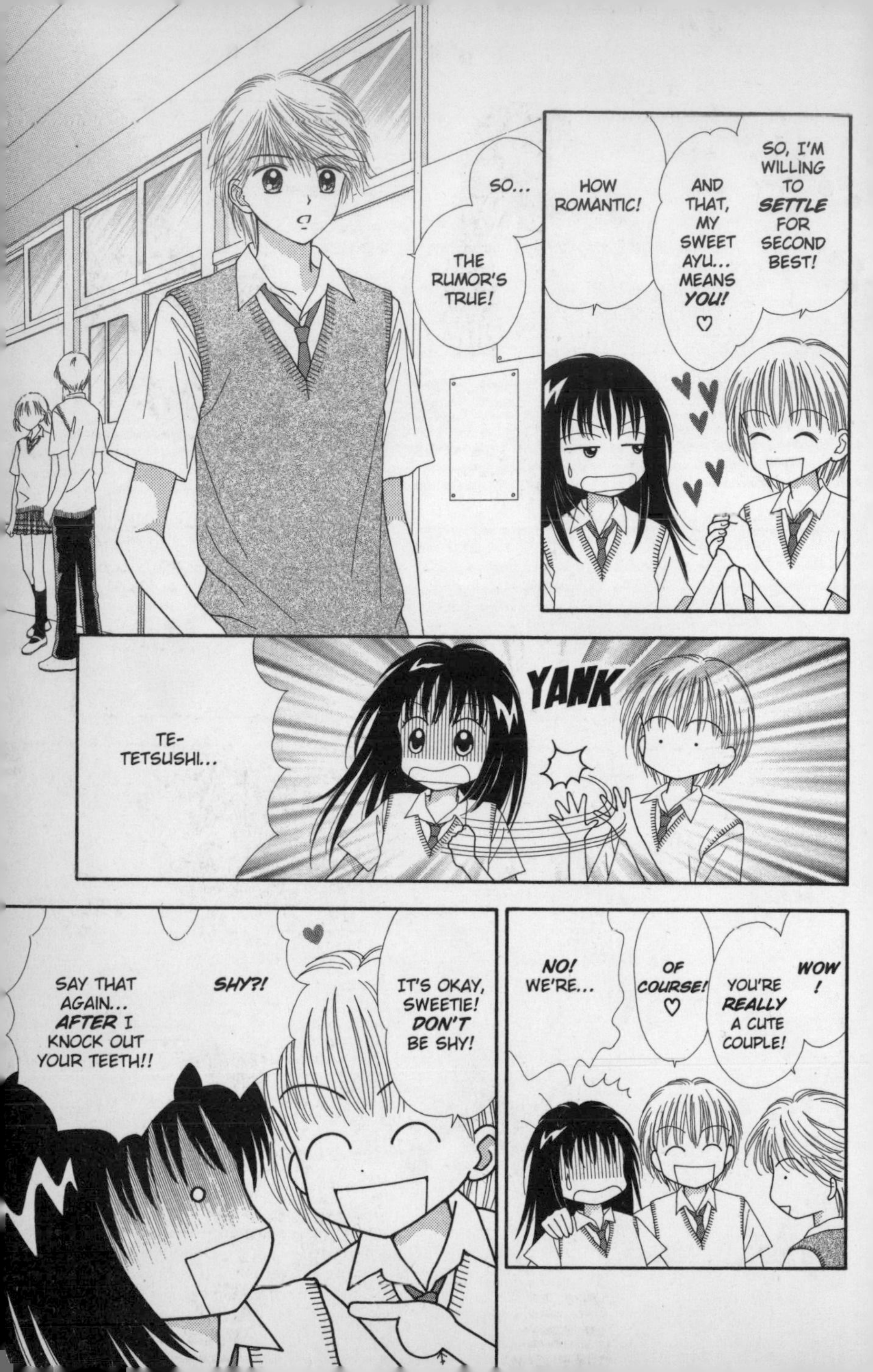
SO, I'M WILLING TO **SETTLE** FOR SECOND BEST!
AND THAT, MY SWEET AYU... MEANS **YOU!** ♡
HOW ROMANTIC!
SO... THE RUMOR'S TRUE!
YANK
TE- TETSUSHI...
WOW! YOU'RE **REALLY** A CUTE COUPLE!
OF **COURSE!** ♡
NO! WE'RE...
IT'S OKAY, SWEETIE! **DON'T** BE SHY!
SHY?!
SAY THAT AGAIN... **AFTER** I KNOCK OUT YOUR TEETH!!

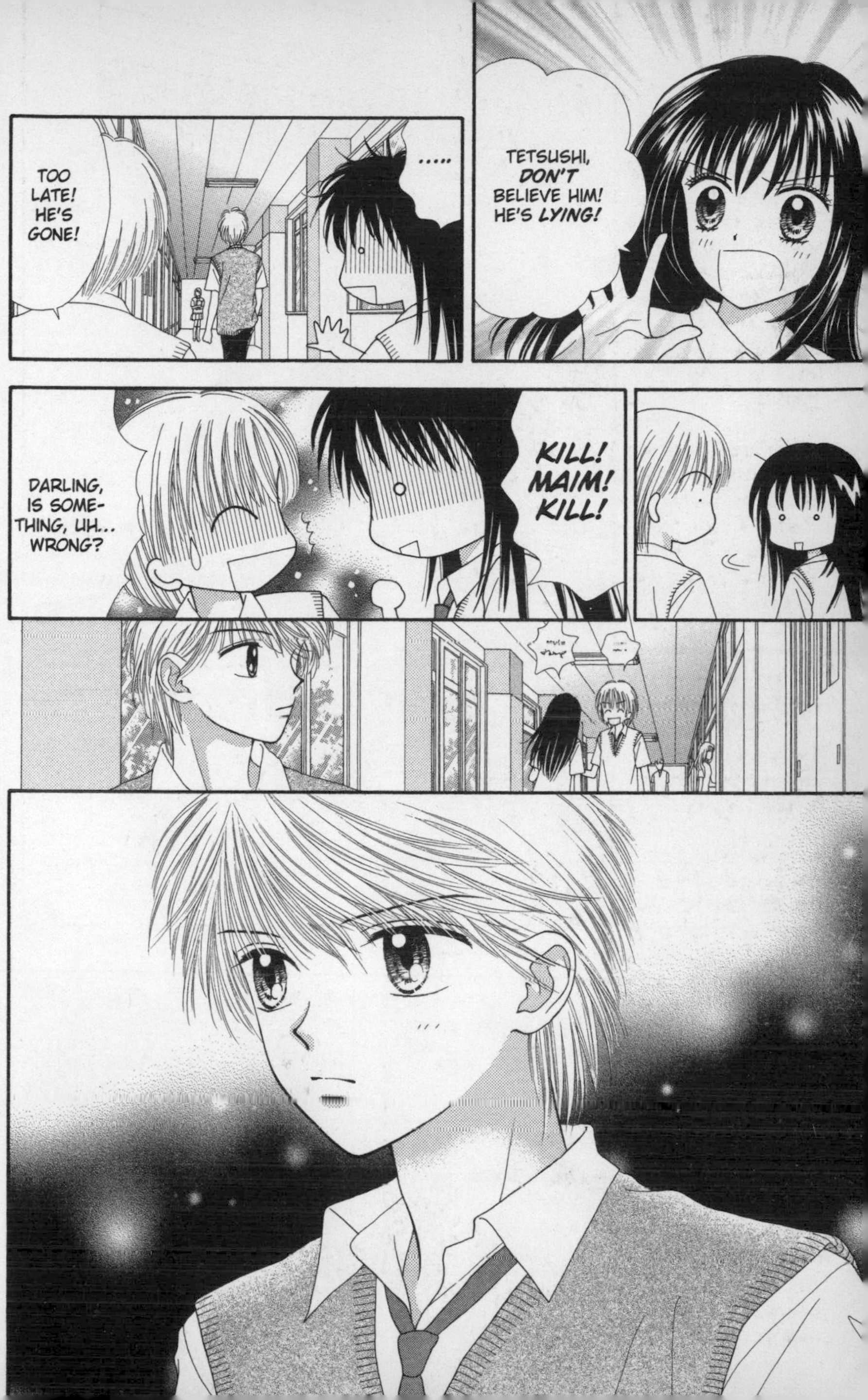
TETSUSHI, DON'T BELIEVE HIM! HE'S LYING!
.....
TOO LATE! HE'S GONE!
KILL! MAIM! KILL!
DARLING, IS SOME-THING, UH... WRONG?

FREE TALK 4

When Nina casts spells with her PC, she always says "**Spamola.**" It's a silly, made-up word that works for the English version of **Ultra Maniac.** But when I was coming up with a magic word for the original, Japanese version, I chose "**Practice!**"

I wanted a word associated with a computer function. But why did I choose "Practice" instead of the more common "Enter" or "Return"? It's because when I looked things up in my Japanese-to-English dictionary it showed that the Japanese term "to put into effect" equaled the English word "practice." It also said that the Japanese term of "casting a spell" translated to "practicing magic."

In addition, there is an American movie called "Practical Magic" starring Sandra Bullock and Nicole Kidman as two witch sisters. (The two main characters are **totally cute!** I really like this movie!) Does the movie's title mean "a practical kind of magic"? I don't know. It could actually mean "practice magic."

Anyway, that's why I chose "Practice." But the official language of the Magic Kingdom isn't supposed to be English. So I really could have used **any** word.

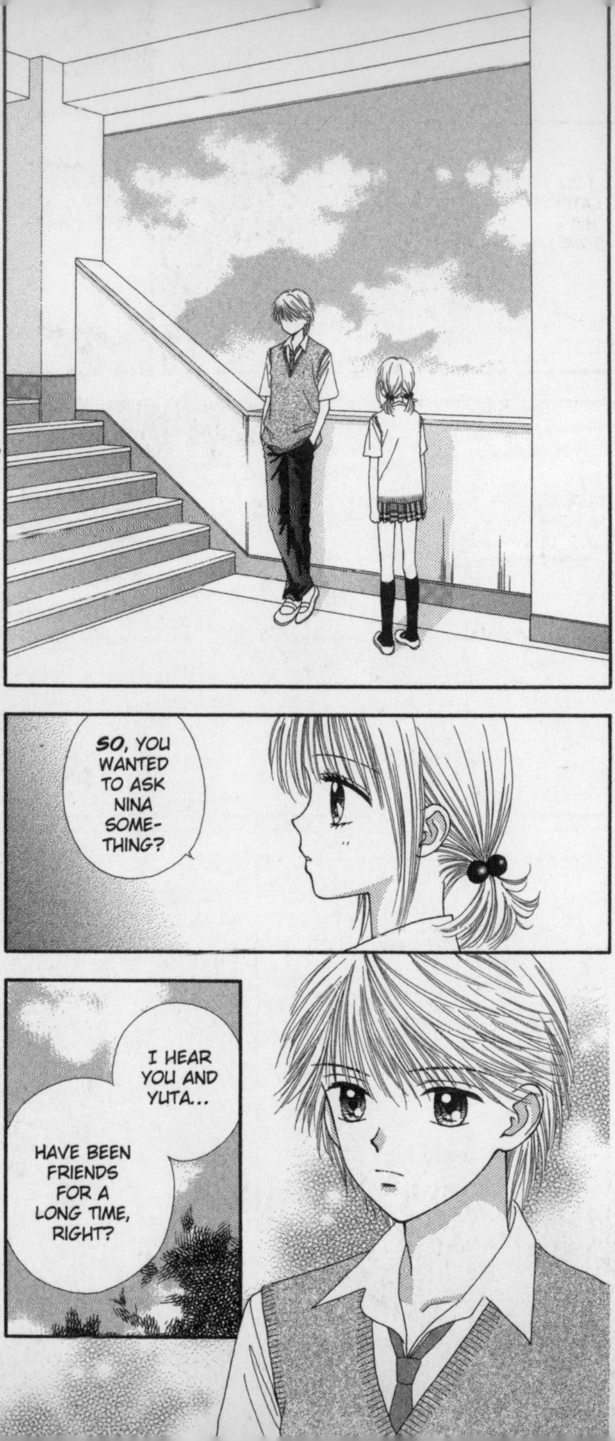
SO, YOU WANTED TO ASK NINA SOMETHING?
I HEAR YOU AND YUTA...
HAVE BEEN FRIENDS FOR A LONG TIME, RIGHT?

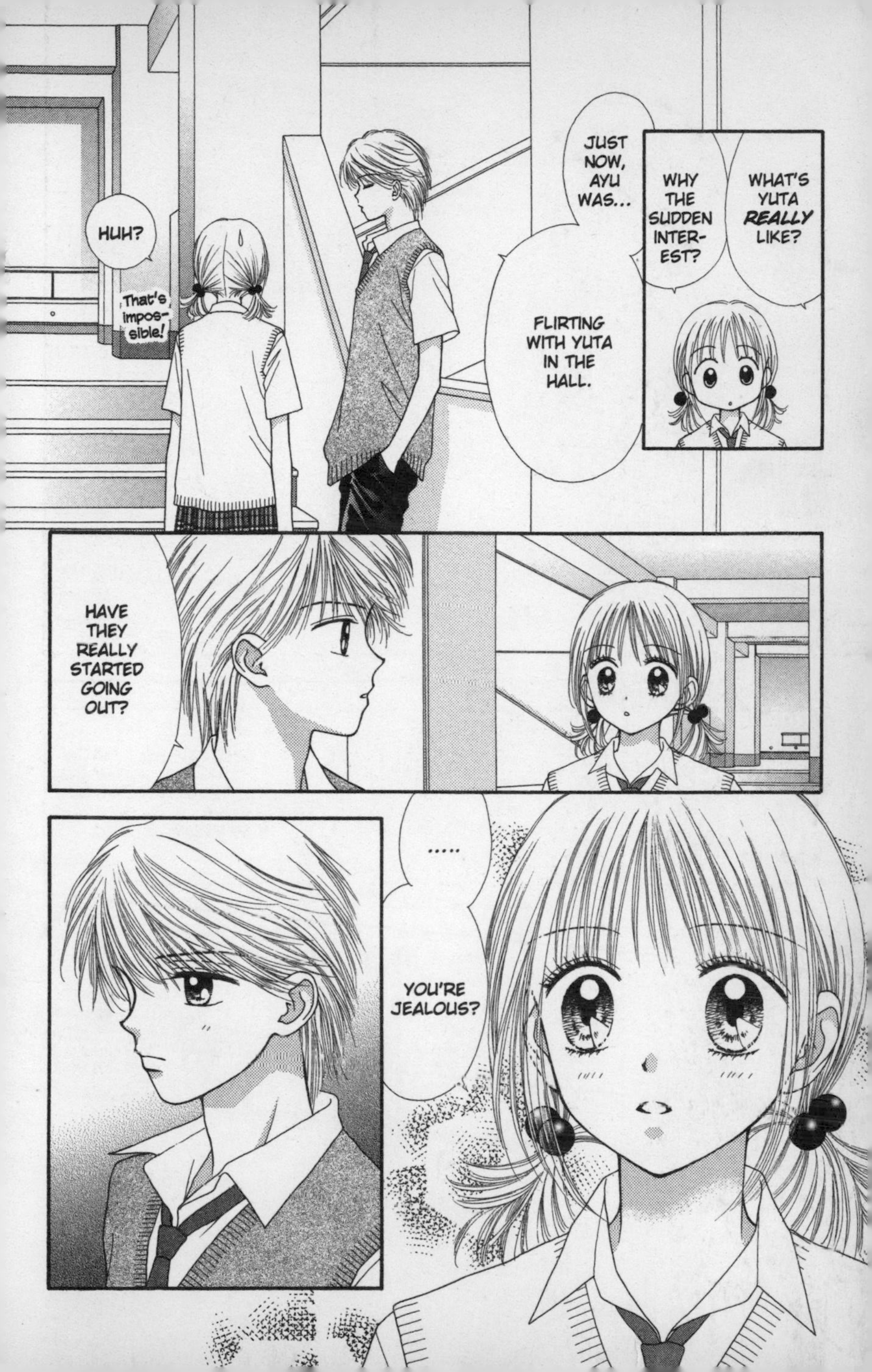
WHAT'S YUTA *REALLY* LIKE?
WHY THE SUDDEN INTER-EST?
JUST NOW, AYU WAS...
FLIRTING WITH YUTA IN THE HALL.
HUH?
That's impos-sible!
HAVE THEY REALLY STARTED GOING OUT?
.....
YOU'RE JEALOUS?

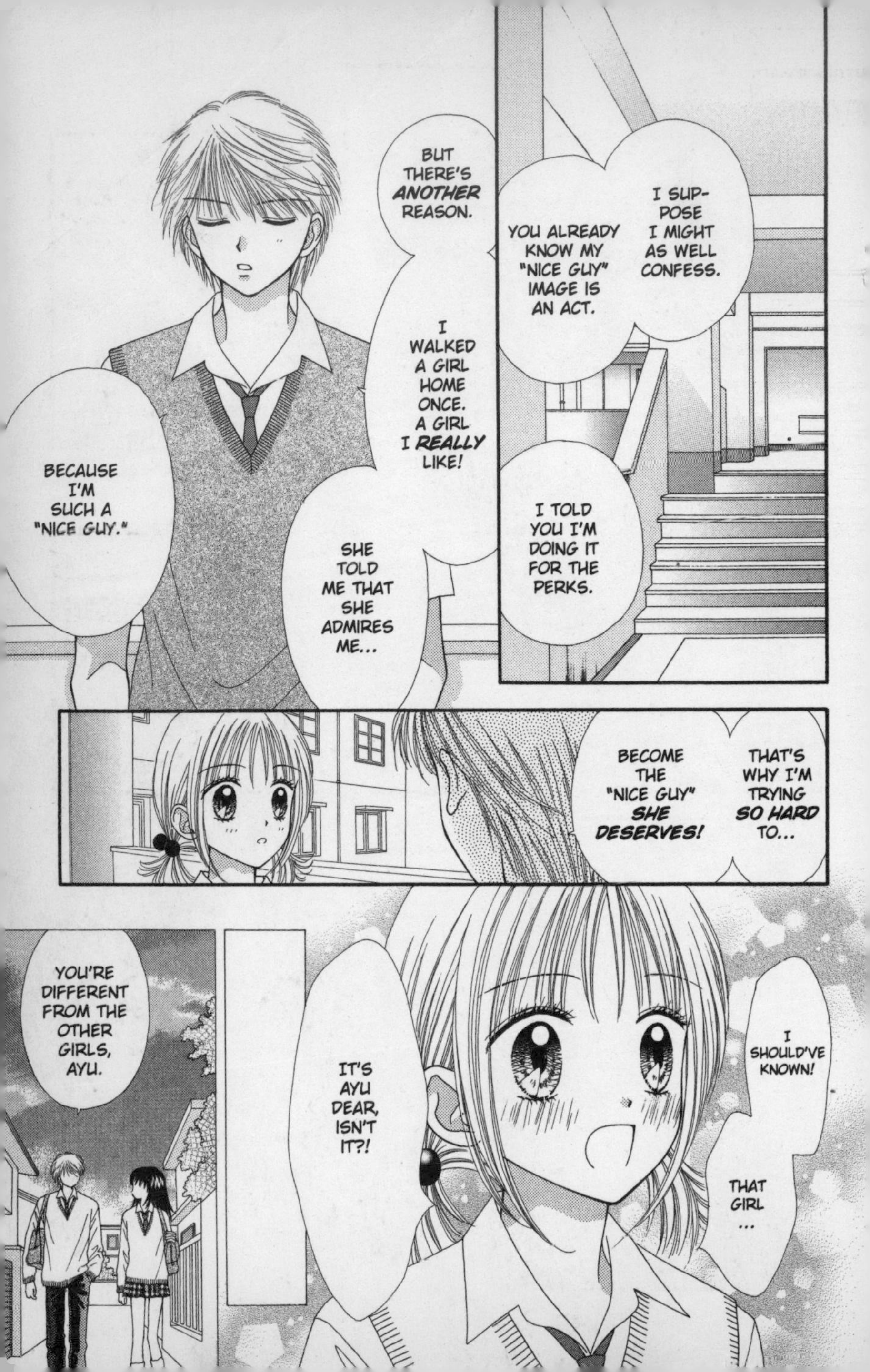
I SUPPOSE I MIGHT AS WELL CONFESS.
YOU ALREADY KNOW MY "NICE GUY" IMAGE IS AN ACT.
I TOLD YOU I'M DOING IT FOR THE PERKS.
BUT THERE'S ANOTHER REASON.
I WALKED A GIRL HOME ONCE. A GIRL I REALLY LIKE!
SHE TOLD ME THAT SHE ADMIRES ME...
BECAUSE I'M SUCH A "NICE GUY."
THAT'S WHY I'M TRYING SO HARD TO...
BECOME THE "NICE GUY" SHE DESERVES!
I SHOULD'VE KNOWN!
THAT GIRL...
IT'S AYU DEAR, ISN'T IT?!
YOU'RE DIFFERENT FROM THE OTHER GIRLS, AYU.

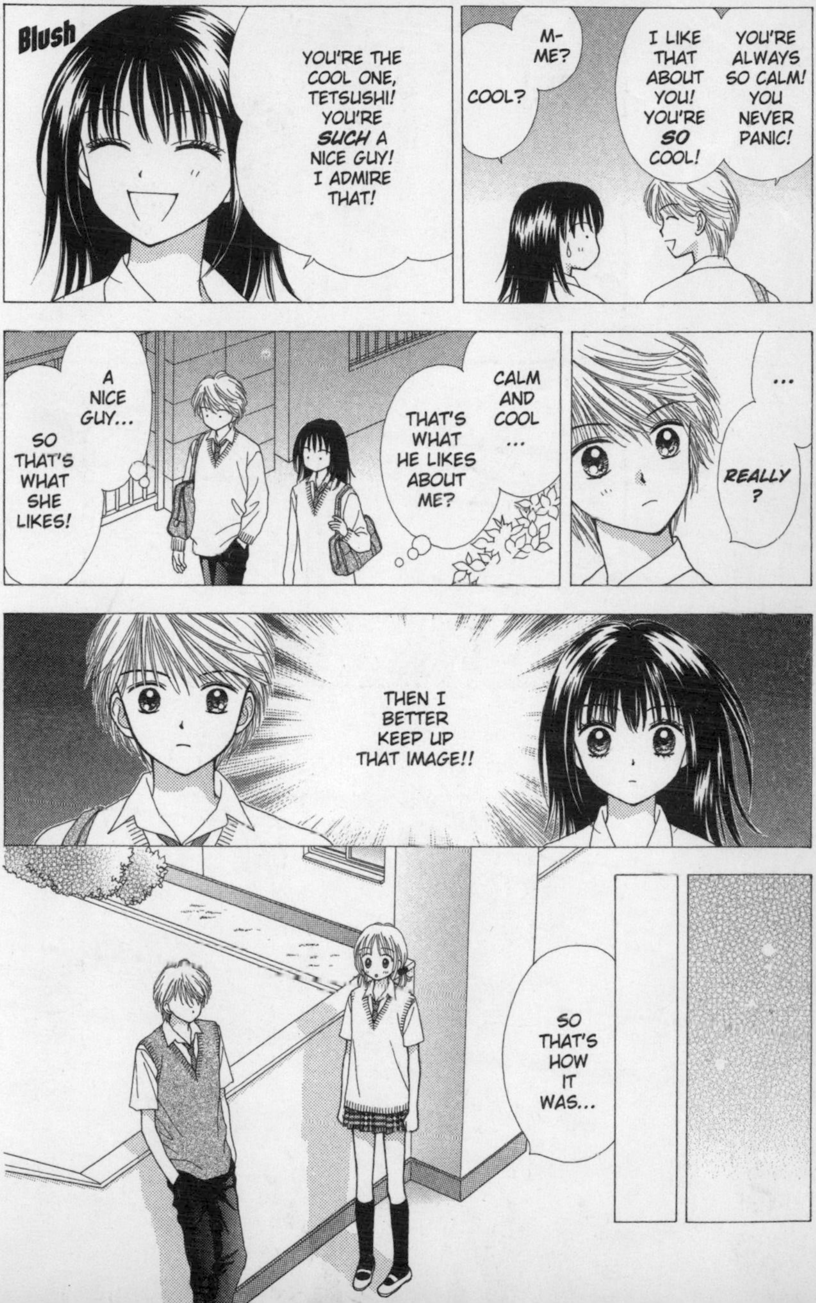
YOU'RE ALWAYS SO CALM! YOU NEVER PANIC!
I LIKE THAT ABOUT YOU! YOU'RE *SO* COOL!
M-ME? COOL?
Blush
YOU'RE THE COOL ONE, TETSUSHI! YOU'RE *SUCH* A NICE GUY! I ADMIRE THAT!
... *REALLY*?
CALM AND COOL...
THAT'S WHAT HE LIKES ABOUT ME?
A NICE GUY...
SO THAT'S WHAT SHE LIKES!
THEN I BETTER KEEP UP THAT IMAGE!!
SO THAT'S HOW IT WAS...

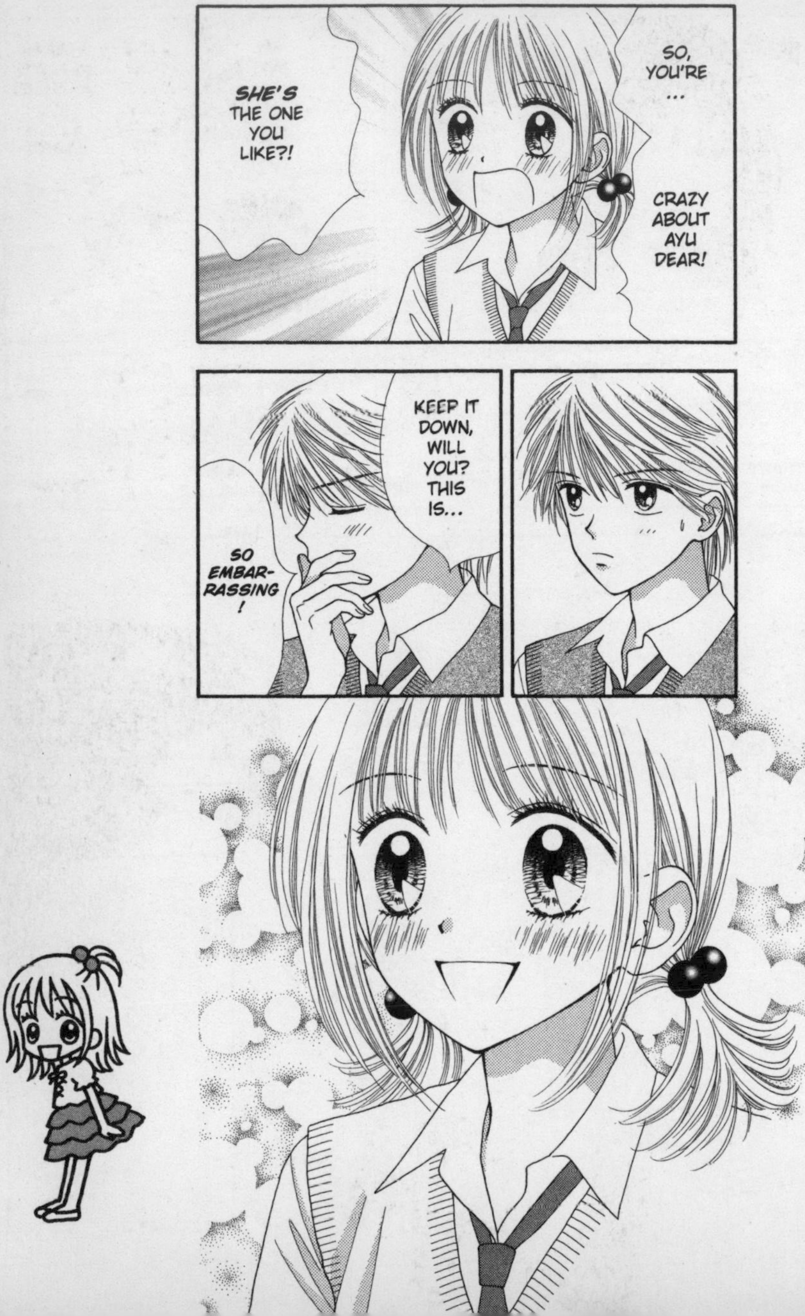
SO, YOU'RE ...
CRAZY ABOUT AYU DEAR!
SHE'S THE ONE YOU LIKE?!
KEEP IT DOWN, WILL YOU? THIS IS...
SO EMBARRASSING!

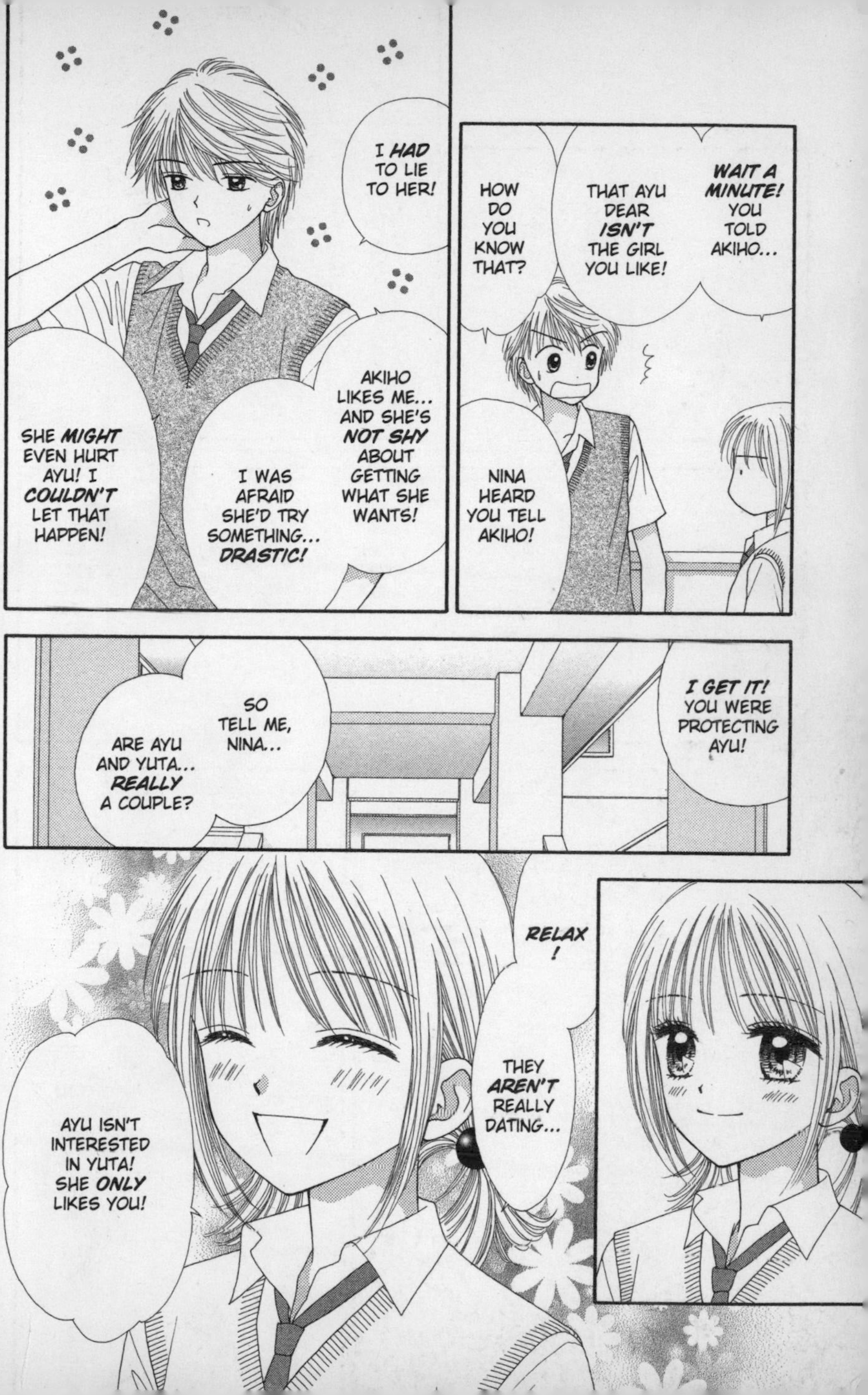
WAIT A MINUTE! YOU TOLD AKIHO...
THAT AYU DEAR ISN'T THE GIRL YOU LIKE!
HOW DO YOU KNOW THAT?
NINA HEARD YOU TELL AKIHO!
I HAD TO LIE TO HER!
AKIHO LIKES ME... AND SHE'S NOT SHY ABOUT GETTING WHAT SHE WANTS!
I WAS AFRAID SHE'D TRY SOMETHING... DRASTIC!
SHE MIGHT EVEN HURT AYU! I COULDN'T LET THAT HAPPEN!
I GET IT! YOU WERE PROTECTING AYU!
SO TELL ME, NINA...
ARE AYU AND YUTA... REALLY A COUPLE?
RELAX!
THEY AREN'T REALLY DATING...
AYU ISN'T INTERESTED IN YUTA! SHE ONLY LIKES YOU!

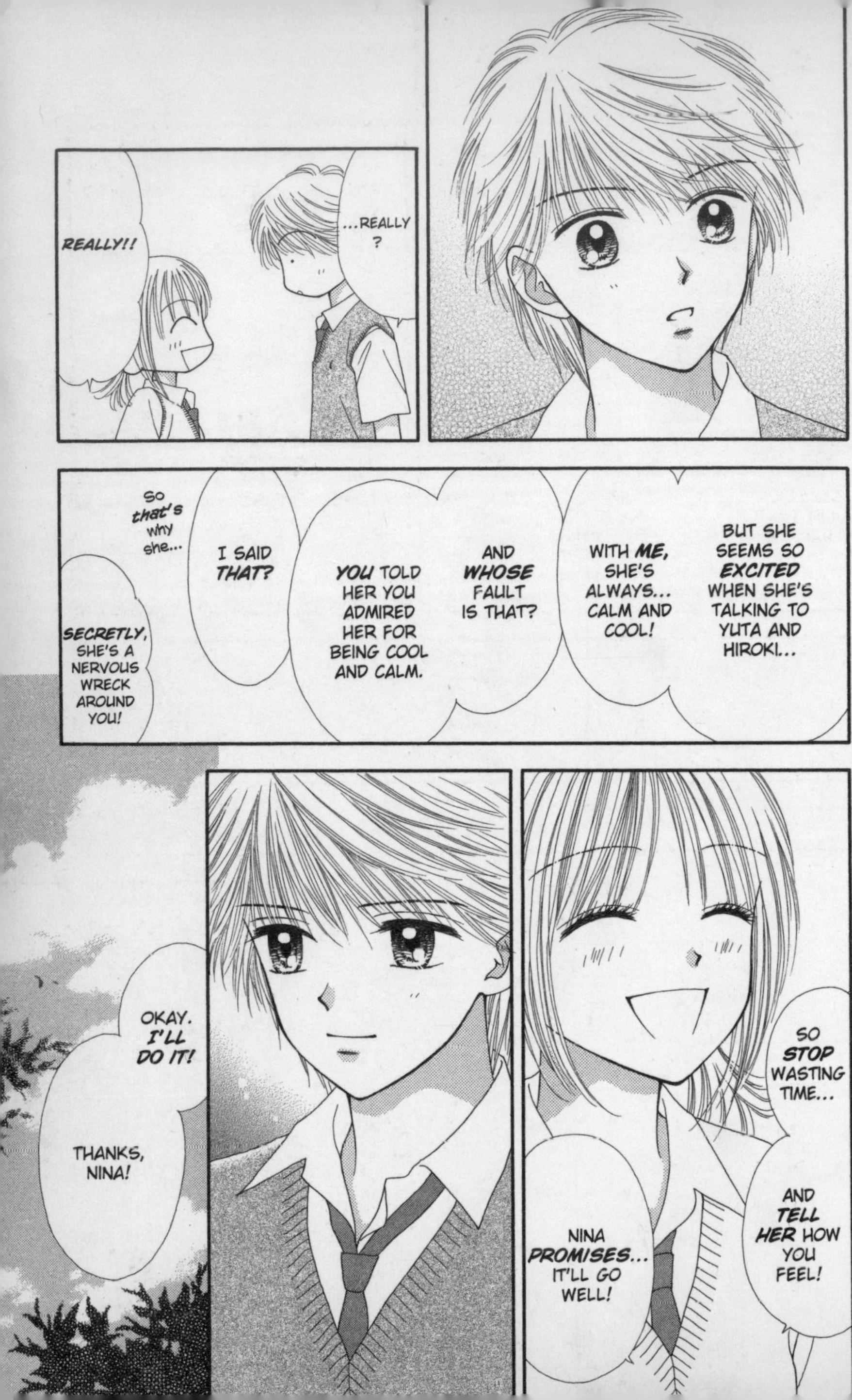
...REALLY ?
REALLY!!
BUT SHE SEEMS SO EXCITED WHEN SHE'S TALKING TO YUTA AND HIROKI...
WITH ME, SHE'S ALWAYS... CALM AND COOL!
AND WHOSE FAULT IS THAT?
YOU TOLD HER YOU ADMIRED HER FOR BEING COOL AND CALM.
I SAID THAT?
So that's why she...
SECRETLY, SHE'S A NERVOUS WRECK AROUND YOU!
SO STOP WASTING TIME...
AND TELL HER HOW YOU FEEL!
NINA PROMISES... IT'LL GO WELL!
OKAY. I'LL DO IT!
THANKS, NINA!

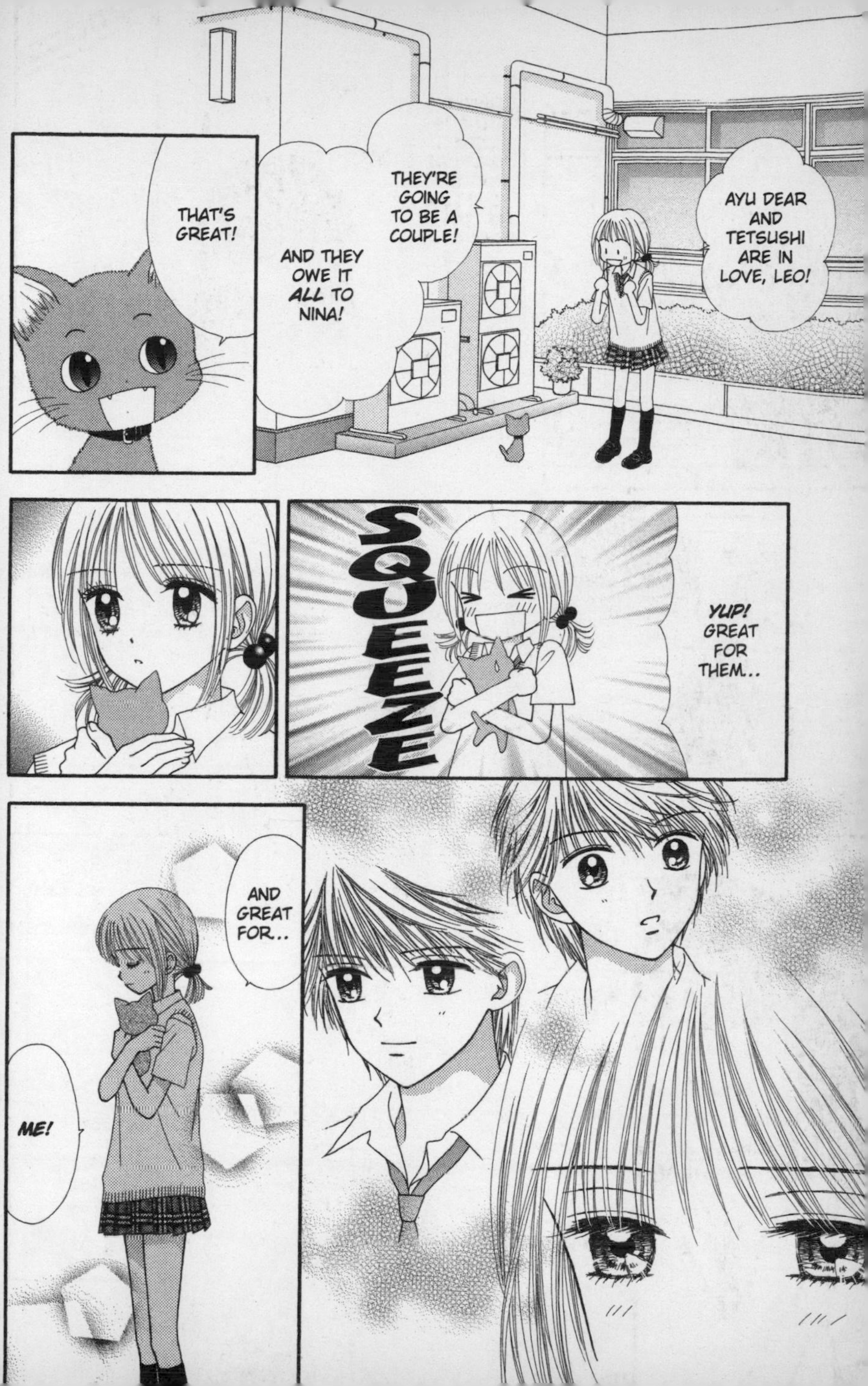
AYU DEAR AND TETSUSHI ARE IN LOVE, LEO!
THEY'RE GOING TO BE A COUPLE!
AND THEY OWE IT *ALL* TO NINA!
THAT'S GREAT!
YUP! GREAT FOR THEM..
SQUEEZE
AND GREAT FOR..
ME!

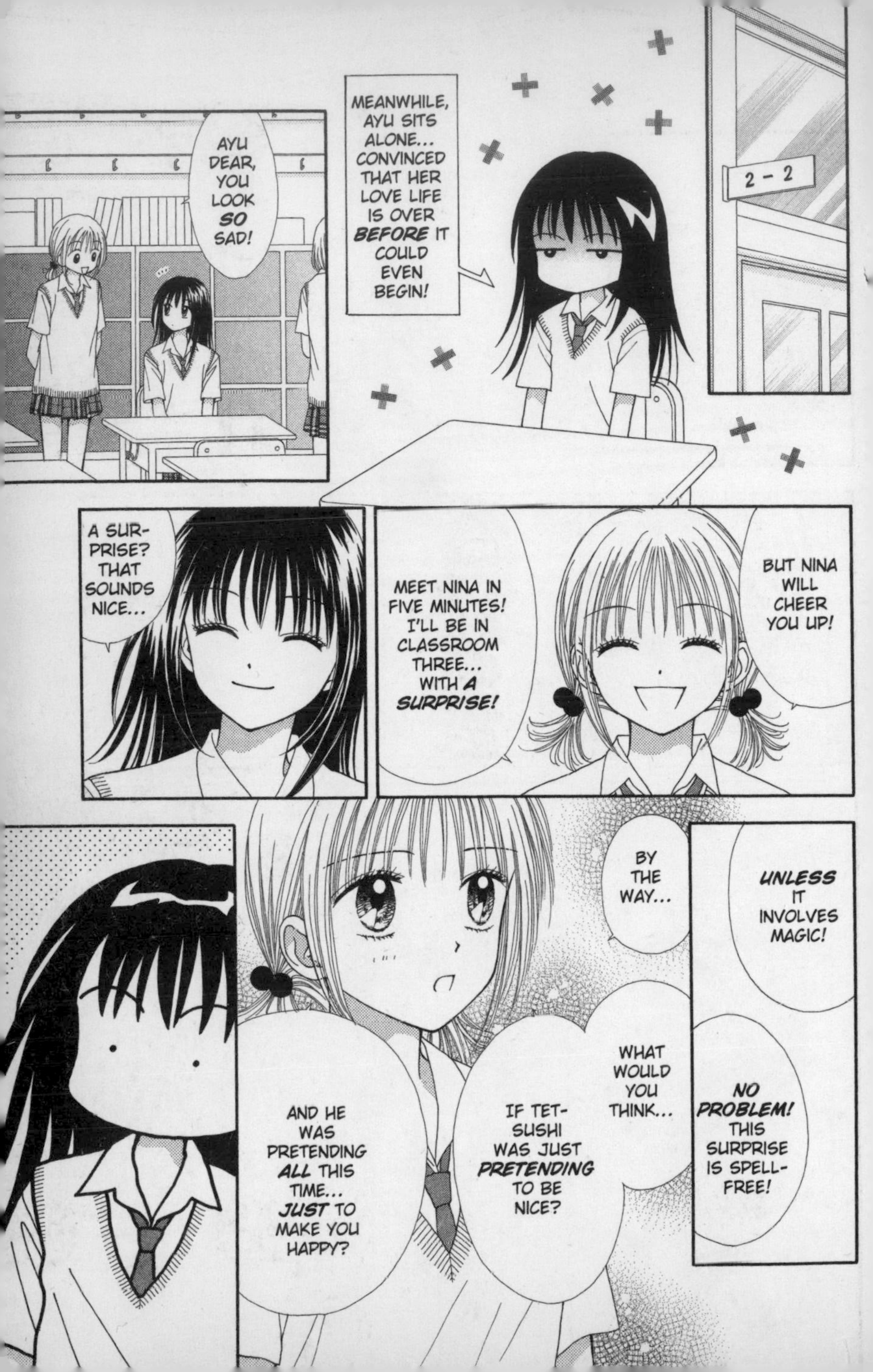

2 – 2
MEANWHILE, AYU SITS ALONE... CONVINCED THAT HER LOVE LIFE IS OVER BEFORE IT COULD EVEN BEGIN!
AYU DEAR, YOU LOOK SO SAD!
BUT NINA WILL CHEER YOU UP!
MEET NINA IN FIVE MINUTES! I'LL BE IN CLASSROOM THREE... WITH A SURPRISE!
A SURPRISE? THAT SOUNDS NICE...
UNLESS IT INVOLVES MAGIC!
NO PROBLEM! THIS SURPRISE IS SPELL-FREE!
BY THE WAY...
WHAT WOULD YOU THINK...
IF TETSUSHI WAS JUST PRETENDING TO BE NICE?
AND HE WAS PRETENDING ALL THIS TIME... JUST TO MAKE YOU HAPPY?

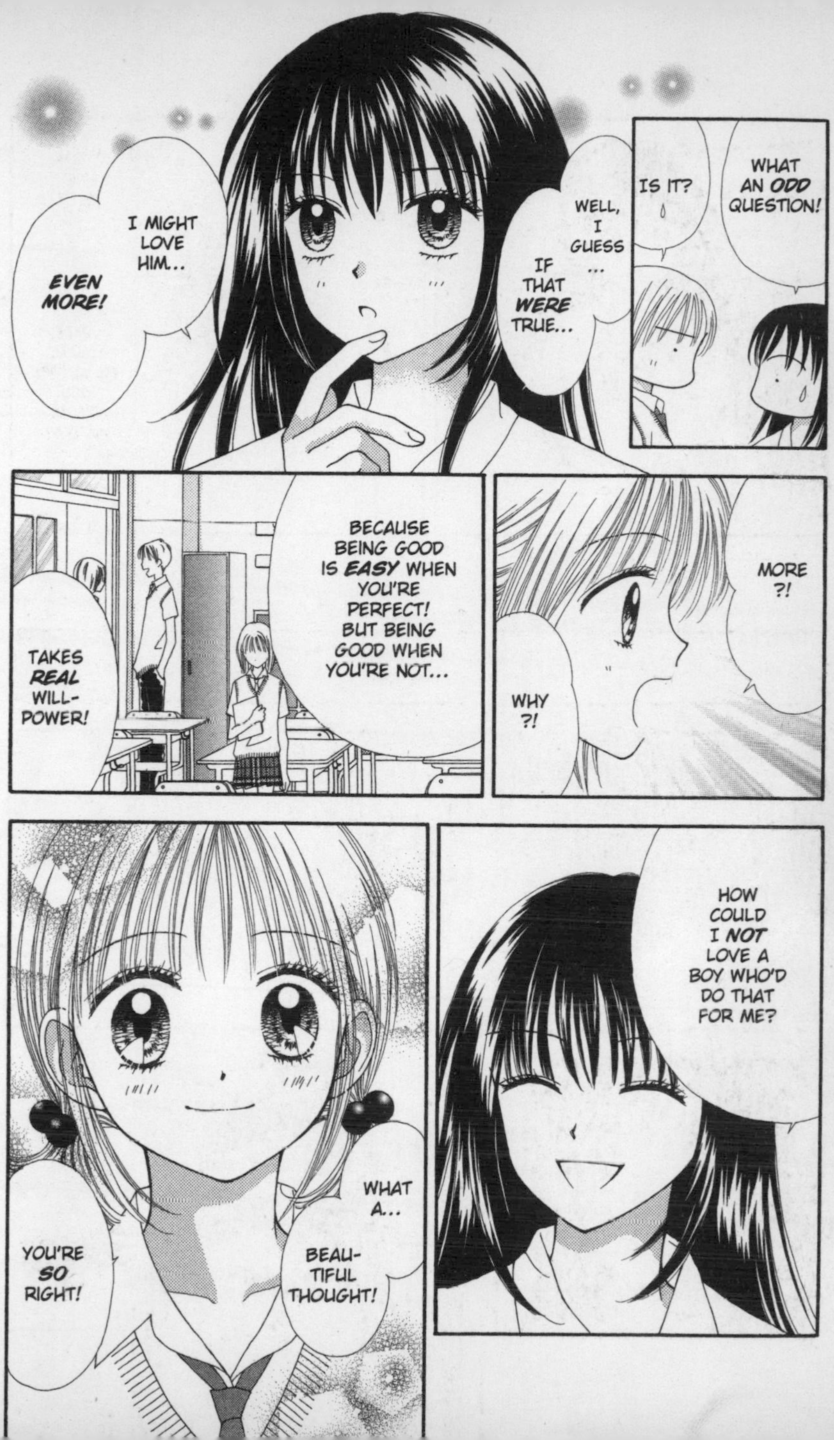
WHAT AN ODD QUESTION!
IS IT?
WELL, I GUESS ...
IF THAT WERE TRUE...
I MIGHT LOVE HIM... EVEN MORE!
MORE?!
WHY?!
BECAUSE BEING GOOD IS EASY WHEN YOU'RE PERFECT! BUT BEING GOOD WHEN YOU'RE NOT...
TAKES REAL WILL-POWER!
HOW COULD I NOT LOVE A BOY WHO'D DO THAT FOR ME?
WHAT A...
BEAU-TIFUL THOUGHT!
YOU'RE SO RIGHT!

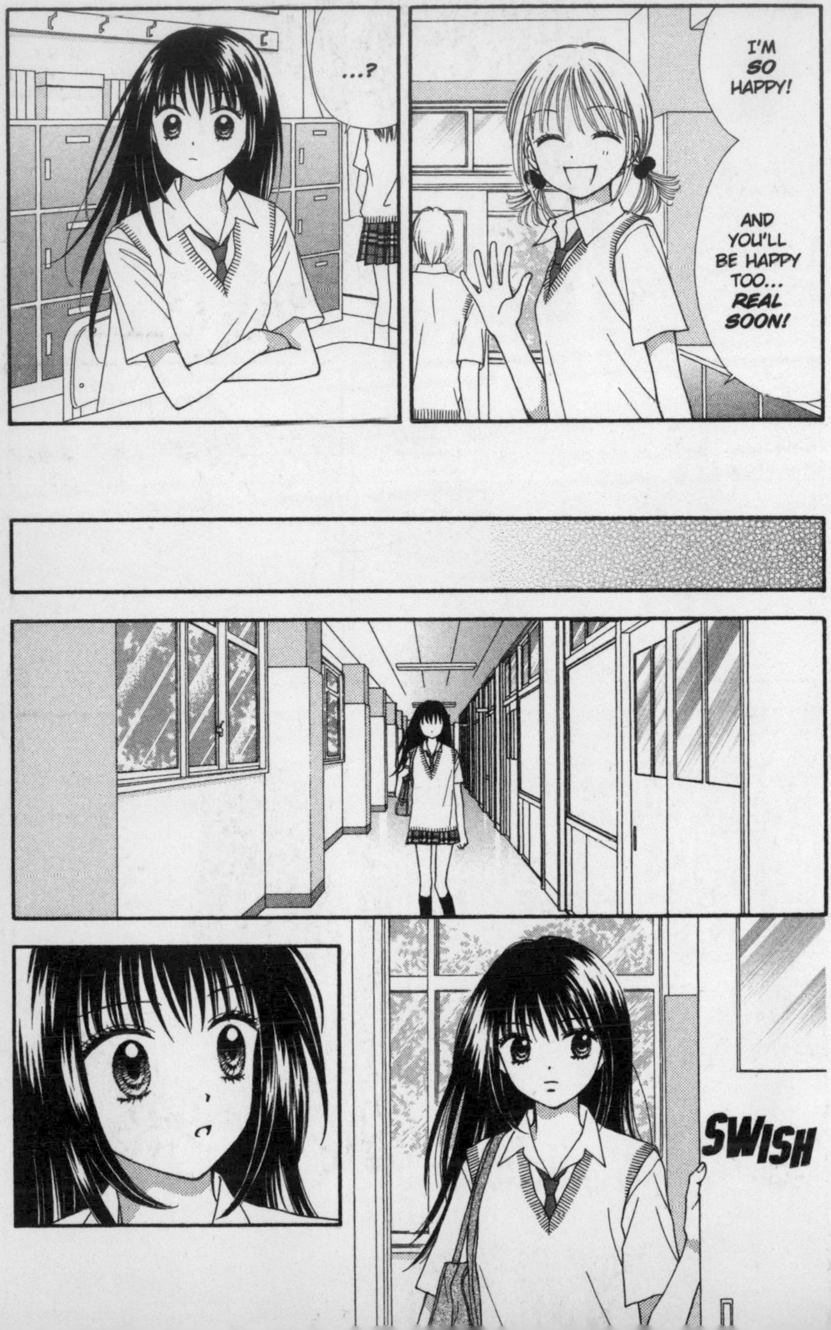
I'M SO HAPPY!
AND YOU'LL BE HAPPY TOO... REAL SOON!
...?
SWISH

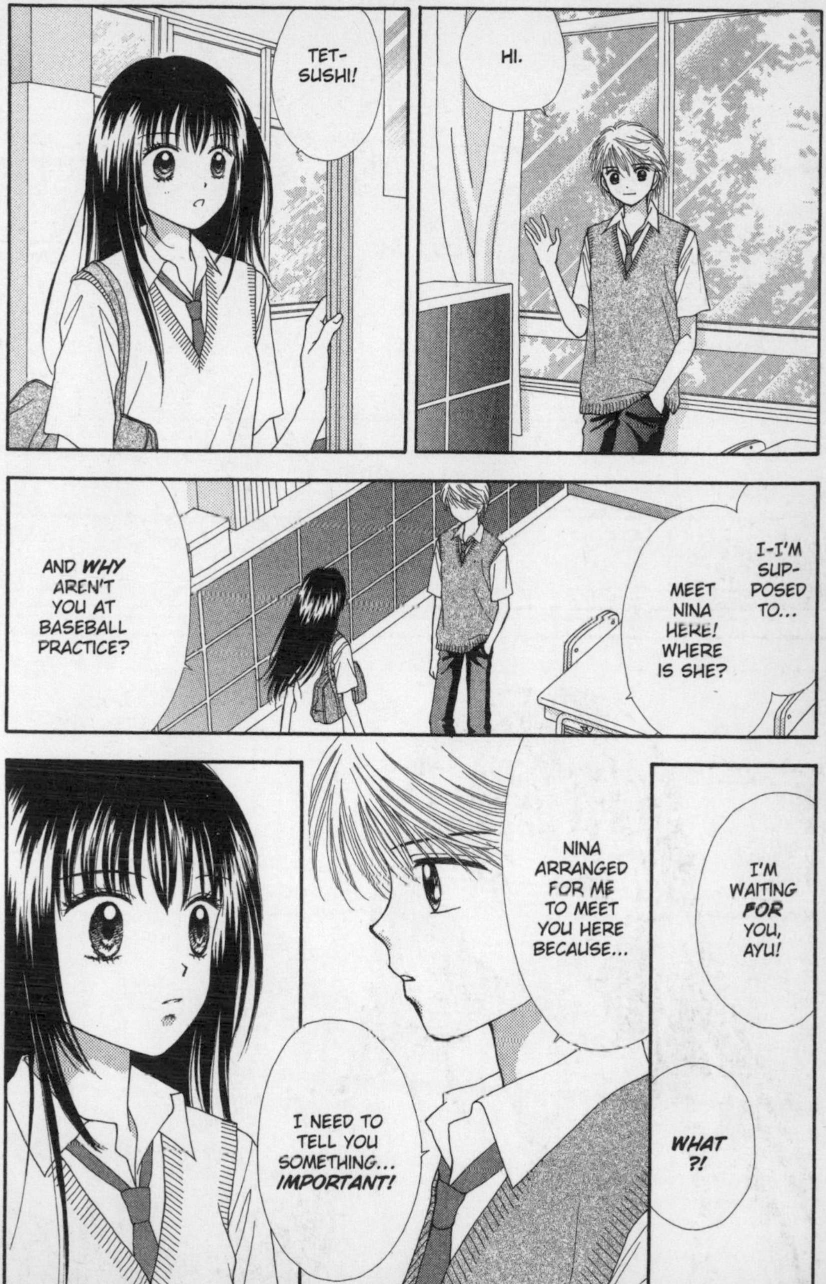
HI.
TET-SUSHI!
I-I'M SUP-POSED TO...
MEET NINA HERE! WHERE IS SHE?
AND WHY AREN'T YOU AT BASEBALL PRACTICE?
I'M WAITING FOR YOU, AYU!
WHAT?!
NINA ARRANGED FOR ME TO MEET YOU HERE BECAUSE...
I NEED TO TELL YOU SOMETHING... IMPORTANT!

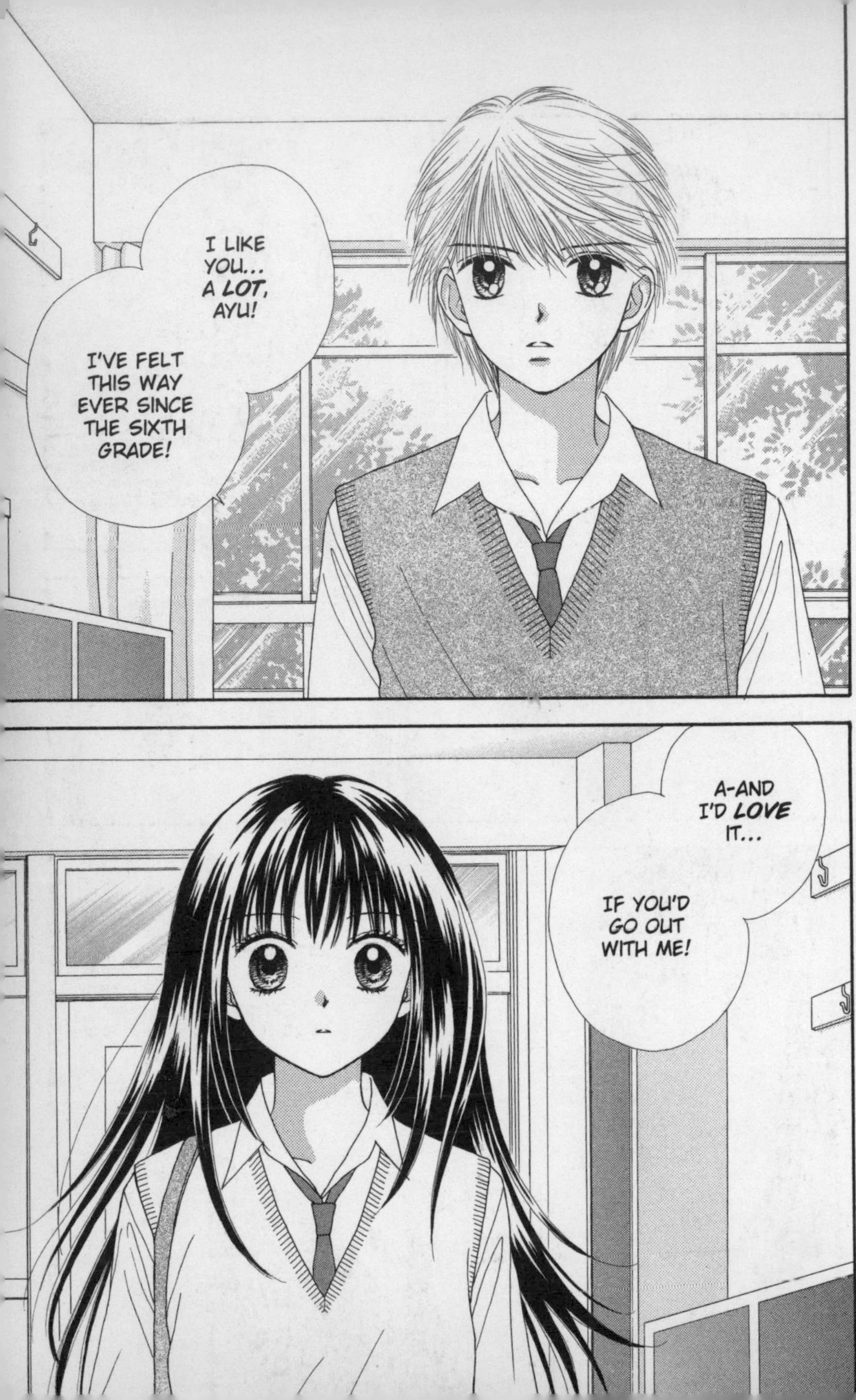
I LIKE YOU... A *LOT*, AYU!
I'VE FELT THIS WAY EVER SINCE THE SIXTH GRADE!
A-AND I'D *LOVE* IT...
IF YOU'D GO OUT WITH ME!

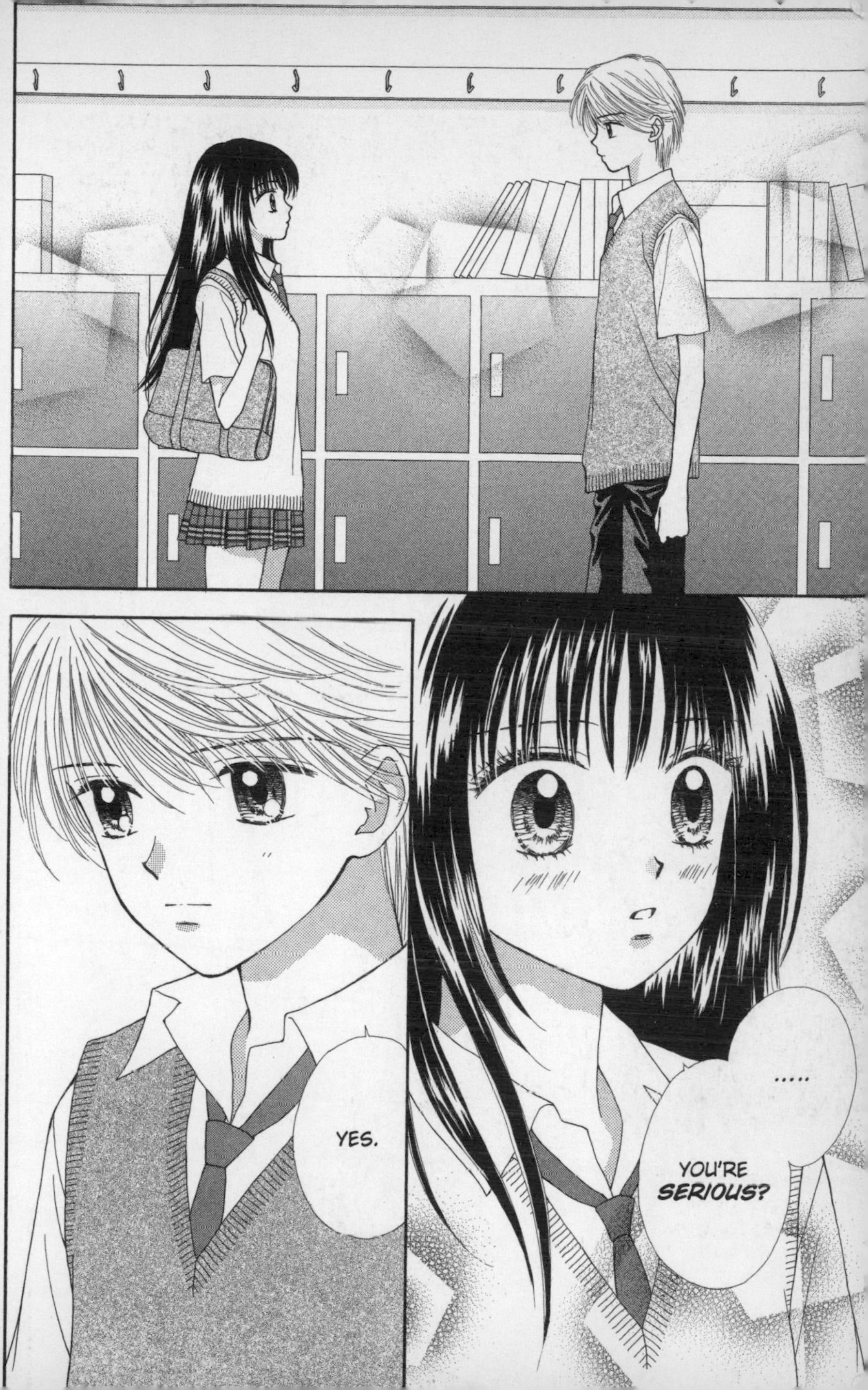
.....
YOU'RE SERIOUS?
YES.

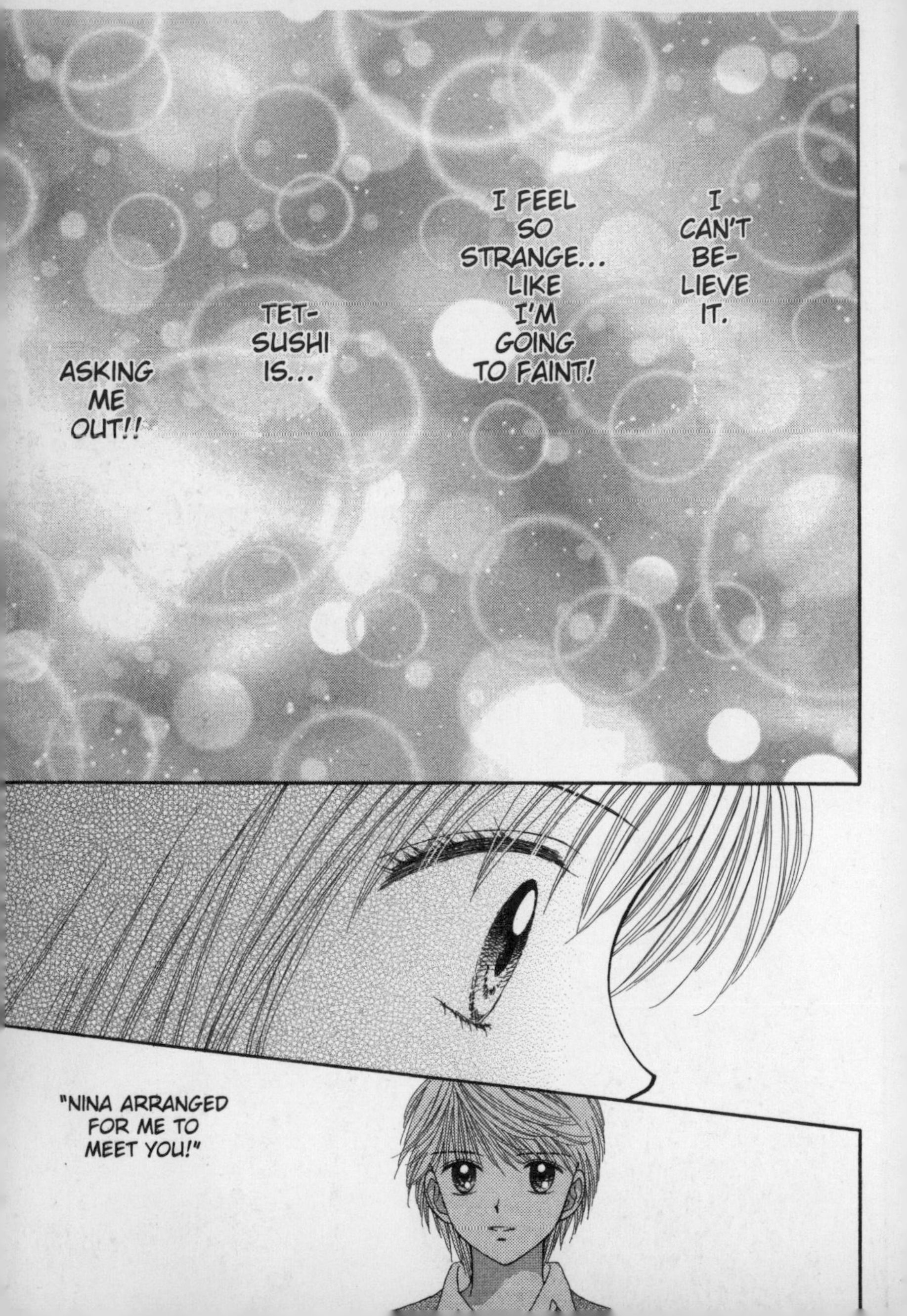
I CAN'T BE-LIEVE IT.
I FEEL SO STRANGE... LIKE I'M GOING TO FAINT!
TET-SUSHI IS...
ASKING ME OUT!!
"NINA ARRANGED FOR ME TO MEET YOU!"

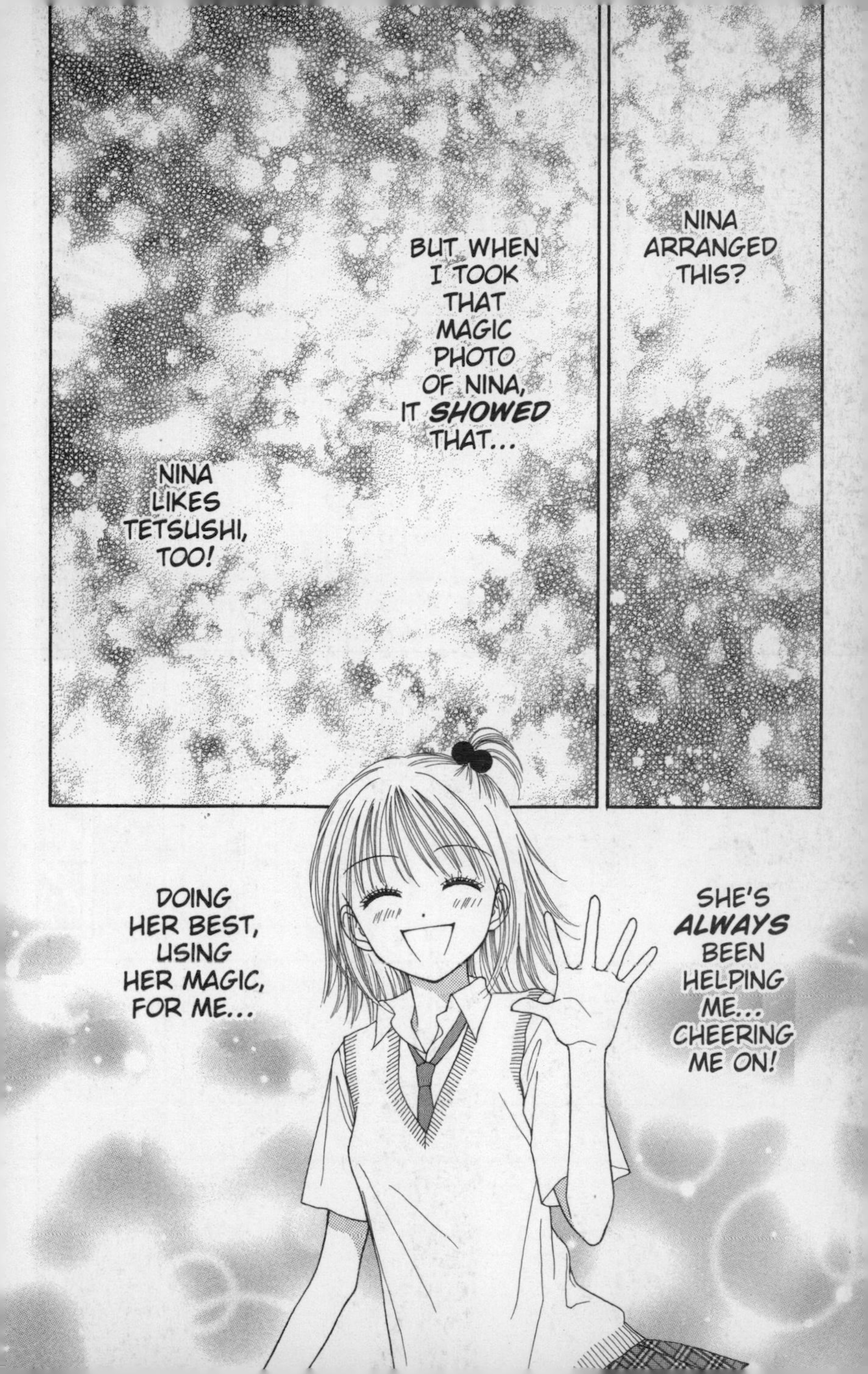
NINA ARRANGED THIS?
BUT WHEN I TOOK THAT MAGIC PHOTO OF NINA, IT SHOWED THAT...
NINA LIKES TETSUSHI, TOO!
SHE'S ALWAYS BEEN HELPING ME... CHEERING ME ON!
DOING HER BEST, USING HER MAGIC, FOR ME...

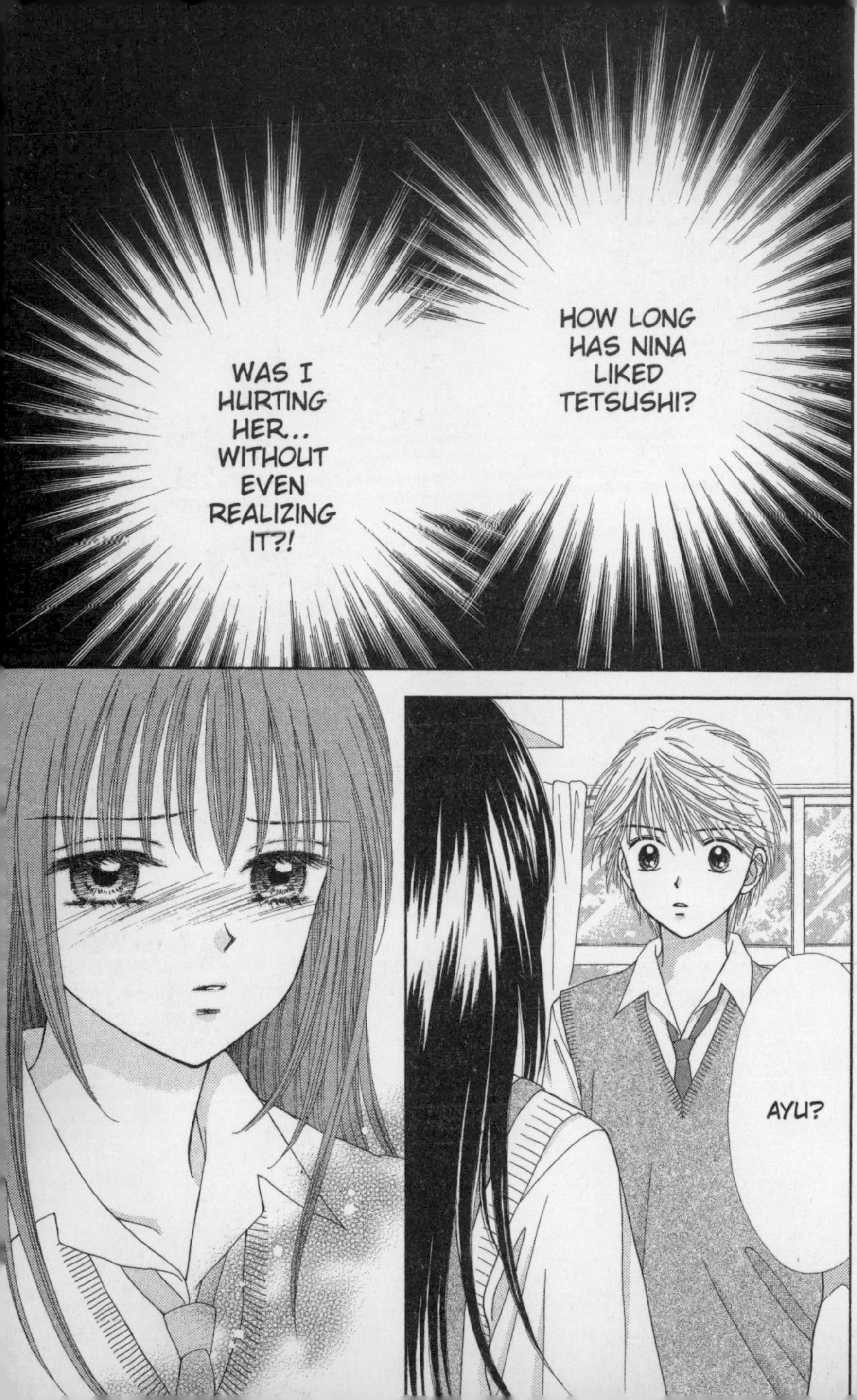
HOW LONG HAS NINA LIKED TETSUSHI?
WAS I HURTING HER... WITHOUT EVEN REALIZING IT?!
AYU?

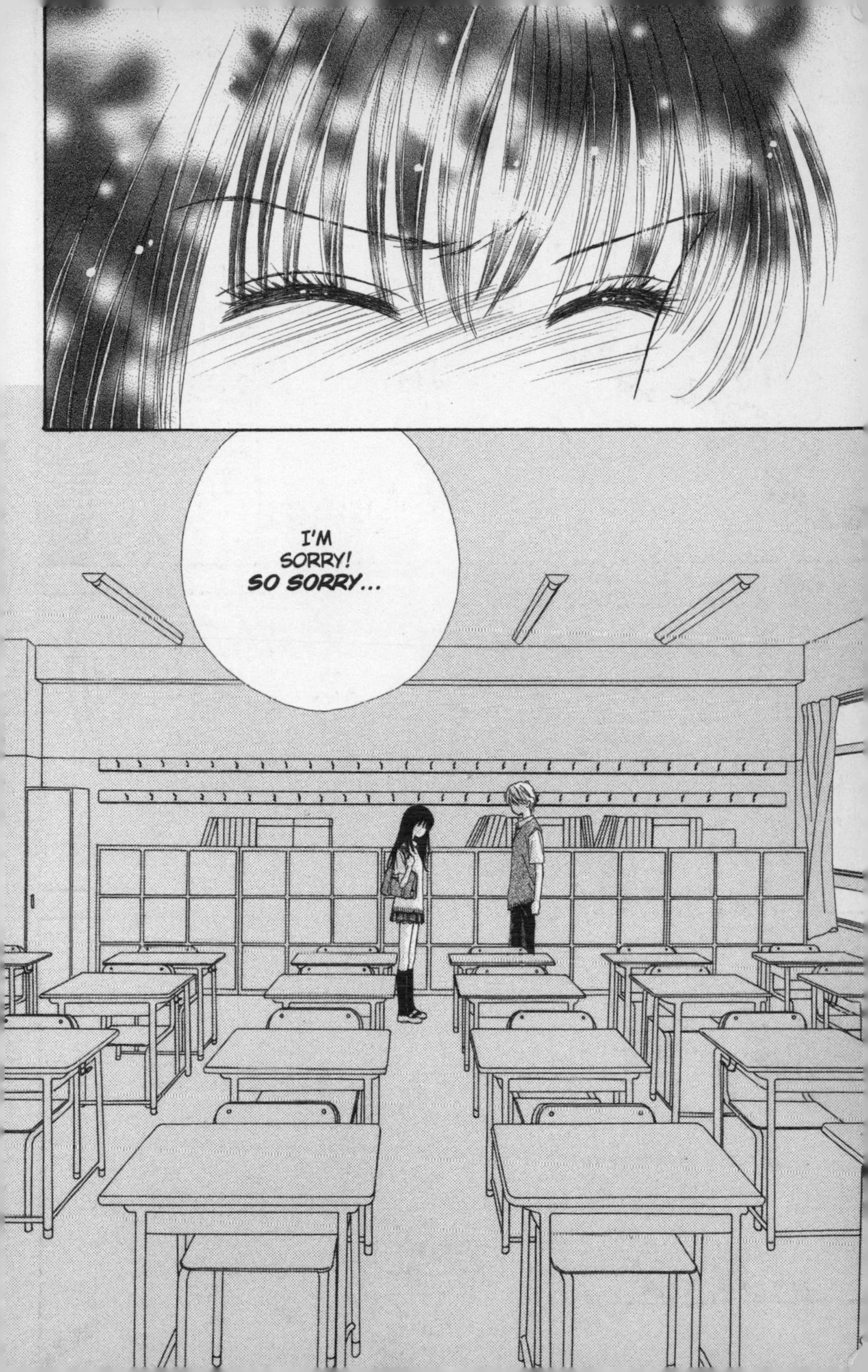
I'M SORRY! SO SORRY...

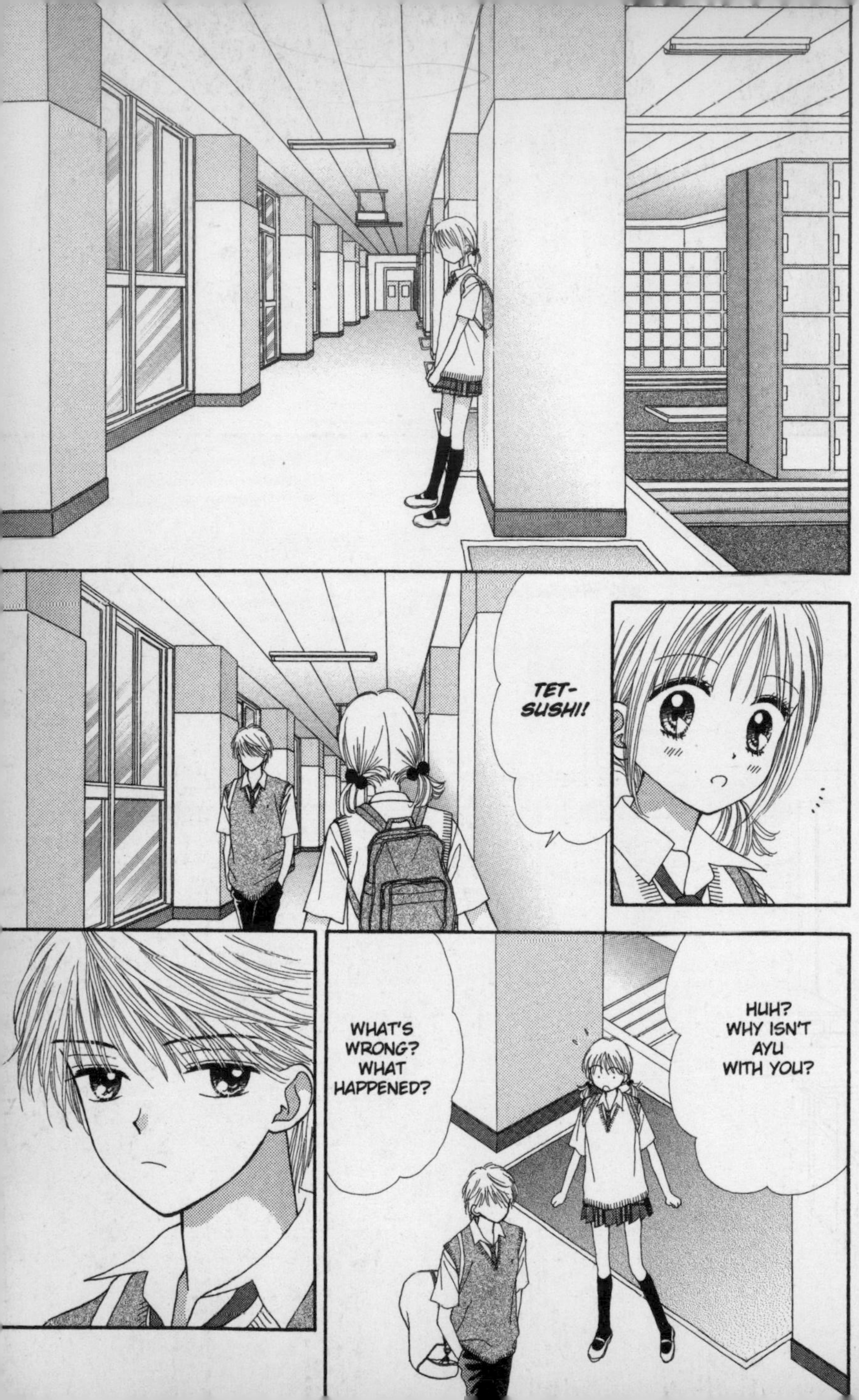
....
TET-SUSHI!
HUH? WHY ISN'T AYU WITH YOU?
WHAT'S WRONG? WHAT HAPPENED?

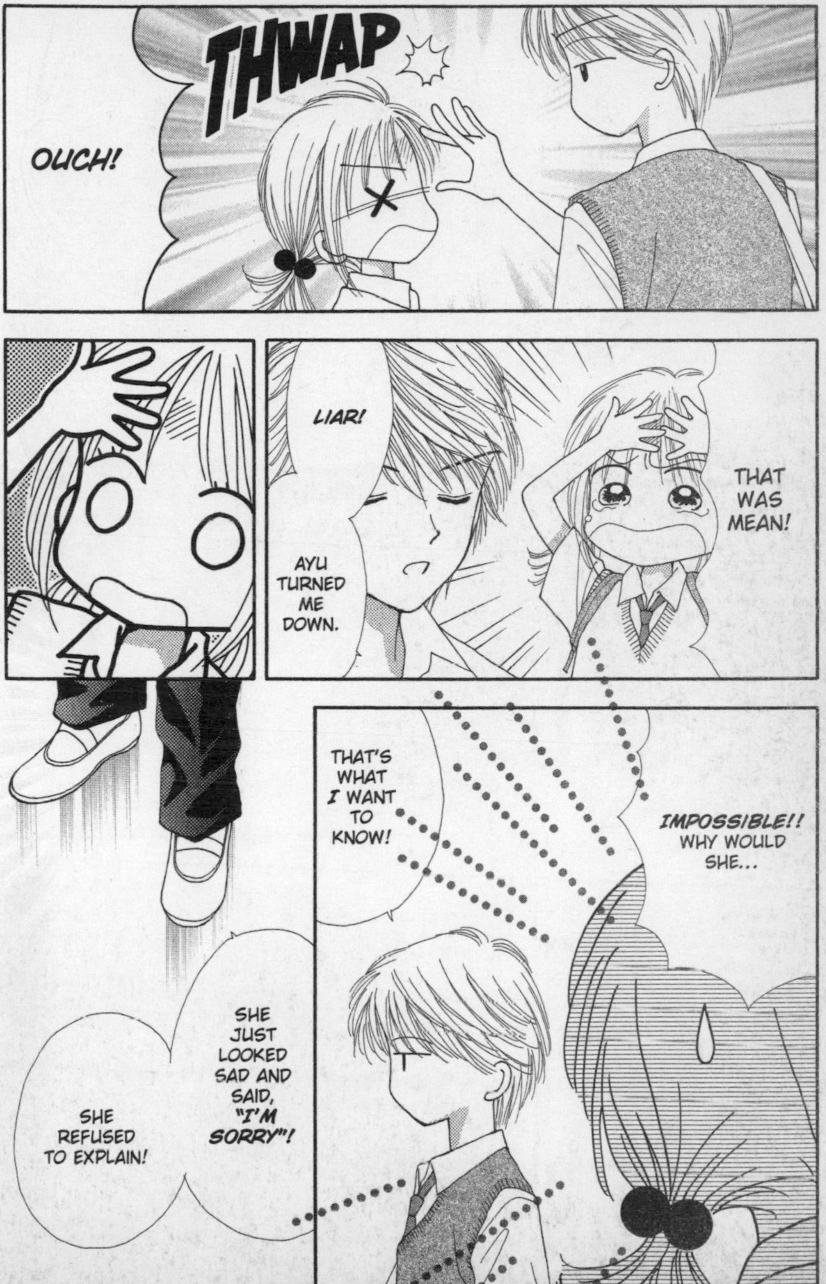
THWAP
OUCH!
THAT WAS MEAN!
LIAR!
AYU TURNED ME DOWN.
IMPOSSIBLE!! WHY WOULD SHE...
THAT'S WHAT *I* WANT TO KNOW!
SHE JUST LOOKED SAD AND SAID, *"I'M SORRY"!*
SHE REFUSED TO EXPLAIN!

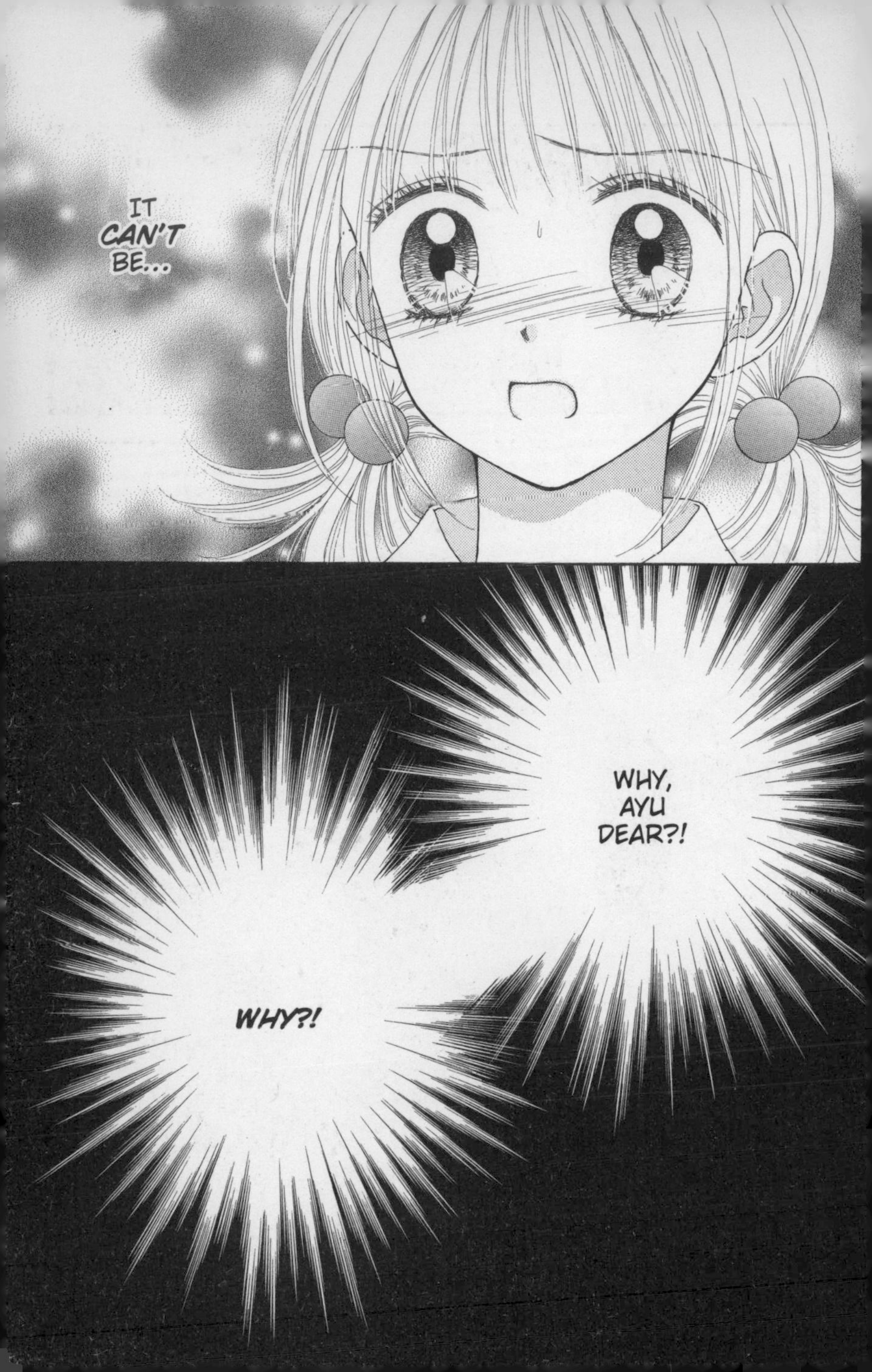
IT CAN'T BE...
WHY, AYU DEAR?!
WHY?!

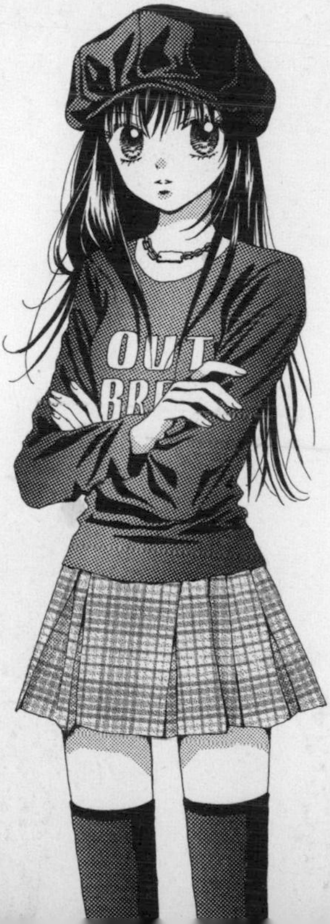
OUT

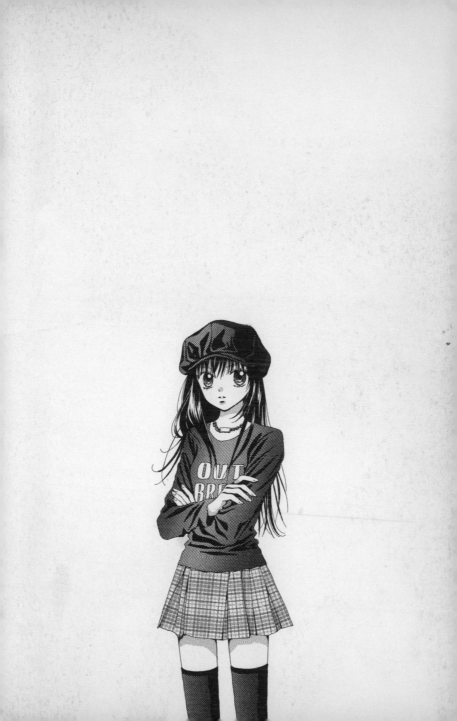

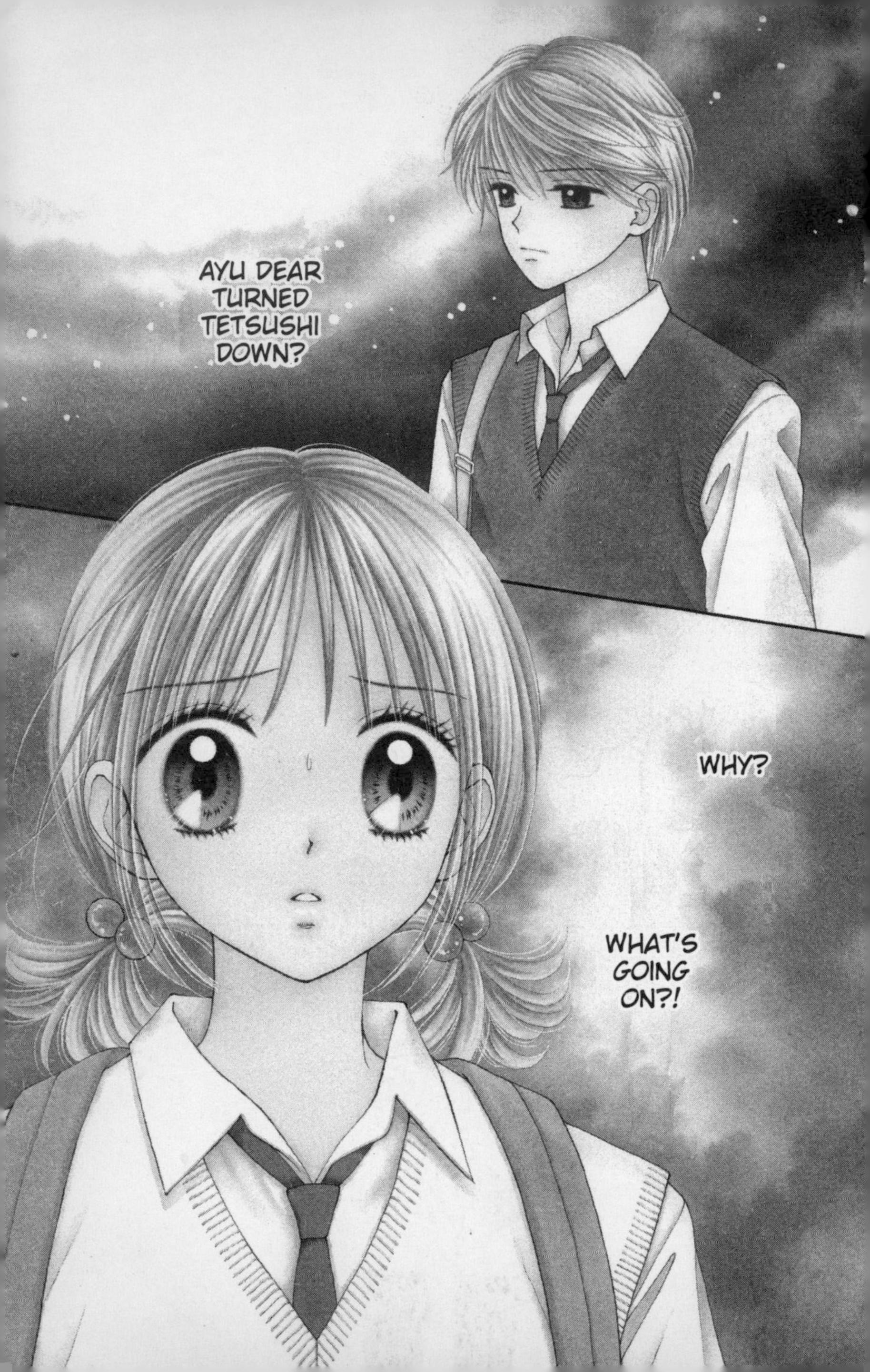
AYU DEAR TURNED TETSUSHI DOWN?
WHY?
WHAT'S GOING ON?!

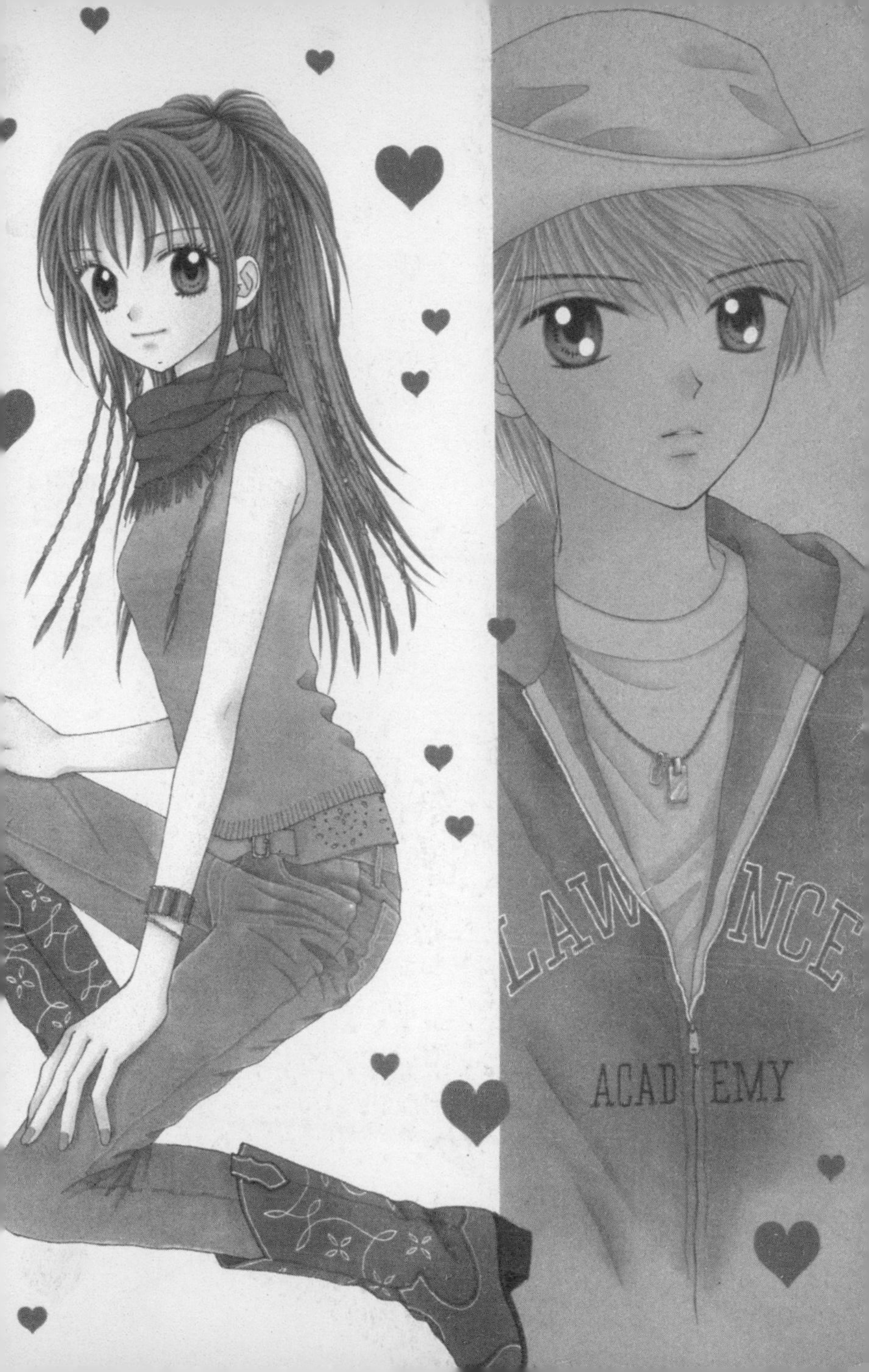
LAW NCE
ACADEMY

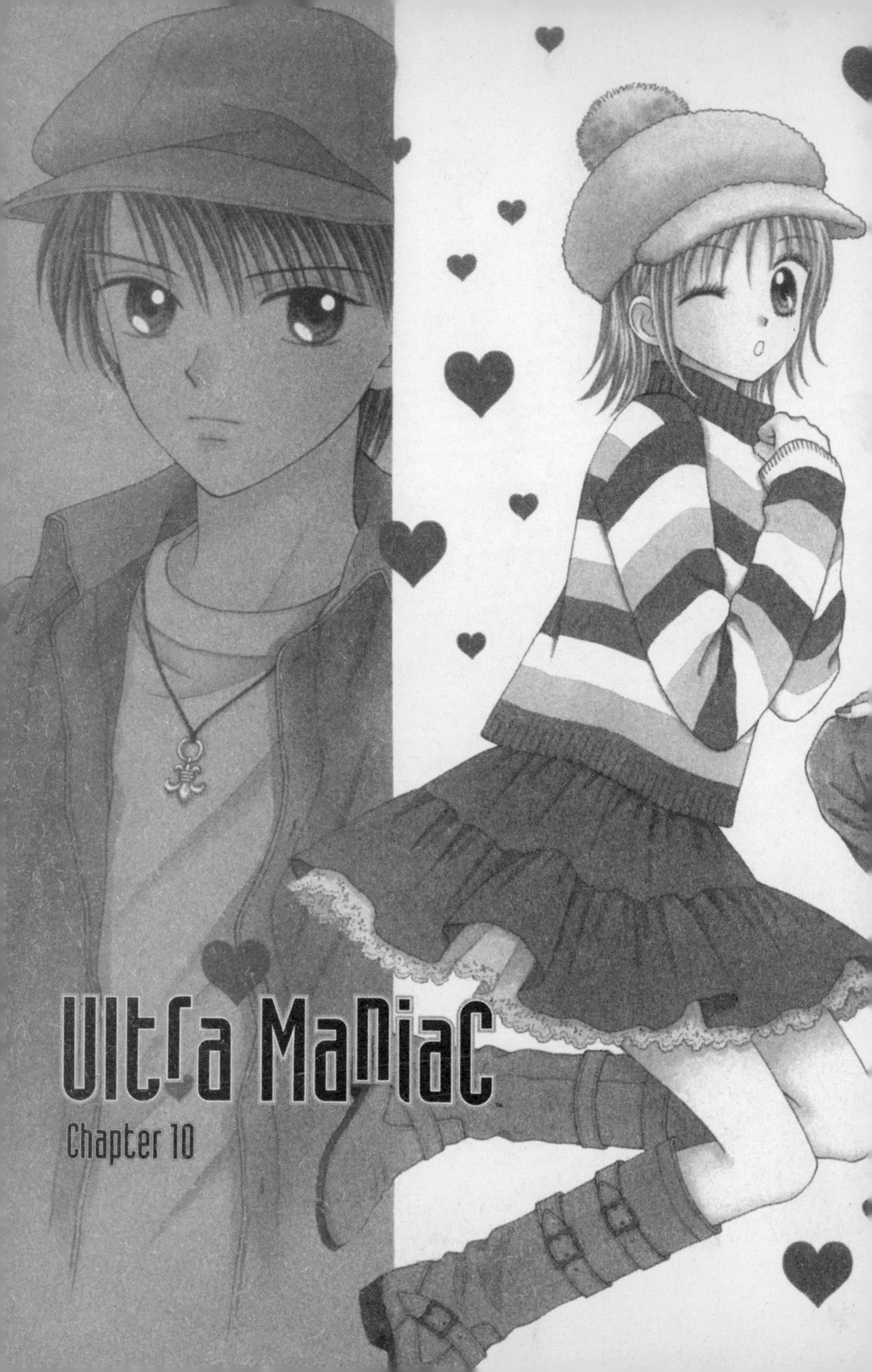
Ultra Maniac
Chapter 10

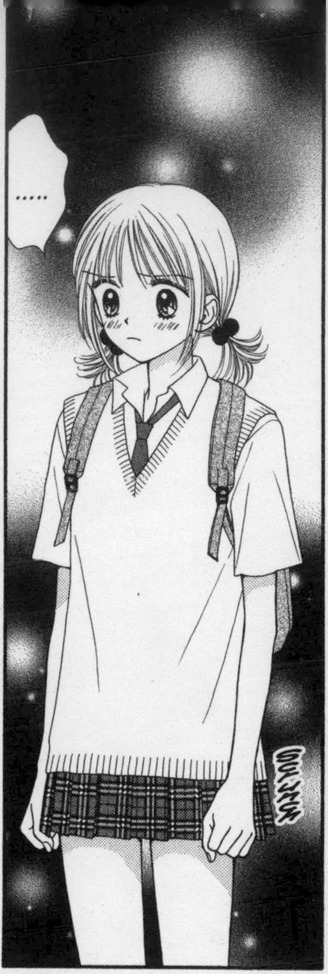
.....

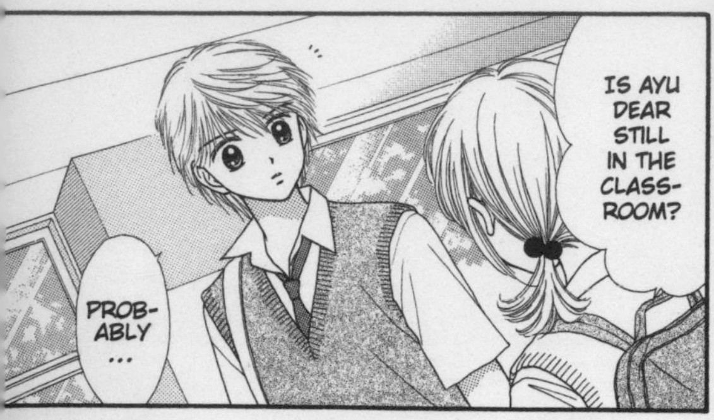
IS AYU DEAR STILL IN THE CLASS-ROOM?
...
PROB-ABLY ...

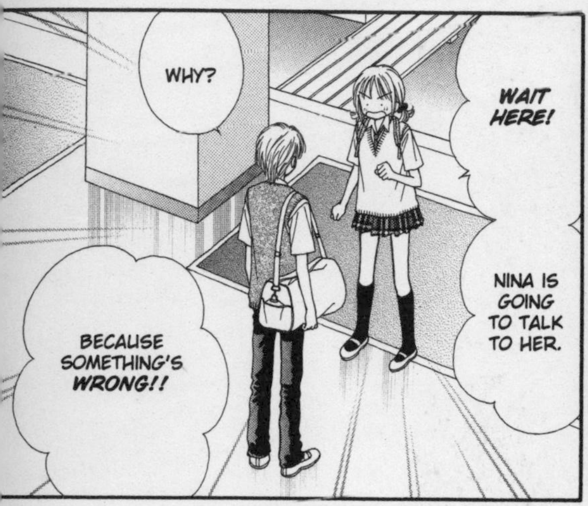
WAIT HERE!
NINA IS GOING TO TALK TO HER.
WHY?
BECAUSE SOMETHING'S *WRONG!!*

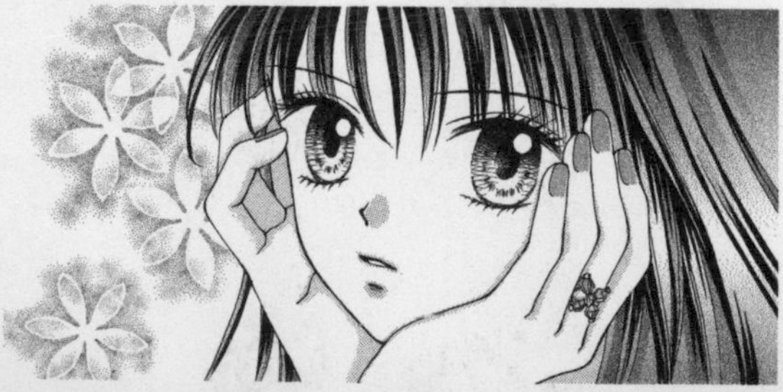

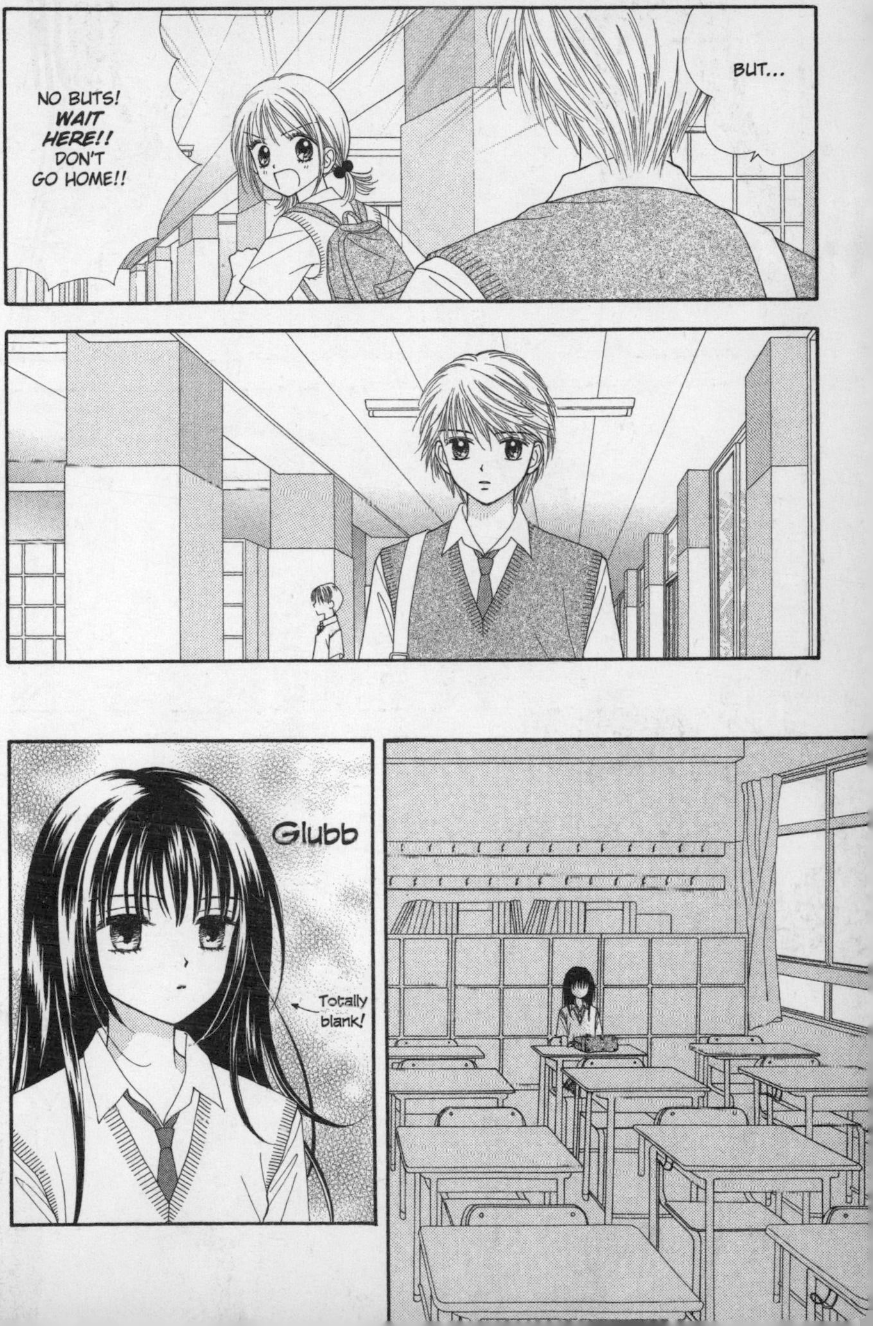
BUT...
NO BUTS! WAIT HERE!! DON'T GO HOME!!
Glubb
Totally blank!

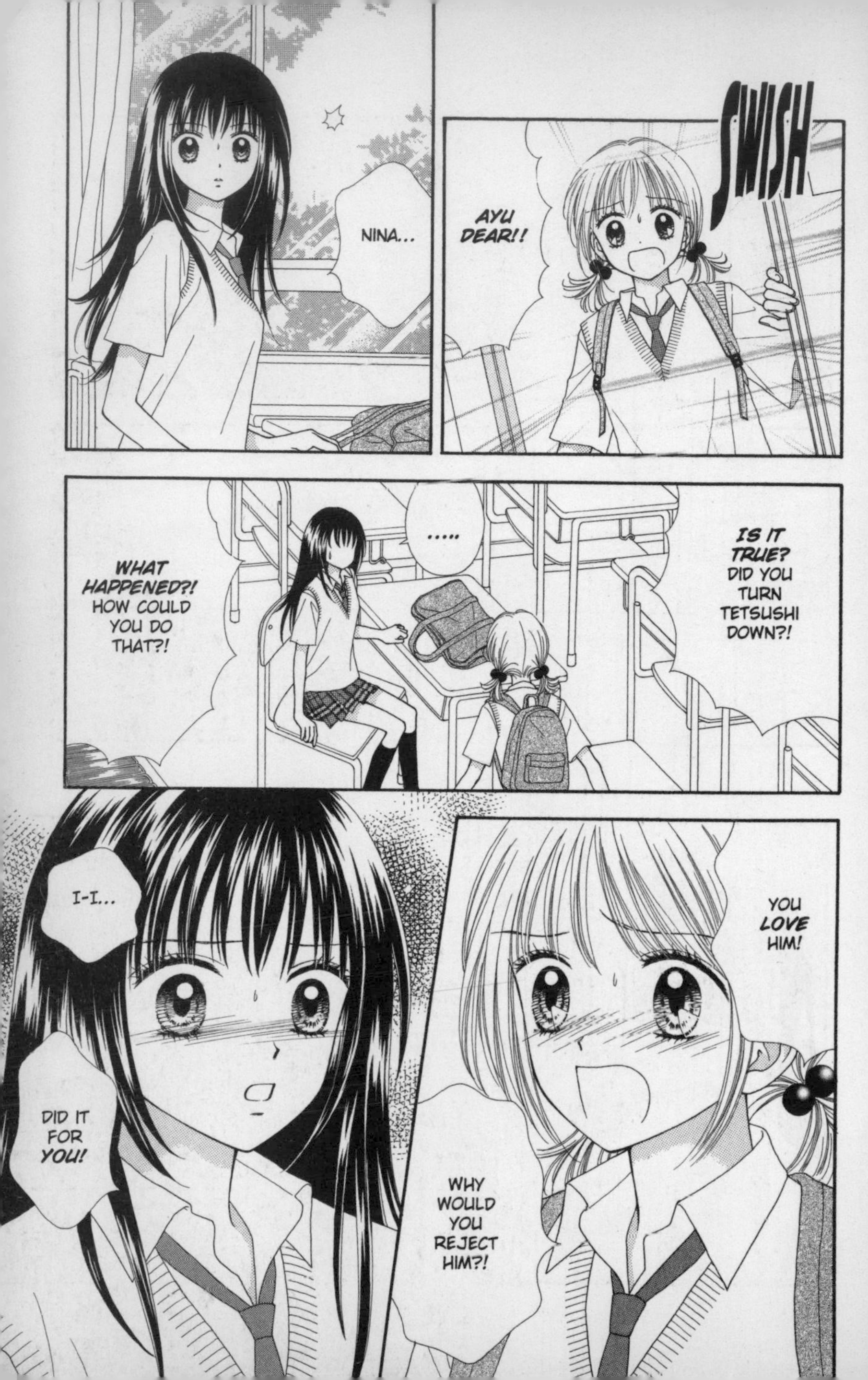
SWISH
AYU DEAR!!
NINA...
IS IT TRUE? DID YOU TURN TETSUSHI DOWN?!
.....
WHAT HAPPENED?! HOW COULD YOU DO THAT?!
YOU LOVE HIM!
WHY WOULD YOU REJECT HIM?!
I-I...
DID IT FOR YOU!

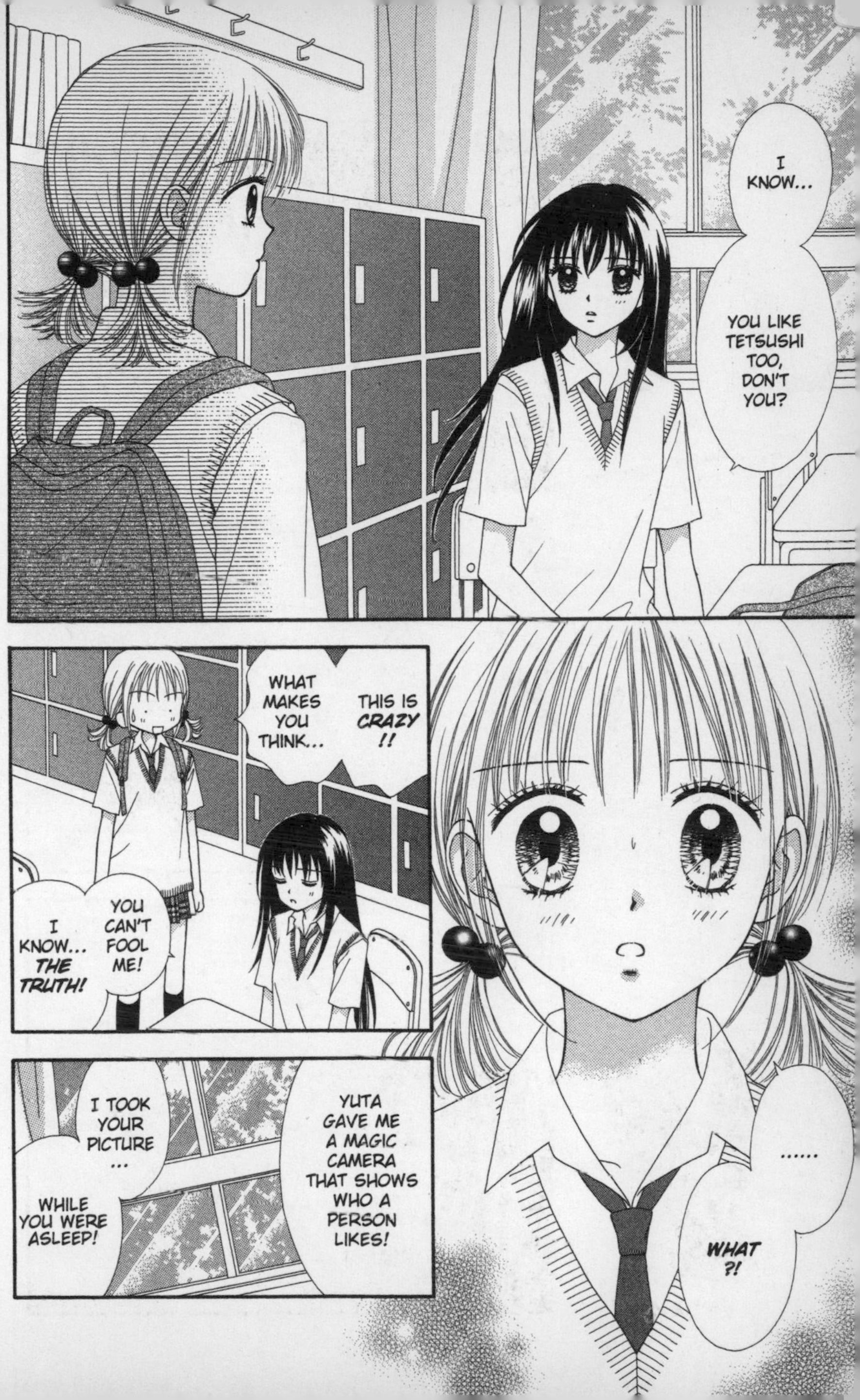
I KNOW...
YOU LIKE TETSUSHI TOO, DON'T YOU?
......
WHAT ?!
THIS IS CRAZY !!
WHAT MAKES YOU THINK...
YOU CAN'T FOOL ME!
I KNOW... THE TRUTH!
YUTA GAVE ME A MAGIC CAMERA THAT SHOWS WHO A PERSON LIKES!
I TOOK YOUR PICTURE ...
WHILE YOU WERE ASLEEP!

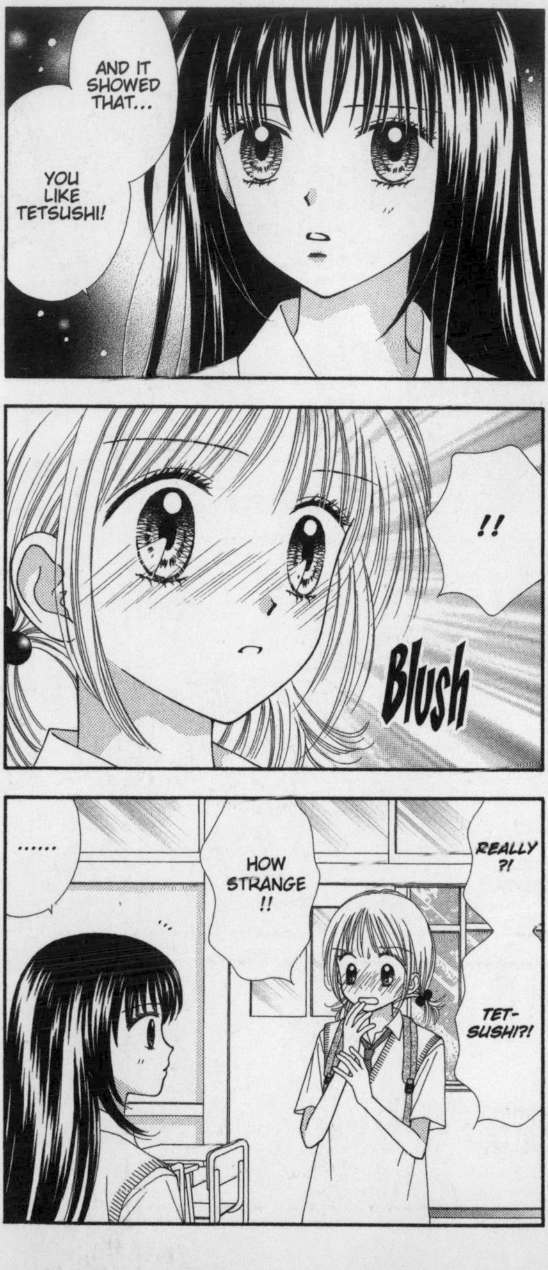
AND IT SHOWED THAT...
YOU LIKE TETSUSHI!
!!
Blush
REALLY ?!
TET-SUSHI?!
HOW STRANGE !!
......
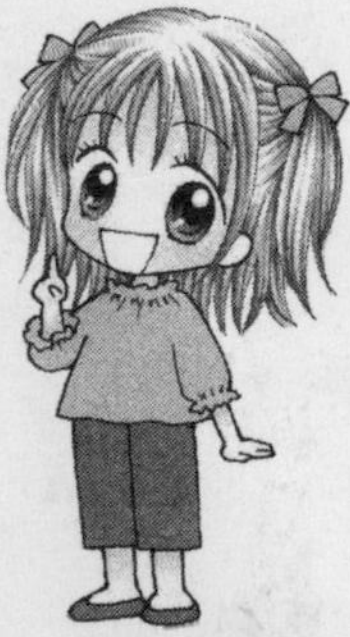

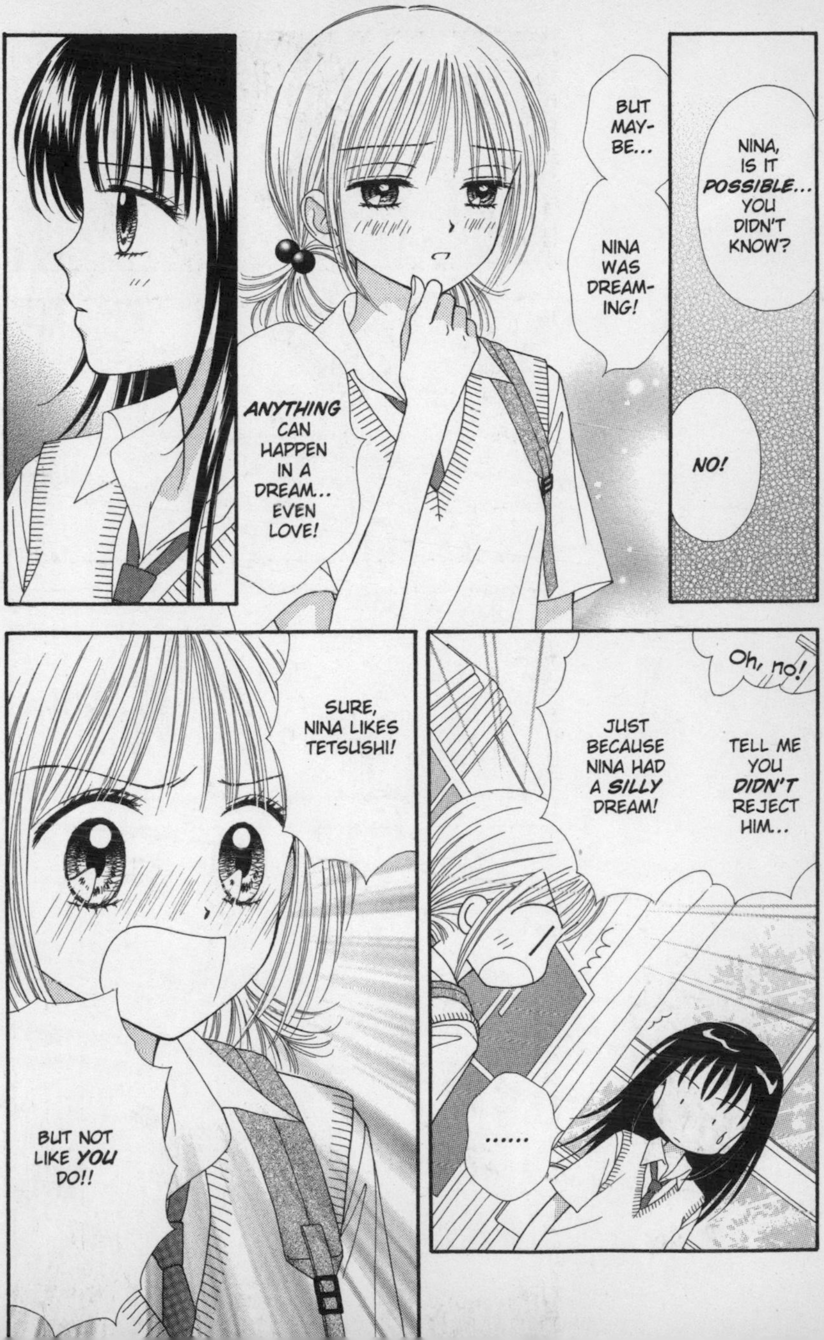
NINA, IS IT POSSIBLE... YOU DIDN'T KNOW?
NO!
BUT MAY-BE...
NINA WAS DREAM-ING!
ANYTHING CAN HAPPEN IN A DREAM... EVEN LOVE!
Oh, no!
TELL ME YOU DIDN'T REJECT HIM...
JUST BECAUSE NINA HAD A SILLY DREAM!
......
SURE, NINA LIKES TETSUSHI!
BUT NOT LIKE YOU DO!!

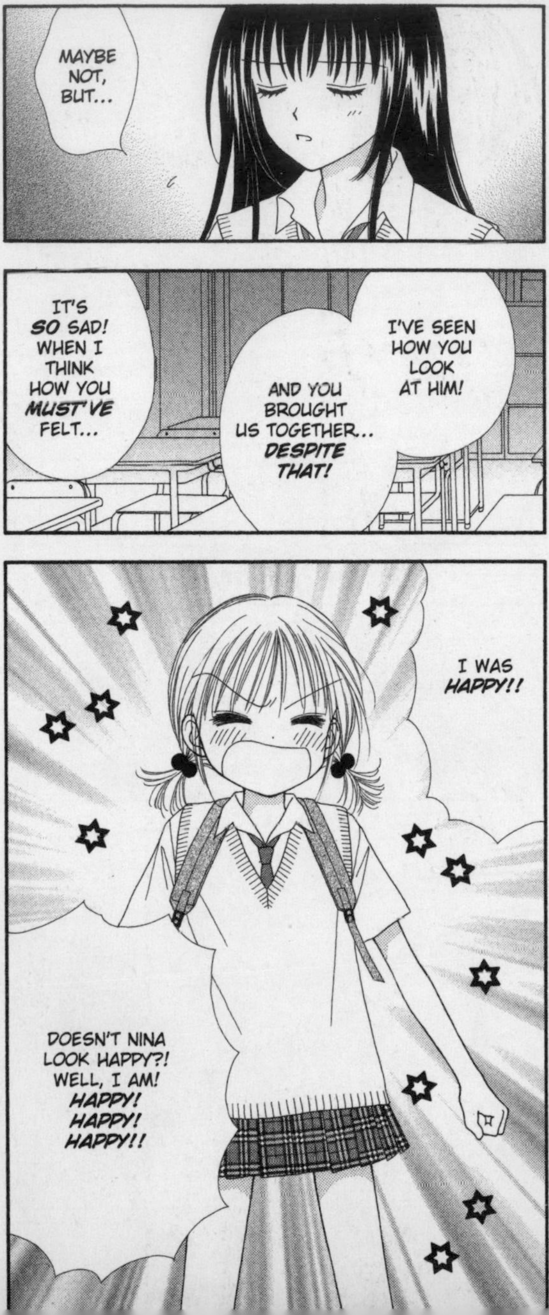
MAYBE NOT, BUT...
I'VE SEEN HOW YOU LOOK AT HIM!
AND YOU BROUGHT US TOGETHER... DESPITE THAT!
IT'S SO SAD! WHEN I THINK HOW YOU MUST'VE FELT...
I WAS HAPPY!!
DOESN'T NINA LOOK HAPPY?! WELL, I AM! HAPPY! HAPPY! HAPPY!!

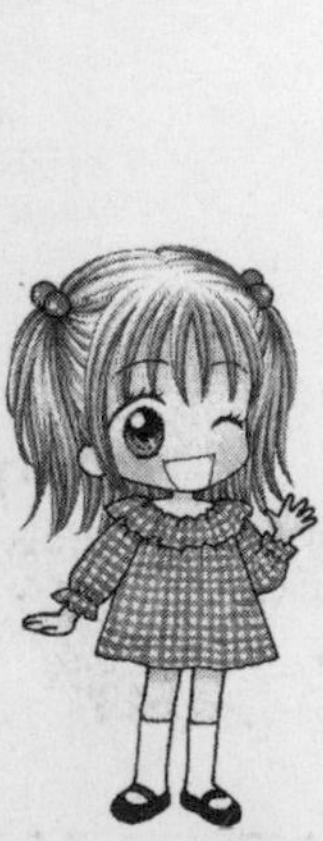

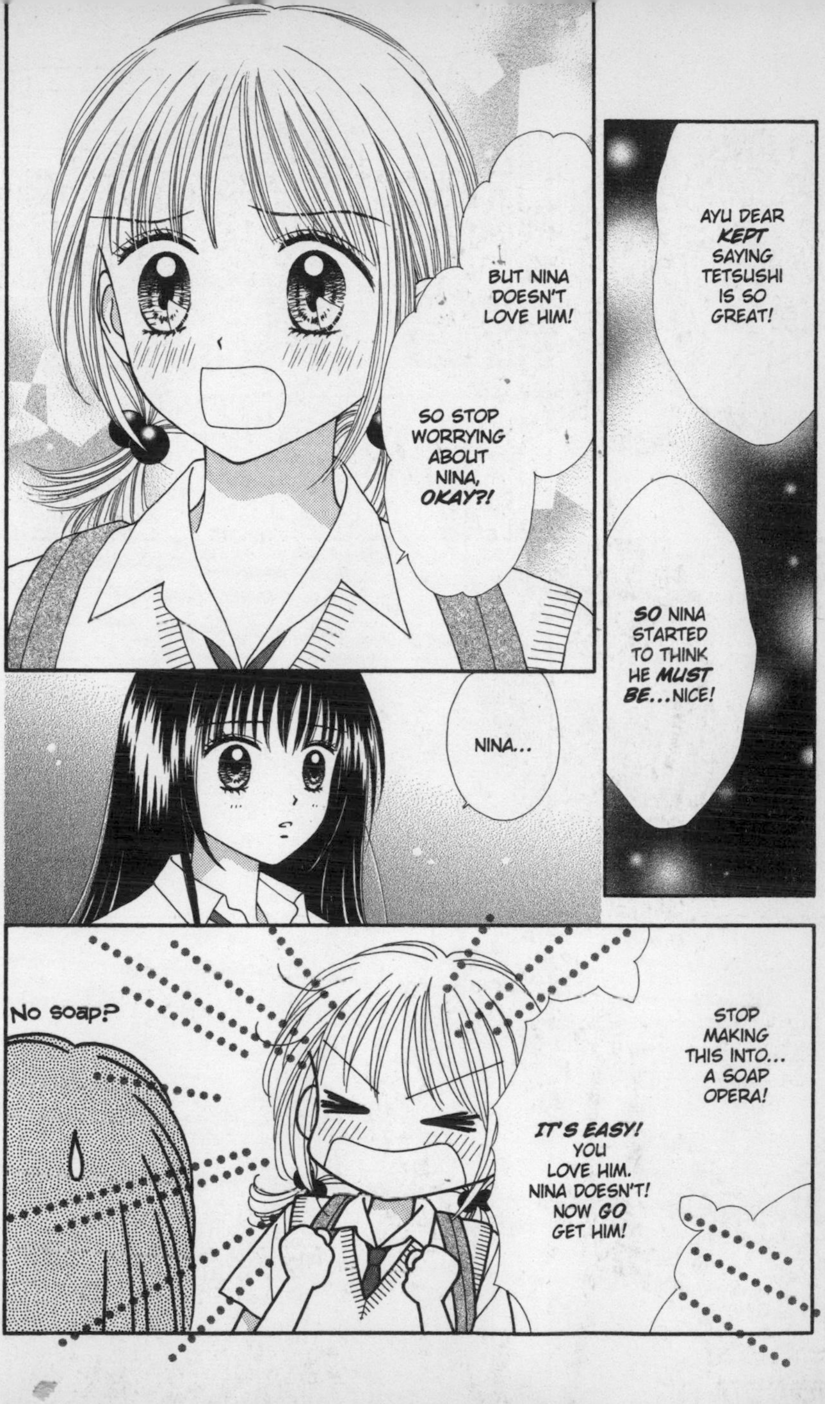
AYU DEAR ***KEPT*** SAYING TETSUSHI IS SO GREAT!
SO NINA STARTED TO THINK HE ***MUST BE***...NICE!
BUT NINA DOESN'T LOVE HIM!
SO STOP WORRYING ABOUT NINA, ***OKAY?!***
NINA...
STOP MAKING THIS INTO... A SOAP OPERA!
IT'S EASY! YOU LOVE HIM. NINA DOESN'T! NOW ***GO*** GET HIM!
No soap?

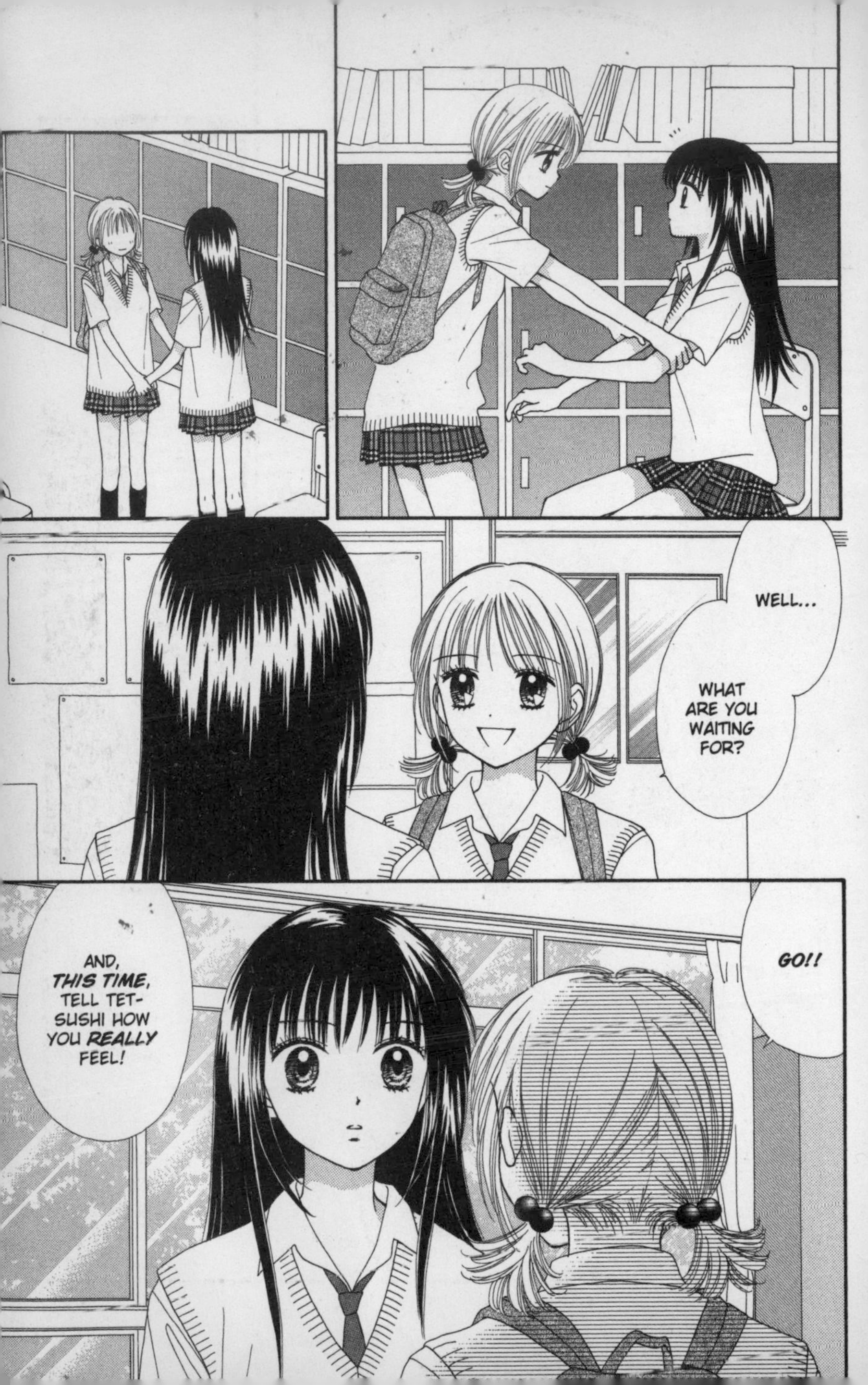
WELL...
WHAT ARE YOU WAITING FOR?
GO!!
AND, *THIS TIME,* TELL TET-SUSHI HOW YOU *REALLY* FEEL!

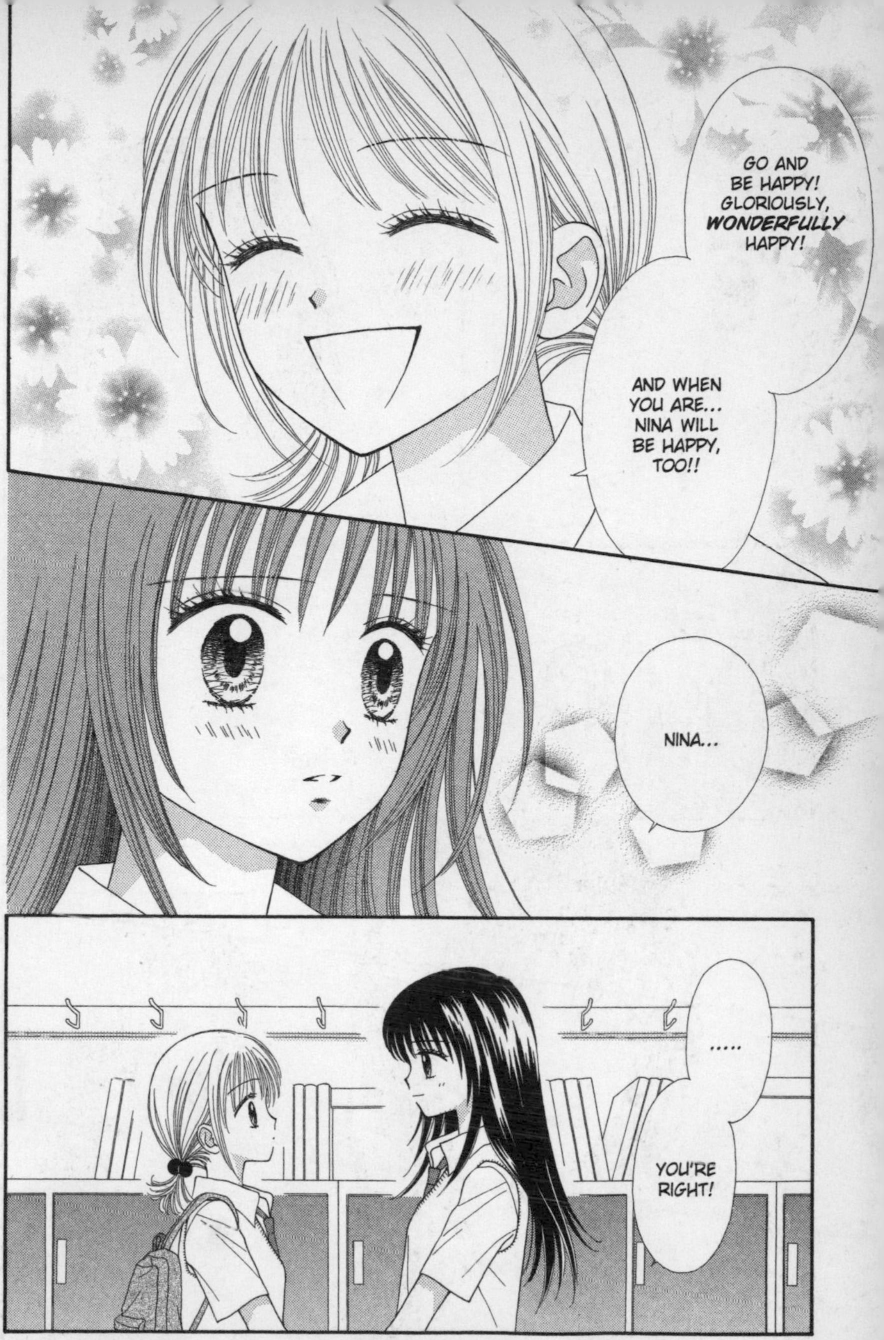
GO AND BE HAPPY! GLORIOUSLY, **WONDERFULLY** HAPPY!
AND WHEN YOU ARE... NINA WILL BE HAPPY, TOO!!
NINA...
.....
YOU'RE RIGHT!

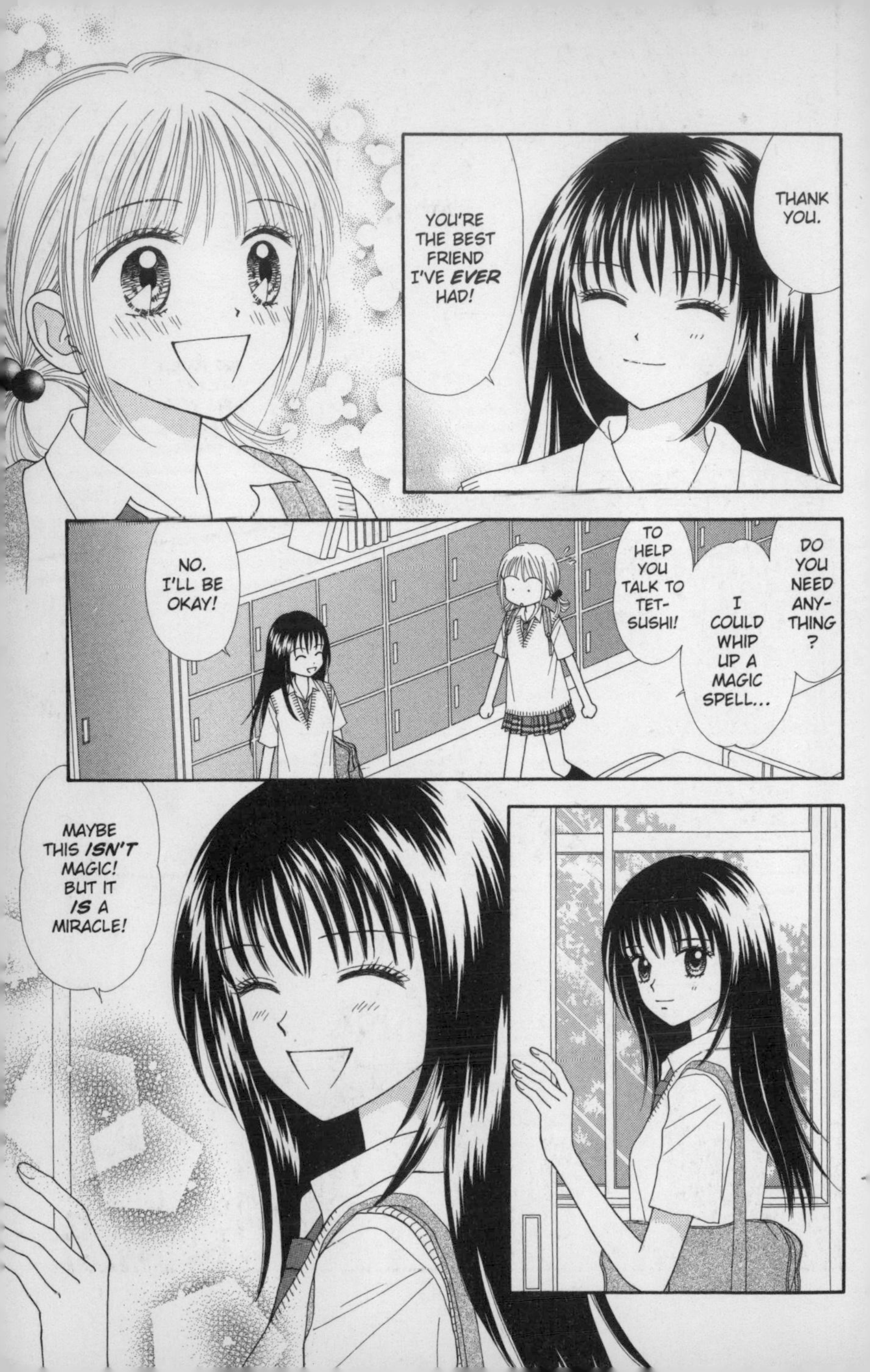
THANK YOU.
YOU'RE THE BEST FRIEND I'VE EVER HAD!
DO YOU NEED ANYTHING?
I COULD WHIP UP A MAGIC SPELL...
TO HELP YOU TALK TO TET-SUSHI!
NO. I'LL BE OKAY!
MAYBE THIS ISN'T MAGIC! BUT IT IS A MIRACLE!

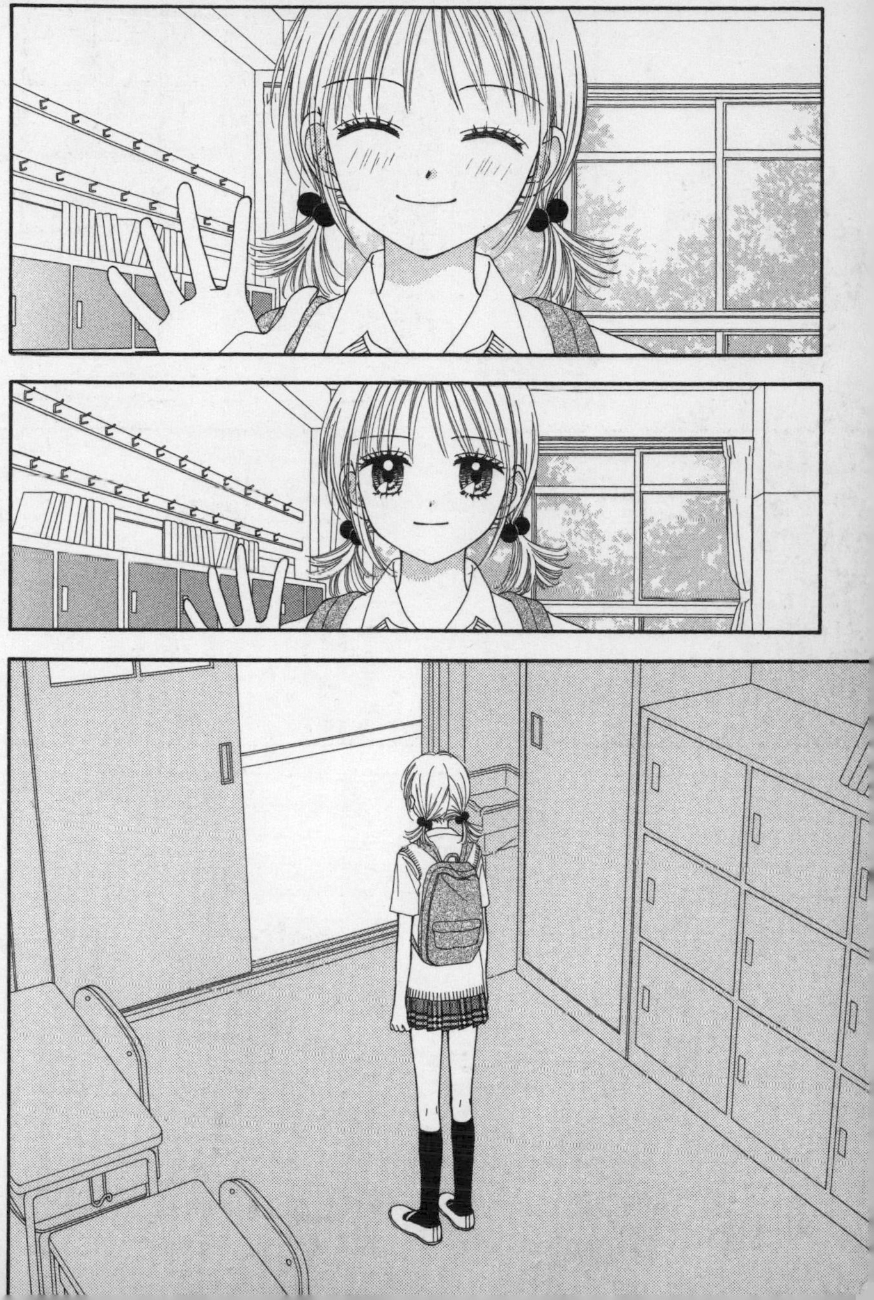

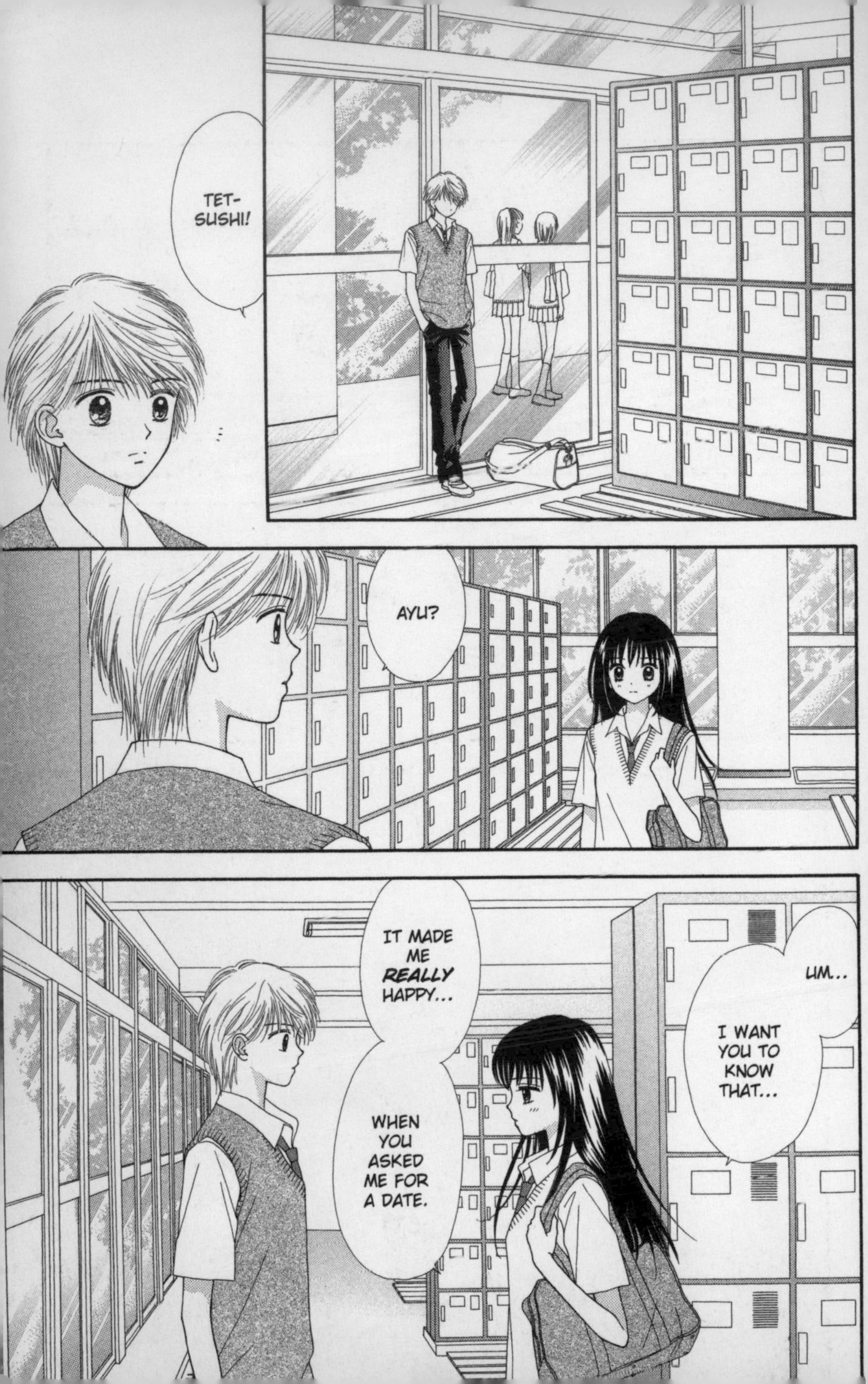
TET-SUSHI!
...
AYU?
UM...
I WANT YOU TO KNOW THAT...
IT MADE ME REALLY HAPPY...
WHEN YOU ASKED ME FOR A DATE.

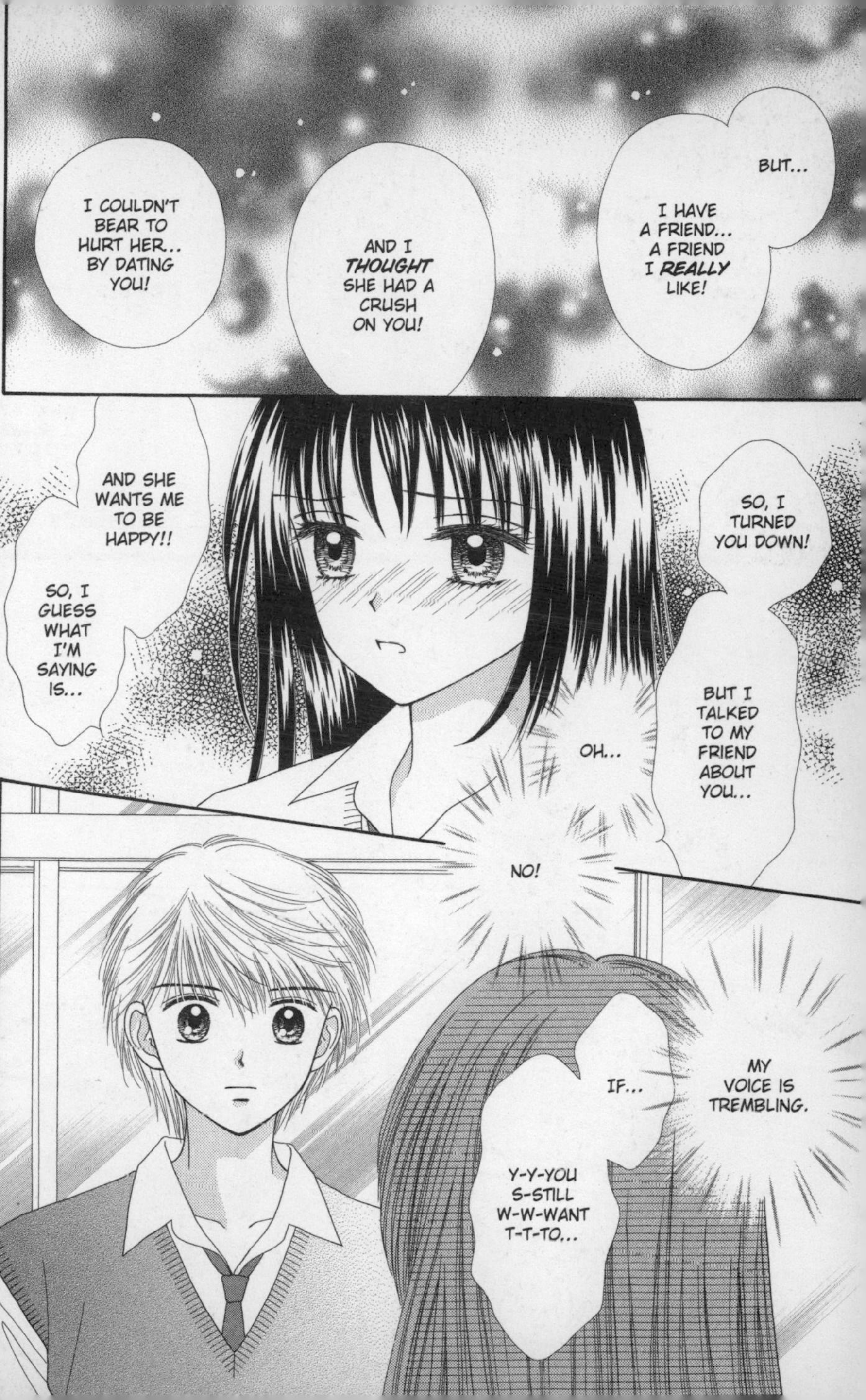
BUT...
I HAVE A FRIEND... A FRIEND I *REALLY* LIKE!
AND I *THOUGHT* SHE HAD A CRUSH ON YOU!
I COULDN'T BEAR TO HURT HER... BY DATING YOU!
SO, I TURNED YOU DOWN!
BUT I TALKED TO MY FRIEND ABOUT YOU...
OH...
AND SHE WANTS ME TO BE HAPPY!!
SO, I GUESS WHAT I'M SAYING IS...
NO!
MY VOICE IS TREMBLING.
IF...
Y-Y-YOU S-STILL W-W-WANT T-T-TO...

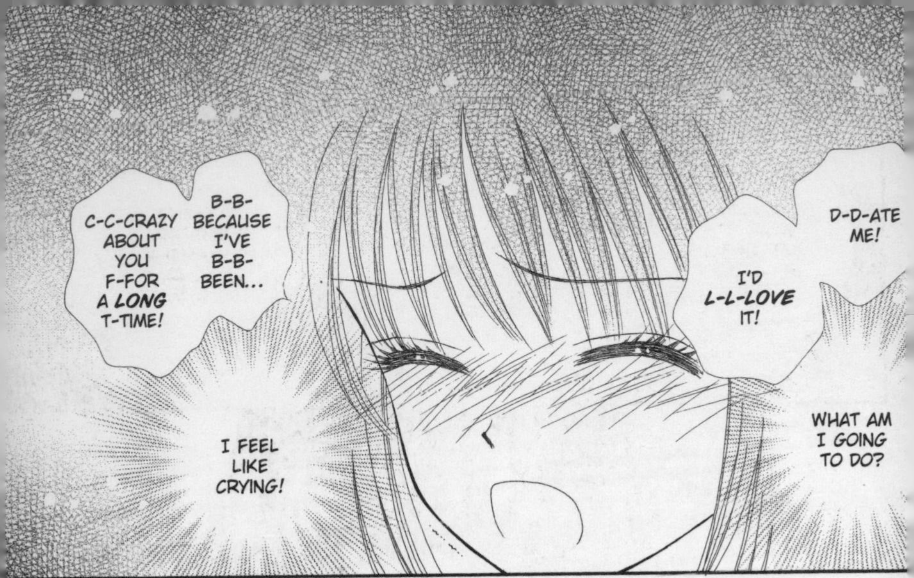
D-D-ATE ME!
I'D L-L-LOVE IT!
WHAT AM I GOING TO DO?
B-B-BECAUSE I'VE B-B-BEEN...
C-C-CRAZY ABOUT YOU F-FOR A LONG T-TIME!
I FEEL LIKE CRYING!

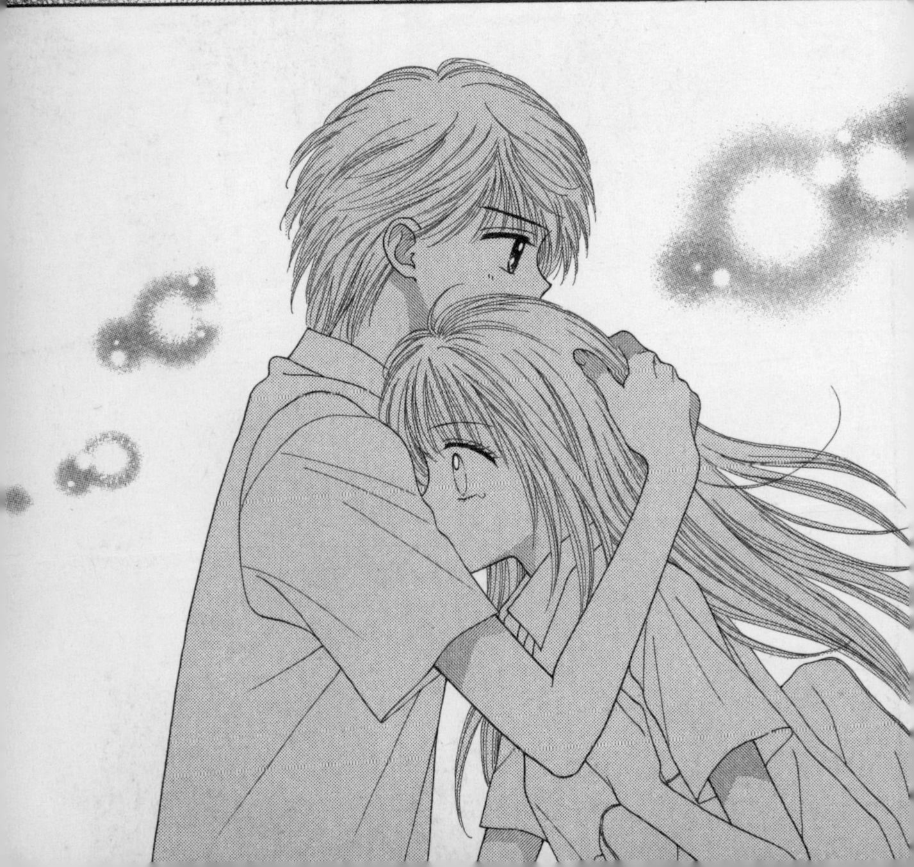

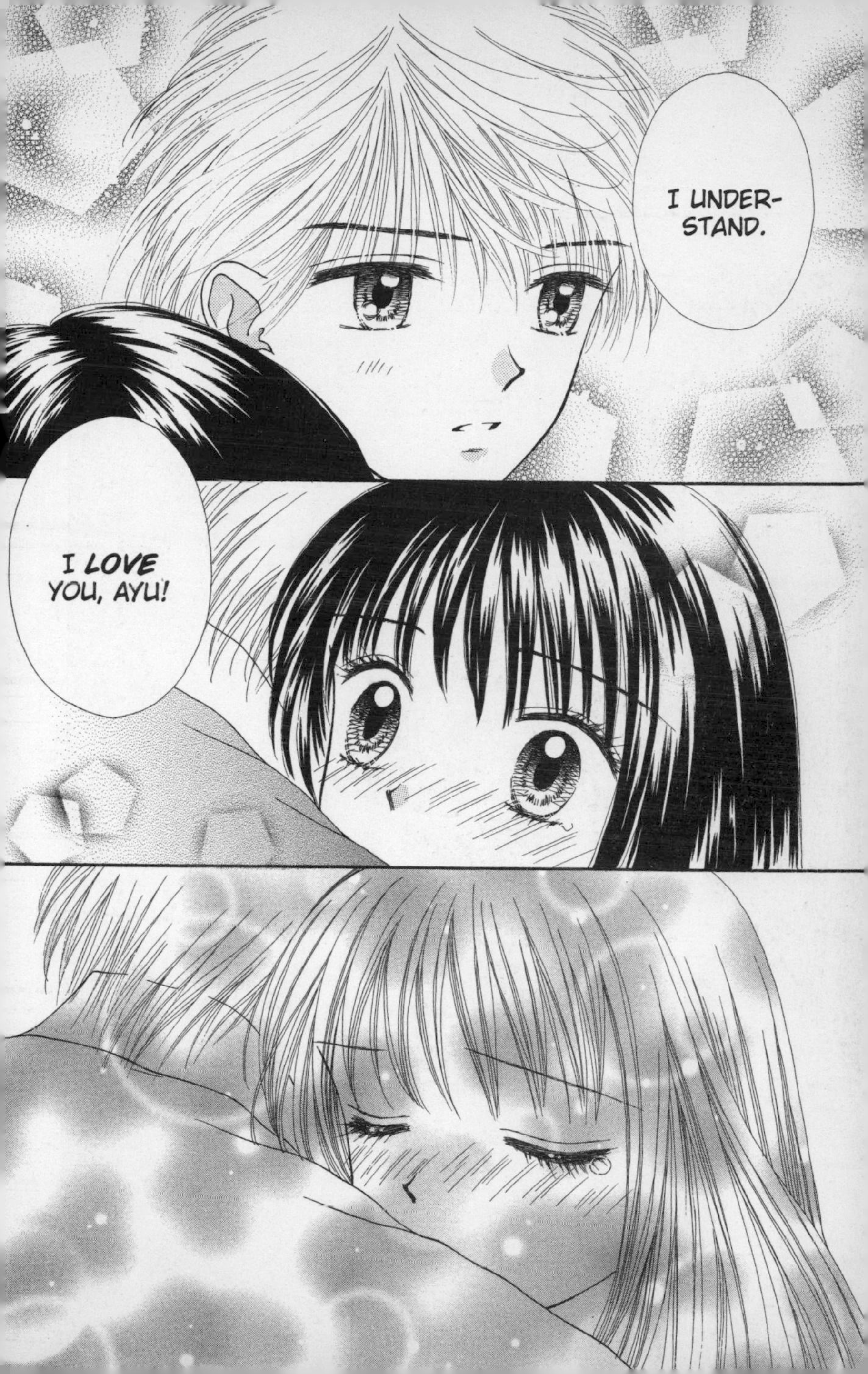
I UNDER-STAND.
I LOVE YOU, AYU!

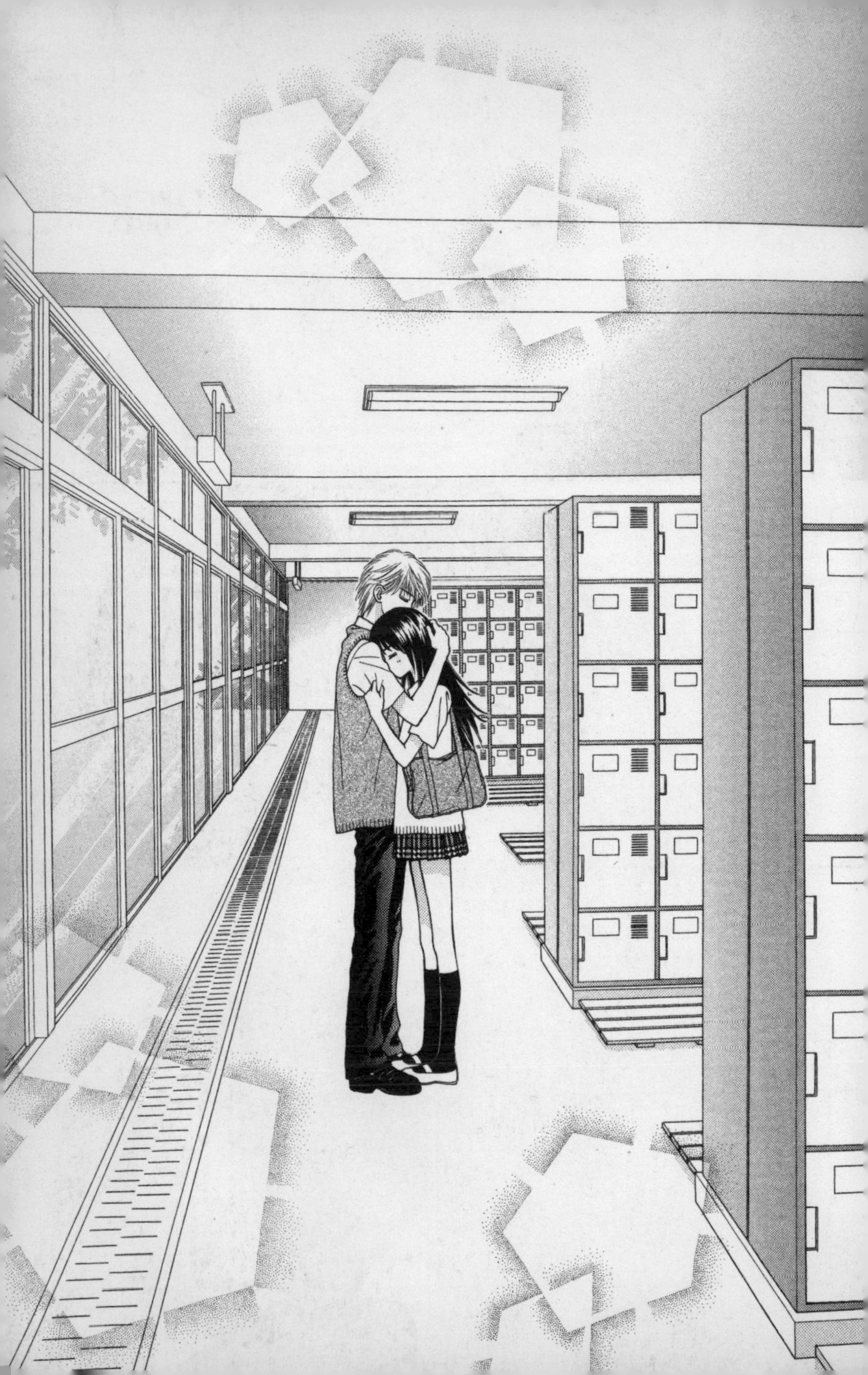

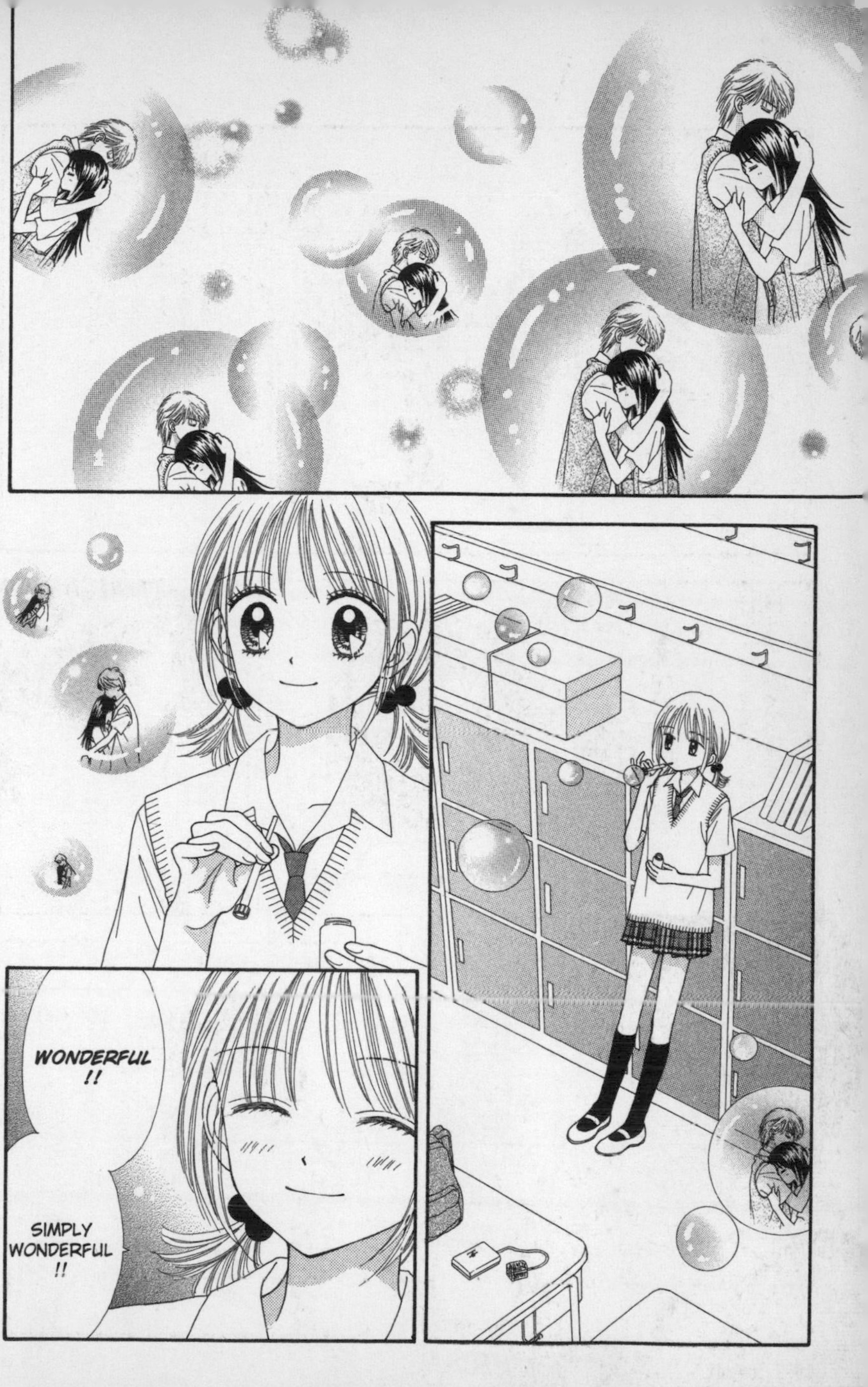
WONDERFUL !!
SIMPLY WONDERFUL !!

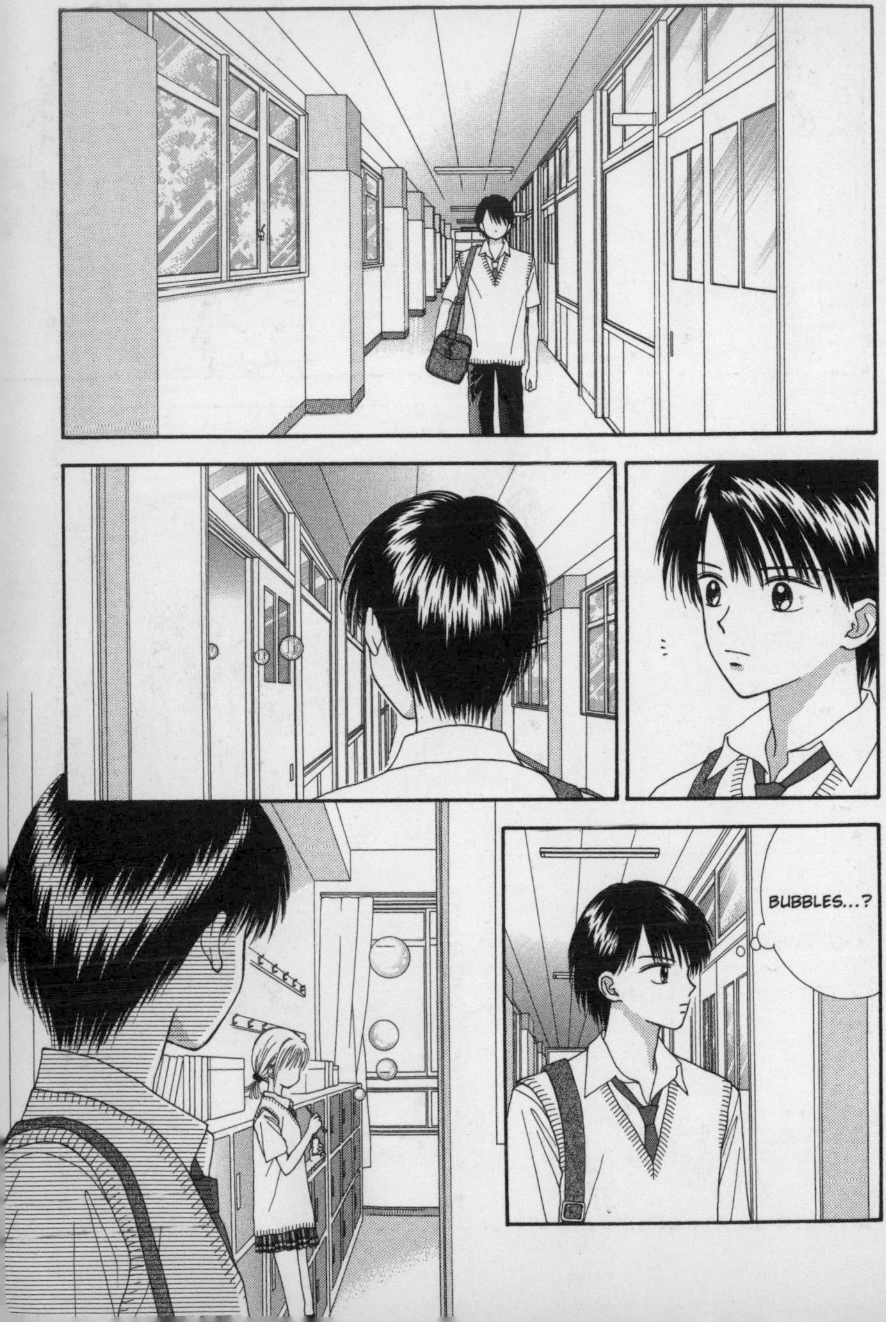
BUBBLES...?

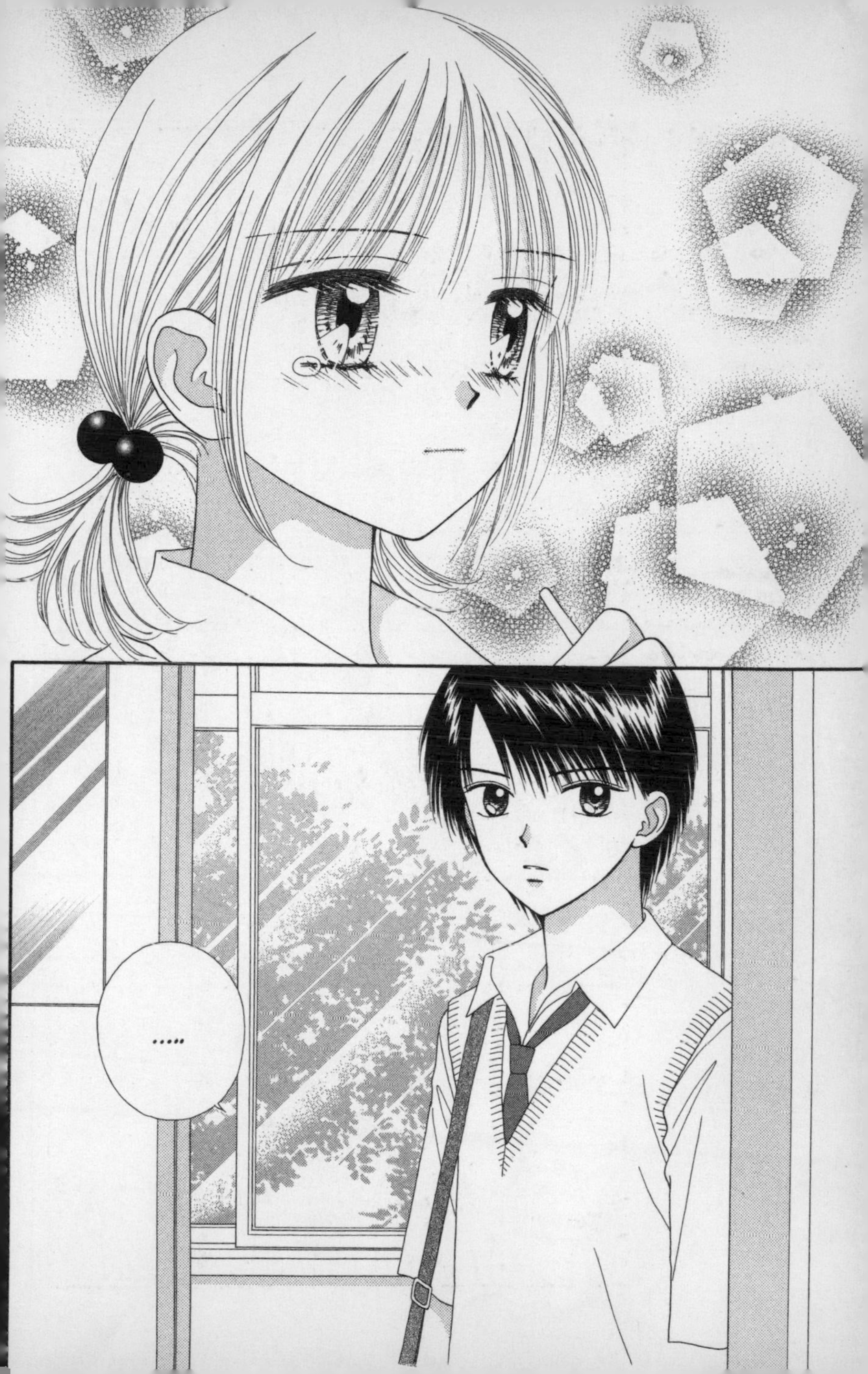
.....

FREE TALK 5

So, how did you like Ultra Maniac Volume Two? Volume One had a sort of "magic amuck" feel to it. But Volume Two set aside the magic to concentrate more on the romance. I'd love to hear what you think. Write to me at:

Ultra Maniac
c/o Shojo Beat
VIZ Media
P.O. Box 77010
San Francisco, CA 94107

See you in Volume Three!

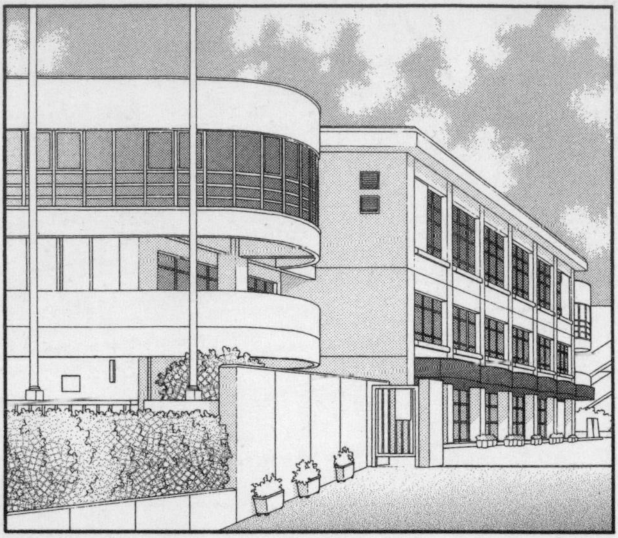

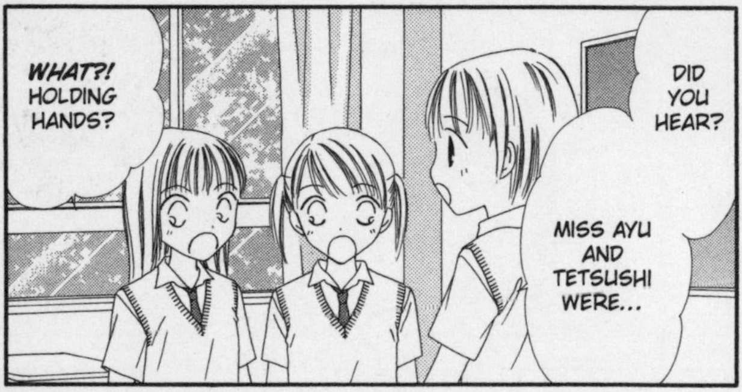

DID YOU HEAR?
MISS AYU AND TETSUSHI WERE...
WHAT?! HOLDING HANDS?

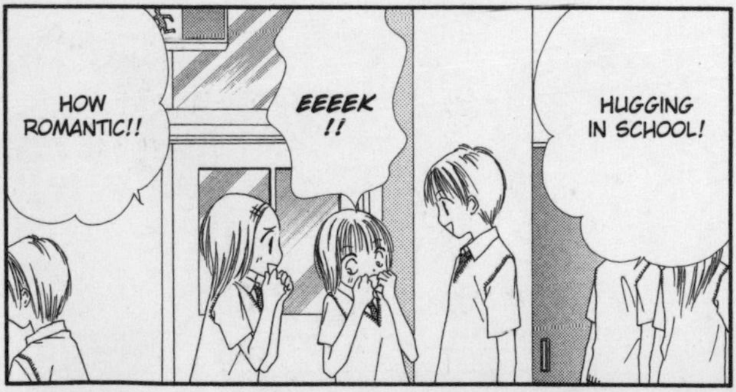

HUGGING IN SCHOOL!
EEEEK !!
HOW ROMANTIC!!

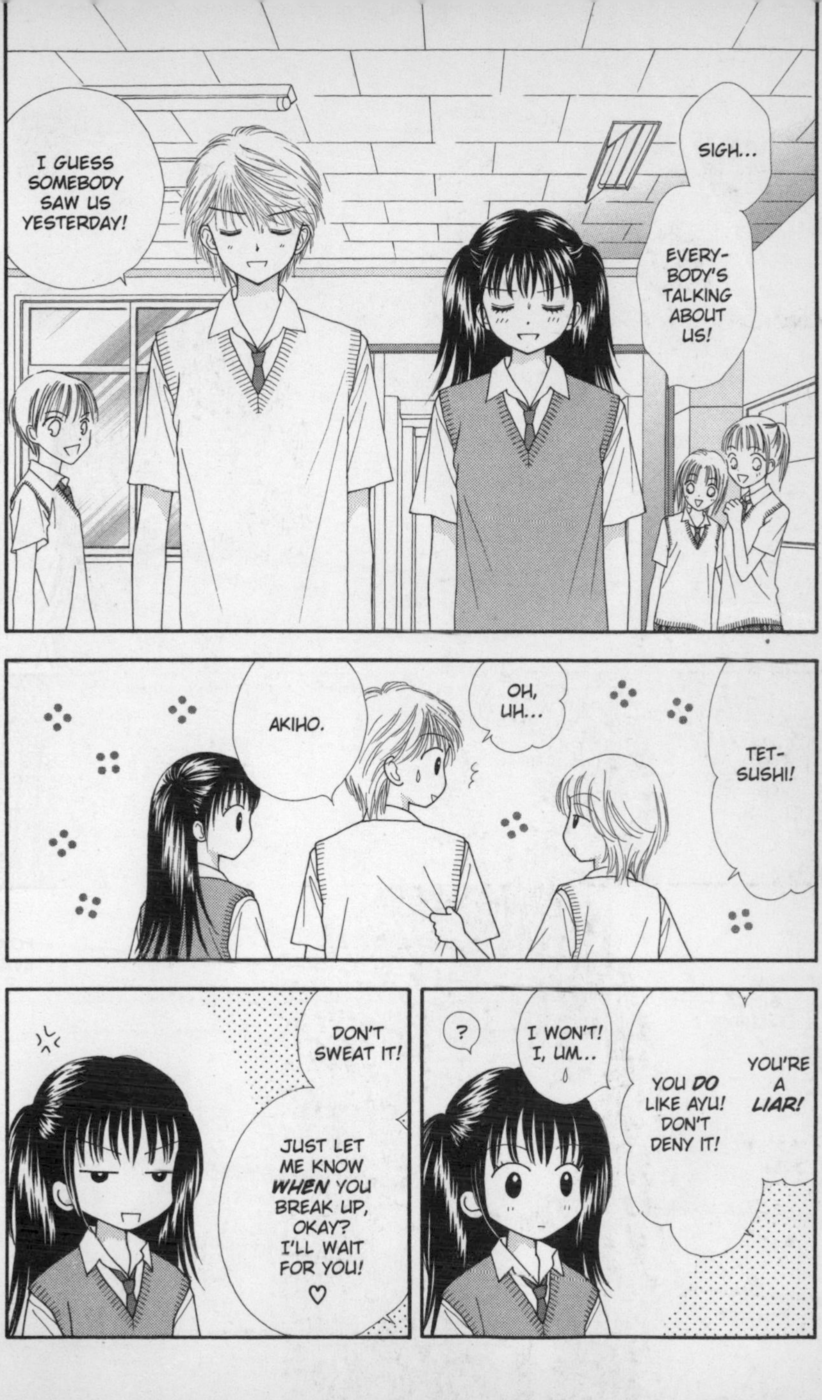
SIGH...
EVERY-BODY'S TALKING ABOUT US!
I GUESS SOMEBODY SAW US YESTERDAY!
TET-SUSHI!
OH, UH...
AKIHO.
YOU'RE A LIAR!
YOU DO LIKE AYU! DON'T DENY IT!
I WON'T! I, UM...
?
DON'T SWEAT IT!
JUST LET ME KNOW WHEN YOU BREAK UP, OKAY? I'LL WAIT FOR YOU! ♡

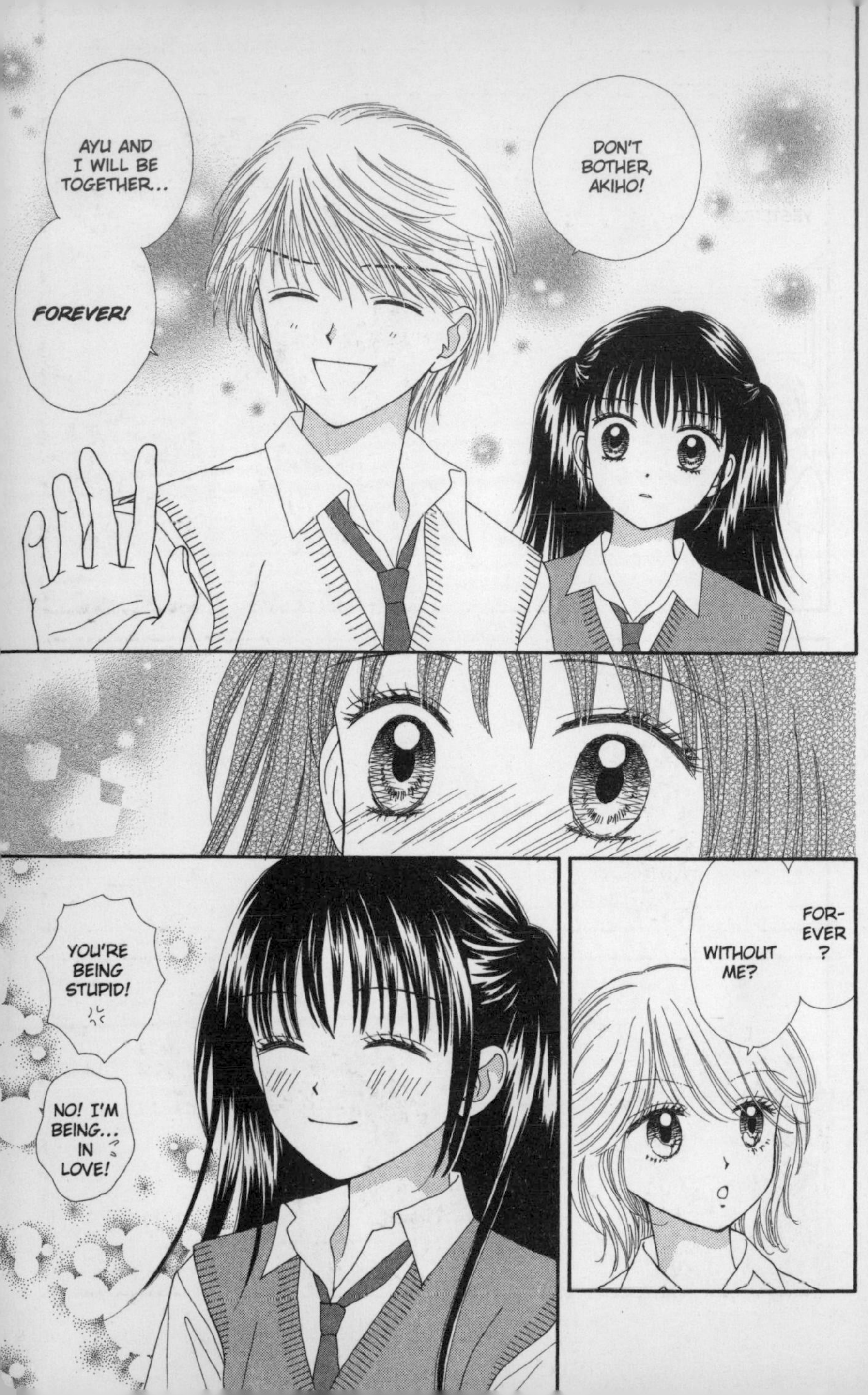
DON'T BOTHER, AKIHO!
AYU AND I WILL BE TOGETHER...
FOREVER!
FOR-EVER?
WITHOUT ME?
YOU'RE BEING STUPID!
NO! I'M BEING... IN LOVE!

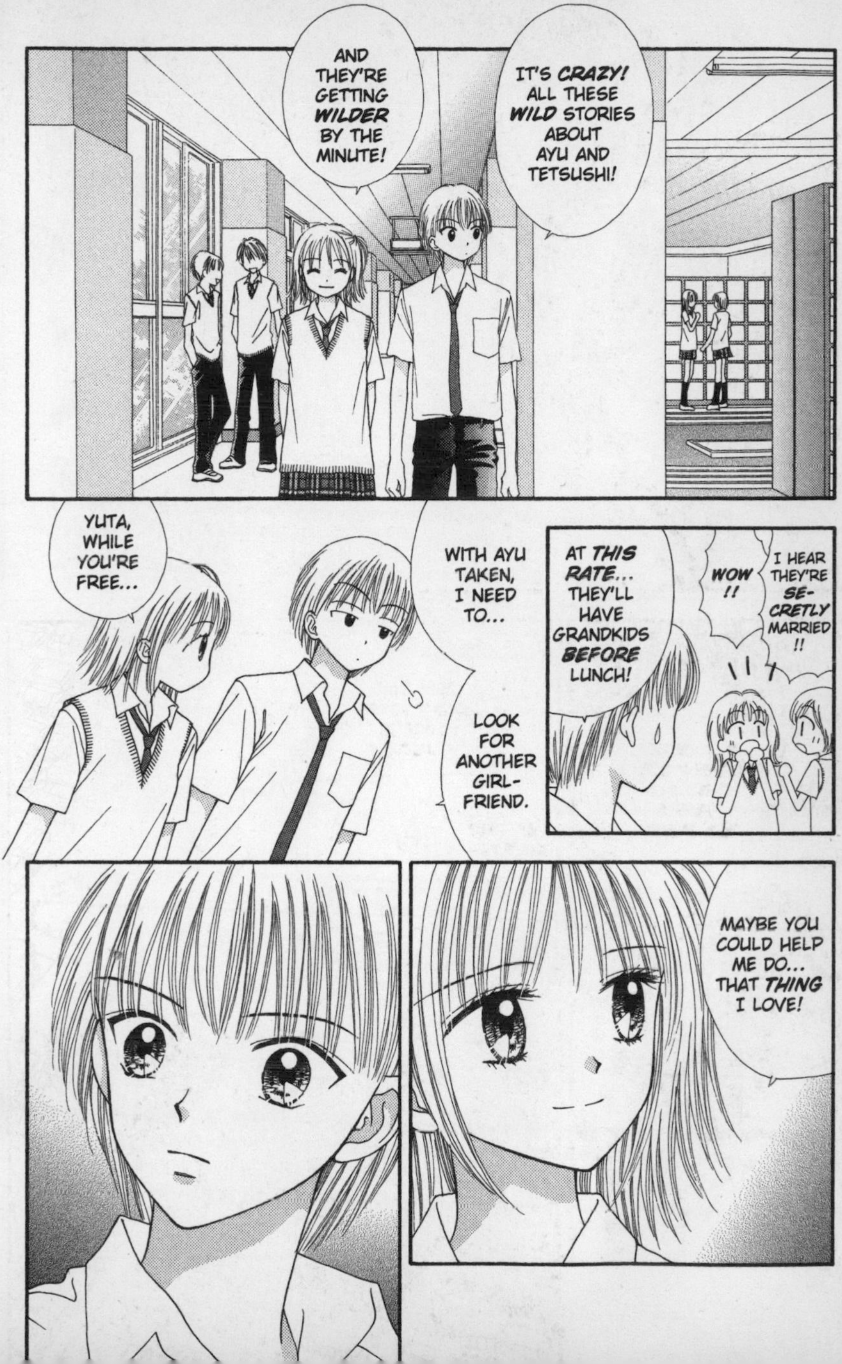
IT'S CRAZY! ALL THESE WILD STORIES ABOUT AYU AND TETSUSHI!
AND THEY'RE GETTING WILDER BY THE MINUTE!
I HEAR THEY'RE SE-CRETLY MARRIED !!
WOW !!
AT THIS RATE... THEY'LL HAVE GRANDKIDS BEFORE LUNCH!
WITH AYU TAKEN, I NEED TO...
LOOK FOR ANOTHER GIRL-FRIEND.
YUTA, WHILE YOU'RE FREE...
MAYBE YOU COULD HELP ME DO... THAT THING I LOVE!

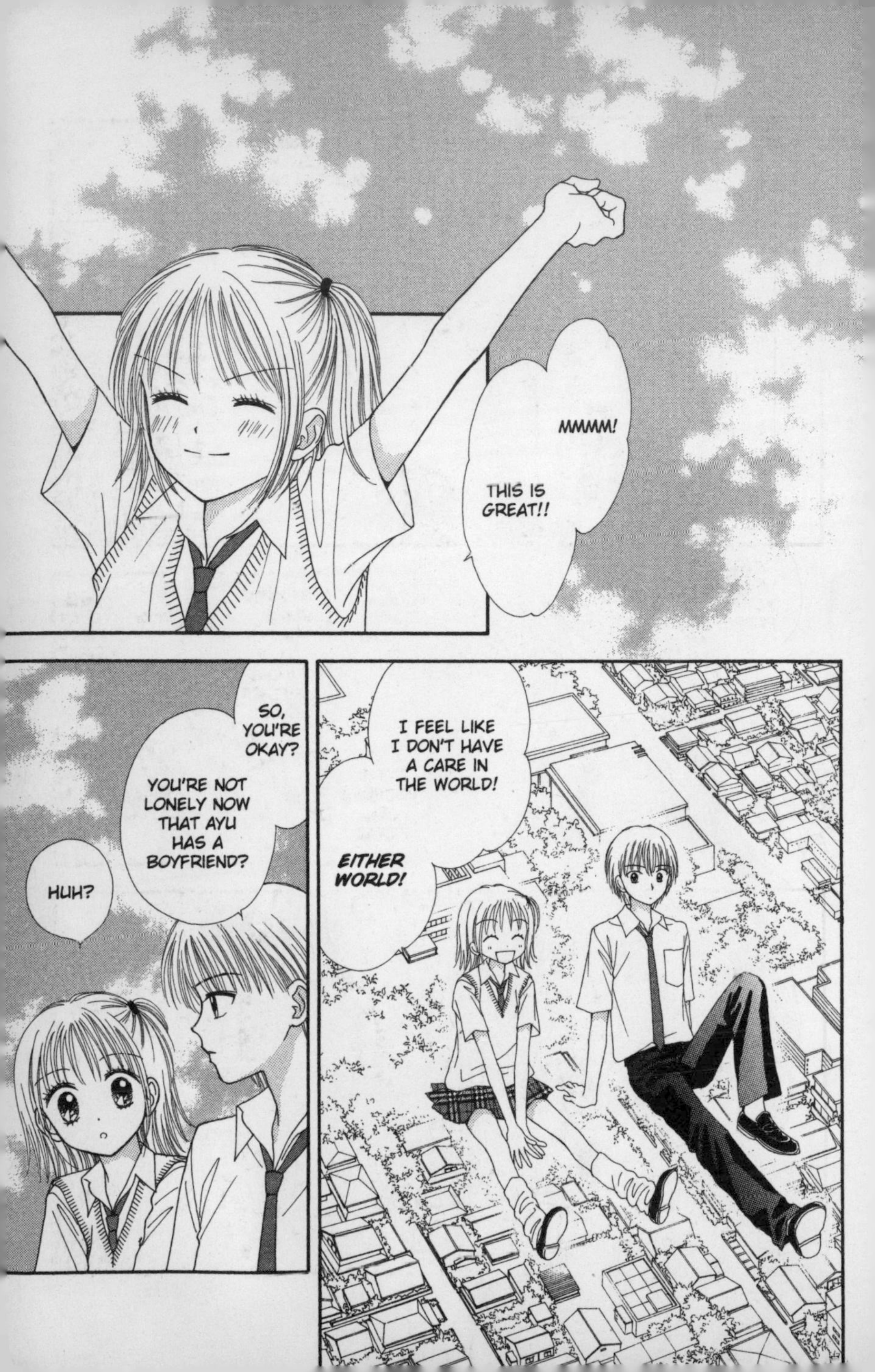
MMMM!
THIS IS GREAT!!
I FEEL LIKE I DON'T HAVE A CARE IN THE WORLD!
EITHER WORLD!
SO, YOU'RE OKAY?
YOU'RE NOT LONELY NOW THAT AYU HAS A BOYFRIEND?
HUH?

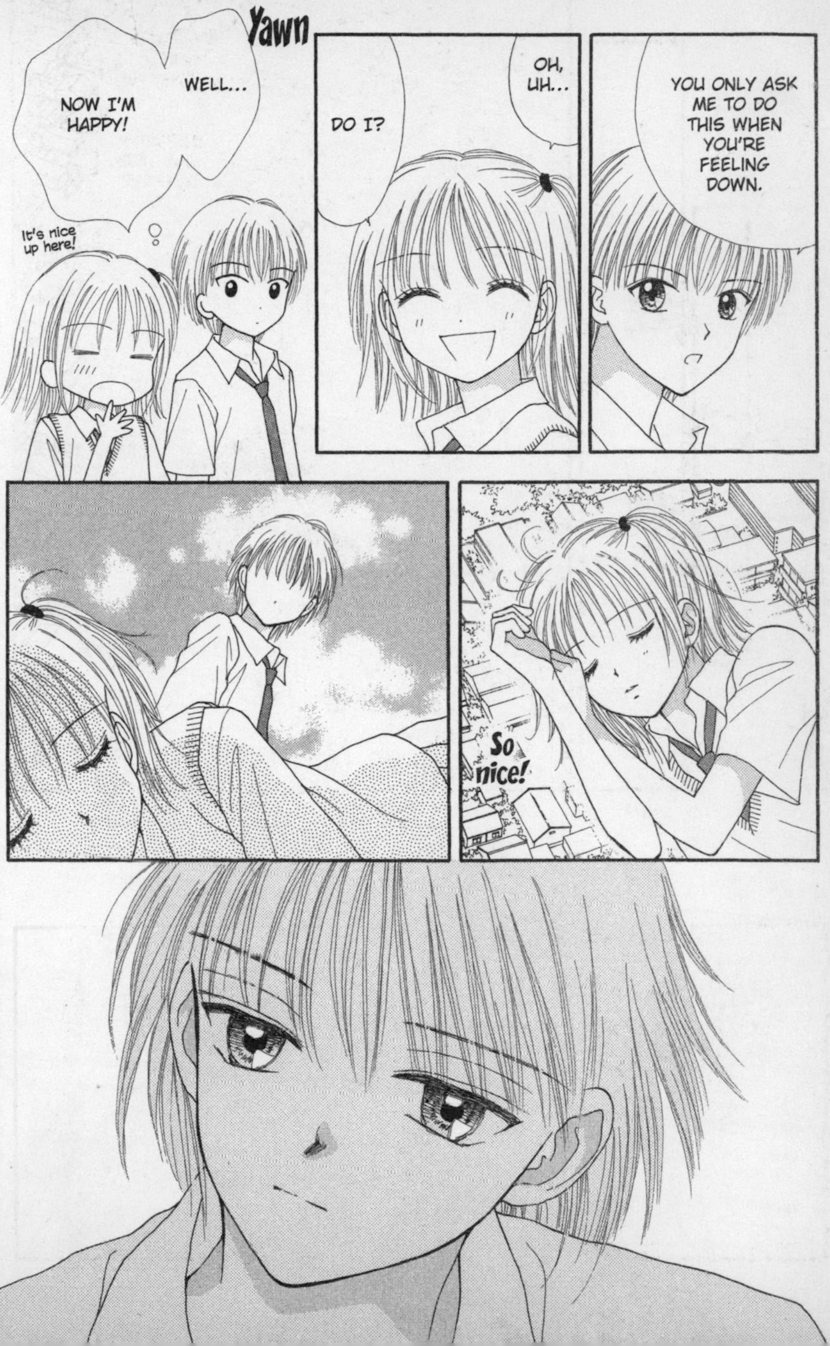
YOU ONLY ASK ME TO DO THIS WHEN YOU'RE FEELING DOWN.
OH, UH...
DO I?
Yawn
WELL...
NOW I'M HAPPY!
It's nice up here!
So nice!

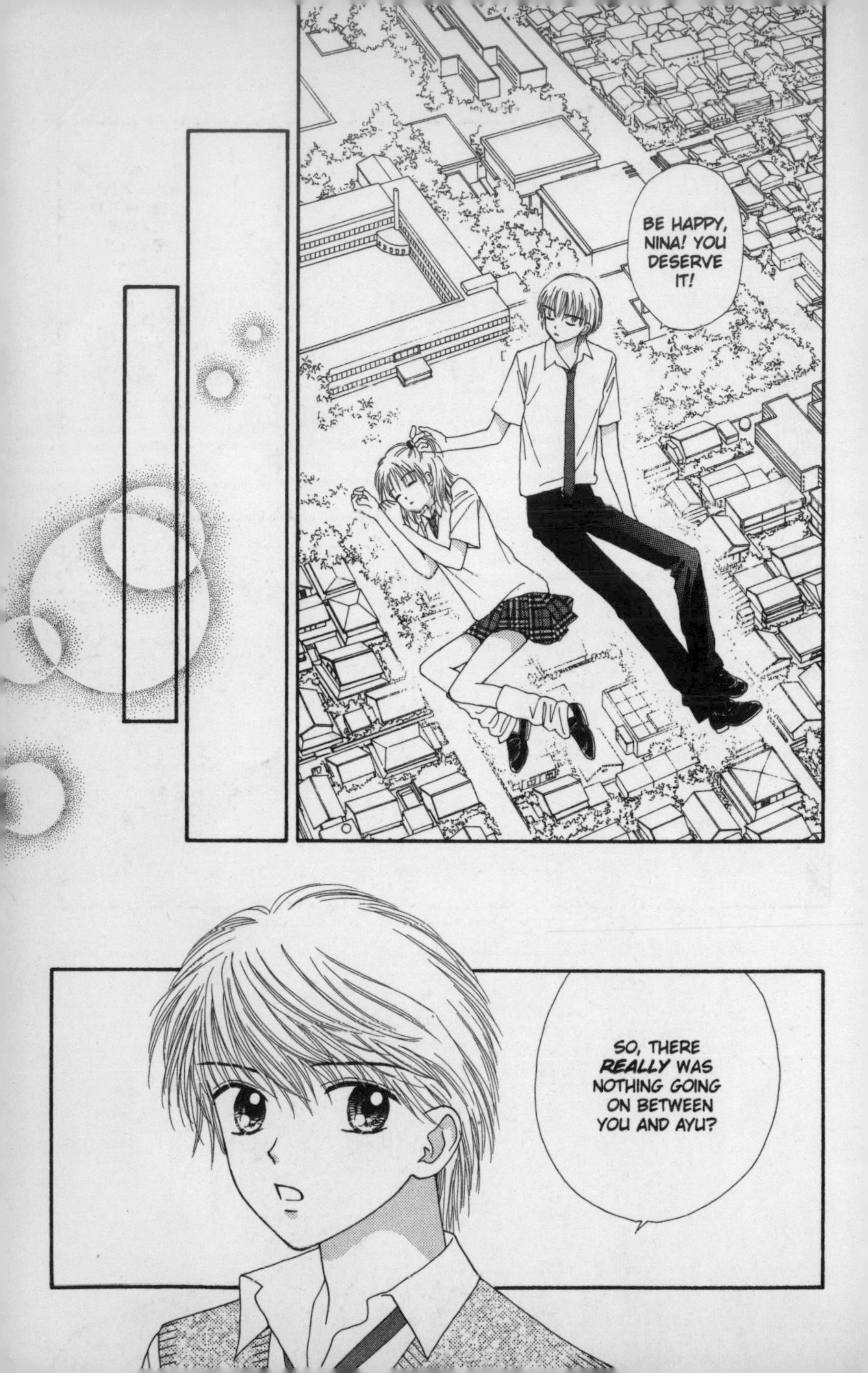
BE HAPPY, NINA! YOU DESERVE IT!
SO, THERE *REALLY* WAS NOTHING GOING ON BETWEEN YOU AND AYU?

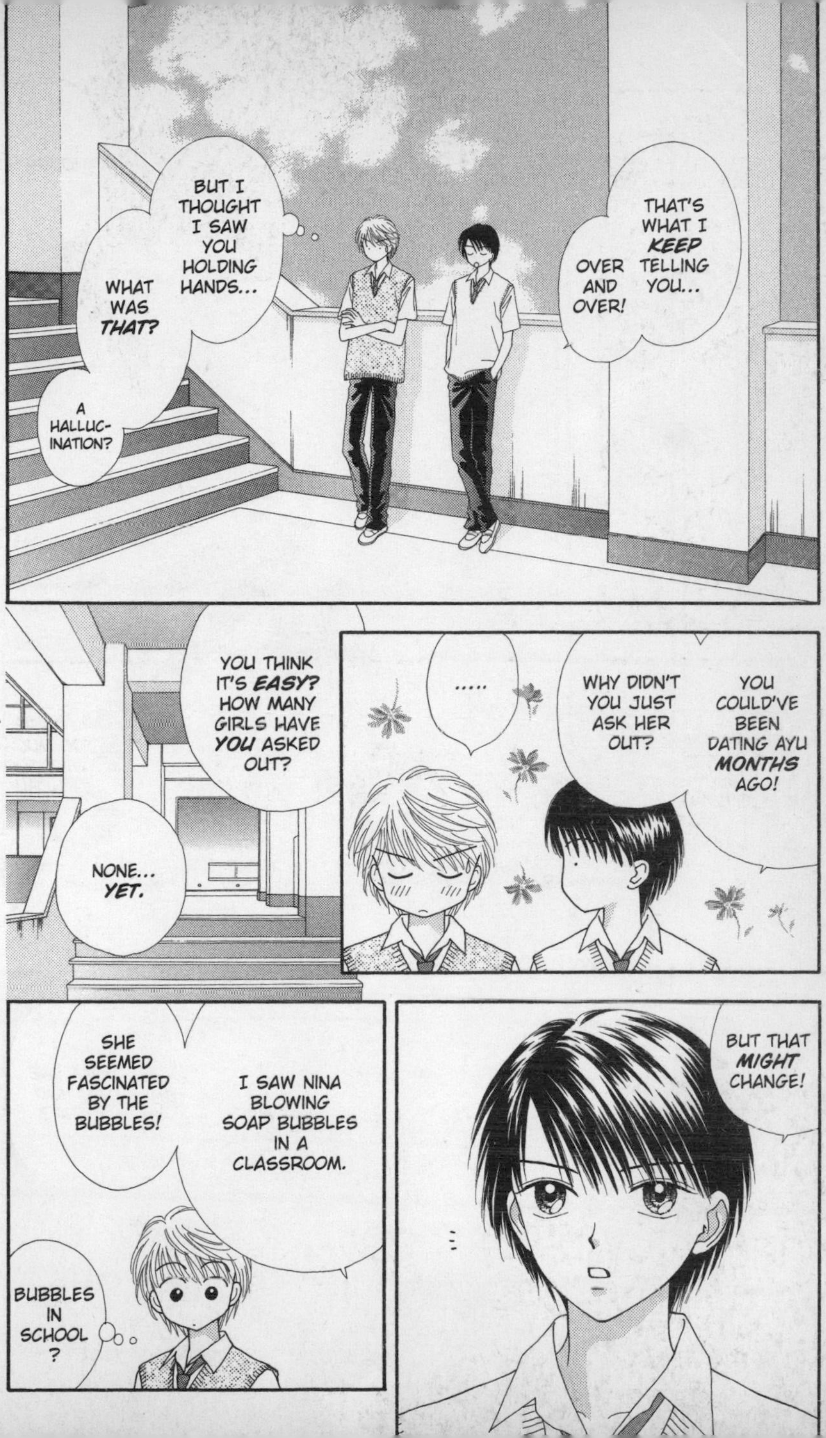
THAT'S WHAT I KEEP TELLING YOU... OVER AND OVER!
BUT I THOUGHT I SAW YOU HOLDING HANDS...
WHAT WAS THAT?
A HALLUCINATION?
YOU COULD'VE BEEN DATING AYU MONTHS AGO!
WHY DIDN'T YOU JUST ASK HER OUT?
.....
YOU THINK IT'S EASY? HOW MANY GIRLS HAVE YOU ASKED OUT?
NONE... YET.
BUT THAT MIGHT CHANGE!
I SAW NINA BLOWING SOAP BUBBLES IN A CLASSROOM.
SHE SEEMED FASCINATED BY THE BUBBLES!
BUBBLES IN SCHOOL?

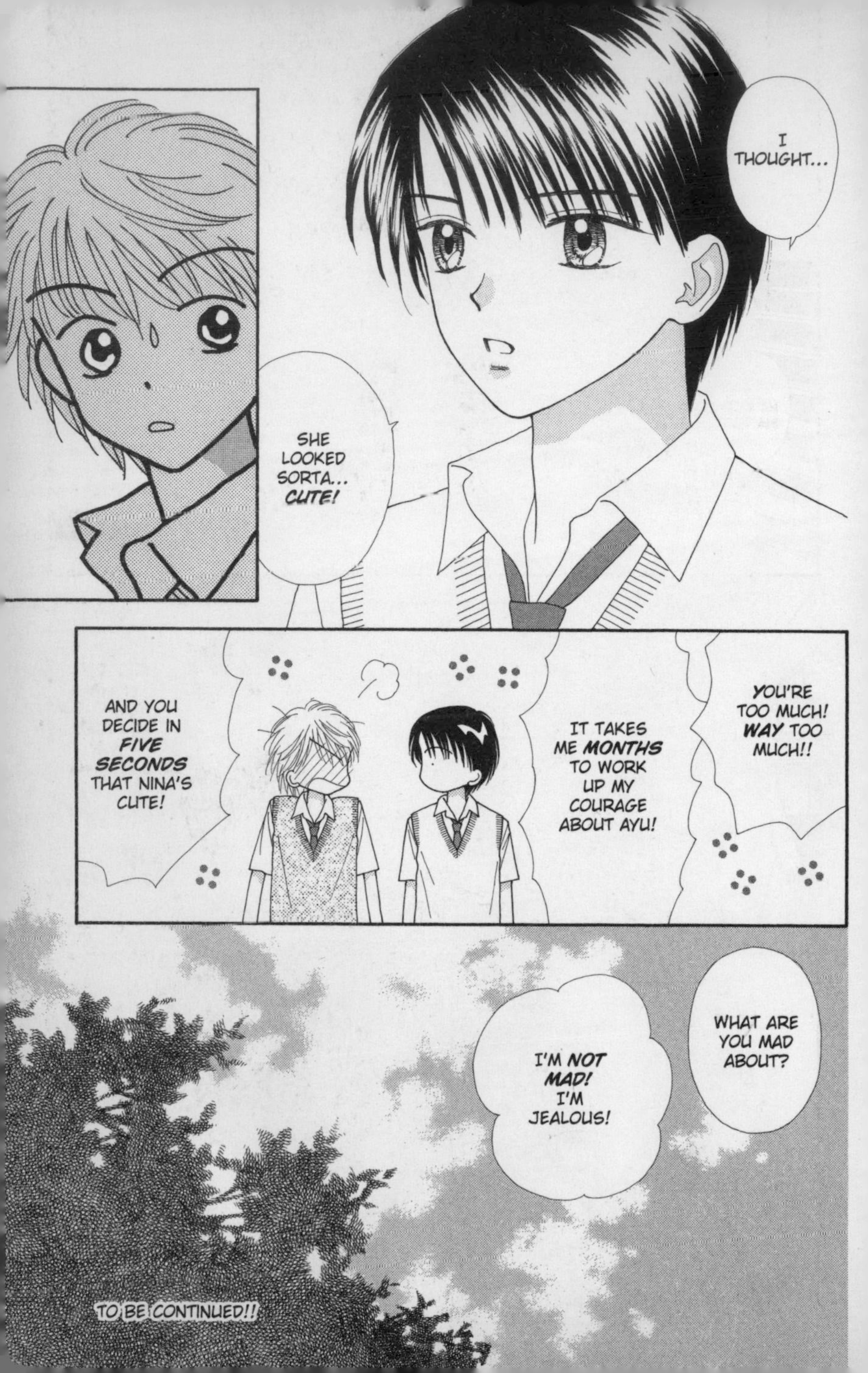
I THOUGHT...
SHE LOOKED SORTA... CUTE!
YOU'RE TOO MUCH! WAY TOO MUCH!!
IT TAKES ME MONTHS TO WORK UP MY COURAGE ABOUT AYU!
AND YOU DECIDE IN FIVE SECONDS THAT NINA'S CUTE!
WHAT ARE YOU MAD ABOUT?
I'M NOT MAD! I'M JEALOUS!
TO BE CONTINUED!!

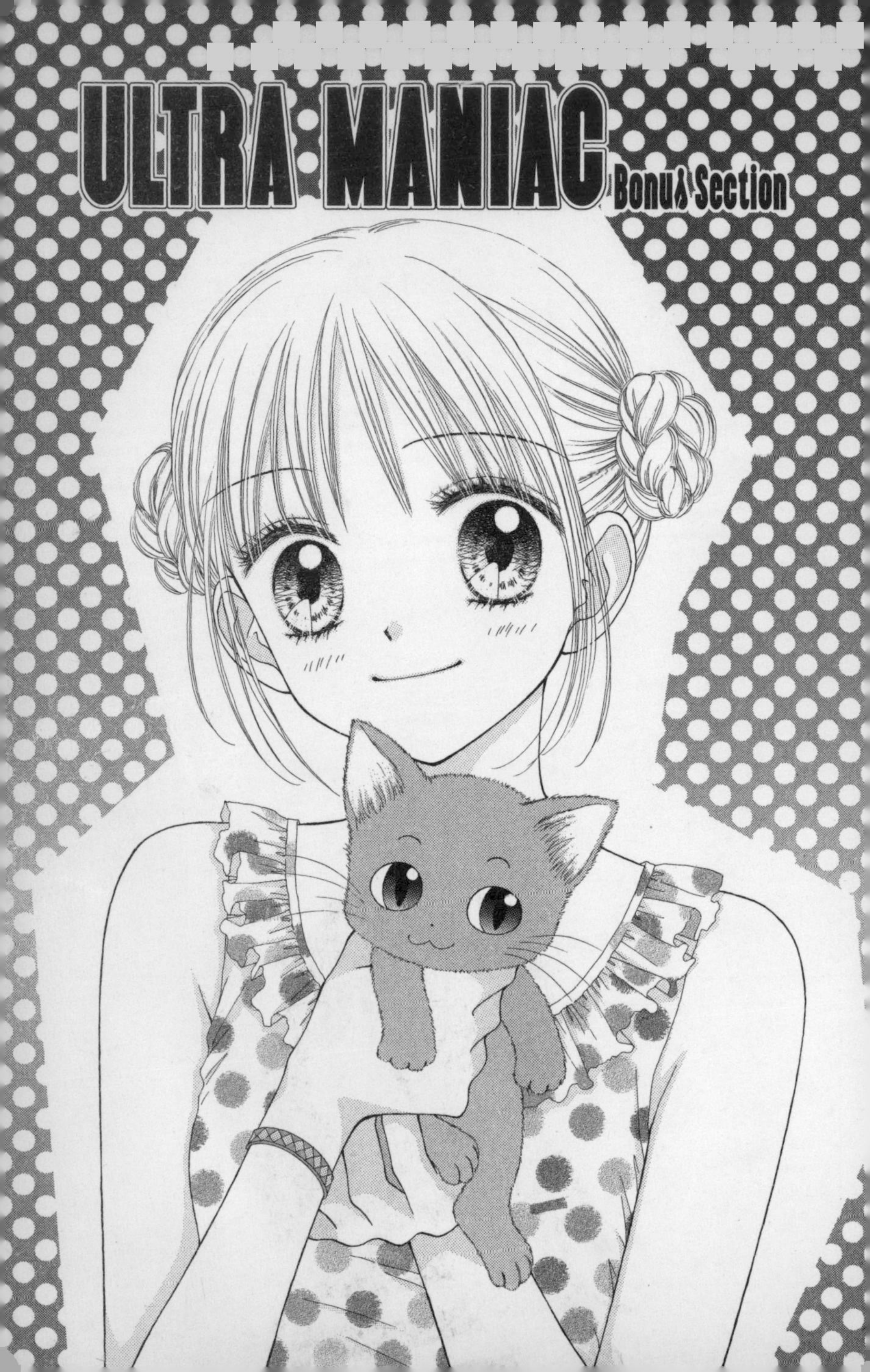
ULTRA MANIAC
Bonus Section

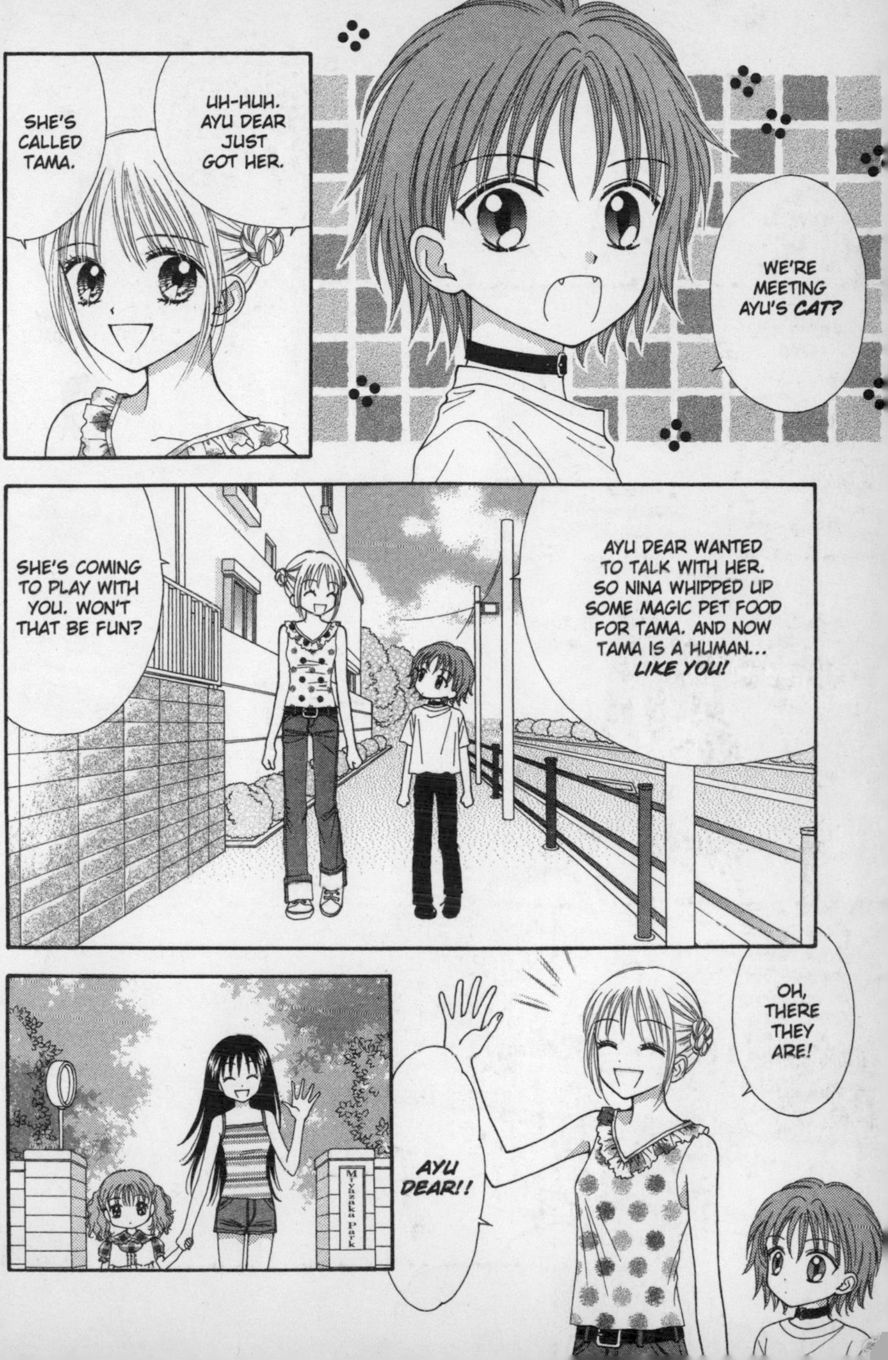
WE'RE MEETING AYU'S *CAT?*
UH-HUH. AYU DEAR JUST GOT HER.
SHE'S CALLED TAMA.
AYU DEAR WANTED TO TALK WITH HER. SO NINA WHIPPED UP SOME MAGIC PET FOOD FOR TAMA. AND NOW TAMA IS A HUMAN... *LIKE YOU!*
SHE'S COMING TO PLAY WITH YOU. WON'T THAT BE FUN?
OH, THERE THEY ARE!
AYU DEAR!!
Miyazaka Park

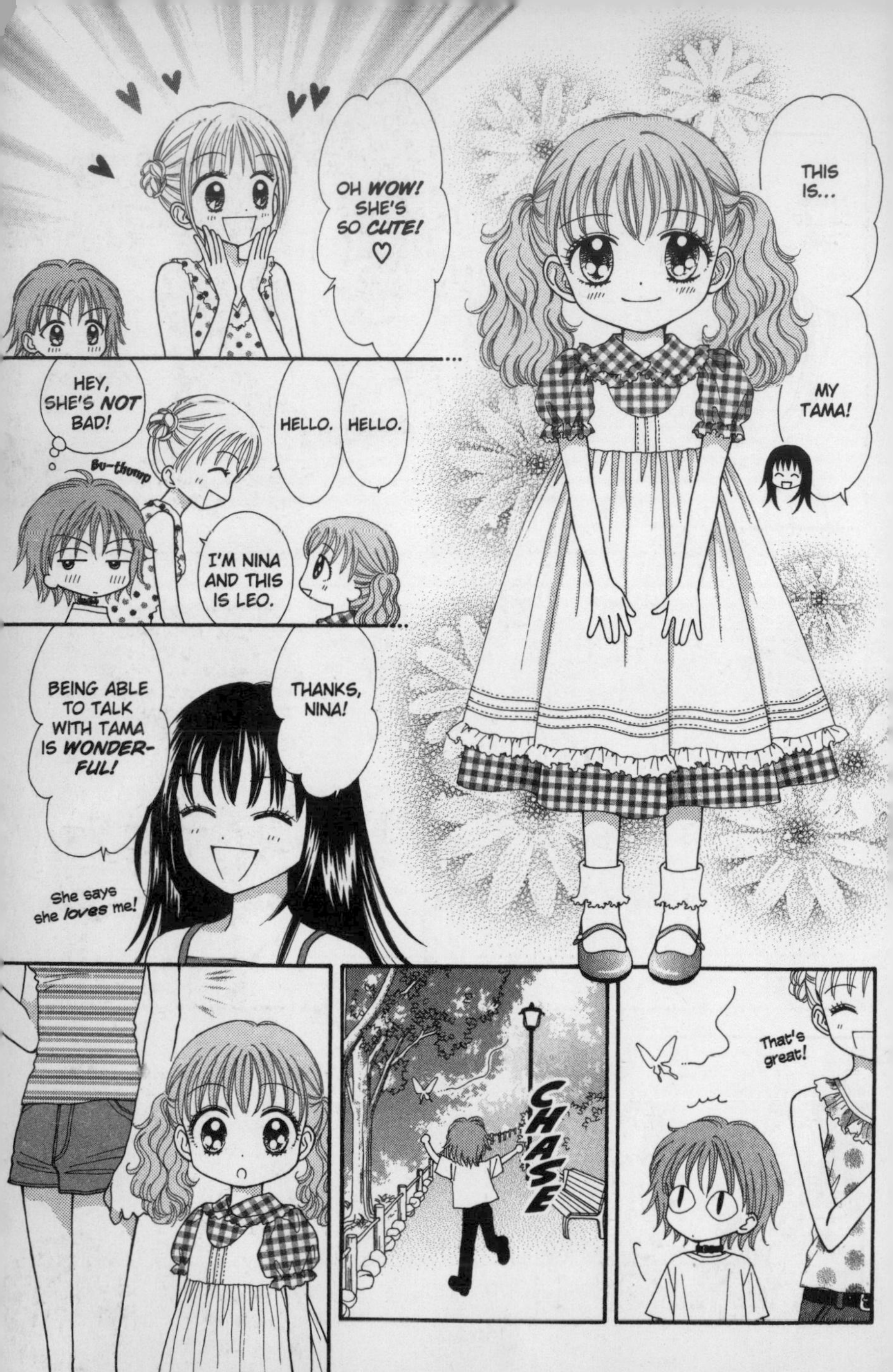

THIS IS...
MY TAMA!
OH WOW! SHE'S SO CUTE! ♡
HELLO.
HELLO.
HEY, SHE'S NOT BAD!
Bu-thump
I'M NINA AND THIS IS LEO.
THANKS, NINA!
BEING ABLE TO TALK WITH TAMA IS WONDERFUL!
She says she loves me!
That's great!
...
CHASE

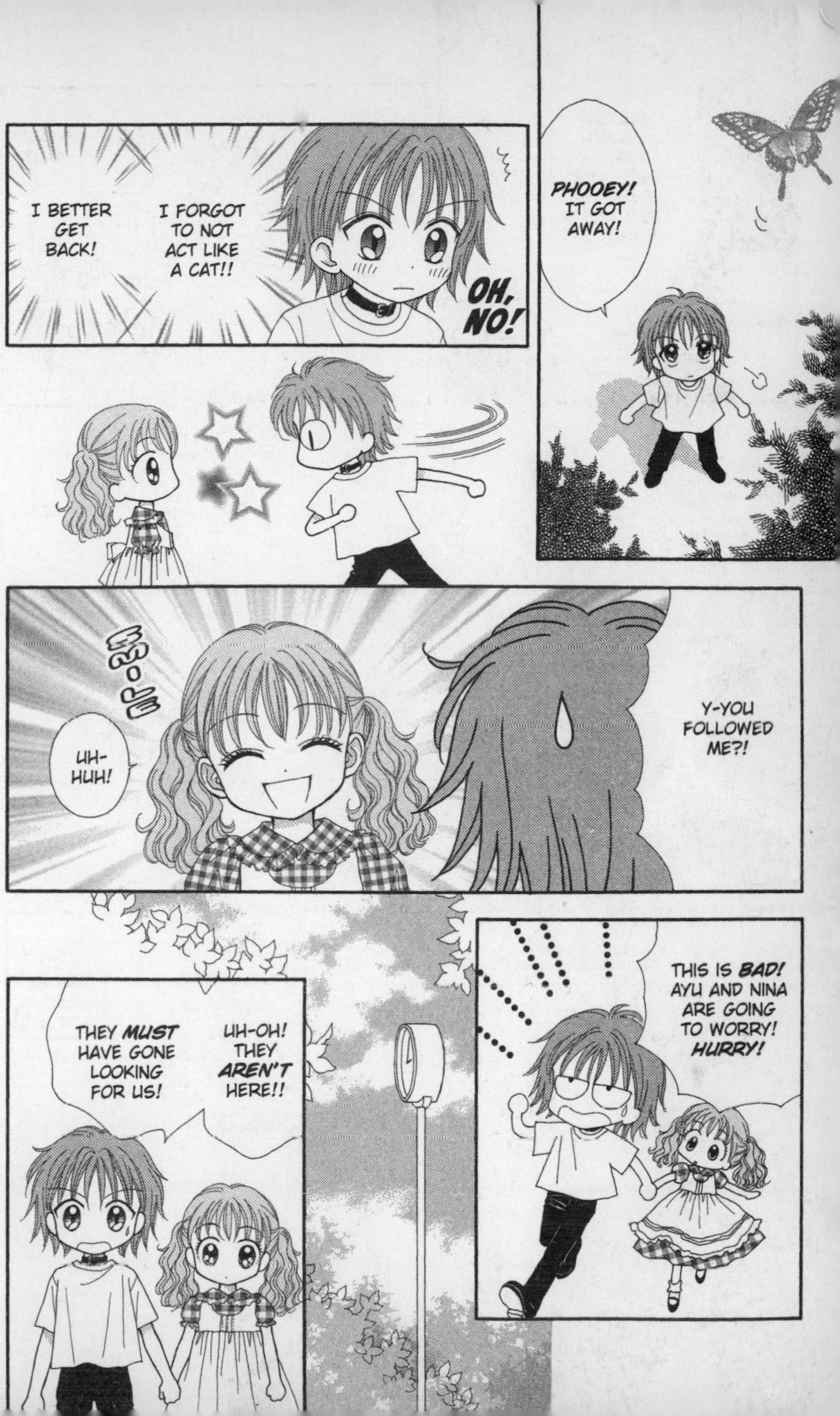
PHOOEY! IT GOT AWAY!
I FORGOT TO NOT ACT LIKE A CAT!!
I BETTER GET BACK!
OH, NO!
Y-YOU FOLLOWED ME?!
UH-HUH!
THIS IS BAD! AYU AND NINA ARE GOING TO WORRY! HURRY!
UH-OH! THEY AREN'T HERE!!
THEY MUST HAVE GONE LOOKING FOR US!

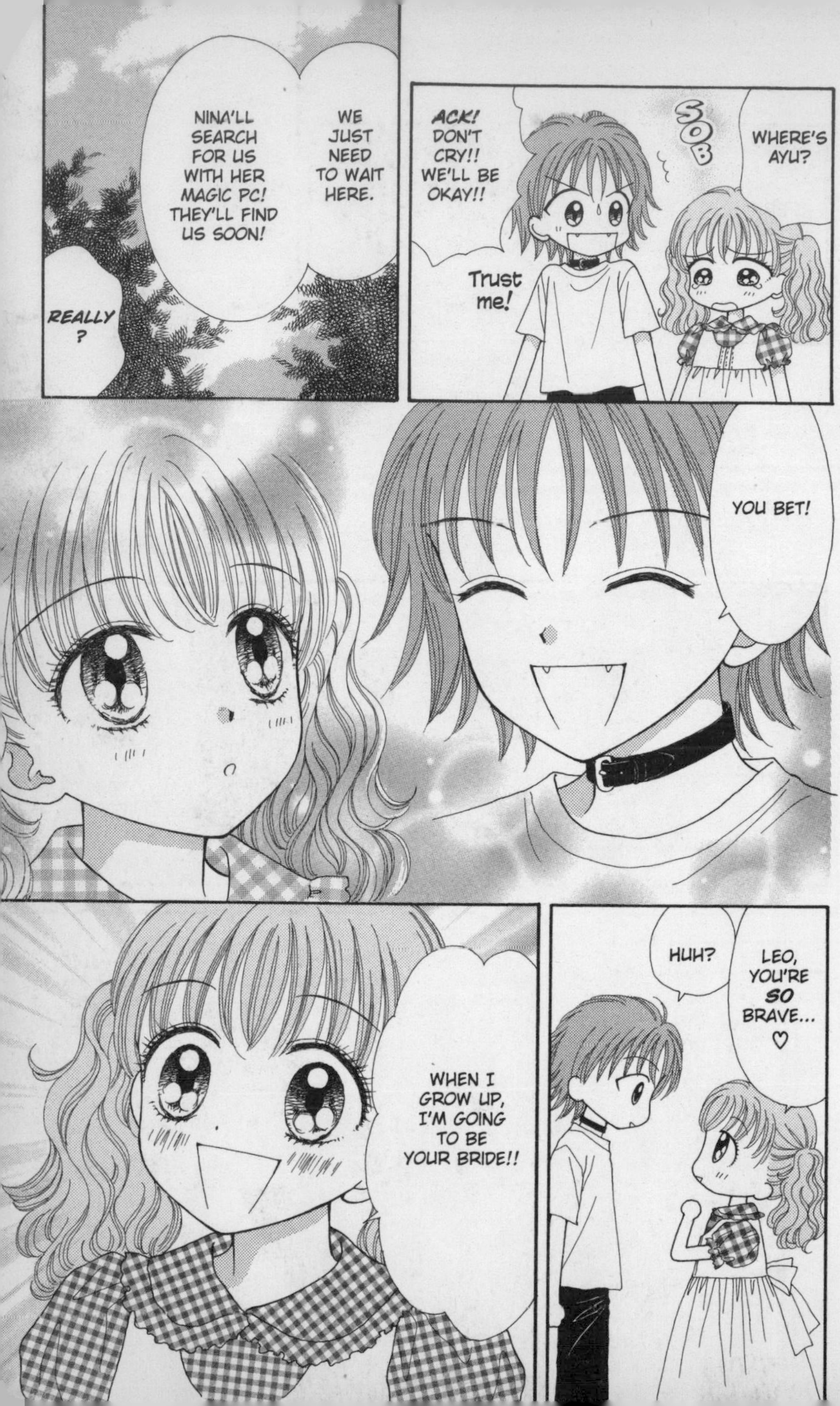
WHERE'S AYU?
SOB
ACK! DON'T CRY!! WE'LL BE OKAY!!
Trust me!
WE JUST NEED TO WAIT HERE.
NINA'LL SEARCH FOR US WITH HER MAGIC PC! THEY'LL FIND US SOON!
REALLY?
YOU BET!
LEO, YOU'RE SO BRAVE... ♡
HUH?
WHEN I GROW UP, I'M GOING TO BE YOUR BRIDE!!

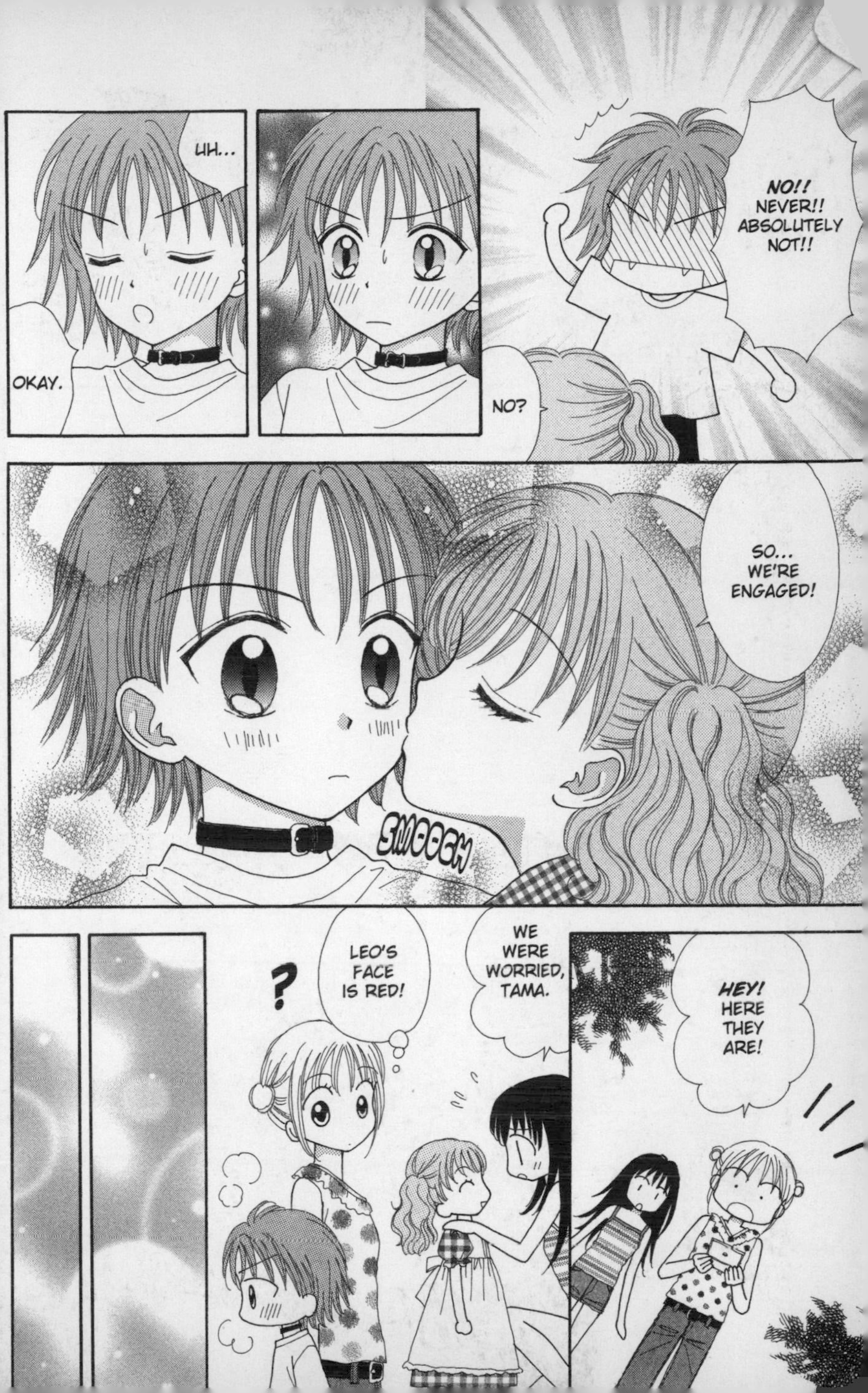
NO!! NEVER!! ABSOLUTELY NOT!!
NO?
UH...
OKAY.
SO... WE'RE ENGAGED!
SM-OOCH
HEY! HERE THEY ARE!
WE WERE WORRIED, TAMA.
LEO'S FACE IS RED!
?

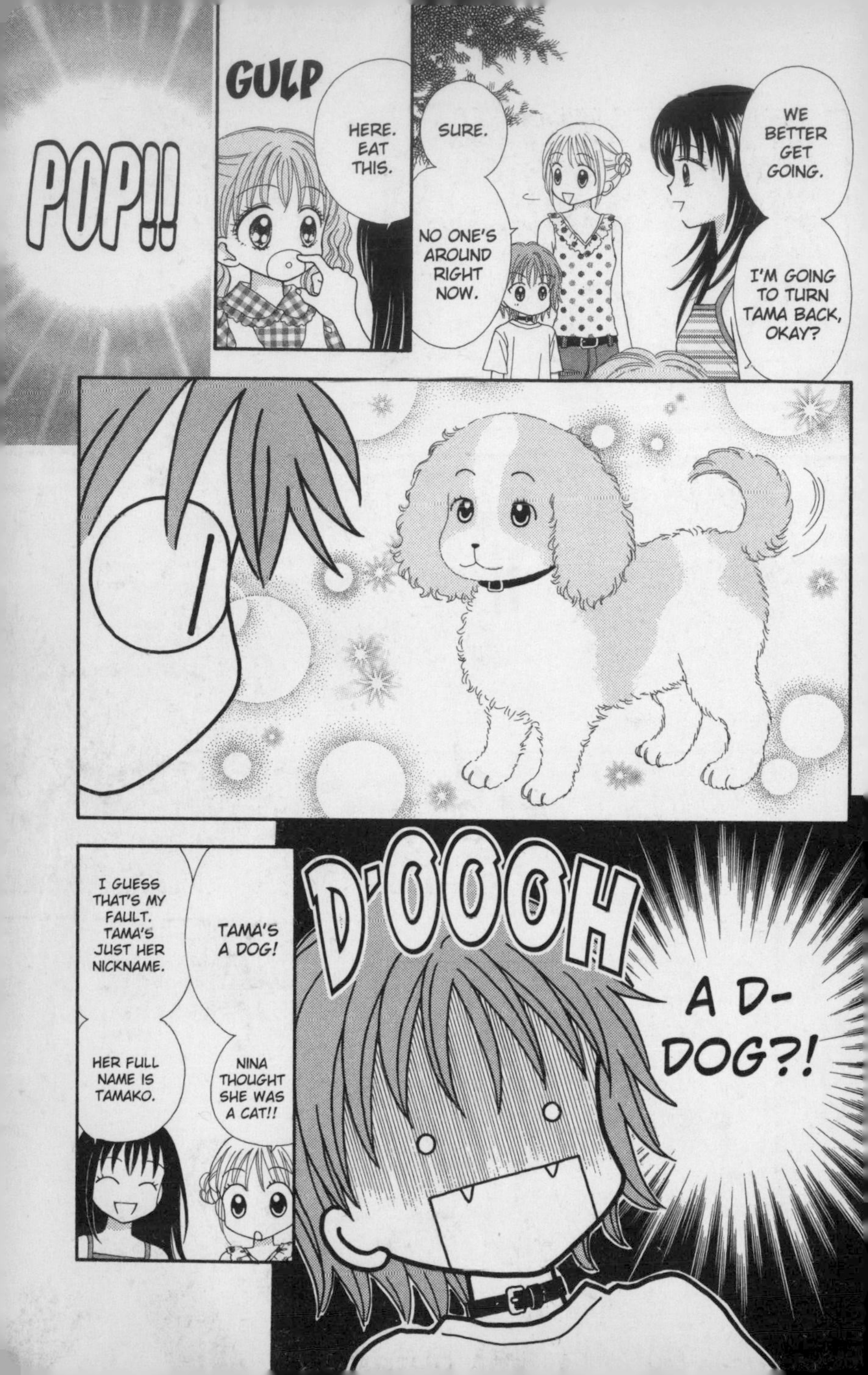
WE BETTER GET GOING.
I'M GOING TO TURN TAMA BACK, OKAY?
SURE.
NO ONE'S AROUND RIGHT NOW.
HERE. EAT THIS.
GULP
POP!!
D-OOOH
A D-DOG?!
TAMA'S A DOG!
NINA THOUGHT SHE WAS A CAT!!
I GUESS THAT'S MY FAULT. TAMA'S JUST HER NICKNAME.
HER FULL NAME IS TAMAKO.

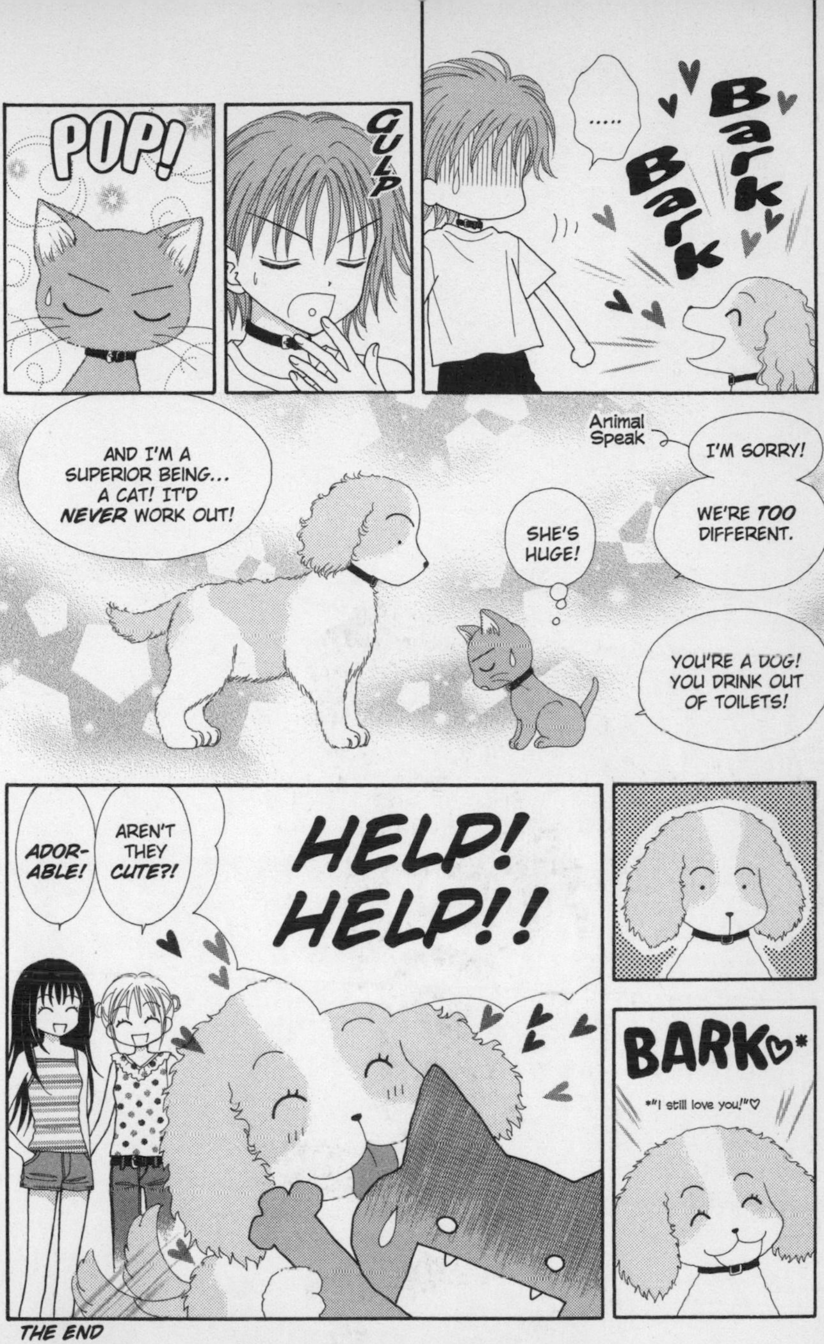
......
Bark Bark
Bark Bark
GULP
POP!
Animal Speak
I'M SORRY! WE'RE TOO DIFFERENT.
YOU'RE A DOG! YOU DRINK OUT OF TOILETS!
SHE'S HUGE!
AND I'M A SUPERIOR BEING... A CAT! IT'D NEVER WORK OUT!
BARK♡*
*"I still love you!"♡
HELP! HELP!!
AREN'T THEY CUTE?!
ADORABLE!

THE END

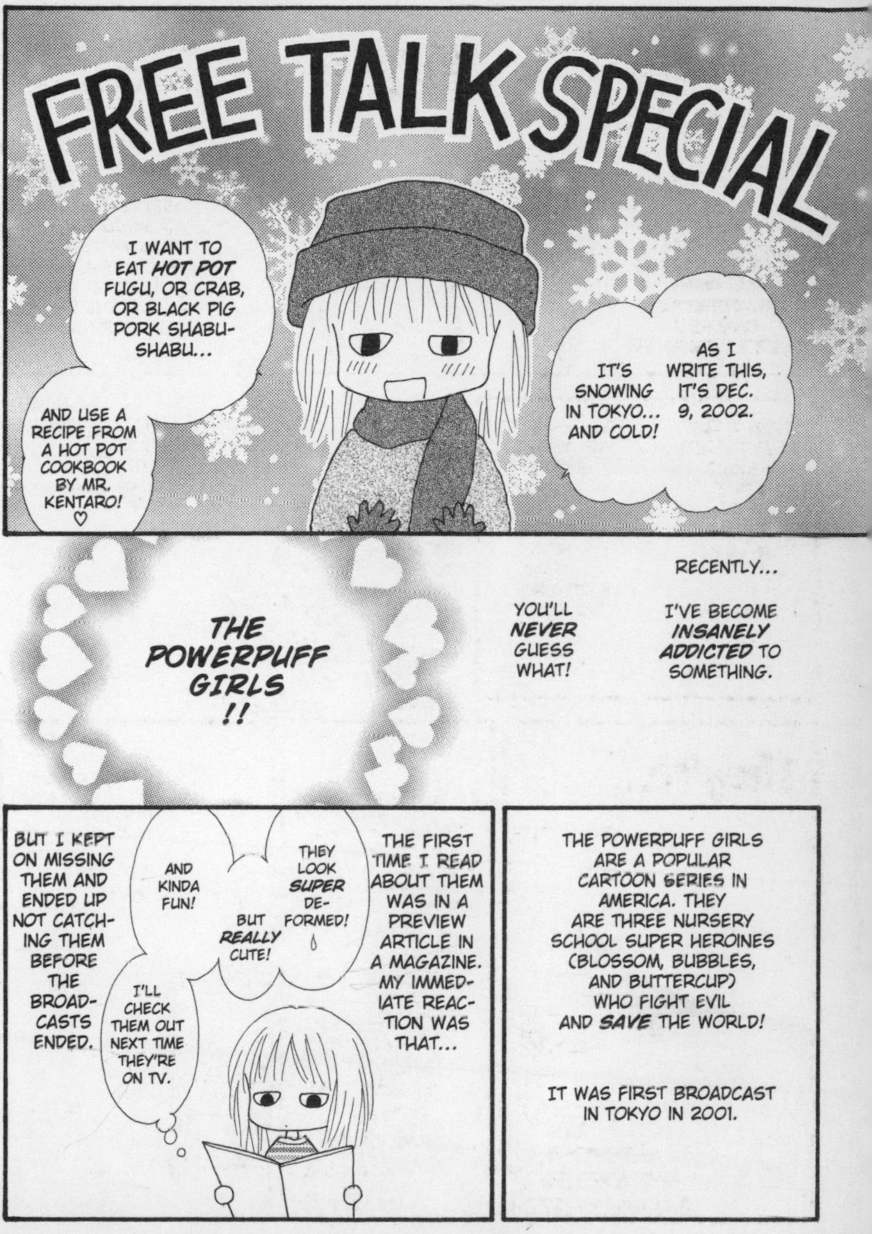
FREE TALK SPECIAL
AS I WRITE THIS, IT'S DEC. 9, 2002.
IT'S SNOWING IN TOKYO... AND COLD!
I WANT TO EAT HOT POT FUGU, OR CRAB, OR BLACK PIG PORK SHABU-SHABU...
AND USE A RECIPE FROM A HOT POT COOKBOOK BY MR. KENTARO! ♡
RECENTLY...
I'VE BECOME INSANELY ADDICTED TO SOMETHING.
YOU'LL NEVER GUESS WHAT!
THE POWERPUFF GIRLS !!
THE POWERPUFF GIRLS ARE A POPULAR CARTOON SERIES IN AMERICA. THEY ARE THREE NURSERY SCHOOL SUPER HEROINES (BLOSSOM, BUBBLES, AND BUTTERCUP) WHO FIGHT EVIL AND SAVE THE WORLD!
IT WAS FIRST BROADCAST IN TOKYO IN 2001.
THE FIRST TIME I READ ABOUT THEM WAS IN A PREVIEW ARTICLE IN A MAGAZINE. MY IMMEDIATE REACTION WAS THAT...
THEY LOOK SUPER DE-FORMED!
BUT REALLY CUTE!
AND KINDA FUN!
I'LL CHECK THEM OUT NEXT TIME THEY'RE ON TV.
BUT I KEPT ON MISSING THEM AND ENDED UP NOT CATCHING THEM BEFORE THE BROADCASTS ENDED.

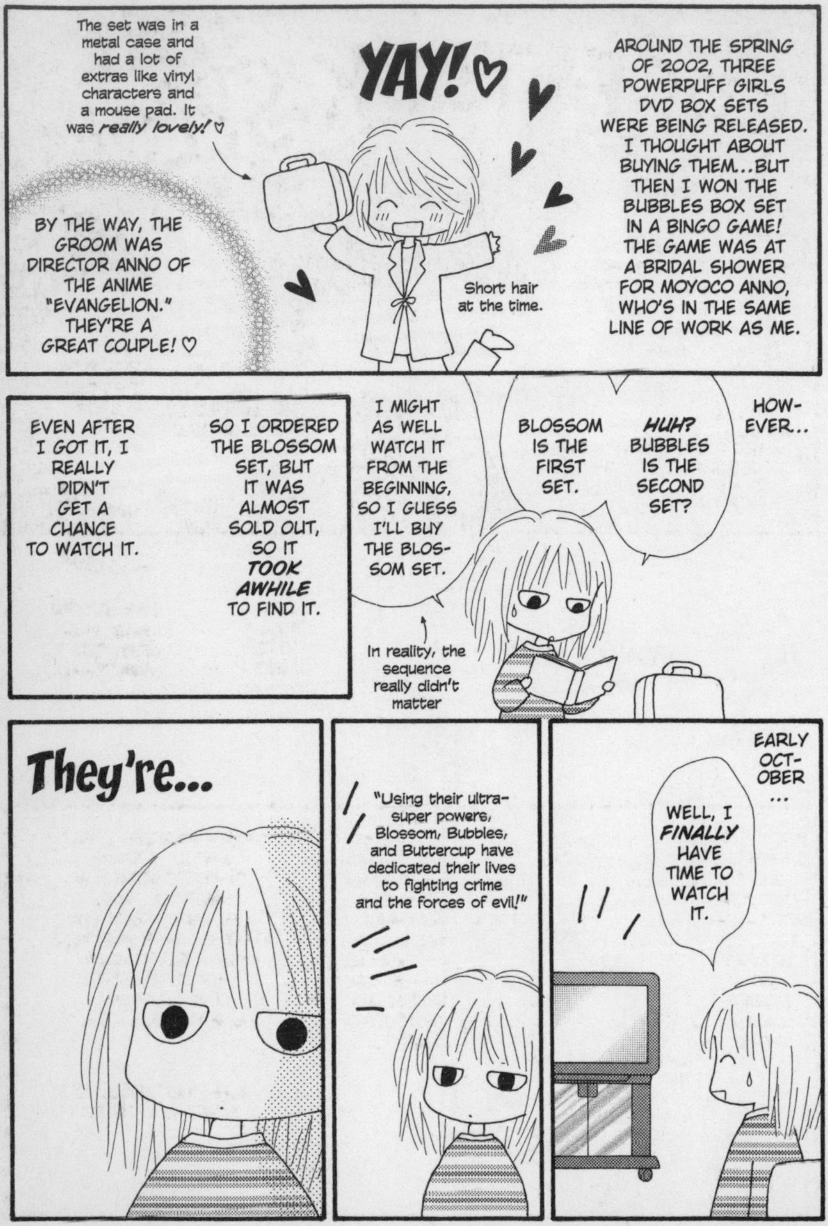
AROUND THE SPRING OF 2002, THREE POWERPUFF GIRLS DVD BOX SETS WERE BEING RELEASED. I THOUGHT ABOUT BUYING THEM...BUT THEN I WON THE BUBBLES BOX SET IN A BINGO GAME! THE GAME WAS AT A BRIDAL SHOWER FOR MOYOCO ANNO, WHO'S IN THE SAME LINE OF WORK AS ME.
YAY! ♡
The set was in a metal case and had a lot of extras like vinyl characters and a mouse pad. It was *really lovely!* ♡
Short hair at the time.
BY THE WAY, THE GROOM WAS DIRECTOR ANNO OF THE ANIME "EVANGELION." THEY'RE A GREAT COUPLE! ♡
HOW-EVER..
HUH? BUBBLES IS THE SECOND SET?
BLOSSOM IS THE FIRST SET.
I MIGHT AS WELL WATCH IT FROM THE BEGINNING, SO I GUESS I'LL BUY THE BLOS-SOM SET.
In reality, the sequence really didn't matter
SO I ORDERED THE BLOSSOM SET, BUT IT WAS ALMOST SOLD OUT, SO IT *TOOK AWHILE* TO FIND IT.
EVEN AFTER I GOT IT, I REALLY DIDN'T GET A CHANCE TO WATCH IT.
EARLY OCT-OBER ...
WELL, I *FINALLY* HAVE TIME TO WATCH IT.
"Using their ultra-super powers, Blossom, Bubbles, and Buttercup have dedicated their lives to fighting crime and the forces of evil!"
They're...

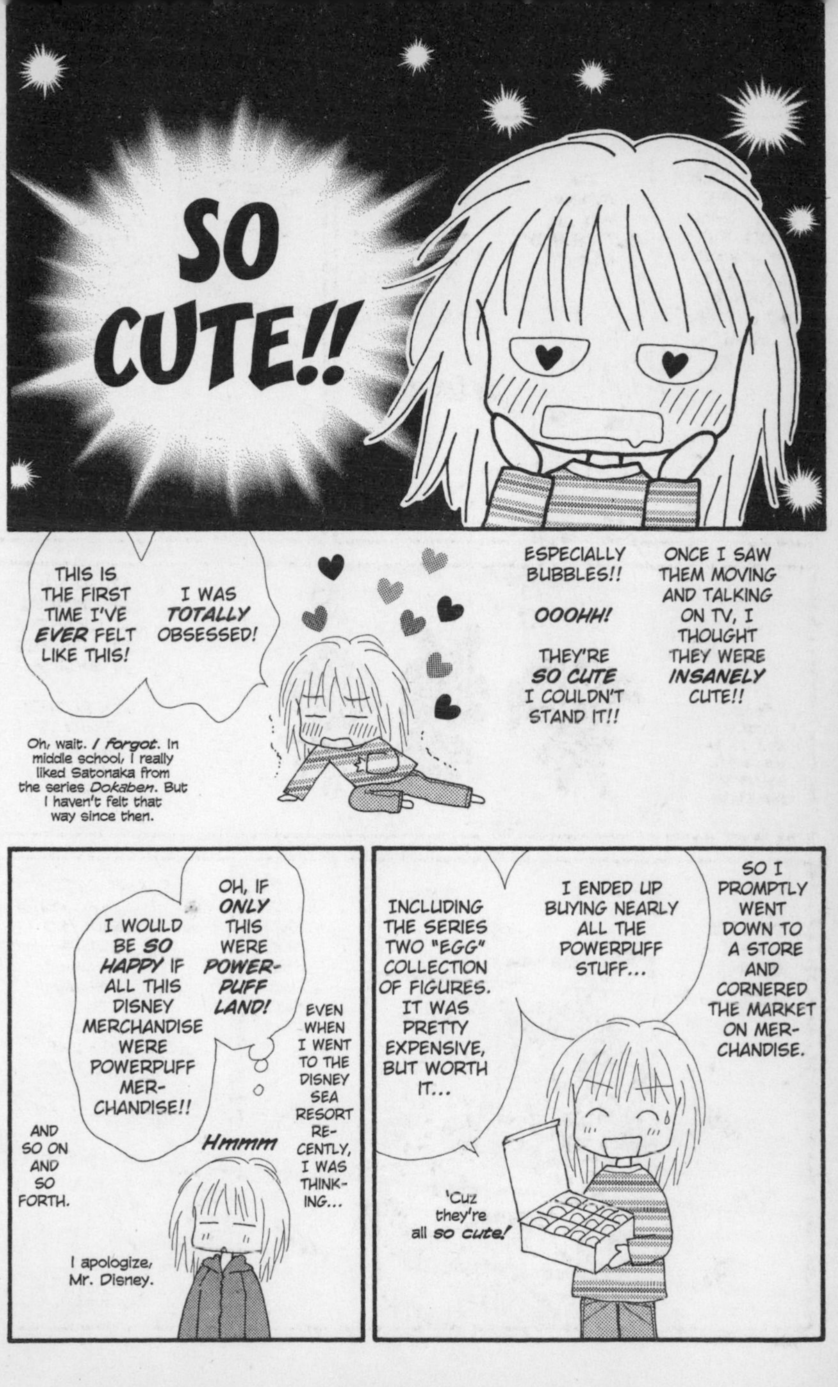
SO CUTE!!
ONCE I SAW THEM MOVING AND TALKING ON TV, I THOUGHT THEY WERE *INSANELY* CUTE!!
ESPECIALLY BUBBLES!!
OOOHH!
THEY'RE *SO CUTE* I COULDN'T STAND IT!!
I WAS *TOTALLY* OBSESSED!
THIS IS THE FIRST TIME I'VE *EVER* FELT LIKE THIS!
Oh, wait. *I forgot*. In middle school, I really liked Satonaka from the series *Dokaben*. But I haven't felt that way since then.
SO I PROMPTLY WENT DOWN TO A STORE AND CORNERED THE MARKET ON MER-CHANDISE.
I ENDED UP BUYING NEARLY ALL THE POWERPUFF STUFF...
INCLUDING THE SERIES TWO "EGG" COLLECTION OF FIGURES. IT WAS PRETTY EXPENSIVE, BUT WORTH IT...
'Cuz they're all *so cute!*
EVEN WHEN I WENT TO THE DISNEY SEA RESORT RE-CENTLY, I WAS THINK-ING...
OH, IF *ONLY* THIS WERE *POWER-PUFF LAND!*
I WOULD BE *SO HAPPY* IF ALL THIS DISNEY MERCHANDISE WERE POWERPUFF MER-CHANDISE!!
Hmmm
AND SO ON AND SO FORTH.
I apologize, Mr. Disney.

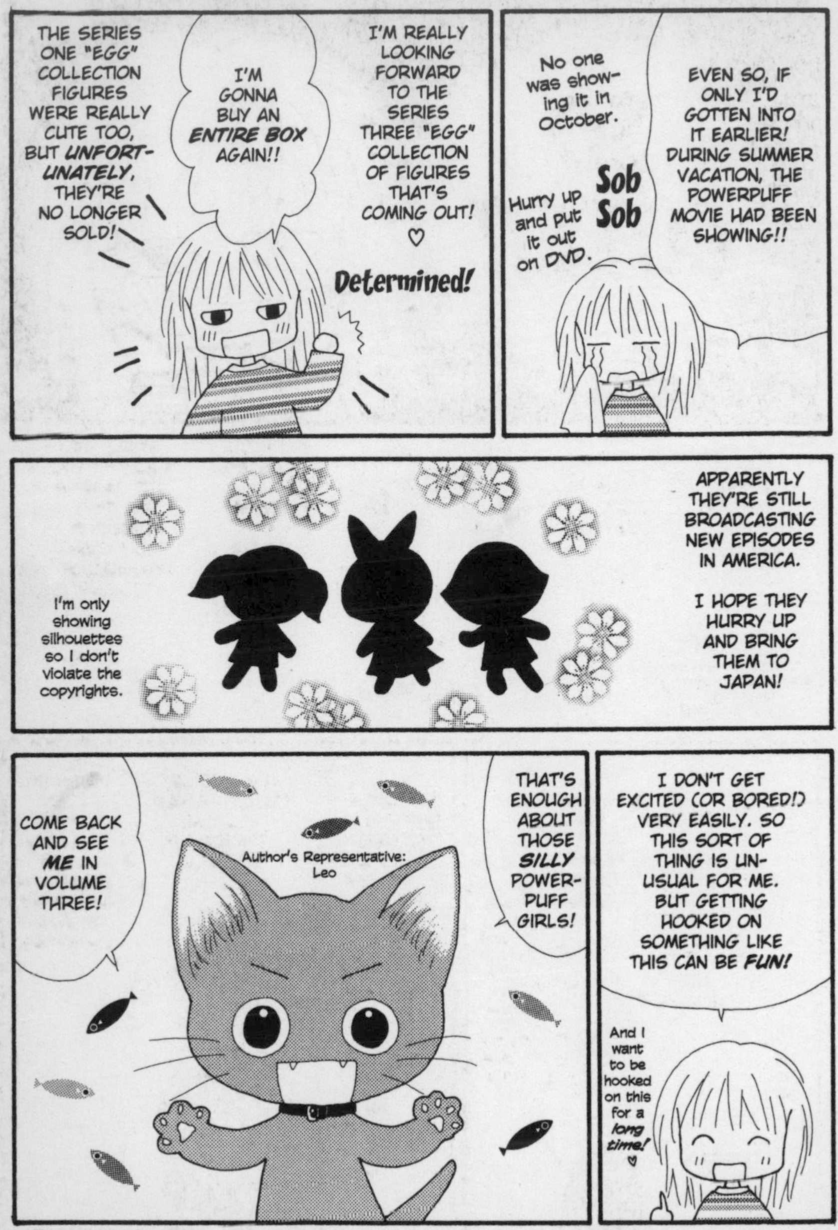
EVEN SO, IF ONLY I'D GOTTEN INTO IT EARLIER! DURING SUMMER VACATION, THE POWERPUFF MOVIE HAD BEEN SHOWING!!
No one was showing it in October.
Sob Sob
Hurry up and put it out on DVD.
I'M REALLY LOOKING FORWARD TO THE SERIES THREE "EGG" COLLECTION OF FIGURES THAT'S COMING OUT! ♡
I'M GONNA BUY AN ENTIRE BOX AGAIN!!
THE SERIES ONE "EGG" COLLECTION FIGURES WERE REALLY CUTE TOO, BUT UNFORTUNATELY, THEY'RE NO LONGER SOLD!
Determined!
APPARENTLY THEY'RE STILL BROADCASTING NEW EPISODES IN AMERICA.
I HOPE THEY HURRY UP AND BRING THEM TO JAPAN!
I'm only showing silhouettes so I don't violate the copyrights.
I DON'T GET EXCITED (OR BORED!) VERY EASILY. SO THIS SORT OF THING IS UNUSUAL FOR ME. BUT GETTING HOOKED ON SOMETHING LIKE THIS CAN BE FUN!
And I want to be hooked on this for a long time! ♡
THAT'S ENOUGH ABOUT THOSE SILLY POWERPUFF GIRLS!
Author's Representative: Leo
COME BACK AND SEE ME IN VOLUME THREE!

FIN.

Wataru Yoshizumi

Comments
The author, Wataru Yoshizumi, told us: "I wrote this story with the intention of making both Ayu and Nina the main characters, but in reality, the ratio is more like six-to-four in Ayu's favor. Actually, it's easier to draw Nina, and she's easier to manipulate as a character."

Bio
Wataru Yoshizumi hails from Tokyo and made her manga debut in 1984 with *Radical Romance* in *Ribon Original* magazine. The artist has since produced a string of fan-favorite titles, including *Quartet Game, Handsome na Kanojo* (*Handsome Girl*), *Marmalade Boy*, and *Random Walk. Ultra Maniac,* a magical screwball comedy, is only the second time her work has been available in the U.S. Many of her titles, however, are available throughout Asia and Europe. Yoshizumi loves to travel and is keen on making original accessories out of beads.

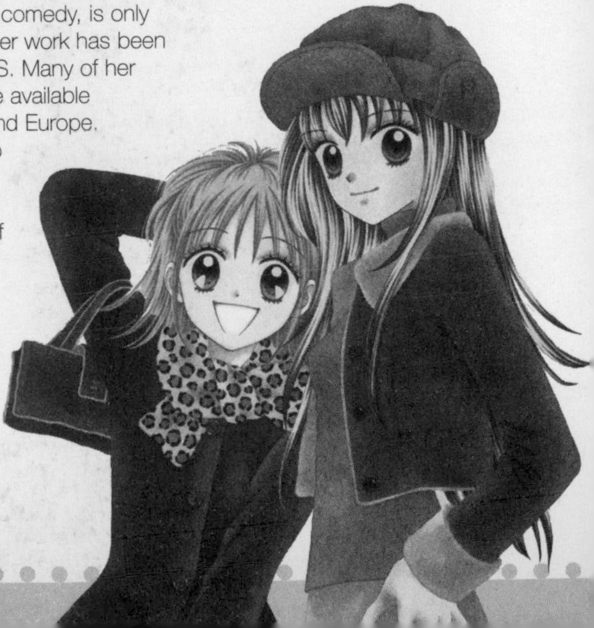

ULTRA MANIAC VOL. 2

The Shojo Beat Manga Edition

STORY AND ART BY
WATARU YOSHIZUMI

English Adaptation/John Lustig
Translation/Koji Goto
Touch-up Art & Lettering/Elizabeth Watasin
Cover & Graphic Design/Izumi Evers
Editor/Eric Searleman

Editor in Chief, Books/Alvin Lu
Editor in Chief, Magazines/Marc Weidenbaum
VP of Publishing Licensing/Rika Inouye
VP of Sales/Gonzalo Ferreyra
Sr. VP of Marketing/Liza Coppola
Publisher/Hyoe Narita

Printed in the U.S.A.

Published by VIZ Media, LLC
P.O. Box 77010
San Francisco, CA 94107

Shojo Beat Manga Edition
10 9 8 7 6 5 4 3
First printing, August 2005
Third printing, July 2007

store.viz.com

RATED A FOR ALL AGES

PARENTAL ADVISORY
ULTRA MANIAC is rated A and is recommended for readers of all ages.

ratings.viz.com

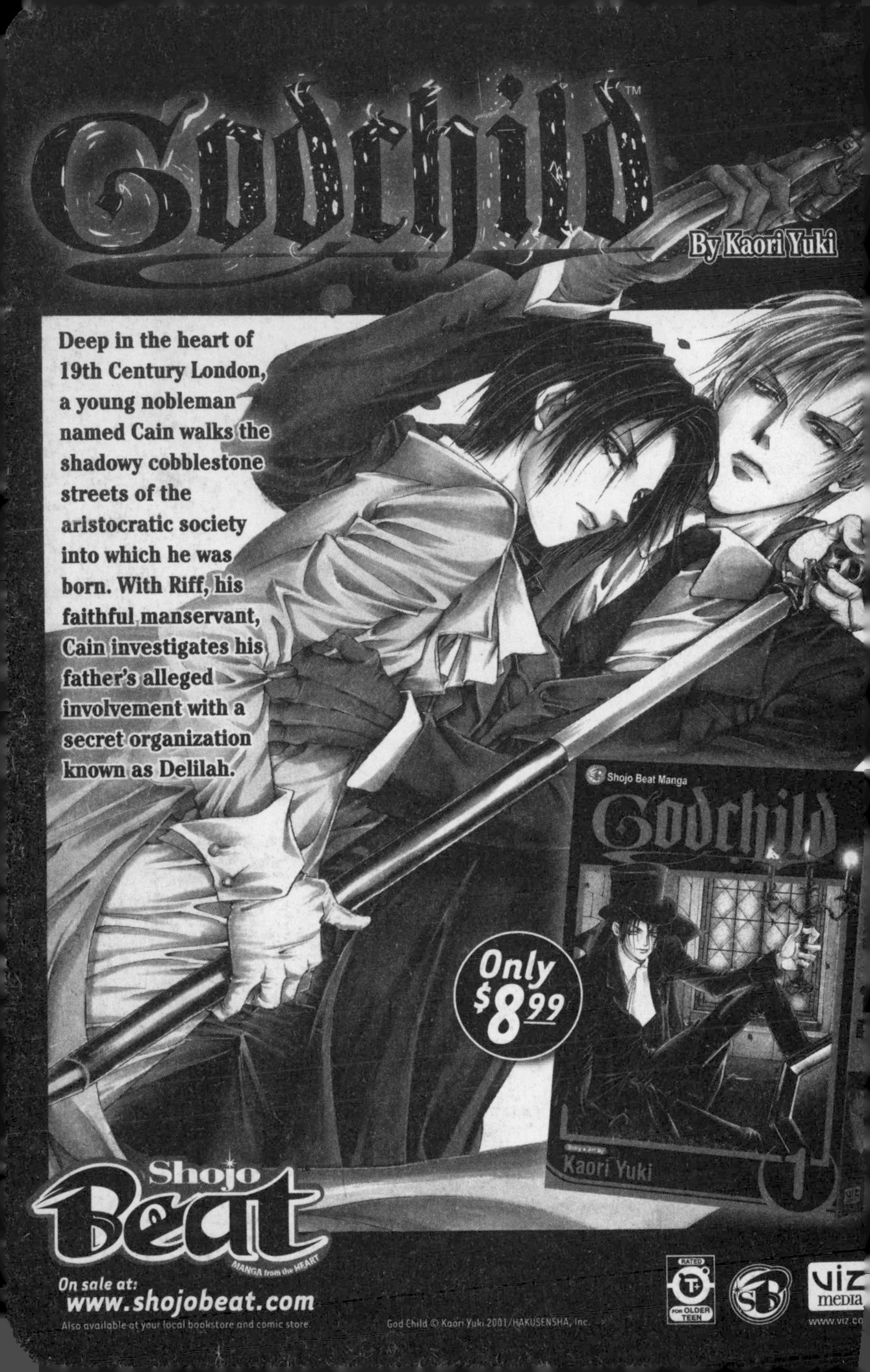
Godchild™
By Kaori Yuki
Deep in the heart of 19th Century London, a young nobleman named Cain walks the shadowy cobblestone streets of the aristocratic society into which he was born. With Riff, his faithful manservant, Cain investigates his father's alleged involvement with a secret organization known as Delilah.
Shojo Beat Manga
Godchild
Kaori Yuki
Only $8.99
Shojo Beat
MANGA from the HEART
On sale at:
www.shojobeat.com
Also available at your local bookstore and comic store.
God Child © Kaori Yuki 2001/HAKUSENSHA, Inc.
RATED T+ FOR OLDER TEEN
viz media
www.viz.co

you think
Beat Manga!

Our survey is now
available online. Go to:

shojobeat.com/mangasurvey

Help us make our
product offerings
better!